LONGING TO BELONG

To Fr. Anthony Brunning
From
The Medina Family!
(Victoria, Anya, Tegan, Astrel & Kiara)
(Trinidad & Tobago)

MARK TIERNEY
FILIP VANDENBUSSCHE

LONGING TO BELONG

THE LIFE OF
DOM MAYEUL DE CAIGNY
(1862-1939)

FOUNDER OF THE
MOUNT ST. BENEDICT MONASTERY
TRINIDAD, WEST INDIES IN 1912

MOUNT ST. BENEDICT
TRINIDAD

MMXII

This first edition of "Longing to Belong" was published in commemoration
of the 100th Anniversary of Mount St. Benedict.

The Abbey of Our Lady of Exile
Mount St. Benedict
St. John's Road
Tunapuna
Trinidad and Tobago
West Indies

www.pariapublishing.com

Typeset in Centaur by Paria Publishing Company Limited
and printed by Lightning Source, U.S.A.

ISBN 978-976-8242-01-3

Other publications by Mount St. Benedict:

The Abbey - Mount St. Benedict - A Popular Guide
by Mark Tierney, O.S.B., 2005 (Prospect Press)

Dedication

To

Monique De Caigny

grand-niece of Dom Mayeul De Caigny
who died on 11 March 1998,
spouse of Filip Vandenbussche,
co-author of the book,

and to

Dom Mark Tierney, OSB

co-author of the book,
who died on 31 December 2011.

Contents

Prologue

MONIQUE De Caigny, a granddaughter of Alois De Caigny, the younger brother of Dom Mayeul De Caigny, was the first family member to visit his final resting place in St. Leo Abbey, Florida. This happened in 1994, at which time she conceived the idea of finding more information about her grand-uncle, realizing that the St. Leo Abbey archives contained a major source for the life of Dom Mayeul. When Monique died in 1998 from a termi-nal illness, Filip, her husband, vowed to honour her memory and her wishes.

During the following years Filip Vandenbussche continued to mull over the idea on how to achieve this goal. Having contacted the monastery of Mount St. Benedict in Trinidad, also called the Mount, founded in 1912 by Dom Mayeul, he discovered that the history of the Mount had recently been written by Dom Mark Tierney from Glenstal Abbey, Ireland. In that book there was a major chapter on the life of Dom Mayeul, opening a number of interesting questions regarding his life. At the time, Dom Mark, the author, was spending six months each year at the Mount in Trinidad, putting the archives there into proper order. In the meantime he had become an authority on the subject of the Mount and its history, including the life of the founder, Dom Mayeul. Dom Mark had also spent considerable time at the archives at St. Leo, Florida. Combining his knowledge of the contents of both archives, Father Mark was, for Filip, the ideal person to bring to fruition the publication of a biography on Dom Mayeul. For both Filip and Dom Mark, the writing of the biography was very much a labour of love, not just honouring Monique, but also putting the record straight regarding the much misunderstood life of Dom Mayeul. The wealth of information available allowed for a full analysis of Dom Mayeul's character, values, achievements, his deep religious convictions and profound spirituality. It took much time and patience to put all the pieces together, resulting in this book *Longing to Belong*.

Dom Mayeul, who had been born Peter De Caigny in 1862, in Iseghem, Belgium, had an extraordinary life, both as a child and an adult. He had been deeply influenced and fascinated by the controversies surrounding the Catholic Church of his day. His achievements were numerous and sometimes extraordinary. Throughout his life he travelled a great deal, and at one time or other lived in Belgium, Brazil, Trinidad, USA and France. Before finishing his secondary education, at the age of seventeen, he joined the Redemptorist Order, experiencing the trials and hardships of religious life in the late nineteenth century. As a Redemptorist priest and later on in life, he became involved in local conflicts, and showed himself to be both uncompromising and unwavering when faced with opposition. All his life, he believed that he had moral right on his side. He gradually developed a sincere devotion to the person of the Pope, to the extent that he was prepared to shed his blood for the papal cause. Having spent eighteen years as a Redemptorist, he decided that their kind of life did not suit him. He then became a Benedictine monk, at which stage he received the Benedictine name Dom Mayeul. In making this move from one religious Order to another, he was seeking somewhere to begin a new start in life and hopefully find somewhere he could sink his roots permanently.

Throughout his life, Dom Mayeul related well to most people. Whenever he moved on, he left behind him a large number of admiring disciples and friends, who had come to love him, and who depended on his spiritual guidance and teaching. Many called him a living saint. However, there were others who felt hurt or angry at his attitude towards them and at his undiplomatic style. These two opposing groups, one who adored him and the other who could never agree with his actions, appeared at almost every moment in his life. As a result, he had to face a number of sad conflicts, which took up much of his time, and caused him considerable frustration, if not annoyance.

When Dom Mayeul started writing his memoirs, especially Volume II, which he intended as his apologia, he knew it might be difficult, if not impossible, to publish them during his life-time. Some of the material in the book was controversial, and could be an embarrassment to his Benedictine brethren. However, he expressed the hope that someone, later on, would pick up the story where he left off, and tell his story to the world. In his last will, written on his sickbed in 1939, he expressed the firm wish that his memoirs remain untouched for 10 years after his death. This implied an opening of the door to a future publication. He told his successor in Trinidad that "one day the truth will come out". We hope that his wish has now been fulfilled.

As Abbot of Mount St. Benedict in the one hundredth year of its founding, I am very happy to have been associated with this project and with the co-authors. Dom Mark Tierney first came to our Abbey at my invitation in 2004, soon after my election as the fifth Abbot of Mount St. Benedict in November 2003. We are very grateful for his tremendous work in restoring our monastery's archives and for writing *The Abbey, Mount St. Benedict – A Popular Guide* which was published in December 2005. It is our hope that *Longing to Belong* will truly do justice to the founder of Mount St. Benedict, who has long been misunderstood and misrepresented. We see this book as an important addition to the repository of historical research in the world of religious life in the late nineteenth and early twentieth century.

Without Dom Mayeul there would have been no Mount St. Benedict. And without Mount St. Benedict, Trinidad would not have been the same. The story of Dom Mayeul needed to be told at some point in time. There seemed to have been no better time to do so than in this one hundredth and fiftieth year of the anniversary of the birth of Dom Mayeul and in this one hundredth year of the founding of the Mount. Dom Mark Tierney has done a wonderful labour of love in bringing this to fruition. Unfortunately, he is unable to see the completed work, having gone to his eternal reward on 31 December 2011. He has now joined Monique De Caigny whose first visit to the resting place of Dom Mayeul in 1994 was an important impetus in the quest for the truth about her grand-uncle. By Divine Providence, her husband Filip Vandenbussche and Dom Mark were brought together. And this book is the fruit of that quest for truth which transcended time, continents and personalities.

JOHN PEREIRA, O.S.B.
ABBOT, MOUNT ST. BENEDICT
TRINIDAD, EASTER 2012

CHAPTER I

The Beginnings
(1862 – 1879)

IF IT IS TRUE that the child is father of the man, it is also true that the man is the reflection or mirror of the child. In the case of Peter De Caigny, later called Dom Mayeul, his childhood days certainly left an indelible mark on him. His upbringing was quite unusual, with most of it spent outside his parents' home. His brothers and sisters were almost strangers to him, and he missed out on the usual inter-family relationships, especially with his parents and siblings. He led a lonely, sheltered existence, which forced him to fall back on inventing games in which he was the sole participant. He also had time enough on his hands to become an avid reader of books. There is no reason to believe that his was an unhappy childhood, but he never experienced what most people call a 'normal home life'. As we embark on a study of his life, it is necessary to reflect that, during his early childhood, up to the age of 13, he was nearly always on his own, living with an aunt and uncle, and that in his last thirteen years, he became a hermit, living most of the time in a lonely farmhouse in Florida, U.S.A.

What is the key to his unsettled, ever changing career? He never seemed to sink his roots anywhere for more than a short length of time. There is a certain restlessness about him, a seeking for something, though this 'something' always seemed to elude him. The simplest way to explain his situation is this: he spent his life longing to belong; seeking for a permanent and stable home-base. At least four times in his life he thought he had found just such a home-base, but, owing to circumstances, was forced to move on. It was not that he found it difficult to settle in anywhere, whether as a child in his aunt's and uncle's home, or a boarder in a junior seminary, or a novice with the Redemptorists and Benedictines. One could, perhaps, say that fate, or Providence, played a large part in his life. He seemed at times to be the victim of circumstances beyond his control. At other times the life-changing events looked to be of his own making or to say the least, could perhaps have been avoided. Yet he achieved a great deal in his life. He had his moments of success and even fame, but also many major setbacks. He always had friends, and throughout his life he related well to most people. One could hardly call him a lonely person, a loner, in the extreme sense of the word. Rather, he sought solitude, preferably in nature, and peace in a world that he did not always understand or relate to. This is only one of the many paradoxes it will be necessary to unravel, in order to understand the very complex personality of Peter De Caigny.

Fortunately, he has left us a detailed account of his life, contained in three sizeable volumes of memoirs, written in French, soon after his 60th birthday. Looking back on his long and interesting life, he was proud of what he had achieved as a missionary monk and priest in Brazil and Trinidad. Thus the first volume (referred to as Volume I), written in 1924, is entitled *"Twenty-Five Years as a Missionary in the Tropics"*. It is a moving story covering the years in Brazil and Trinidad (Nov 1897-April 1923). In 1930 he started writing the second volume (Volume II) of his memoirs, the most compelling one. He writes about his entire life, telling a story which is credible, and, at times, very fascinating and revealing in-depth details on most of the crucial years of his life. It includes also a chapter on the genealogy of the family. Hence it forms the basis for most chapters in this biography. It is also important to mention that Volume II was an evolving work. For each year that passed by, he added paragraphs and chapters, covering special events and summarizing that year. His last entry is dated January 1939. The third volume is mostly taken up with letters, pictures, obituaries and other souvenirs of the De Caigny family and friends. Among the large selection of original letters, are several from his sisters and mother, in Flemish, which is the Dutch language spoken in the Flanders area of Belgium. Volume III also includes many letters and documents from various confidants and people he held in high regard, for example from the abbot primate. Most of these letters and documents are related to important changes in his life, and are many times referred to in his Volume II, to prove or to document what he was writing.

THE 3 VOLUMES OF THE MEMOIRS OF PETER DE CAIGNY

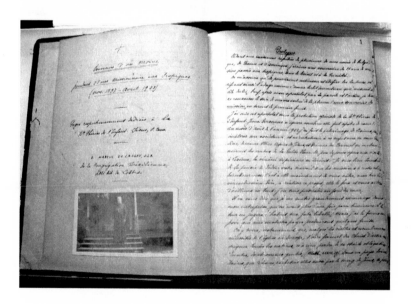

MEMOIRS VOLUME I: 25 YEARS AS A MISSIONARY IN THE TROPICS

MEMOIRS VOLUME III CONTAINS MANY FAMILY PICTURES AND LETTERS

In writing his memoirs, he set himself a daunting task, re-living his entire life, and analyzing his changing situations. Possessing a natural gift for writing, he gradually developed a very distinct literary style. The three volumes are written in a clearly legible longhand, every page presenting an incredible uniformity of script, in steady straight lines. This was an amazing achievement. He could not have done a better job with a typewriter or computer. There is not a single spelling mistake, neither is there any sign of corrections. Altogether it presents an extraordinary feat of penmanship, reflecting a disciplined mind. Having started with what the Latins called a *tabula rasa* (a blank slate), he managed to fill more than a thousand pages, without blot or smudge. It is almost certain that he was using detailed diaries or notes, in much the same way that medieval monks copied from some ancient manuscript. However, he had to put it all together, and make it credible and readable. He evidently had the gift of *total recall*, a kind of photographic memory, coupled with a sense of history. At the same time he possessed great powers of concentration, a sure and steady eye, and an untiring hand. His memoirs have never been published, although Volume I (i.e. *Twenty-Five Years as a Missionary in the Tropics*) has been hand copied, in a limited number, by sisters of the abbey of Clervaux, Luxemburg, for the use of his extended family in Belgium, and for the monks of the abbey of Bahia, Brazil. Nonetheless, he expressed the hope that one day they would eventually see the light of day. By request in his last will, Volume II could only be read and published at least 10 years after his death. The reader of this book will clearly understand why he made this request in his last will. The time has now come to set the record straight, to provide a full account of the life and times of this remarkable man, not in his own words, but using his memoirs and the thousands of letters and documents we have in the various archives, as a constant check or source.

He was born on 29 March 1862, in Iseghem, a little town in the province of West Flanders, Belgium. Receiving the name Peter at baptism, he was the 4th child of Felix De Caigny (1828-1892) and Ursula Neyrinck (1829-1900). In time, the family consisted of nine children: 4 boys and 5 girls. His father was a hard-working small farmer who existed just above the poverty line. His mother was a very religious woman, anxious for the spiritual welfare of her family. It is no wonder that all five of the girls became religious sisters, while one of the boys, Peter, became a religious priest. Iseghem

HIS PARENTS, FELIX DE CAIGNY AND URSULA NEYRINCK

was at the heart of Catholic Flanders, and Flemish (same as Dutch) the language spoken in Flanders, the northern part of Belgium. Religion was the life-blood of his family, not just taken for granted, but practised with conviction and enthusiasm.

The earliest memory young Peter retained of life under his parents' roof was a very startling one. He was five years old at the time. Their house, situated close to a railway line, had a thatched roof, which was set on fire by some sparks from a passing train. The family got out just in time, but the father, hoping to save the cows, which were housed in the adjoining cow barn, was badly injured when the roof fell on him. He was eventually rescued, but suffered terrible burns. The family house was a complete shell, which had to be abandoned until such time as it could be re-built. In his memoirs he comments on this tragic event:

The first impression that remained in my memory as a child is that of a heavy cross: the fire of our house and the groaning of my father, terribly burnt. As he wanted to save the cows, he was crushed by the burning roof which fell on him. It was extremely difficult to rescue him from under the wreckage. My father was very devoted to the Sacred Heart...every Friday of the month he received Holy Communion,... he refrained from smoking during Lent. He loved the Blessed Virgin Mary very much, every evening the rosary was recited in common and for that he demanded much respect. In the fire his clothes were consumed by the flames but his scapular and the skin underneath remained intact. For many, Mary saved his life (Vol. II, 8).

The family was forced to seek refuge with a helpful neighbour. Young Peter was taken in the arms of a girl cousin to the house of one of his uncles, Joseph Neyrinck (1827-1911), who was doubly related, being his mother's brother, while his wife, Amelia De Caigny (1832-1916) was a sister of Peter's father. The couple lived in the nearby village of Cachtem. Having no children of their own, they were happy to take little Peter into their home. He remained under their care until his adolescent years. Someone suggested at the time that Peter had started the fire, as he was seen earlier playing with a box of matches, and that he was sent away, even banished, as a kind of punishment. This is hardly credible, but if it is true, then it was the first, but not the last, time in his life that he was accused unjustly of doing something wrong. In any case, he was too young at the time to reason out this matter for himself, though he later wondered if he had been the cause of the family tragedy. Whatever the reason, and most probably it was a practical one, Peter was brought up outside his own family, deprived of the constant presence of his parents, and without the companionship of his brothers and sisters. He made the following reflection on this fact in his memoirs:

> Surely God had His plans when he allowed me to be brought up out of my family. I do not know these plans of God, but the formation of my character was strongly marked by the fact that I did not live under my parents' eye, in the company of my brothers and sisters (Vol. II, 11).

He was the only child in his uncle's and aunt's house. His uncle was a rather stern man, who only allowed Peter to receive his friends at his house, under his uncle's supervision. It appears that during these early years, Peter's health was very frail. However, thanks to the excellent care of his aunt, he overcame his weakness, and was later able to pursue his studies without serious interruption. It may well be that, during his formative years, he had no experience of real love, and that he spent the rest of his life looking for it. He developed the mentality of a displaced person, not sure if he really belonged anywhere. From time to time he went to his parents' house, which had been rebuilt, but he always felt a stranger, if not an outsider, there. He described his feelings as follows:

> At times I went to my parents' house; but I experienced there a certain uneasiness. Undoubtedly they were good to me, and I liked to play with my little sisters, driving them full-speed in the wheelbarrow. One day the little barrow broke, and I did not know what to do when I saw my little sister crying. . . . I experienced in an undefined way the feeling that I never really had a "home". God deprived me of those delights that so many others enjoy as a matter of course. Was I not in a way a stranger everywhere, even in the bosom of my family? My heart was thirsting for caresses which I scarcely knew. Because of this, I suffered as a child, although I was not able to recognize it then (Vol. II, 12-13).

As a boy, Peter was fascinated by the stories coming from Rome, where Pius IX, (1846-1878) was fighting to retain the Papal States. He was only five when, in 1867, the children of his village were encouraged to prepare bandages for Belgian soldiers in the papal army, called zouaves, who had been wounded in the latest campaign. His young heart was thrilled by the account of the exploits of these brave zouaves. He had a vivid imagination, perhaps living in a dream world, so that he vowed to become a 'zouave' when he grew up. Later, in 1870, a glorious reception was prepared in Iseghem for the returning Belgian zouaves, which left a lasting impression on young Peter. It is significant that when it came to composing a subtitle for the second volume of his memoirs, he put himself down as a "faithful papal zouave".

Yet he was blessed and privileged, thanks to the care and attention of his aunt and uncle. He always had sufficient food and shelter, books to read, and he was secure in the belief that God was watching over him. He led an almost idyllic, though sheltered, existence in this lovely Flemish village, which allowed him to live close to nature, to form a relationship with trees, flowers, birds and all wild things. The place ever after retained a kind of nostalgic hold over him, and he loved to return there in his later years. His roots and most intimate memories lay in the villages and towns of Iseghem, Emelghem, Cachtem and Roulers (minor seminary) marking him out as a convinced Flemish patriot.

He must have been six or seven years of age when he was sent to the municipal school in Iseghem, to complete his primary studies. To get to that school he had to walk about an hour, since he lived with his uncle and aunt in Cachtem, the neighbouring village. He enjoyed the daily walk in nature and he avoided when possible the crowded market days. At school he had a brilliant and pious teacher, Mr. August Vermeire, who made a deep impression on him, giving him a deep love for the Flemish language and literature, a love he retained for the rest of his life. Like many Belgians, young Peter hailed Pius IX as a martyr after the fall of Rome and its annexation by the Italian kingdom in 1870. He had an almost fanatical attachment to the Pope (Pius IX) and the Catholic Church. Throughout the days of his youth, Peter was caught up in this Flemish-Catholic ideology, which called for the creation of a Catholic state, and a confessional Catholic movement led by the bishops.

That resulted in what has been called 'the battle for souls', fought out on several fronts. The parish became the main centre of ecclesiastical endeavour, with innumerable societies such as that of St. Vincent de Paul and the Francis Xavier Associations, attracting large numbers of supporters. Newspapers, pamphlets and bro-

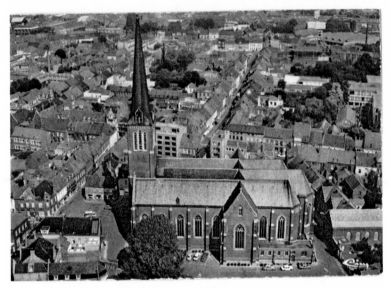

THE CITY OF ISEGHEM, THE CHURCH WHERE HE WAS BAPTIZED

MUNICIPAL SCHOOL, THE SCHOOL THAT FOREVER LEFT A POSITIVE MARK ON HIM,
ESPECIALLY HIS TEACHER AUGUST VERMEIRE

CACHTEM, THE VILLAGE WHERE PETER GREW UP, AWAY FROM HIS BROTHERS AND
SISTERS, BUT UNDER THE GOOD CARE OF HIS UNCLE AND AUNT. AT THE RIGHT,
THE SMALL RIVER "DE MANDEL", CUTTING THROUGH THE MEADOWS AND ALONG
WHICH YOUNG PETER ENJOYED PLAYING AND CLIMBING IN THE TREES. AT THE
VERY TOP ON THE RIGHT, THE CANAL WHICH WAS HANDMADE, 17 KM IN LENGTH.
PETER MENTIONED IN HIS MEMOIRS THE LONG SWIMS IN THE CANAL. IT TOOK TEN
YEARS TO FINISH AND THE FIRST BARGE NAVIGATED THE CANAL IN 1872.
(PICTURE COURTESY OF TEN MANDERE)

chures set the tone, while public meetings often led to aggressive confrontations. It affected every aspect of social life, even leisure activities, and led Catholics to create their own theatre companies, libraries, brass bands and cultural associations. It spilt over to such vital matters as cemeteries and burials. Only Catholics could be buried in official burial sites, as the burial of others would desecrate the site. Civil burials were considered as a scandal, and were condemned by priests from the pulpit. Young Peter was marked for life by these religious rivalries, which involved taking sides, and indulging in polemics. In later years, in Brazil and Trinidad, he allowed himself to become involved in serious disputes with his religious superiors, refusing to compromise or consider the fact that he might be wrong.

By 1873, his parents had established themselves in the village of Emelghem, bordering Iseghem, where they rented a larger farm. Their financial situation had improved considerably since the days of the fire, thanks mainly to the hard work and enterprise of the father. That same year, 1873, a minor domestic hiccup occurred when Peter was due to make his First Communion. It was the accepted custom of the time, that a child would receive his First Communion in the same parish as his school, which in Peter's case was Iseghem. However, his parents decided that he should make it in their new parish church of Emelghem. Both parish priests fought over the little boy, claiming him for themselves. Fortunately, common sense and parental rights prevailed in the end. Everything was amicably arranged, and Peter received his First Communion in Emelghem, on the 1st of April 1873. After the ceremony, his mother took him for a festive meal to the house of one of her brothers, Peter's godfather, who was very fond of him. A few months later, Peter was confirmed in Iseghem.

At the age of thirteen, Peter was in his final year of elementary education, and arrangements had to be made for his continued education. On the 12th of January 1875 Peter was godfather at the christening of his younger brother to whom he gave the name of Alois, after St. Aloysius. At the end of the scholar year 1874-1875, Peter received the gold medal for good behaviour and the silver medal for his other achievements at school, much to the delight of his mother. It seems that he already felt the call to the priestly life, and hoped he might be able to attend one of the minor semi-

THE FARM HOUSE IN EMELGHEM. AFTER THE TERRIBLE FIRE THE FAMILY
MOVED TO THIS LITTLE FARM ABOUT 1 KM FROM THEIR FIRST FARM IN ISEGHEM.
EMELGHEM AND ISEGHEM ARE IN FACT BORDERING AND THE TOWN-VILLAGE
CENTRES ARE VERY CLOSE. ALTHOUGH STILL SMALL, THIS FARM WAS LARGER AND
NOT ANY LONGER CLOSE TO THE RAIL TRACKS.

THE CHURCH OF EMELGHEM IN WHICH HE DID HIS FIRST COMMUNION ON
1 APRIL 1873.

naries, which existed at this time in Belgium. These were second-ary boarding schools, run by the Catholic Church, which provided educational facilities for talented students, also with the hope to steer them to religious life. He discussed the matter of his future education with his aunt and uncle, and also with his confessor, the Rev. Benoot, vicar of Cachtem where young Peter still resided. The latter arranged for Peter to be accepted into the minor seminary of Roulers, where he began his secondary studies in October 1875. He revealed his intentions to his parents, who had considered send-ing him, for economic reasons, to the Jesuit Apostolic School at Turnhout. But they readily gave their consent to the Roulers pro-posal strongly backed as it was by Peter's aunt. His schoolmaster, Mr. Vermeire at the municipal school of Iseghem, got to know about this decision and he tried with all means to convince Peter's parents to keep young Peter for one more year in his school to bet-ter prepare him for the studies at the minor seminary. However it was Peter's ambition to be, as quickly as possible, nearer to the goal of his life. ⸺

At last my parents yielded to my insistence. I was at the height of joy! It was a great step forward in my career (Vol. II, 16).

Thus, in the autumn of 1875, Peter set out on the next stage of his career, which was to provide him with new opportunities and challenges. Roulers proved to be an excellent choice, giving him the chance to develop his mental faculties, and teaching him to stand on his own two feet. In addition, Roulers was conveniently located, bordering the village of Cachtem where Peter resided. The distance between Cachtem and Roulers was a mere 6 kilometres and the distance between Iseghem and Roulers about 8 km, distances that were, in those days, easy to cover on foot. Or, considering he had to take his luggage for the boarding school, young Peter may have trav-elled by train. The train connection between Courtrai and Bruges, inaugurated in 1847, made a stop at Iseghem and Roulers.

He spent four years in Roulers, which he considered the happiest time of his life. Again, as in his primary school, he was fortunate in having a number of excellent teachers, all priests, who inspired him to work hard and expand his mind. In his memoirs, he gives their names: Fr. Jules Delorge for science, Fr. Hugo Verriest for literary studies, and Fr. Victor Lanssen his boarding-master, who gave weekly conferences to the students on a wide range of subjects.

THE SILVER MEDAL (1874) PETER RECEIVED AT THE MUNICIPAL SCHOOL

MONUMENT OF GUIDO GEZELLE, THE PRIEST-POET. HE IS ONE OF THE
LEGENDARY FOUNDERS OF THE FLEMISH MOVEMENT. HE WAS A STUDENT AND
TEACHER AT THE MINOR SEMINARIE OF ROULERS.

Roulers was in the heartland of Flanders, but French was the language of everyday use in the seminary. The mid-1870s witnessed a resurgence of the Flemish Movement, which had as its objective the preservation of Flemish language and literature, as well as the Christian traditions of the region. Many of Peter's teachers however were members of the Flemish movement and they tried to give their courses, as often as possible and tolerated, in Flemish. It is a fact that the Flemish Movement found an excellent breeding ground at the minor seminary in Roulers, during the years that Peter was at school there. The young Peter De Caigny thus found himself caught up in this exciting socio-political movement, and became personally acquainted with its chief initiators. One of the leaders of the movement was a Catholic priest and poet, Fr. Guido Gezelle (1830-1899), for whom Peter had a high regard. In his memoirs Peter wrote:

> *I learned to love in a special way my homeland, as I witnessed the Christian beginnings of the famous Flemish Movement, born within the very walls of this minor seminary (Roulers)...My soul was delighted at reading various masterpieces written by Guido Gezelle: "De kerkhof bloemen" (The churchyard flowers), "O 't ruisschen van het ranke riet" (Oh, the rustling of the slender reeds). This movement was begun by G. Gezelle. It was nurtured and developed by H. Verriest and his famous disciple Albert Rodenbach, and had as its objective the preservation of the Flemish language and the Christian traditions of our region; could there be anything more appropriate? I readily joined in the movement (Vol. II, 18).*

It is necessary to remember this Flemish background as it gave him a sense of patriotism, as well as a loyalty, to a particular group. On the first page of Volume II he wrote the famous Flemish saying: *"Met 't kruis in top, Zo varen wij, Door 't wereldtij, Ten hogen hemel op!"* (With the cross as our flag, so we sail through the world's oceans, to the high heavens). And on the envelopes of his letters, he wrote "For God and Flanders". This Flemish nationalist legacy instilled a kind of die-hard mentality, which served him badly in later life, as it led him to see most situations as black or white, as right or wrong. It meant that he became an idealist, rather than a realist, reaching out for some supposedly worthy cause, which he pursued with all his energy. In such a climate there was no room for compromise.

North
Sea

Netherlands

Brugge

West-
Vlaanderen

Thielt
Roulers Iseghem

Gent

Oost-
Vlaanderen

Antwerpen

Antwerpen

Limburg

Hasselt

Germany

Vlaams Brabant

Leuven

Brussel

Waver

Waals
Brabant

Luik

Luik

Henegouwen

Bergen

Namen

Namen

Namen

Luxemburg

Aarlen

Luxembourg

Luxembourg

France

BELGIUM

EUROPE

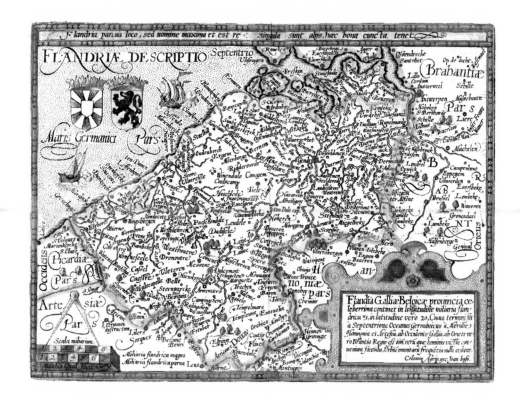

COUNTY OF FLANDERS IN THE 15TH CENTURY: THE NORTH SEA AT THE TOP
LEFT, CALLED THE ENGLISH CHANNEL. ON THE LEFT IS FRANCE AND ON THE
RIGHT TOP CORNER, THE RIVER THE SCHELDT AND PORT OF ANTWERP. ON THE
RIGHT, THE PROCINCE BRABANTIA, NOW ALSO PART OF BELGIUM,
WITH THE CAPITAL BRUSSELS.

Map of the county of Flanders by Matthias Quad (cartographer) and Johannes Bussemacher (engraver & publisher, Cologne). This image is in the public domain. http://en.wikipedia.org/wiki/File:Quad_Flandria.jpg

He recognised, of course, that Flemish was a minority language, and if he wished to travel, and become a missionary, he would have to learn other languages. By the end of his life, he spoke and wrote fluently the following languages: Flemish, French, Brazilian-Portuguese, English and Latin. His other abiding interest, while in Roulers, was history, especially the history of the Church. His two favourite books were: *"Fabiola"* by Cardinal Wiseman, and *"The Monks of the West"* by Montalembert.

Peter's time in Roulers coincided with a movement on the part of the Belgian Liberal government to control education in the country. The progressive liberals, which included the masonic lodges, began a campaign of anti-clericalism, and made it clear that they sought to eliminate the Catholic dominance in education. Roulers, along with many other Catholic schools, survived the government's move to impose a secular school system everywhere in Belgium. In fact, the attempt by the government to secularise education back-fired, and it is calculated that some 3,385 new Catholic schools were created in the late 1870s *(See Els Witte, The Battle for monasteries, cemeteries and schools in Belgium, in Culture Wars. Eds. C. Clark and W. Kaiser. Cambridge University, Press. 2006).*

While enjoying his many intellectual successes and interests, Peter had one constant worry at the back of his mind, namely his health. In order to become a priest, he would have to be in good health. At certain moments of his life he suffered from various health problems. In his memoirs he refers to the fact that from the age of seven he suffered from rheumatism. He also had a weak chest and found the long, cold winters of Flanders sapped his energy and brought loss of weight. His aunt, in whose house he continued to live when not at the seminary, was well aware of these problems. She visited him regularly at Roulers, especially during Lent, when the seminary food was reduced, and brought him a fair supply of eggs, chocolate and figs. He was also given permission to have a cup of soup at 10.30, after the morning classes. Whenever he was at home with his aunt, she made him take cod liver oil, usually accompanied by a glass of wine to make the bad taste disappear. One day, the bishop of Bruges visited the seminary to inspect the corps of the zouaves. He stopped in front of Peter and told him that he should develop his chest.

De Brauwer-Stock, Grand'Place, Roulers.   ROULERS. Panorama Sud.

Zicht van 't Klein Seminarie, op St Michielstoren. – In 1896.

THE MINOR SEMINARY IN 1896 AT ROULERS
(ARCHIVES MINOR SEMINARY ROULERS)

21

He never forgot the terrible epidemic of smallpox which struck Flanders in 1878. Among those who died during the plague was his class friend, Francis Hoste. It made a strong impression on him and Peter kept the obituary card all his life in Volume II. There is a clear possibility that his moves to Trinidad, and later to Florida, were partly motivated by reasons of health. It would seem that throughout his life he was constantly seeking a healthy place of refuge, a kind of Shangri-La. At least three times in his life he thought his dream had come true, in Santa Cruz (Brazil), in Mount Thabor (Trinidad), and the College Farm of St Leo Abbey (Florida).

Apart from his health problems, he had to deal with some personal shortcomings, mostly relating to his character. He suffered from an extreme sensitivity, which led him to resent any criticism, no matter how slight. He describes all this, as follows, in his memoirs:

> *I tried to keep down certain bad tendencies of my nature. I reacted badly to any sign of contempt or mockery. I remember that at the beginning of my stay at the seminary, a certain cassock, the cut of which seemed to me ridiculous, became a source of annoyance for me when people started to make comments about it. Mockery and contempt about that and other matters hurt me a lot, and I preferred to wear clothes that were rather simple and poor. One day someone offended me by giving me a nickname. I felt my blood boil in my veins and my heart reacted strongly; it was not for nothing nature had made me ill-tempered. Nature had endowed me with a 'bilious-sanguine' nature, which fortunately I was able to control (Vol. II, 20).*

Peter wrote this in his 60th year, and evidently chose his words carefully. Writing in French, a language which is very precise, he admitted that he was a 'bilious-sanguine' person. Both French and English use the same word, which means someone who sets himself certain aims and ambitions, who likes to win, and is prepared to use every effort to excel. At its most precise meaning, a 'bilious' person is someone who likes to make decisions, to control and direct the lives of others. However, it also lends itself to certain abuses, such as giving way to anger, hardness of heart, even tyranny, as well as impatience and cynicism. Peter admits in his own words that as a child he tried to excel in all games, and that his uncle reproached

VIEW OF THE VILLAGE OF CACHTEM, TAKEN FROM THE SMALL RIVER. YOUNG
PETER LOVED NATURE AND SOLITUDE. HE DESCRIBED IN HIS MEMOIRS THE LONG
WALKS HE MADE ALONG THE CREEK "DE MANDEL" WHICH MEANDERED THROUGH
THE VILLAGE AND ITS FARMLANDS. (PICTURE COURTESY OF TEN MANDERE)

him for his excessive desire to win, and for his recklessness and un-warranted temerity (Vol. II, 11). He had an excessively proud nature and he felt humiliated and ashamed by the poverty of his parents. As a consequence he always tried to establish a certain distinction and superiority for himself, and for his entire family branch.

> *For, if my parents were not endowed with this world's goods, they were rich in faith and sustained by an admirable devotion. How-ever these lofty considerations did not prevent my proud nature from suffering at the sight of my parent's poverty. If the social status of our family was rather humiliating in the eyes of the world, in a sense, it was far from being dishonourable. My parents first, and then my two brothers, managed through their hard work and integrity, to raise their fortunes and their social status (Vol. II, 7).*

Later in his life, his Redemptorist superiors suggested that cer-tain decisions by Peter could possibly be explained as a reaction to excessive inferiority feelings. These shortcomings of character will become much more evident as the story of his life unfolds.

Fortunately, there was, he admits, another side to his personal-ity, summed up in the word 'sanguine'. This indicated that he was extremely sociable, seeking to make contact with persons of his own background or interests, and needing to form innumerable relationships with other people. It also meant that he had a friendly, jovial and generous nature. On top of all this, he had a highly intel-ligent mind, which when allied to all his other exceptional qualities, allowed him to reach high office and to influence a great number of people. But all that was in the distant future.

During his time in Roulers, he made several pilgrimages. Dur-ing the Easter Holidays, together with his elder brother, they went during the night on foot to Bruges to attend the Holy Blood pro-cession. It took them all night to get there but the trip was for him an unforgettable experience. Peter spent part of the long summer holidays at the houses of different members of his family. He made long walks across the cultivated fields. There he found the beautiful nature and horizons that he missed so much at the minor seminary. He was especially fond of the company of one of his cousins, Octave De Caigny, who was studying at the episcopal college of

A PAPAL ZOUAVE.
THE PAPAL ZOUAVES WERE FORMED IN DEFENCE OF THE PAPAL STATES. THE ZOUAVES EVOLVED OUT OF A UNIT, FORMED IN 1860, THE FRANCO-BELGIAN REGIMENT. ON JANUARY 1, 1861 THE UNIT WAS RENAMED THE PAPAL ZOUAVES. THE ZOUAVES WERE MAINLY YOUNG MEN, UNMARRIED AND ROMAN CATHOLIC, WHO VOLUNTEERED TO ASSIST POPE PIUS IX IN HIS BATTLE TO DEFEND THE PAPAL STATES. THE REGIMENT WAS TRULY INTERNATIONAL.

Photographer: Fratelli D'Alessandri, Roma. Lombardi Historical Collection. This image is in the public domain because its copyright has expired. http://en.wikipedia.org/wiki/File:Papal_Zouave.jpg

THE ZOUAVES AT THE MINOR SEMINARY, ROULERS, GUARDING THE BUST OF POPE PIUS IX (ARCHIVES MINOR SEMINARY ROULERS)

25

St. Amand, in Courtrai. The two boys went every year to visit the parish priest of Langemarck, another cousin. Peter describes these visits in his memoirs:

> These visits, to our cousin the parish priest, helped me to get an idea about the life of secular priests. Doubtlessly they render a great service to the Church, being the numerous army of St. Peter; but I did not feel at all attracted to that way of life. On the contrary this experience made my desire for religious life grow ever stronger. Near the village (Langemarck) there was an Abbey of Trappists, in Westvleteren. We decided to call and see the place, and were welcomed quite cordially. It was the first time I was in contact with monks. Their hospitality, so simple and natural, left on me an excellent impression. But I was not drawn to their way of life. My cousin, Octave De Caigny, shared my views on this point. God was calling us elsewhere. Years later, I became a religious, while he joined the Seminary of Foreign Missions in Paris. He was sent to India, and it was during one of his holidays in Flanders that he assisted my mother during her last illness. Both of us had the love of the missions but, as for me, I wished to dedicate myself to that ideal with the backing of a religious rule (Vol. II, 23-24).

During the short Christmas holiday he spent some time with his parents and brothers and sisters. He admits that he still had that kind of uneasy feeling:

> The short Christmas holidays had all the charm of the feasts spent in the intimacy of the family. It is perhaps only in these circumstances that I enjoyed it most. Brought up alone, almost always away from home, I loved to take part in the several entertainments of those long winter evenings, to make up in some way for my privations in that matter. I felt less isolated and, as it were, closer to my family without however being able to get rid of a sort of uneasiness in their presence. So, therefore I always willingly went back to the minor seminary (Vol. II, 26).

Having completed four years studying what was called 'the Humanities', Peter decided the time had come for him to make some kind of commitment to a religious form of life. His superiors in the minor seminary tried to get him to stay on for another two years in Roulers, to complete his secondary education. However, discovering that he already qualified, being over 17 years of age, to enter the novitiate of any religious Congregation or Order of his choice, he discussed his vocation with Fr. Godts, the rector of the Redemptorist monastery in Roulers. Peter told him that he wished to join an Order which was devoted to Mary, the Mother of God, and to the missions. The latter received him kindly and confirmed that his Order, the Redemptorists, had special devotion to Mary, and that they had missions in South America. Not knowing any other Order, Peter decided to apply for entry to the novitiate of the Redemptorists, provided that he received his parents' permission.

In June 1879, Peter took the opportunity to discuss his vocation with his aunt and uncle, who showed no surprise at his decision. A few days later he paid a visit to his parents, and asked their permission. His mother was the only one who offered any discreet opposition, asking if he had consulted his spiritual adviser. She also hoped he had reflected on this serious decision, which he was taking at such a young age. Satisfied with his answers, his parents gave him their blessing and permission. At the minor seminary of Roulers, he kept his decision to himself, until two days before the summer holidays. He discovered then that he would be the first leaving his class to join a religious Order. At the end-of-term prize-giving, the awards were presented by Fr. Godts, the local Redemptorist superior. Peter received the top prizes in History, Geography and Flemish Literature, as well as that of Good Behaviour. He placed second in Christian doctrine and French language. However mathematics was not his cup of tea, he came only sixth in class. Buoyed up by the thought that he was heading for a wonderful life, which would bring him close to God, he left Roulers with a light heart and an easy mind.

A farewell party was given in his parents' house, attended by relatives and friends, as well as many of his classmates. Although he was the 4th by order of birth, he was the first to leave the family circle, and make his permanent home in a religious Order. His five sisters eventually left home to consecrate themselves to God in the religious life. Considering that, since the age of four, he had never really known the happiness of living under his parent's roof, Peter was deeply moved when the time came to say goodbye to his parents. He would always remember the poignant moment when, as he was about to depart, his mother made the sign of the Cross on his forehead.

Surely, as I was not as accustomed as my sisters were to the sweet-
ness of the family nest, the separation did not prove so costly for me.
However, my heart was heavy when I bade farewell to my family,
especially when my mother, whom I loved very much, made on my
forehead, as she used to do, the sign of the cross. Such was the end
of my life in the world (Vol. II, 31).

He considered this as marking the end of his life 'in the world'. Yet he had seen so little of 'the world', from whose dangers he was now escaping. He admitted later that the idea of marriage had never entered his head, for the very reason that he knew nothing about girls or marriage at this moment of his life. It would appear that he was being thrown into the sea of life at the deep end. Yet, from his point of view, he was simply following his vocation, as indicated by the will of God. How he would cope with the challenges of the years to come, time alone would tell.

Peter wrote in his memoirs about this important change in his life:

More and more the world was becoming a burden to me. I vividly
felt that in it, I was not in my element. I experienced a strong
attraction for the cloister. So I left a world I hardly knew. Yet I
disliked it very much. It was not at all heartache for the lost love
of a girl that led me to the cloister. Never had the picture of a girl
touched my imagination. The idea of marriage had never offered
itself to my young heart, completely taken by the love of God alone.
I did not know evil or, at the most, I hardly suspected it. I entered
into the monastery, happy to escape from the dangers of this world,
which I had been taught to fear (Vol. II, 31).

Love for the Pope and Church are part and parcel of my early
infancy. I only heard people talk about Pius IX, the Pope Martyr
and prisoner in the Vatican. Since then I dreamed to be a zouave.
How I regretted it, that I was born too late to go to Rome to shed
my blood in defence of the temporal domain of the Pope! But later,
thinking that the spiritual domain was much more important, and
consequently, he needed a lot more zouaves to defend it. I decided
to be, with heart and soul, the champion of the Pope and Church,
even If I were to lose my life (Vol. II, 5).

PETER AT THE AGE OF 17, BEFORE LEAVING FOR ST. TROND,
THE REDEMPTORISTS.

PETER'S MEMOIRS, VOLUME III, IN WHICH HE RESERVED, ON THE RIGHT OF
HIS PICTURE, A SPACE TO INCLUDE THE PICTURE OF HIS BROTHER MEDARD,
WHO DIED AT THE AGE OF 25.

Later in his life, reflecting on the similarity between his own sufferings and battles he fought, and that of the Pope, he made the following remarks:

> *How many times afterwards did I not think that death, on a battlefield around Rome, would have been much sweeter for me than the many moral sufferings I had to endure during my life, in order to remain faithful to the desires and to the will of the head of the Church. Not only the impious, outside the Church, attack the Pope with violence and tricks, but also Christians, from the inside, making the battle even more distressing (Vol. II, 5).*

This reflection illustrates very well how he felt during the many uphill battles he fought, and how he perceived, rightly or wrongly, the actions of some of the high-ranking members of the clergy.

CHAPTER II

Life as a Redemptorist
(1879 – 1897)

IN MID-SEPTEMBER 1879, Peter De Caigny, accompanied by a few other students of the minor seminary of Roulers, left by train for Saint-Trond, where the novitiate of the Belgian Province of the Redemptorists was located. They stopped at Brussels, to change trains and have something to eat. In a restaurant, they met a friendly priest, who, learning where they were going, offered them some cigars, which they accepted. Peter wrote later that he threw away the butt of the cigar at the door of the novitiate, and never again used tobacco under any form. The novitiate, the building within a monastery that is devoted exclusively to the housing and training of novices, presented a rather sombre, if not forbidding, aspect. To help them over the first hurdle, they had to undergo a fifteen-day retreat, a series of spiritual exercises, from 1-15 October. This was a kind of fast-track initiation into the life of a Redemptorist. On the last day of the retreat, Peter and his companions were clothed in the habit of the Order. The novitiate group was a large and very fervent one, full of exuberance and enthusiasm. However, their spirits were soon to be sorely tested by the novice master, a very austere man, who favoured all kinds of bodily mortifications. Nowadays, it is almost impossible to imagine the indignities and humiliations they had to submit to. In his memoirs, Peter gives some stark details, which sound very medieval and even sadistic *(Vol. II, 28)*. The mortification and penance included fasts and all kind of disciplines. There were the hair-shirts in all shapes, a garment of rough cloth made from goats' hair and worn in the form of a shirt or as a strap or as a belt. Mastication of bitter herbs and deprivation of sleep, mainly because one had to wear a hair-shirt in bed, were not at all uncommon either. All these were their daily fare. He recounts how one Christmas night, the priest, whose job it was to wake the novices for the midnight Mass, found him asleep, and started throwing icy water on his face. But the worst trial of all was the food. He described the problem in his memoirs:

> Having enjoyed a delicate regime at my aunt's, and also at the minor seminary of Roulers, where I had been granted many exceptions, some dishes in the novitiate caused quite a problem for my stomach. For instance, cod provoked terrible cramps in the beginning. I had to remain silent and control myself as best I could. . . .I used a stratagem, taking lots of mustard to overcome my repugnance. But it was mainly the beet-soup that I disliked. . . . I heard one senior member of the community chatting one day with others, and making the remark that I had the appearance of a person affected by tuberculosis (phthisis). Such remarks led me to fear that I would not be admitted to Profession at the end of my novitiate. However, the idea of asking for exceptions did not even come into my mind. . . . The aunt who brought me up was struck, during a visit, at seeing how slim and pale I was. She mentioned it to Fr. Godts, who was now Rector at Saint-Trond. But she was angry to see that her intervention had no result. God alone assisted me in a visible way, even in the matter of my health (Vol. II, 33).

Another cruel act of humiliation came from the novice master himself. Apparently he took pleasure in teasing Peter about his surname, often calling him 'Monsieur le Marquis De Caigny', since in French, the diminutive 'de' indicated noble origin. On arriving at Saint-Trond, Peter had taken care to write his name De Caigny, but it was no use when faced with the malice of his novice master. During Peter's time in Roulers, where Flemish was the language in everyday use, there had been no remarks made about his surname, but they all pronounced his name very incorrectly. But in Saint-Trond, where French was in common use, the name De Caigny stood out a mile and was pronounced the right way. Peter, of course, had known for some time a family tradition regarding their name that the 'De Caigny' were of French origin, and had come into Belgium in the 16th century. They had remained on in Flanders and taken positions in the village of Thielt and surrounding area. Peter had also learned another family tradition, recounted to him by his father, that the family was descended from a French general. However, he had no intention of sharing any such thoughts of grandeur with his novice master, and in the meantime had to endure the teasing and humiliation. Still much later, Peter discovered more about

32

his possible ancestors. However most of the documents and other sources covering the period before the 15th century got lost in the fire of the presbytery of the priest, a genealogist and family friend, who did the research. This was most unfortunate from a genealogical point of view.

But where did the family name originate from? For sure, the name De Caigny did not originate in Flanders. One has to remember that at that time, Belgium did not exist as a country. Flanders was a county (a province) and belonged in the 14th, 15th and 16th century consecutively to France, Duchy de Burgundy, the Habsburg Empire and in the 16th century to Spain. Flanders was already at that time the battlefield of many wars. For the period, starting at the 15th century, there are two sources, both with their own merits. The first source goes back to Jean De Caigny, born in 1468, in Armentieres (France), married in Courtrai-Flanders (1498) with Rebecca Maeseman. Their grandson, Romain De Caigny, born around 1540, settled in Thielt as a builder-carpenter and married Marie-Therese Roelants in 1570. Romain, together with his son Romain II (born in 1572), rebuilt and restored the many houses and structures in the city of Thielt, which were heavily damaged during the Religious Wars and by various invading troops. Thielt had about 3500 inhabitants in 1640. Romain II married Marguerite Van Aelst around 1600. He died in Thielt on 12 June 1653.

The second and more reliable source, Desire De Somviele (1838-1914), the well-known archivist of the city of Thielt and genealogist, concluded that the father of Romain II, was in fact Jerome De Caigny. Romain II, born in Normandy, France, settled around 1598 in Thielt and became later on part of the bourgeoisie. The name was often written in historic documents in Thielt as "Cagny" (instead of Caigny), the name of a village in Normandy. In fact, in Normandy there are many references to the seigniors de Coigny, De Caigny, de Cagny. The 'Chateau de Coigny', near Carentan, Manche, France, which Peter visited in 1923, may have belonged to his ancestors at one time. Unfortunately, during the battle of Normandy in June 1944, the bombardments on Caen destroyed the whole city and reduced the immense and famous archives to ashes.

Without any doubt, Romain De Caigny and Marguerite Van Aelst are in a straight line the ancestors of Peter De Caigny. All the generations up to this date, following Romain from father to son,

CHATEAU DE COIGNY. THE CHATEAU, WHICH IS LOCATED ABOUT 15 KM FROM THE
VILLAGE ST MERE EGLISE, WHERE THE AMERICAN AIRBORNE DIVISION SUFFERED
SO MANY LOSSES IN JUNE 1944, DURING THE LANDING IN NORMANDY.
THE CHATEAU WAS THE HQ OF THE GERMAN STAFF AND IN THE SECOND
WEEK AFTER THE LANDING IT BECAME THE AMERICAN HQ. FORTUNATLEY THE
CHATEAU, UNLIKE MOST STRUCTURES, WAS NOT DESTROYED. THE SMALL ROOMS IN
THE ATTIC STILL SHOW MANY OF THE GERMAN GRAFFITI, MAINLY POETRY, THAT
THE SOLDIERS LEFT ON THE WALLS.

have all been successfully researched and documented. The only unanswered question is from which area in France, Armentieres or Normandy, came the very first De Caigny to settle in Flanders. The name 'De Caigny', with the diminutive 'de', was over time written and interchanged as 'De Caigny' (with capital D), and in one word 'Decaigny'. Romain De Caigny has been remembered in Thielt as an architect, builder and as a man of standing. One of his master-pieces, still standing, is the tower of the belfry of Thielt, restored in 1620 in a rather unique style – in 1598 Flanders had become a county under Spanish governance. His descendants would take up many important positions in the area and surrounding cities. There is a large portrait painting, hanging in the city hall of Thielt, of the military leader Constantin De Caigny, born in 1712. Peter De Caigny referred in his memoirs, at several crucial events of his life, to his ancestors. But more on that in the following chapters.

After one year in the novitiate, Peter was accepted for religious profession on 15 October, 1880. This ceremony meant that he had to take the three vows, of Poverty, Chastity and Obedience, binding for three years. A short time before his profession, he experienced a serious doubt, which troubled his mind and heart, for he began to ask himself if the life of a Redemptorist was really meant for him. These doubts were centred on the very nature of the life as led by the Redemptorists. He wished for more silence, more enclosure, more liturgical and contemplative life, than was provided by the Rule of St. Alphonsus. He gradually began to think that the daily activities and duties of the Redemptorists were similar to that of "secular priests", whereas his own inclinations were towards a mo-nastic kind of life. Within his close family circle there were several parish priests. He appreciated the great service they rendered but his heart and mind were longing for something else, although he didn't know where to look for what he really wanted. This idea was to haunt him for a long time. He explained his hesitations in the following words:

> I mentioned my problem to the novice master, who dismissed my doubts as a temptation which I should disregard. That was more easily said than done. First of all, was it a temptation? I found it difficult to believe that either the evil one or my nature were responsible for my doubt. In the meantime, I remained very per-plexed. Besides, at the time, I hardly knew any other religious

Thielt. — Le Beffroi.

THE BELFRY OF THIELT WITH THE TOWER OF 1620

Order, except the Franciscans and the Trappists. My reading of Montalembert's "Monks of the West" had only provided me with a historical knowledge of the past. But where then should I go? Still more, there was no hurry. The wisest thing was to wait. And last of all, the uncertainty of such a change frightened me. Nevertheless, my doubt was there (Vol. II, 31).

He spent three years in Saint-Trond, under a regime which would have broken the spirit of most people. It is difficult to understand, let alone explain, the mentality of his superiors, who subjected him, and all the other young men in their charge, to such treatment. One of the punishments imposed for a so-called sin of the tongue (i.e. speaking ill of someone), was to make the guilty person go down on his knees and lick the ground for ten minutes or even longer. This was done in the church, or one of the corridors of the house, and involved licking the tiles. Often this punishment was imposed without any definite proof, but on the word of another student, who acted as a 'zealot'. Peter explains this particular custom:

On several occasions I was appointed 'zealot'. This office consisted in publicly accusing those who committed faults against the Holy Rule. This function, as delicate as unpleasant, taught me to fulfil my duties without preoccupying myself with human respect. I only had in mind the Holy Rule, without partiality. Evidently, as one discharges that obligation in all conscience, because of human weakness one cannot expect to please everybody. I was zealot on several occasions, first in the novitiate, then in the clericate in Saint-Trond, then in Beauplateau, and after ordination, for the whole community. Thank God, this duty was nowhere for me a seed-bed of enmity (Vol. II, 29-30).

After his profession, he proceeded to a two-year period of study in Saint-Trond, though still under the eye of his superiors. This was nothing more than a continuation of his former studies in the Humanities, which he had begun at Roulers. He found this intellectual work very satisfying, and life became more bearable. There were less bodily mortifications, though the humiliations continued to be frequent. One day he had to dance in public. The rule was to accept everything with calm and a smile (Vol. II, 33). Outwardly, he observed the rule in all its details, especially where silence and custody of the eyes were concerned. All this, together with a certain gravity of bearing, earned him the nickname "Desert Father". One suspects a certain naivety or docility on his part, in thus leaving himself open to such criticism, perhaps even to ridicule. There are several examples in his memoirs, where he seemed to show a lack of tact or diplomacy. The following is a typical such incident:

> *One of my superiors told me to go to his cell every evening for a short manifestation of conscience. At this time the Holy See had not yet issued the regulations that were published later on that matter (In 1917, the new Code of Canon Law forbade superiors to demand any revealing of conscience from their subjects). In my genuine simplicity, I thought I should let him know even about the involuntary thoughts that, at times, came spontaneously to my mind against him. This was for me the cause of a lot of trouble. Although I told that superior that I did not entertain these unintentional thoughts, he could not conceive that anyone could possibly have ideas of that kind about him! He justified and defended himself, as though I was the cause of these ideas. Our relations became quite difficult (Vol. II, 34).*

Such treatment from his superiors in Saint-Trond was in no way helpful to the healthy development of his general character and well-being. If anything, it only contributed to complicating and confusing Peter's life. He could, of course, do nothing to rectify the situation, as he was always at the receiving end of these difficult situations. At best one can say that it was all part of the growing up process of candidates for religious life in the late nineteenth century. It undoubtedly led to a negative and unhealthy mentality in these unfortunate young men. The wonder is that they survived such a regime, and retained so much of their sanity.

In September 1882, Peter was sent for further studies to Beauplateau, between Bastogne and St. Hubert, in the Province of Belgian Luxembourg, to study philosophy and Theology. This was a newly established Redemptorist convent, built in 1880, and also contained a house of studies. The property had been donated to the Redemptorists by the du Bus family, who lived in a nearby chateau. During the first year, the students suffered greatly from the lack of essential amenities, such as heating, furniture, baths, etc., which were in the process of being installed. They found themselves in the heart of the Ardennes, a rather cold and damp environment, especially in the winter months. The house of studies, called a Scholasticate, was miles from any town, surrounded by forests and perched on a plateau, hence the name *Beauplateau*. The "beau" (beautiful) part of the name referred rather to the view than the site itself. The convent was located in the perimeter of Bastogne, and during the Battle of the Ardennes and Bastogne in the winter of 1944 many refugees took shelter in the convent buildings. During the fierce battle, the buildings changed hands several times between the Germans and the Americans, leaving the convent in ruins.

These years of study in Beauplateau made a deep impression on Peter. He experienced a great spiritual profit since the formation at Beauplateau complemented harmoniously the one he got at Saint-Trond. Fr. Dubois, as holy as learned, was his new prefect. Under this wise and enlightened guide, Peter's soul began soon to expand. The first two years were spent studying philosophy. He had been given to understand, when in Saint-Trond, that he would never succeed in grasping this subject, and so he had approached it with a certain fear. However, he soon became fascinated, and eventually excelled in it to an eminent degree. Indeed, he ended his two years of philosophy by pouring out his love for the subject in Flemish verse. It was probably during his years in Beauplateau that he developed a literary style of his own. Unfortunately, the texts of his writings at this stage of his life seem to have been lost. They were mostly in the form of essays or theses, offered to his professors, and probably thrown, by them, into the waste paper basket.

Having completed the two-year course in philosophy, he started a four-year course of studies in Theology, which consisted of several sub-divisions; Dogmatic Theology, Moral Theology, Sacred Scripture, the Liturgy, etc. The study of the Holy Bible filled him with awe. Evidently this was the first time he had seriously come face to face with the Word of God. He describes his reactions in his memoirs:

> *The study of the Holy Bible, more than any other, filled me with a pure joy. I had the feeling that God was talking to my soul and revealing His secrets. I made a collection of sacred texts: some forming the theoretical part, others the practical. The first was related to the different attributes of the Three August Persons of the Blessed Trinity; for instance the majesty and supreme power of God the Father, the wisdom and beauty of the Word, and love and goodness of the Holy Spirit. In the practical part, the texts recall and explain our duties towards the three Persons of the adorable*

Trinity. All this formed a biblical bouquet, containing the honey of the purest asceticism (Vol. II, 38).

We also had a class of sacred literature that I liked very much, especially as it was delivered by our Prefect, Fr. Dubois. He left us entire freedom of choice of our compositions. I took this opportunity to write an essay that brought deep emotion, it seems, in the soul of many a young confrere. The subject was "The theory of true happiness according to the sacred poetry of the heart". In prose and verse, I celebrated God, our principle and end, the only source of true happiness for men. To my great surprise, I received a spontaneous and quite unusual ovation (Vol. II, 39).

Unfortunately, neither of the above compositions: "*The collection of sacred texts*", nor "*The theory of true happiness*", has survived.

There was only one downturn during these years of studying Theology. It came to him in the form of scruples, and concerned his attitude towards women. His problem is best described in his own words:

These studies were accompanied for some time by a crisis of scruples; several times a week I had to apply to the kind offices of our venerated Prefect (Fr. Dubois), who always welcomed me with a fatherly solicitude. The idea of, the very word, "woman", became for me an occasion of temptation that unsettled me without knowing why. The impression left on me by my education, made me fear that every woman could be a serpent ready to seduce me. Actually, I knew no woman, save those in my family: hence, wherefrom could arise this instinctive and mysterious fear of any daughter of Eve? The speculative knowledge I had of women's nature and role, and of the way to behave towards them, left me in some frightening obscurity from the practical point of view (Vol. II, 50).

Such thoughts were nothing more than the musings of a young celibate, who has not yet come to terms with the role that women could play in his life. Later, in a gloss on the side of the page, he added these words: "*And the Lord God said: It is not good for man to be alone. Let us make him a help like unto himself (Genesis, ii. 18). Not exclusively as a wife, but as a true helpmate in various respects. What a pity that in this matter we have not conformed to the divine plan!*"

After five years in Beauplateau, Peter was due to receive the three Major Orders: Subdiaconate, Diaconate and Priesthood, spread over three days, 9th, 10th and 11th October 1887, while his First Mass was scheduled for 12th October. Peter had nine companions, all candidates for the priesthood. They approached the big day of their ordination with fervour and recollection. However, they were to receive a big shock, a few days beforehand. The rector decided, at the last moment, that there would be no guests for the occasion. He cited as an excuse for this decision, the unusual number of candidates, and the altogether unacceptable number of guests, presuming there would be at least six guests per candidate. The rector maintained that such crowds of guests would serve as a distraction to the young men, who should be thinking only of the solemnity of the occasion, and not worrying about their parents' feelings. Peter was deeply disappointed, knowing how much his dear mother was looking forward to attending the ordination ceremony and his first Mass, and getting his first priestly blessing. There certainly was a serious lack of sensitivity in the way the rector handled this matter. He must have been aware of the long tradition in every religious Congregation or Order, to invite parents and close relatives to an Ordination and a First Mass. This was just another of the innumerable crosses, or mortifications, which Peter had to bear during his time as a Redemptorist. He just could not understand why his mother had to suffer along with him.

However, circumstances unforeseen either by himself or his superiors intervened several days later, which gave him the opportunity of singing Mass at Emelghem, in the presence of his family and the whole parish. He was almost a complete stranger to them, as he had not once visited home during his six years in Beauplateau. The 'unforeseen circumstance' which allowed this visit was a local election in Iseghem, which he was obliged by law to attend. Peter described the situation in his memoirs:

> The occasion was a local election at Iseghem, my birth place, which was sharply contested between Catholics and Liberals. As I was an elector, I had to take part in it. Since this was to take place on a Sunday, I left Beauplateau on the Saturday before, to spend the night in Brussels; the following day I took an early train to vote, and afterwards, travel to Emelghem to sing the high Mass. It was a great consolation for my dear parents, who had been deprived of the

PETER AS A REDEMPTORIST WITH THREE OF HIS FIVE SISTERS,
ALL RELIGIOUS SISTERS (NUNS)

joy of attending my ordination. After the consecration, my brother Medard sang a solo beautifully; it caught my attention, as I could not recognize his voice: he was so young when I had left home. Only a few years later he was to leave this world (i.e. to die), to sing the praises of God in heaven (Vol. II, 46).

Peter still had to complete his final academic year in Beauplateau, where he returned immediately after his visit to Emelghem. Whether he realized it or not, but the six years in Beauplateau had taken its toll on his health. His parents noticed how pale and thin he had become, and expressed their anxiety and solicitude. They had, in fact, hardly recognized him. The breaking point came during the final days of the summer term of 1888, when Peter was called on to publicly defend a thesis, and fainted before he even began to speak. This caused quite a stir among his superiors, who immediately suspended the procedure. However, the more important consequence of this was that, instead of entrusting Peter with the chair of philosophy in Beauplateau – as had been agreed on – the superiors deemed it wise to give him a year of rest. He received an order to proceed at once to Brussels, to St. Joseph's, the main location of the Redemptorist Order in Belgium and called the provincial house, and to stay there for the remainder of the year 1888-1889.

Besides the fainting fit, another serious matter worried Peter. His upper lip had been slightly deformed, apparently during a bitterly cold winter when he was a child. Then, in his final year in Beauplateau he began to witness something similar happening to his nose. This double disfigurement of his face was particularly embarrassing, now that he was a priest. He realized that he would soon be called upon to face crowds of people, conducting missions, preaching sermons, celebrating Mass. He admitted in his memoirs that the disfigurement did not leave him unmoved and that he struggled to accept it. For this reason, he probably was glad to leave Beauplateau, where he had no opportunity to consult a doctor, which is what he most likely did once he arrived in Brussels. During the rest of his life the matter never again troubled him and was never mentioned again in his writings. Nor was there anything noticeable on the many pictures taken over the years.

— Two incidents of family interest occurred during his year in Brussels. Both throw light on the deep religious atmosphere of their home. He wrote of these events in his memoirs:

43

While I was in Brussels, I had the pleasure of guiding one of my sisters in the choice of a religious community. Three of my sisters had already entered religious life, and my elder sister only waited for some improvement of her precarious health to consecrate herself also to the Spouse of our souls. As I learned to know and appreciate the Sisters of Charity whose founder was the holy Canon Triest, of Ghent, I took my sister to them. . . . She was not long in deciding to join this flourishing Congregation, and in a short time she became among them an excellent nun.

On the 9th of September of this same year 1889, my brother Medard departed for heaven; his holy death was that of a predestined soul. He was only 25 years old. Since he was quite talented and the world smiled on him, my mother became frightened and she repeated with fervour the prayer of Blanche of Castile for her son Louis. But that Queen of France kept her son, whereas my mother saw hers carried away by a mysterious illness. I know all this from the very words of our holy mother, who preferred to see her son die young and faithful, rather than to be exposed to the dangers of this world at the peril of his soul (Vol. II, 50).

More importantly, from Fr. Peter's point of view, was the opportunity to observe at first hand in Brussels the working life of a Redemptorist priest. He was called on to spend long hours hearing confessions. He tells how one day he spent 10 hours in a confessional box, and in the end was so overcome by sleepiness, that he could no longer hear what people were saying to him. The most common duty demanded of him was to participate in a parish mission. This involved giving catechism classes to children in the morning, and preaching sermons to adults and hearing confessions in the evening. He found it an exhausting ordeal, especially as he could not trust himself to preach spontaneously, but had to learn his sermons by heart. At the same time, he could not avoid being critical of, and even saddened by, the material side of these parish missions. He admitted that the missions were worthwhile, and even necessary, to keep the faith and religious practice alive in people. But there were two side effects of these apostolic duties, which presented a danger or temptation to the Redemptorist priests: (i) the exaggerated praise and respect offered by the people to the priests, leading to a false opinion of oneself, and (ii) being obliged daily to partake of a table richly laid with abundant and delicate food, which was hardly in keeping with the spirit of mortification expect-ed from religious. In each parish, they were invited, on a daily basis, to join with the neighbouring priests in a festive banquet, during which the conversation was not always edifying, while the amount of drink consumed was often excessive. Peter eventually resorted to the ploy of leaving the table after one hour, under the pretext of having to prepare his instructions for the following day.

While in Brussels, the question of his vocation once more came under scrutiny, and he asked himself if this was the life he really aspired to. However, he was not given much time to brood over this matter, since the provincial (the head of the Belgian Redemp-torists) had already decided to send Peter back to Beauplateau as professor of philosophy. Thus, in October 1889, he began teaching philosophy, and soon found himself in his element. He was exempt from all apostolic work, while at the same time his living condi-tions were now greatly improved. He was given comfortable living quarters, with a fire in his room. He no longer had to suffer the harsh cold of the long winters in the Ardennes. Furthermore, he was free to give himself over to teaching, study and prayer, which suited him admirably. He enjoyed teaching, and seemed to have the gift of imparting knowledge to his students in a gentle and convincing manner.

One house custom, however, had not changed since he was last in Beauplateau: the weekly manifestation of conscience to one's supe-rior, which was strictly compulsory according to the Constitutions. This was not a great problem, providing one had a sympathetic and friendly superior. However, in 1890, there was a double change of superiors in Beauplateau, of both the rector and the prefect. His old friend, Fr. Dubois, had been sent to the Generalate House to Rome, and the replacement rector and prefect proved quite unsym-pathetic to Peter. The incidents, which he describes in his memoirs, concern petty domestic matters, but were nonetheless annoying (*Vol. II, 51-52*).

As already mentioned, Peter had a very sensitive side to his nature, and found it difficult to cope with criticism. The house regime in Beauplateau, under the new superiors, became an occasion of real suffering for him. He states that he felt like a naughty schoolboy, up to the moment of knocking at the door of the rector for these weekly manifestations of conscience. This strange exercise was supposed to accustom the religious to see God's authority in the orders of the superior. For Peter, however, during his remaining years in Beauplateau, it remained a weekly nightmare. He never knew when he might be accused of some fault or misdemeanour. The problem may well have been propounded by a clash of personalities. His superiors may have found him just a little too perfect, and wished to take him down a peg or two. Peter, on his side, found it difficult to suffer 'fools' gladly, and, in any case, was never happy when dealing with any criticism from his superior. In later life, he often judged his superiors – were they abbots or bishops – to have acted rather foolishly, if not unjustly, towards him. All this led him to suffer intermittent moments of unhappiness, and gave him reason, once again, to question his vocation as a Redemptorist. He summed up his reaction to all this in a significant sentence: *Actually to be accused falsely seems to me more painful than many other trials that usually affect us (Vol. II, 51).*

Yet, life was not entirely unbearable for him. During the summer holidays, he made several interesting excursions in Belgium, the Netherlands, the Grand-Duchy of Luxemburg and Germany. One particular visit remained in his mind for a long time, namely his first visit to the abbey of Maredsous, in Belgium. He described this visit in his memoirs:

> *On another occasion, I visited the famous Benedictine Abbey of Maredsous. It was the 8th of September, Feast of the Nativity of the Blessed Virgin Mary. After Vespers, in the Chapter Room, I attended the beautiful ceremony of an investiture. From that day, the fine melody, and the words "Beati eritis", were constantly in my mind. I did not know that a few years later the same ceremony would be performed on me! God was secretly preparing his ways (Vol. II, 53).*

During one of the summer holidays he took part in a mission to East Flanders. This triggered again in Peter's mind a strong doubt about his current vocation. He wrote on this in his memoirs:

> *The mission was a great success. But from the material point of view, it was the same abundance of refined food, of exquisite wines and long meals, of visits of neighbouring priests, of conversations which, most times, I got tired of. What pleased others usually was quite far from my personal taste. Truly I felt that this type of life was not*

meant for me and as a consequence, the question of my vocation came up into my mind in a more insistent way (Vol. II, 66).

After four years of teaching philosophy, he was appointed spiritual director of the clerics in Beauplateau, while still retaining his professorship of philosophy. He found this new position very satisfying. In addition to being spiritual director of the clerics (i.e. those preparing for ordination), he also had to give them weekly spiritual conferences. This added workload, which called for a study of ascetical theology, opened up new vistas for Peter. However, his main interest still centred on philosophy. It seemed to him that there was a need for a thorough study of the moral system of St. Alphonsus Liguori, the founder of the Redemptorists. Eventually, in 1894, he produced a book called *"An Apologia for the Moral and Philosophical Teaching of St. Alphonsus"*. The book was written in Latin, on what today would seem a very obscure subject: *Aequiprobabilism*. However, it was very well received, both by his Redemptorist brethren and the general public. Apparently, it was the first book to state clearly the dependence of St. Alphonsus on St. Thomas Aquinas. Praise for the work came from both within the Congregation and outside, as can be seen from the flattering reviews in such journals as the *"Revue Thomiste"*, *(1895, May, 277)*, the *"Irish Ecclesiastical Record"* *(1895, Sept)* and the *"American Ecclesiastical Review"* *(1895, June, 503)*. He kept copies of these reviews, and quoted extensively from them in his memoirs (Vol. II, 56-57). He found himself suddenly in the limelight, with congratulations coming from all sides. He was especially pleased to receive the approval of the new superior general of the Redemptorists, Fr. Matthias Raus, who at the same time confirmed him in his double responsibility as professor philosophy and spiritual director of the clerics in Beauplateau.

About this time, there was talk among the Belgian Redemptorists of establishing a new editorial board for their theological review *"Nouvelle Revue Theologique"*, which had been established in Louvain, in 1869. Fr. Peter De Caigny's name was mentioned as one of the possible candidates for this position. However, fate intervened in a rather strange way, to prevent this happening. He describes the situation in his memoirs:

But soon Divine Providence allowed something to happen that was to generate very serious consequences for my future. By his Encyclical "Aeterni Patris" (4 August 1879), Pope Leo XIII had laid

THE REDEMPTORIST HOUSE AT BEAUPLATEAU

down that St. Thomas Aquinas be taken as the guide in the study of Philosophy. This measure, so wise and timely, met with serious opposition, even from priests and religious whom he had much trusted to attain his objective. The illustrious Pontiff had to take a tough line towards the main ecclesiastical opponents. Well known professors were withdrawn from their chairs in Rome and exiled. At Beauplateau, professors and students had conformed with docility to the views of Leo XIII. But in 1894, we received some German students, who were hostile to this reform because, they said: "in the name of scientific progress, modern learning would disapprove of it, because scholastic (i.e. St.Thomas Aquinas's) principles were antiquated! The Pope's attempt was quite clumsy and would not survive him; it was condemned in advance" (Vol. II, 71-72).

Thinking back to the time of his youth, when he had enthusiastically endorsed the principles of the papal zouaves, any such open criticism of a Pope, as that proposed by the German students in Beauplateau, was anathema to Fr. Peter. He soon decided that, in his capacity as prefect and professor, he could not tolerate the censorious attitude of those young German students. To begin with, he tried using kindness and persuasion, but it was in vain. Finally, he felt himself forced to assert his authority, forbidding them to criticize the prescriptions of the Pope or to talk about them among themselves. But he was wasting his time. Their opposition only increased. They made an appeal to their superiors in Bavaria (Germany) and maintained that they felt supported by the answers they received. Fr. Peter explained the situation to the Redemptorist provincial who took the side of the German students, saying that these latter were guests, and had the right not to be molested or antagonized. Eventually a German Redemptorist was called in to examine the problem. His proposal was quite bizarre, as Fr. Peter recounts in his memoirs:

"It would be all right" he said, "to give the public the impression that we obeyed the Sovereign Pontiff while, inside the house, we would feel free to do what we thought appropriate, holding for true what, in our eyes, was in keeping with modern science!" Calmly but firmly, I replied that, in conscience, I could not adopt his views which, manifestly, were in contradiction to genuine obedience (Vol. II, 58).

Fr. Peter felt so strongly about the matter that he wrote immediately to the superior general in Rome, stating his views, and adding that if measures were not taken to impose the prescriptions of the Pope, he would find himself obliged to inform the nuncio in Brussels. He got an immediate reply from Rome, assuring him that "measures in keeping with the Encyclical of the Pope will be taken without delay, but your resignation is now unavoidable". Some of his fellow Redemptorists had come to resent Fr. Peter's general attitude, declaring him to be "self-willed and intellectually superior". Certainly he had become something of an enigma. Fr. Dubois, Fr. Peter's friend and former superior, summed up his feelings in a telling phrase, calling Fr. Peter: *"an angel of purity and a demon of pride"* *(Kadoc, Leuven)*. It was clear to everyone – and even himself – that he had become *'persona non grata'* in Beauplateau. Although the superior general invited him to come to Rome, and take up a post there, Fr. Peter turned this down. He came to realize that the occasion offered him the opportunity to carry out his desire to join a stricter Order, one that would be contemplative. By a strange twist of mind, he decided to enter the Carthusians. He had, of course, first to obtain the permission of his superiors, and then to be accepted by the Carthusians.

He was fortunate in having a very wise superior general in Rome, namely Fr. Matthias Raus (1829-1917), who held this office from 1894-1909. He received Peter's request to join the Carthusians with sympathy, and offered his full support. However, he added one condition: that if it proved unsuccessful, Fr. Peter would return to the ranks of the Redemptorist Congregation. Touched by this paternal advice, Peter agreed to these conditions. The Belgian and Canadian clerics in Beauplateau did not conceal their sadness, at the thought of losing Fr. Peter. Some of them left the expression of their feelings in writing. One of these, who signed himself Augustin Philippe, wrote at the back of a picture card, which he gave to Fr. Peter: *"Please never forget him who will always remember you, who for the rest of his life will boast of having been your disciple and who hopes, thanks to your wise direction, to make further progress in virtue and perfection"*. There is no doubt that Fr. Peter had made a very great impression on his students, who loved and respected him. One has to presume that he was equally attached to them, and that he shed a tear of two at this separation. He wrote of this moment of departure in his memoirs:

THE ABBEY, LA GRANDE CHARTREUSE (ORDER OF THE CARTHUSIANS)
IN FRANCE

If the step I was about to take was regretted by those who loved me, it was misinterpreted by others. It is true that it could be seen as a rash act of mine, provoked by disappointment. They had no idea of the long uncertainties I had passed through concerning my vocation. . . . In the depths of my soul I was convinced that God, in His paternal providence, would sooner or later take me, through severe trials, to the place he had chosen for his glory and the good of my soul. . . . If I did not succeed at the Carthusians, I would, in some other place, where and when God would deem appropriate. I left Beauplateau at the beginning of February 1895. The farewell they bade me was touching and sad (Vol. II, 61).

The Carthusian (Ordre des Chartreux) adventure was a complete failure. Fr. Peter first of all went to the famous monastery, La Grande Chartreuse, situated in the high valley of the Alps of Dauphine, France, but remained there only a few days, because of the severe cold of the place. The prior then arranged for him to be received in the monastery of Valbonne, another Chartreuse house, in the region of Gard, in the south of France where the climate was not so harsh. He lived there for several months, and threw himself into the life of the monks, enjoying the solitude and the silence. He was clothed in the habit of St. Bruno, and given the name St. Ayrald as his patron saint. He made a courageous attempt to live the monastic rule without any mitigation, if only to see how strong he was, physically and morally. However, in the end he had to admit that his health was gradually being undermined by the austere rule. The greatest physical strain was the lack of sleep. Little by little, he had to admit that he was attempting the impossible. Yet, the thought of returning to the Redemptorists was equally daunting, as he wrote in his memoirs:

Returning to the Congregation would be a great failure, the consequences of which would not be pleasant for my nature. For some, I would be an object of compassion, but for many others? I would meet mockery, disdain, indifference, whereas thus far I had been surrounded by respect and attention as a result of success. And during the long hours of my solitude I had ample opportunity to wonder why God had allowed this experiment at the Carthusians. It was in October 1895 that I left the beloved Charterhouse of Valbonne, and went straight to our (i.e. Redemptorist) house in Valence. Our confreres, startled at the sight of the walking skeleton

*I had become, warmly welcomed me. I was able to recover a little,
and then write to the Superior General, who eventually decided to
send me to Kansas City, in the United States, to teach Philosophy
(Vol. II, 62-63).*

Throughout his time in the Carthusians, his thoughts often
turned to his dear mother, who must have been very perplexed by
his recent adventures. At the same time, he knew he could always
rely on her prayers for his future destiny. Even though it seemed
as if he was moving away from his goal, he was actually drawing
near to his final destination, for it was in the United States that he
received the advice to enter the abbey of Maredsous.

In November 1895, Fr. Peter, after a brief visit to his mother
and family, boarded a steamer at Antwerp for New York. This was
the first of many such transatlantic crossings he made in the years
ahead. He marvelled at the beauty and the extent of the waters, and
enjoyed the company of his fellow passengers. He spent a few days
sightseeing in New York, but was not impressed by the skyscrapers,
though he did admire St. Patrick's Cathedral. He then took a train
to Kansas City, where he was expected to begin teaching philosophy
at the Redemptorist house of studies. However, he found himself
facing one obvious difficulty: his classes had to be given in English,
a language he hardly knew. He followed some courses in English,
but, despite his determination, failed to make any serious impact
on his students, and after three months was relieved of his post.
This experience meant another failure, a fact which did nothing to
boost his morale and general well-being. With time on his hands,
he was given permission to do some travelling, and soon discovered
that there were several newly established Benedictine abbeys in the
United States. He was especially impressed by Belmont Abbey, in
North Carolina. However, before deciding on any definite move, he
consulted the future apostolic delegate to the United States, Mgr.
Frances Satolli (1839-1910), who was in Canada at this time, and
had himself been a Benedictine monk of Monte Cassino. Mgr.
Satolli received him kindly, and advised him, being a Belgian, to
apply to the abbey of Maredsous. Fr. Peter wouldn't forget Mgr.
Satolli's advice.

The provincial of the Belgian Redemptorists was visiting Canada
at this time, and asked Fr. Peter to come to see him in Montreal.
After hearing of Fr. Peter's experience in Kansas City, the provincial

decided to recall him to Belgium. The two boarded a Dutch steamer in New York and arrived in Rotterdam in the summer of 1896. Some documents in the archives of the Redemptorists refer to the fact Fr. Peter was ordered to go for 3 months in penitence to the house of Redemptorists at Tournai, but that he refused. He went almost immediately to Bavaria, to one of the houses in Gars-am-Inn, where he spent several very unhappy months confined in his room. The superior was unable to offer him any work (preaching, hearing confessions, etc.) because he could not speak German.

During his time in Bavaria, he came across an article in *"La Revue des Missions"* (abbey of St. Andre, Bruges), written by Dom Gerard van Caloen, a monk of Maredsous, who had been put in charge of restoring the Benedictine Congregation in Brazil. This set him thinking of the advice given him by Mgr. Satolli, that he should join the Benedictines in Maredsous. He wrote at once to Fr. Coppin, a Redemptorist he had known in Beauplateau, and who was now assistant to the superior general in Rome, outlining his recent experiences, and mentioning his desire to enter Maredsous. Fr. Coppin replied very positively, giving his approval to the proposal. He ended his letter with the words: *"I am morally certain that the Benedictines will receive you. Go ahead!" (Vol. II, 67)*. Some months later, the superior general Fr. Raus contacted him, assuring him of his support and goodwill, and suggesting that he first seek a dispensation from his vows as a Redemptorist. Thus Fr. Peter, after some hesitation and fervent prayers, made a formal application to Rome for a dispensation. He gives the account of this affair in his memoirs:

I received my dispensation, worded in the following terms: "By the kindness of his Ecclesiastical Superiors, we recommend the priest, Peter De Caigny, who, after taking his vows for the Belgian Province of our Congregation in 1880, sought their dispensation, which has been granted to him this very day. His motive being that he felt his vocation was not for our Institute. Without hesitation we can bear witness of his high learning in sacred science and of the irreproachability of his life while he was among us. Given at Rome, Generalate of St. Alphonsus. On the 9th of March 1897." I was deeply touched. Without delay, I bade farewell to our good Bavarian confreres who had treated me so kindly. I was not used to putting on the soutane of a secular priest, but I knew that soon I would wear the Benedictine habit.

A LA PIEUSE MÉMOIRE

DU

T. R. P. Ernest DUBOIS

de la Congrégation du T. S. Rédempteur

Né à Verviers, le 23 juin 1835,
Admis à la profession religieuse, le 18 juillet 1858,
Ordonné prêtre, le 22 mars 1862,
Pieusement décédé à Jette, le 25 août 1911.

Fr. Ernest Dubois, his superior and confidant.
Peter held Fr. Dubois in very high regard.

55

I owe a great and sincere gratitude to the Redemptorists, especially to the Belgian Province of the Congregation, where, I am happy to say, I received an excellent religious formation, both from the ascetic and scientific point of views. As I left the Congregation, my intention was quite clearly to remain on excellent terms with all, especially with the Superiors. I walked out carrying with me my devotion for St. Alphonsus and for St. Bruno (Vol. II, 84).

It is evident that he left the Redemptorists much enriched in mind and soul. He had been given the chance to develop a brilliant intellect, as well as many other qualities, which served him so well in the years ahead. In any case, he had not walked out, but followed the necessary canonical procedures. The fact that he had left with the blessing and good will of his superiors was a point in his favour. He always kept Fr. Ernest Dubois in high regard. Whenever he could, Fr. Peter would visit him at the Redemptorist house in Brussels. He kept Fr. Dubois's letters and obituary card in Volume III.

I owe especially an eternal debt of gratitude to venerable Fr. Dubois, prototype of a true religious. As I left the Redemptorist Congregation, my intention was clearly, to always remain in excellent terms with all, especially with my former superiors (Vol. II, 84).

Dom Odo van der Heydt, archivist at Mount St. Benedict wrote in his history of the Mount:

Fr. Peter had been a brilliant student and professor, an accomplished preacher, an able conversationalist, capable of approaching any subject and speaking about it intelligently and entertainingly. According to trustworthy witnesses, the Belgian Redemptorist fathers have not had a man of Fr. Peter's abilities ever since he left them to join the Benedictines (MSB, Dom Odo, History of MSB).

At the moment of his departure there may have been some strong heartbreaks, but there were no hard feelings, while his honour and reputation were untarnished.

From his Redemptorist time on, all the major changes in Fr. Peter's life resulted from an escalating conflict because of his unwavering attitude. He was convinced he had the papal, Church and moral rights on his side and in addition, his pride and honour did not allow for any compromise. This undiplomatic approach always resulted in a drastic change in his life and a new start of "Longing to Belong".

However, he always left behind a great number of people that were really devoted to him because of his guidance, counselling, spiritual teachings and the overall religious attitude he radiated. Others were hurt and felt angry because they knew that the conflict could have been avoided.

At Beauplateau, when Fr. Peter announced his resignation many of his students were bewildered. They lost their main guide to a better spiritual life and to make further progress in virtue and perfection. He was loved and respected by those who had the same desire for spiritual perfection. Fr. Peter was for them an *"angel of purity".*

On the other hand some of his fellow Redemptorists had come to resent Fr. Peter's general attitude, declaring him to be self-willed and intellectually superior. For them Fr. Peter was a *"demon of pride".* In the Redemptorist archives we found documents from his superiors, indicating that he was too impulsive and that the crisis with the German students could have been solved differently, in a less drastic way. In the same documents some expressed their doubts on Fr. Peter's future with the Redemptorists and that the German student crisis was merely an excuse to explore something better. Fr. Peter's superiors attributed his attitude and character to the fact that he suffered from an inferiority complex, said to be rooted in the young child's original experience of early separation, weakness and dependency (Kadoc, Leuven, archives of the Redemptorists).

These two opposing groups, the group that adored Fr. Peter and the group that couldn't agree with his actions and attitude, would be the common result of all his future actions in Brazil and Trinidad.

CHAPTER III

Becoming a Benedictine
(10 April 1897 - 2 January 1902)

FROM THE MOMENT he left the Redemptorists, Fr. Peter found himself in a kind of religious limbo. He was literally on his own, without any religious vows, and without any superior. The first thing he had to do was to find a bishop to grant him a 'celebret', i.e. a license to celebrate Mass. He thus headed straight for Bruges, the diocese in which he was born, where the bishop Mgr. Waffelaert, received him kindly, and gave him the required celebret. The bishop already knew of Fr. Peter, having read his book *"Apologia for the System of St. Alphonsus"*, and, in fact, invited him to join the ranks of his clergy. Fr. Peter thanked the bishop, but explained that he intended becoming a monk in the abbey of Maredsous. Another source gives a totally different story. According to a letter found in the archives of the Redemptorists, Fr. Peter tried to enter in the diocese of Bruges, but the bishop declined his application. It is impossible to know which story, the one from his memoirs or the one mentioned in the letter, is the correct one.

He next had to make an appointment with the abbot of Maredsous, Dom Hildebrand de Hemptinne, with a view to seeking admission to Maredsous. At this time, Dom Hildebrand held a double post, being abbot of Maredsous and also abbot primate of the Benedictine Order. Since his election as abbot primate in 1893, Dom Hildebrand spent six months each year in Rome and six months in Maredsous. Fr. Peter was fortunate in finding the abbot in residence in Maredsous. They immediately struck up a friendship, especially after Dom Hildebrand told Fr. Peter that he had been an officer of the papal zouave army before becoming a monk. The abbot listened with interest to Fr. Peter's request, but said that before he could give a definite reply he would need more information. This meant contacting the Redemptorists for their views on Fr. Peter. Within a few days Abbot Hildebrand got a posi-

DOM HILDEBRAND DE HEMPTINNE, ABBOT OF MAREDSOUS (1890-1909) AND
NOMINATED THE FIRST ABBOT PRIMATE OF THE ORDER OF SAINT BENEDICT.
DOM HILDEBRAND, WHO HAD ACCEPTED DOM MAYEUL IN MAREDSOUS, ALWAYS
HAD A SPECIAL ATTENTION AND WORD OF SUPPORT FOR DOM MAYEUL.

ABBEY OF MAREDSOUS

tive reply from Fr. Coppin, a Redemptorist, well-known in Mared-sous, having preached several retreats to the students of the abbey school. With this last obstacle removed, the road was now clear for his entrance to Maredsous, set for 10th April 1897.

Before starting his new life, he decided to visit his mother in Emelghem, to break the news of his intention to enter the ab-bey of Maredsous. Being a holy woman, her only concern was the spiritual well-being of her son, and she readily gave her blessing to the proposal of his becoming a Benedictine monk. He arrived in Maredsous in time for Holy Week, and on 19 April, was given the Benedictine habit and the name Mayeul. St. Mayeul was one of the four Saintly Abbots of Cluny, who resigned his abbacy of Cluny in his old age. This marked the beginning of a three months trial pe-riod as a postulant. During the clothing ceremony, Abbot Hildeb-rand made a very touching gesture, by giving the novice one of his own cinctures or belts, which Dom Mayeul wore for the rest of his life, out of respect and gratitude. One may wonder why Abbot Hil-debrand gave such a warm welcome to his latest recruit, especially as Dom Mayeul was 35 years of age, and a priest. Maredsous had been founded in 1872, by monks from Beuron, in Germany, who were forced into exile under Bismarck's Kulturkampf. More than half the novices joining Maredsous during the first twenty years of its existence were already ordained priests, most of them diocesan. Dom Mayeul's novice master in Maredsous, Dom Benoit d'Hondt, was a diocesan priest before joining the monastery, while the as-sistant novice master, Dom (later Blessed) Columba Marmion, was also a former diocesan priest, from Dublin, Ireland. Dom Mayeul described in his memoirs his feelings on that memorable day, when he was clothed as a monk:

> It is impossible to realize what happiness peacefully flooded my soul on that blessed day. All the troubles of the past - and they were not insignificant - seemed nothing compared with the joy I expe-rienced to be, at last, after so many storms, in the safe harbour of monastic life. I really felt "at home" in the great and Holy Order of our Blessed Father Benedict, and this conviction never left me thereafter. Did I not find here all the beauties of liturgical life, the charm of solitude and silence, pleasure to study without feeling bound by scholastic sectarianism, and that sweet peace which is the lot of monks? Finally, the thought that I would dedicate myself to

S·MAJOLO·ABBADE·DE·CLVNY·906-994.

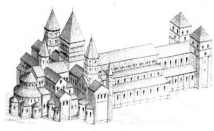

THE ABBOT OF CLUNY: ST. MAYEUL
(WITH THE ABBEY TO THE LEFT)
CLUNY WAS FOUNDED IN 910 AND BECAME THE CENTER FOR THE ESTABLISHMENT
AND EXPANSION OF THE BENEDICTINE ORDER WHICH WAS A KEYSTONE TO THE
STABILITY OF EUROPEAN SOCIETY THAT WAS ACHIEVED IN THE 11TH CENTURY. IN
1793 DURING THE FRENCH REVOLUTION, THE ABBEY WAS SACKED AND MOSTLY
DESTROYED. THE THOUSANDS OF FAMOUS ANCIENT MANUSCRIPTS AND BOOKS
WERE BURNED. UNTIL 1813, THE ABBEY WAS USED AS A STONE QUARRY TO BUILD
HOUSES IN THE TOWN. ONLY A SMALL PART (10%) OF THE ORIGINAL
BUILDINGS REMAINS.

GRAVESTONE IN THE ABBEY CHURCH OF DOM COLUMBA MARMION, ABBOT
OF MAREDSOUS. HE WAS BEATIFIED BY POPE JOHN PAUL II ON SEPTEMBER 3,
2000. MARMION WAS ONE OF THE MOST POPULAR AND INFLUENTIAL CATHOLIC
WRITERS OF THE 20TH CENTURY. HIS BOOKS ARE CONSIDERED SPIRITUAL CLASSICS.
THE CO-AUTHOR OF THIS BIOGRAPHY, FR TIERNEY, WAS A KEY PARTNER IN
THE BEATIFICATION PROCESS AND WROTE THE BIOGRAPHY OF DOM COLUMBA.
DOM MARK TIERNEY, WAS THE EUROPEAN VICE-POSTULATOR OF MARMION'S
BEATIFICATION CAUSE.

the mission in Brazil, as had been agreed upon, fulfilled my wishes.
And what is more, I received shortly after this two letters, one from
the Superior General of the Redemptorists, and the other from Fr.
Dubois (Assistant-General), assuring me that in these last events
they recognised the action of Divine Providence, and expressed
their best wishes for my perseverance. At the back of a picture of
St. Alphonsus, Fr. Raus, the Superior General, wrote: "United in
prayer and in sincere love". This picture meant a lot to me and I
treasure it (Vol. II, 71-72).

Evidently, Dom Mayeul had written to Frs. Raus and Dubois
soon after receiving the habit in Maredsous. He kept the reply he
received from Fr. Mathias Raus, dated Rome, 28 April 1897, and
had it bound into Volume III, the third volume of his memoirs in
which he kept the letters from confidants. This letter, in French, is
worth quoting, as it shows the high regard in which Dom Mayeul
was held by his former superior general:

Behold you are now a Benedictine! I have the confidence and the
certitude that you will be a good, solid son of St. Benedict, a man
of prayer and of virtue, of work and study, according to the spirit
of your great Patriarch. Your letter filled my soul with an immense
joy, and I now thank you with all my heart for the good news
which you have shared with me. All my life I have had a great love
for the Benedictine Order, and, whenever I could, always visited
one of your monumental monasteries. Confidence, courage and
perseverance, my dearly beloved Father! Let us pray every day one
for the other, and continue to correspond whenever we can. As you
have made the request, I send you my blessing, and remain ever
yours in St. Benedict and St. Alphonsus (Vol. III, xiv).

Life in Maredsous turned out to be everything the new postulant
had hoped for. Throughout his time there he was filled with eu-
phoria. Indeed, it soon became clear to himself and his immediate
superiors, that he had an innate Benedictine spirit. He experienced
no difficulty conforming to the customs of Benedictine life and
was quite happy sweeping the cloisters, cleaning the shoes of the
senior monks, working in the sacristy, and so on. Most important
of all, he felt loved by everyone, even by his novice master, Dom
Benoit d'Hondt, who was a venerable old man, austere, simple and
straightforward. He considered the assistant novice master, Dom

ABBEY OF MAREDSOUS, VIEW FROM THE INSIDE CLOISTER GARDEN

Columba Marmion, to be a monk of great holiness and learning. During their recreations and long walks, he had some interesting conversations about asceticism with this latter monk, which left a lasting impression on him.

Having completed his three months as a postulant, he was received into the novitiate on 26 July 1897, by the prior of Maredsous, Dom Basil de Meester. This next stage of his initiation into monastic life normally lasted for one year, though in his case, it was soon to be interrupted. When Dom Mayeul had first offered himself as a monk in Maredsous, he was asked the usual question: "Why do you wish to be a monk?" He replied that he sought the silence of the cloister, but also expressed the hope that one day he might be sent to the missions in Brazil. However, it must have come as something of a surprise, when, in early November, 1897, though still a novice, Dom Mayeul was told by Abbot Hildebrand, that he was being sent to Brazil, along with another monk, Dom Maur Desrumeaux.

Some years previously, Leo XIII had confided the Brazilian Benedictines, who were in a crisis situation, to the care of the Beuronese (Germany) Congregation, of which Maredsous formed a part. The responsibility for this task had fallen on a monk of Maredsous, Dom Gerard van Caloen. In 1897 he made an urgent appeal for monks to come to Olinda, on the northern coast of Brazil, where Dom Gerard was abbot. In answer to this urgent appeal, Dom Mayeul and Dom Maur Desrumeaux were asked to leave Maredsous at such short notice.

This sudden move to Brazil seemed to be in complete contradiction to the spirit of contemplation, silence and prayer, which Dom Mayeul had been cultivating since his arrival in Maredsous. More important still, he had not yet completed his formation as a Benedictine monk. Some years later, this fact came back to haunt him, when he was accused of being a half-baked (the word used was *"an aborted"*) Benedictine. The formation period in most monasteries lasted four years: one year of novitiate, followed by three years in temporary, or simple, vows, still under the eye of the novice master, after which one made solemn profession. The truth is Dom Mayeul never completed this normal initiation course into monastic life.

His fellow novices in Maredsous were evidently saddened at the thought of losing him, and gave a farewell party in his honour. The group had been together for six months or so, and a close bond of friendship had already been formed between them. Most of them were outstanding personalities, with distinguished careers ahead of them. Br. Raymond Thibaut, the future editor and biographer of Blessed Columba Marmion, showed his nascent literary talent, by composing a poem in French entitled: *"Le Rendez-Vous"*, dated 13 November 1897, and addressed to "Our dearest brother Mayeul". Two other fellow novices remained lifelong friends of Dom Mayeul: Br. Adelbert Grisnicht, who became a famous artist and architect, designing the Catholic University of Peking, and doing some wonderful painting in the church of San Bento in St. Paolo, Brazil; and Br. Bede Lebbe, later prior of Glenstal, in Limerick, Ireland, whose letters Dom Mayeul kept carefully, and had them bound into Volume III of his memoirs.

Before departing for Brazil, Dom Mayeul was given permission to visit his mother, a widow since 1892, who lived in the family home in Emelghem. He spent a few days with her, on his way from Maredsous to Antwerp. It was an emotional experience, which he describes in his memoirs:

> *I was able to celebrate the feast of St. Ursula (21 November), my mother's patron saint, at home. My mother consulted me on the question of her will. I wrote it out for her and I later found that everyone was happy with it. After all the events of the last two years, and it being the eve of my departure for Brazil, my meeting with my mother, although naturally filled with melancholy, was touching and very consoling. I had the opportunity to clarify my past conduct. And the sight of my present happiness was a guarantee of stability for the future. I will never forget the moment of our last goodbye, nor ever, above all, my kind and saintly mother's words: "Peter", she said, "I would have liked to see you stay in Belgium so as to be able to close my eyes at the hour of my death; but since God has other arrangements, go where he calls you". Then, like when I was a child, she marked the sign of the cross on my forehead. I was pretty heavy-hearted, and I had a foreboding that I would never see her again in this world. I admired her Christian strength of will in making this great sacrifice for God. When I said goodbye to my mother I shed a lot of tears. My heart is connected with many strings to my homeland and family (Vol. II, 84 and Vol. I).*

GRAVESTONE AT CEMETERY OF EMELGHEM. BESIDES PETER'S PARENTS, HIS BROTHER ALOIS AND HIS SPOUSE SILVIE, WERE ALSO BURIED UNDER THIS HEADSTONE.

In Antwerp, he had the joy of spending the night at the convent of his youngest sister Pharailde, also called Sister Marie Alida, her religious name at the convent. They had not seen each other for many years, and spent what little time they had together, talking of the old days, and discussing his future. She was obviously worried about him, and made him promise that he would make no further radical change in his religious status. It was the last time they were to meet. She became seriously ill soon after his visit, and died a few years later, at the age of thirty one.

On the morning of 23 November 1897, Dom Mayeul joined his confrere, Dom Maur Desrumeaux, at the quayside in Antwerp. Later that day, they boarded a German steamer, bound for Brazil. The two monks were setting out on a missionary journey to a distant land, ready for all eventualities, and filled with enthusiasm and good will. Dom Mayeul knew that he was not the original choice of either Abbot Hildebrand, or Abbot Gerard, for this mission. Their first choice fell on Dom Columba Marmion. However, on second thoughts Abbot Hildebrand decided to keep Marmion in Belgium, to spearhead a new foundation in Louvain, which took place some years later, in 1899. He also rightly felt that Dom Marmion's health would never support the heat of Brazil. This explains why Abbot Hildebrand's choice fell on the novice Mayeul, as he stated in a letter to Abbot Gerard, dated 13 October 1897:

> I have ordered R. Fr. Mayeul, to accompany Dom Maur Desrumeaux for the mission to Brazil. Fr. Mayeul had personally asked to be allowed to go. You know the past history of this novice. He was a Redemptorist for 20 years, professor of Philosophy and of Moral Theology, as well as master of clerics. If he perseveres, you will have in him an excellent support. His health is much better than that of Dom Columba, to cope with the heat of the tropics. I told him (Dom Mayeul) that he would have to re-commence his novitiate in Olinda, an order he received with good grace (ASA, G.v.C. Papers).

Dom Mayeul, who had already come to consider himself a 'missionary monk', wrote a very detailed account of the sea voyage to Brazil (Vol. I, 102). Their first port of call in Brazil was the city of Salvador in the state of Bahia, which they reached on 4 December 1897. For a long time, the city of Salvador was simply known as 'Bahia', and appears on many maps and books under that name, to differentiate it from other Brazilian cities, also named Salvador. The city made a great impression on the travellers. Also, the great ethnic diversity was something they had never experienced before and it was a bit of a culture shock. They proceeded at once to the Benedictine monastery of San Sebastian in Salvador-Bahia, henceforth referred to as the 'abbey of Bahia'. They were received by Abbot Gerard van Caloen, who had come from Olinda to meet them. They were also very graciously welcomed by Abbot General Domingo Machado, and the only other monk in the monastery, Frey Carneiro da Cunha. Little did Dom Mayeul realize that, in less than ten years, he would be elected abbot of this monastery. The buildings were in a deplorable state of neglect or disrepair, following several years of civil unrest, which had only ended on 5 October 1897. During that time, the monastery had been occupied by combatants, and later turned into a hospital for the wounded. The travellers spent only two days in Bahia, before taking ship for Recife and Olinda.

The two monks arrived in Olinda on 8 December 1897. Since the combined novitiate for the Brazilian Benedictine Congregation was housed in Olinda, the novice Mayeul now joined this group. He was very impressed by the monastery, with its wonderful façade, and baroque church. However, he had little time for sightseeing. His first task was to learn to speak, read and write Brazilian Portuguese, the language spoken throughout Brazil. His second priority was to re-start his full year as a novice. This meant that, in fact, he was embarking on his third novitiate, having already endured one as a Redemptorist and the other in Maredsous. He was 35 years of age, and a priest, and must have felt a very mature novice.

In the meantime, Abbot Hildebrand, who never lost interest in the progress of his two monks, wrote again to Abbot van Caloen, on 20 December 1897:

> *I hope that the two Maredsous Fathers are proving helpful to you. If Fr. Mayeul perseveres he will be a real treasure for Olinda, as he is very learned and virtuous (SAZ, G.v.C. Papers).*

These words set Abbot Gerard thinking. He knew that the Brazilian mission was very close to the heart of the Roman authorities, and that they would look with a sympathetic ear on any demand he might make. He had two problems: a group of novices on his hands, but no novice master, and a group of philosophers, and no

FRONT VIEW OF THE ABBEY OF OLINDA

one to teach this subject. His eye fell on the novice Dom Mayeul, who had all the qualities for both jobs, but he would not be available for another half year. On the spur of the moment, he sent a telegram to Rome, asking for a special dispensation for Dom Mayeul, to have his year's novitiate reduced by several months. At the same time, he asked that another novice, Miguel Kruse, who, like Dom Mayeul, was already an ordained priest, have his novitiate reduced in a similar manner. The matter should have been dealt with by the Congregation for Religious, but they passed it on to the Congregation for Extraordinary Affairs, as it was, in truth, an 'extraordinary' request. This latter department of the Holy See considered the matter, and gave a favourable answer in a letter, addressed to Abbot Gerard, dated Rome, 27 April 1898:

> *We hereby dispense the priest De Caigny from fulfilling the usual year's novitiate, and declare that it may now be advanced by three months. The dispensation of five months to be applied to Miguel Kruse, also a priest. The matter has been brought to the attention of the Holy Father, who has graciously acceded to this request. Signed: S. Cavagnis, Secretary (SAZ, G.v.C. Papers)*

On the strength of this document, Abbot Gerard held a Chapter (i.e. Community Council) meeting on 27 May, in Olinda, at which Dom Mayeul and Dom Miguel Kruse were both accepted for simple profession. Two days later, 29 May 1898, the Feast of Pentecost, they made their simple professions. On 30 May, Dom Mayeul was appointed novice master, professor of philosophy, and confessor to the whole community in Olinda *(Olinda, Chronica, Vol. II)*. Abbot Gerard was a good judge of character, as both these monks were destined for high office in later years – Dom Mayeul as abbot of Bahia, and Dom Miguel Kruse as abbot of San Paolo. For the next twelve months, Dom Mayeul had his hands full in Olinda, giving classes on the Rule of St. Benedict to the novices, and teaching philosophy to the clerics. There were twelve young monks in this group, most of them had come from Belgium, Holland or Germany.

Dom Mayeul gave his first sermon in Portuguese on the Feast of the Immaculate Conception, 8 December 1898, in the abbey church of Olinda. At Christmas that same year, he celebrated midnight Mass at a church in Recife, the city near Olinda, and again preached in Portuguese. As he gradually came to explore the surrounding district, Dom Mayeul was both surprised and delighted to find two communities of Belgian religious women living within a few minutes of the monastery in Olinda. They had recently come from the diocese of Ghent, in Belgium. The Sisters of Christian Doctrine, from Dooreseele (Belgium), had been given the bishop's palace in Olinda (the bishop now lived in Recife), where they were splendidly installed, and had already started a primary school, while the Sisters of St. Vincent de Paul, from Gyseghem (Belgium), were in the process of setting up a home for the elderly. Dom Mayeul celebrated Mass in their convents from time to time, and always enjoyed the opportunity to speak Flemish with the sisters, and share memories of their homeland.

—— These early months in Olinda, as he slowly adapted to Brazilian life, proved to be an idyllic time for him. The younger members of the monastery were caught up in the pioneering spirit, full of generosity and good will towards each other and their superiors. Abbot Gerard van Caloen departed by boat for Europe early in 1899, leaving another monk of Maredsous, Fr. Feuillen Lhermitte, as prior, and Dom Mayeul as subprior (2nd in command). The atmosphere in this lovely abbey was conducive to monastic living, with a round of liturgical prayer, studies, reading, and long walks in the surrounding countryside. Dom Mayeul described the scene in his memoirs:

> My time at this point was taken up mainly by all the novitiate and scholastic (i.e. teaching philosophy) duties. To facilitate our adaptation, we went for numerous walks, which I liked taking charge of. Since Olinda Abbey was situated by the sea, we only had to take a few steps to find ourselves outside the town and in natural tropical surroundings. Also, the beautiful beach offered us the best walk in the area. On one side we had the ocean with its breeze and its salutary bathing, and on the other the forests with their soothing foliage and delicious fruits. Everywhere we were blissfully alone, and simple and friendly gaiety reigned supreme on these excursions. But this almost complete happiness was too beautiful to last (Vol. II, 86-87).

Abbot Gerard returned from Europe in time for Easter 1899. Some weeks later, disaster hit the community in Olinda, in the form of the dreaded yellow fever. Little was known at the time of the cause of this scourge. In fact, the source of the illness was the mosquito *stegomyia fasciata*, which propagates the yellow fever virus when it bites. Two of the clerics were infected, and Dom Mayeul was called to hear their confessions. One of them died a few days later, while the other suffered from the effects for the rest of his life. Within days, Dom Mayeul was also struck down with the fever, and was transported in a hammock to the hospital of St. Agatha, near Recife, where the Daughters of St. Anne served. The sister superior, who nursed him through his long illness, held out no hope for his recovery, as he was experiencing what they called "the black vomiting", a symptom which is usually a premonition of death. Abbot Gerard was distraught at the prospect of losing his novice master and professor of philosophy, and began praying to Our Lady of Pompeii, for whom he had great personal devotion, to grant him a cure. Almost miraculously, Dom Mayeul gradually came back to life, thanks to the excellent care he received from the sisters. As soon as he was strong again, and wishing to show his gratitude for their wonderful care, he arranged to preach a retreat to the nuns, who, for the past nine years had been deprived of any such spiritual exercises *(Bull. O.B.B., No. 4. Dec.1899)*. Then, after a long convalescence, he returned to Olinda. Sadly, within a week of his return to the monastery, Prior Feuillen Lhermitte caught the yellow fever, and died on 16th September 1899. Dom Mayeul felt this as a great personal loss, since Dom Feuillen, a Belgian, had originally been a monk of Maredsous.

Even before this last tragedy, Abbot Gerard, seeing the dangers of the yellow fever epidemic in Olinda, and fearing that he would lose his entire community to this dreadful illness, decided to seek a suitable (i.e. healthier) place in the interior of the country, to house his younger monks. On 12 July he wrote to the Benedictine house St. Andre, Bruges. This Belgian foundation coordinated the Benedictine restoration in Brazil:

> *It is now imperative to think of the future. As soon as it is possible to re-organise all the community, I will have to make a journey to the interior of the country, to look for a place which is healthy and at a distance from the sea, outside the yellow fever zone, which will serve as a kind of sanatorium. For it is evident that the greatest obstacle at present to our work of restoration of the Brazilian Congregation is this illness, which could destroy in a very short time the fruits of so many years of hard work (Bulletin des oeu-*

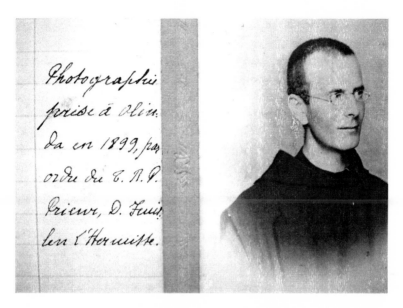

DOM MAYEUL AT OLINDA IN 1899

HEADSTONE OF PRIOR FEUILLEN IN THE OLINDA ABBEY CHURCH.
HE DIED FROM YELLOW FEVER IN 1899.

vres Benedictines au Bresil, henceforth Bull.O.B.B., SAZ, no. 3, September 1899).

Why was Abbot Gerard so concerned about the situation in Brazil at this very moment? And how could the yellow fever threaten to derail all the 'hard work' of the previous four years? The answer to these two questions lay in the areas of finance and recruitment. When, in 1890, Frey Domingo Machado, the abbot general of the dying Brazilian Congregation, consisting of eleven monks in all, applied to Rome for help to restore Benedictine life in his country, the situation looked hopeless. Three years later, in 1893, when Dom Gerard van Caloen was asked by the Pope to undertake the task, almost overnight there seemed to be some hope of a solution. He put all his energies, as well as the considerable financial resources of his own family, into the enterprise. Recently, in January 1899, he had established a recruiting, as well as a fundraising, centre near his family home in Bruges, called Saint Andre. By providing this 'home base' in Belgium, he hoped to attract young men from Europe to volunteer for missionary work in Brazil, and also to encourage wealthy Belgians to finance the growing needs of the Brazilian Benedictine restoration programme. This house, a combination of minor seminary and clearing-bank, had been established with the special blessing of the Pope, and by the summer of 1899 was in full swing with a newly appointed director superior, Dom Maur van Emelen, in charge. Abbot Gerard wanted this house, which later developed into an abbey (St. Andre), to be the power house of the Brazilian restoration movement. However, he feared that if it became known that yellow fever faced the young missionary recruits once they put foot in Brazil, the whole enterprise could be aborted. Hence the urgent need for a healthy, safe, monastery in Brazil, to receive these young Belgian/European men, where they could be trained as monks, and initiated into the Brazilian way of life.

Abbot Gerard spent the month of August 1899 exploring the interior of the north-eastern Brazilian countryside, searching for a place free of yellow fever. No sooner had he found an ideal site at Santa Cruz, close to the town Quixada in the province of Ceara, when he was suddenly called back to Olinda, for the funeral of his prior, Dom Feuillen, who had succumbed to the yellow fever. This last experience unnerved Abbot Gerard so much that in late September, he set his mind to organizing the transfer of the younger monks to Ceara, with Dom Mayeul as superior of the new founda-

THE COMMUNITY OF THE ABBEY OF OLINDA WITH ABBOT GENERAL MACHADO.
DOM MAYEUL, SEATED SECOND ROW, SECOND FROM LEFT, NEXT TO
DOM MACHADO.

DOM MAYEUL WITH THE COMMUNITY OF OLINDA
DOM MAYEUL, SEATED IN THE FIRST ROW, THE FOURTH FROM THE RIGHT.

tion. Thus, at the beginning of October, 1899, Dom Mayeul was once again on the move, facing a new challenge. Altogether there were fifteen monks in his party, leaving Olinda. These included a priest-monk from the United States, while the remainder were novices or young clerics. After a short trip by boat, the party reached Fortaleza, the capital of Ceara, where they purchased some essential goods, such as cooking utensils and food. They then proceeded, by horse and mule, to a place called Guaramiranga, situated on the top of the Serra de Baturite. Here they took up temporary residence in an abandoned college, in order to find their bearings, and get used to the high altitude of the place. Early the following year, 1900, they moved higher still, to their final destination, at Santa Cruz de Quixada. This was the site chosen by Abbot Gerard, and though it seemed to lack all basic facilities, they had no option but to stay there. It was the first, but not the last, time that Dom Mayeul faced the task of trying to turn what looked like a wilderness into a monastic settlement. The group spent the first months living in clay huts (called mocambo), which were thatched to begin with, but later covered with tiles of poor quality. They must have asked themselves many times: how were they going to transform the place into a monastery? It seemed an almost impossible task. What made their task all the more difficult was the fact that neither Dom Mayeul, nor any of the younger monks, had any experience in the art of building a monastery. Neither had they any experience in looking after livestock, such as cows, or ploughing the fields for crops. They urgently needed expert help, in the form of lay brothers (i.e. monks who were able to give all their time to manual work).

At the beginning of April 1900, Dom Mayeul received a letter, informing him that his mother had been very ill, but that she was well on the way to recovery. In fact, she had already died. He described his feelings in his memoirs:

> *Then a telegram came informing me of her death on March 28th aged 71 years. On hearing this news I fell into a state of absolute grief which lasted several days. The world seemed empty and void of attractions, and I found it difficult to perform my duties. But soon, however, the memory of her pious life, and the certainty of her glory in heaven, helped me considerably to emerge from my state of numbness and resume my regular life (Vol. II, 89).*

Dom Mayeul, because of his unusual upbringing, away from his parents' home, would seem to have missed out experiencing a close attachment to his mother. However, this was not so. His mother, by her example and prayers, undoubtedly contributed to his entering religion, first as a Redemptorist and then as a Benedictine. All the evidence points to the fact, that his mother was a remarkable and unusually religious person. Dom Mayeul has left us an interesting and moving account of his mother in chapter IV of his Volume I (61-65). He says that this love for his mother was so great that it blocked out any other human affection. He admired her sanctity, generosity and selflessness, as when she gave him her blessing on his departure for Brazil, knowing they would never meet again in this life. He cherished, as relics, the letters which she wrote to him from time to time, and inserted the originals in his memoirs, Volume III.

— Dom Mayeul quotes from the letter from the priest, Fr. Picavet, who attended her during her last hours. Fr. Picavet who was the priest of another parish, happened to be present and witnessed the final moments before her death. Fr. Picavet wrote the letter in September 1913, thirteen years after her death. After all these years Fr. Picavet had never forgotten how deeply he had been touched by Dom Mayeul's mother. He happened to tell the story about this remarkable woman during a parish gathering. One of the people attending was a niece of Dom Mayeul. She asked Fr. Picavet to share in a letter to Dom Mayeul his story. This is an extract from this letter:

> I can assure you that, throughout my priestly career, I have never encountered anyone so pure, and who waited with such eagerness and calm the moment of her facing the Lord. Your mother appeared to me to be a saint, endowed with the virtues of modesty and righteousness. After all these years, her memory remains clearly with me, as an example of everything that is good and edifying (Vol. III, letter XII).

This image of his mother remained with him all his life. Indeed, he had always been impressed by the wonderful harmony which existed between his father and mother. They had been sorely tried, losing their home in a fire, and suffering hardship and poverty for many years. He considered his father as a Job-like figure, who had come from almost extreme poverty to prosperity, within the span of some twenty years. He retained a respectful memory of both parents, who had given him an inspiring example of true Christian living, as well as teaching him the value of fortitude and hard work *(Vol. I, 64-65)*.

The so-called 'regular life' in Santa Cruz was anything but regular. In fact, with each passing day, he became more and more overwhelmed with work and responsibilities. In two letters, written to the superior of the recruiting house in St. Andre, Bruges, Belgium, dated 8 & 12 July 1900, Dom Mayeul gave details of his situation, as he set about building the monastery of Santa Cruz de Quixada. He regretted that he had no camera to hand, as he wanted his correspondent, Dom Maur van Emelen, to see how things really were. His letter was probably intended as an appeal for funds, but in fact it was nothing more than a travel brochure, describing the incredible scenery and the climate of Santa Cruz and Ceara. In one of these letters he speaks of the long-awaited arrival of Abbot Gerard at Santa Cruz, on 11 July 1900, bringing much-needed funds for the buildings. Since the accommodation in Santa Cruz was both limited and primitive, the abbot was lodged in the nearby village of Santa Anna, though he spent a few days and nights with Dom Mayeul and his monks. It immediately became obvious that Santa Cruz was the apple of Abbot Gerard's eye, the Benjamin of his many foundations.

After spending a month in Santa Cruz, Abbot van Caloen departed, leaving Dom Mayeul to cope with all the problems involved in the construction of the new monastery. He was very happy presiding over these works, especially as it gave much needed employment to the local people. Men, women and even children were willing and anxious to work. Eventually he had about a hundred people on the payroll. The men acted as masons, carpenters, brick-layers, etc, while the rest were asked to transport bricks, wood and sand, usually in small baskets. Unfortunately, after several months, the financial resources at the disposal of Dom Mayeul were depleted, and he found himself in a very difficult situation. He could hardly abandon the work, seeing that he was under obedience to Abbot Gerard to complete the buildings, yet, neither could he dismiss his friendly workers from the local community. He wrote immediately explaining his problem to the abbot general of Bahia and the abbot of Rio, who both sent him substantial sums of money, enough to continue the work. Fortunately for all concerned, at this moment the local authorities in Quixada decided to re-commence work on a large reservoir near Santa Cruz, which provided much needed extra work for many of the local people.

Soon after this turn of events, another crisis hit the community in Santa Cruz, which neither Abbot van Caloen nor Dom Mayeul could have foreseen. Apparently each year there was a serious shortage of water in this mountainous region, caused by prolonged droughts. The monks were thus caught unawares, with the prospect of facing a long six months with no water readily available, as the wells and the streams in the monastery area had all dried up. This meant that water had to be collected by donkeys, in small barrels, from a source several kilometres down the mountain. Even when boiled, this water tasted awful. The monks finally fell on the idea of mixing huge amounts of coffee with it to make it drinkable. The drought also affected the growing of vegetables and other crops. Throughout the winter of 1900-1901, food became scarce, with very little choice or variety. Dom Mayeul feared for the health and morale of the younger monks. There was even talk of a pending famine. To say the least of it, the situation seemed bleak, calling for patience and ingenuity, as well as leadership. Nonetheless, throughout the winter of 1900-1901, the little group managed to survive, while at the same time continuing their studies in philosophy and theology, and the daily round of regular monastic prayer. It was an almost heroic existence.

To their great relief, the spring of the year 1901 came early and brought the rains, so that the parched fields and forests soon became covered with pleasant greenery. Ceara took on a new appearance, and life became bearable once again. Despite the difficulties of the past year, Dom Mayeul knew he had achieved much, and was hopeful for the future of the Santa Cruz monastery. The buildings had been almost completed, and he saw the nascent monastery develop under his eyes. He could even see himself becoming its first abbot. Apart from the buildings, which consisted of cells for the monks, classrooms for teaching the younger monks, a refectory and a chapel, he had not been idle in other departments. First, there was the setting up of the house of studies, with courses in both philosophy and theology. Dom Mayeul acted as the principal professor for both subjects. Finally there was the need of a well-stocked library for the students. Everything was provided within a very short time, almost as by a miracle.

As if all the above-mentioned responsibilities were not enough, Dom Mayeul had begun to make a name for himself as a preacher of missions in Quixada and the surrounding parishes. He preached one such mission at the turn of the century (1900-1901), in Quixada, when people arrived in thousands, and made their peace with God. He saw this as a field of future work for himself and his fellow monks in Santa Cruz. Thirdly, he also found time to finish two dissertations, or books, written in Latin, on St. Alphonsus's moral system. The first was called *"De Gemino Probabilismo Licito"* and the second *"De Genuino Morali Systemate S. Alphonsi"*. Both were published in Bruges, by Desclee de Brouwer, in 1901.

Early in April 1901, Dom Mayeul sent a report of the Santa Cruz experience to Abbot Primate de Hemptinne. The latter replied to him on 9 May with some very encouraging words:

> *I thank you for the details which you have given me about Santa Cruz, which give promise of a happy future for this foundation. May the Lord grant your prayers for the success of your work, and recompense you for your sacrifices (Vol. I, 90).*

Throughout his time in Santa Cruz, Dom Mayeul was forced to consider his own monastic standing. He was not yet a fully-fledged monk, being in simple or temporary vows, with no firm canonical status. He had to ask himself when, and where, he could make his final commitment to the Benedictine way of life. Dom Mayeul decided he had to raise this important matter of his solemn (final) profession, due to take place later that year, with Abbot Gerard. On the one hand, he wanted to be absolutely certain that he was doing the right thing, committing himself to the life of a Benedictine monk. Whether he suffered from genuine doubts, or let his imagination go wild, he ended by making an emotional appeal to Abbot van Caloen on the matter. He asked Abbot van Caloen to allow him to travel to Belgium, to consult his former novice master in Maredsous, Dom Benoit d'Hondt, about his monastic vocation. In a series of letters to Abbot van Caloen, Dom Mayeul wrote very frankly, comparing his life as a Redemptorist and a Benedictine monk. Resulting from this interchange of letters, Dom Mayeul's relationship with Abbot van Caloen deteriorated, especially when Abbot van Caloen accused Dom Mayeul of going behind his back and writing to the abbot primate about the Brazilian situation, which in fact was quite untrue. Dom Mayeul also mentions a growing difficulty

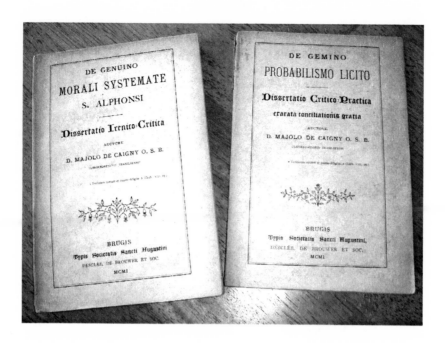

DOM MAYEUL PUBLICATIONS, IN LATIN, ON ST. ALPHONSUS'S MORAL SYSTEM.
A HIGH LEVEL THEOLOGICAL WORK, A MUCH APPRECIATED WORK AMONG
THE THEOLOGIANS.

he has had with some of the German (Beuronese) monks, who were given posts of responsibility in Olinda, San Paulo and elsewhere in Brazil. The following are examples of some of Dom Mayeul's feelings at this time, contained in letters written to Abbot van Caloen from Santa Cruz, in Ceara.

> *I pray with all my heart that the good Lord will arrange for peace to reign between the Beuronese, German monks, who will come to direct the monasteries in Brazil, and the original Brazilian monks. I must admit that the time I spent as novice master in Olinda, was for me a great sacrifice. According to these Beuronese monks, I lacked the true Benedictine spirit. If I live to middle age, being 40, I will ask my Superior to let me live in a hermitage, with a few books. . . . I have lived alone for more than 9 months in Ceara, without being able to open myself to anyone. Even your letters were few and far between. I shall never forget this year. . . (Dom Mayeul to G.v.C., 9 April 1901. SAZ, G.v.C. Papers.).*

> *I feel myself forced to write to you again about my situation. The greatest cross of my life was having, as a spiritual director, a secular priest, who did not understand the kind of religious Order that would suit me, and also having, as Redemptorist novice master, a priest, who took advantage of my youth, to keep me in that Congregation, even though I said to him that I was out of place there, and that I sought a more contemplative kind of life. I have now found such an Order (i.e. the Benedictines), and I am happy, in spite of all the crosses I have suffered. Yet, on account of my having changed religious orders, I will never be in the eyes of my confreres anything more than an "aborted Benedictine". . . .I wish to live in peace with everyone, in spite of being an "aborted Benedictine".(Dom Mayeul to G.v.C. 15 April 1901, SAZ, G.v.C. Papers)*

> *I have had, for a long time, a great desire to consult the novice master in Maredsous, Dom Benoit d'Hondt, whom I believe to be a man of God, on the question of my state of soul and my general situation (Dom Mayeul to G.v.C., 15 May 1901, SAZ, G.v.C. Papers).*

Finally, on 23 June, 1901, still writing from Santa Cruz, Dom Mayeul laid his cards on the table, and sent what sounded like an ultimatum to Abbot van Caloen:

I have the right – before making solemn profession – to consult, in secret, with one or two fathers of Maredsous. I need also to go to Belgium to draw up my last will and testament (monks had to make a will before pronouncing their final vows). And I need to consult with members of my family on this matter. Since you are now in Europe, I can consult both you and my family at the same time, to our mutual satisfaction. I pray your Lordship to banish from your mind any suspicion which my conduct may seem to warrant. I wish to say that I have not the least temptation against my holy vocation. On the contrary, my only desire is to remain in the Brazilian Congregation (Dom Mayeul to G.v.C., 23 June 1901, SAZ, G.v.C. Papers).

All these thoughts were floating through his mind, as he contemplated the scene in Santa Cruz during the late May and early June 1901. He hoped that, after his solemn profession, he would return to Santa Cruz as superior. He was very happy there, and felt in every sense of the phrase "on top of the world". He could have had no idea the he was about to receive a cruel blow. This came at the end of May, 1901, in the form of a telegram from Abbot Gerard, which rocked his monastic life from top to bottom. He described the situation as follows in his memoirs:

The Rt. Rev. Fr. Abbot informed me in a laconic tone of my dismissal as prior of Santa Cruz, and ordered me to leave for Olinda without delay, where I would receive his instructions. I must say this was like a bolt of lightning to me, as harsh as it was unexpected! Yes, this blow was harsh indeed. I had grown fond of the foundation in spite of its initial privations; its ravishing position at the top of the mountain, with views encompassing a vast horizon as far as the eye can see, its charming isolation in the middle of woods, the poverty with its hardships, the devoted affection of the people of our village who were already converted, and that of the neighbouring communities, the ease of preaching the missions in Ceara; in fact, everything came together, both nature and grace, to charm my heart and spirit at Santa Cruz. All these natural and supernatural attractions had conspired to make me believe that this was the blessed place that the Providence of my celestial Father had prepared for me till the end of my days. What a painful surprise! And this blow could not have been more unexpected. I could not explain it (Vol. II, 91-92).

A great sadness descended on Santa Cruz and the district of Ceara, when on the Feast of St. John, 24 June, 1901, Dom Mayeul departed, never to return. He left behind him many disciples and friends. The foundation, which became an abbey in 1903, was suppressed in 1921, and thereafter became a "Home for the Elderly *(Casa de Repouso de Sao Jose)*". Dom Mayeul always maintained that if he had been left there, the monastery of Santa Cruz would have quietly developed and flourished.

Several months later, when in Rome, Dom Mayeul learned from the mouth of Abbot Primate de Hemptinne, one of the reasons why Abbot van Caloen had suddenly dismissed him from his position as prior of Santa Cruz. It was based on a misunderstanding, as well as a misjudgement, on the part of Abbot van Caloen. One of the Brazilian monks had written to the abbot primate, saying that Abbot van Caloen was letting the monks of Santa Cruz die of hunger. Without naming the author of this letter, the abbot primate informed Abbot van Caloen of its contents, and the latter wrongly presumed that Dom Mayeul had written the offending letter. On the strength of this information, Abbot van Caloen decided to take the radical measure of dismissing Dom Mayeul from Santa Cruz. At least, that is the story as told by Dom Mayeul.

However, it is clear that there were several other reasons behind Dom Mayeul's dismissal. One of these related to the latter's overrunning his budget for the construction of Santa Cruz. In a lengthy memorandum, drawn up by Abbot van Caloen some time in 1901, and entitled *"The Case of Dom Mayeul"*, there is a reference to this overspending by Dom Mayeul on the buildings in Santa Cruz. Van Caloen, who was more often than not absent in Europe, had arranged for the abbot of San Paolo to send a substantial sum of money every month to Santa Cruz, to help finance the buildings. However, this money was never paid, a fact which was apparently not revealed to Abbot van Caloen. Under the circumstances, as we have seen, Dom Mayeul had been forced to go begging elsewhere: to Bahia, Rio and Olinda, and, in so doing, incurred the anger of Abbot van Caloen.

There was a final and more pressing reason for asking Dom Mayeul to leave Santa Cruz. This was the crisis looming in the abbey of Rio de Janeiro — a very wealthy and valuable monastery — which, at any moment, was in danger of been expropriated by the state, because there was no one permanently residing there except the elderly and infirm abbot and one other monk. Van Caloen had already decided to appoint Dom Mayeul as prior of Rio to deal with this crisis, if and when it occurred. Thus, at this moment, he wanted Dom Mayeul to be nearer to Rio than in Ceara, which was over a thousand miles up north. Hence the order for Dom Mayeul to move to Bahia was motivated by a multipurpose decision. Van Caloen explained all this in his 'Memorandum' on Dom Mayeul, which he addressed to Dom Benoit d'Hondt, of Maredsous in early August 1901:

> *Soon after my departure for Europe, Dom Mayeul fell into financial difficulties, which was quite beyond my comprehension. He began writing right and left, and went himself to Olinda and Bahia, asking for money. This was the beginning of the present situation. . . . In the meantime, Dom Ulric, the novice master in Bahia, had written several times to me, saying that he was overworked owing to the large number of novices, and asked for a replacement. I decided then to send Dom Mayeul to Bahia as novice master. I had at the back of my mind the idea that Dom Mayeul, if he were in Bahia, would be nearer at hand to be sent to Rio, to deal with a possible crisis in that monastery. It was at this point, when I asked him to go to Bahia as novice master, that he lost control of himself. He wrote me a series of bad letters, accusing me of giving preference to the German/Beuronese monks in Brazil. He obviously resented losing his position as prior of Santa Cruz, and handing over that position to Dom Maurice. I tried to calm him by saying that the appointment in Bahia would only be temporary, and that I intended, as soon as possible, to send him as prior to Rio .(SAZ, G.v.C. Papers)*

On arrival at Olinda from Santa Cruz on 26 June 1901, Dom Mayeul found that Abbot van Caloen was still in Europe. Two weeks went by before he received the awaited letter from Abbot van Caloen, written from St. Andre, Bruges, and dated 24 June 1901. It was nothing more than a blunt order to proceed immediately to Bahia, to take up the post of novice master. Before leaving Olinda for Bahia, Dom Mayeul wrote to Abbot van Caloen, on 13 July 1901:

> *Your Lordship tells me that I am over-excited and troubled. I wish to assure you that I am completely at peace. If I wrote to you in*

ABBOT VAN CALOEN, ARCHABBOT OF BRAZIL.
JOSEPH VAN CALOEN WAS BORN IN BELGIUM (BRUGES) IN 1853, THE SON OF
BARON KARL VAN CALOEN AND HIS WIFE SABINA, COUNTESS OF GOURCY-
SERAINCHAMPS. HE DIED IN 1932 AND HE IS BURIED IN THE ABBEY OF ST.
ANDRE, ZEVENKERKEN (BRUGES) OF WHICH HE WAS THE FOUNDER.

OVERVIEW OF THE BRAZILIAN CONGREGATION, TO WHICH ST. ANDRE
ALSO BELONGED. IN THE MIDDLE, PICTURE OF ABBOT MACHADO AND
ARCHABBOT VAN CALOEN.

somewhat strong language, it was to register my objection to the appointment of Dom Maurice as my successor in Santa Cruz. I wish very much to speak with you, and for several grave reasons I need to come to Belgium. If you refuse me this permission, I shall be forced to write to the Abbot Primate and this will only make our relationship more difficult. I hope we can arrange everything to our mutual satisfaction (SAZ, G.v.C. Papers).

Dom Mayeul spent four weeks in Bahia, and used the occasion to get to know Abbot General Domingo Machado, for whom he retained a great admiration and affection. While there he met Dom Adalbert Surirsen, a monk of Beuron, who was in Bahia as a visitator, on behalf of Abbot van Caloen, examining the situation in Brazil. Dom Adalbert told Dom Mayeul, in confidence, that the relationship between Abbot van Caloen and the abbots of Beuron and Maredsous was not good. At the suggestion of Dom Adalbert, Dom Mayeul then sent a detailed report on the general Brazilian situation to the archabbot of Beuron.

As already mentioned, Dom Mayeul had for some time felt the need to consult with a wise old monk about his vocation. He could not find anyone in Brazil to fit this category. He honestly believed that he needed someone to reassure him of his situation, which had become more complicated of late, due to his differences with Abbot van Caloen and his problems with the German monks. He certainly had no intention of allowing himself to be called an "aborted monk" for the rest of his life. He decided that the only man who could sort out his problems was Dom Benoit d'Hondt, his former novice master in Maredsous.

Dom Mayeul had to wait several weeks before he got any further word from Abbot van Caloen. The latter wrote to him on 8 August 1901, announcing the arrival of Dom Adalbert Surirsen, in Bahia, as his delegate, with full powers to make decisions regarding Dom Mayeul's future movements and advising Dom Mayeul to discuss his problems with this latter monk. Some words in this letter from Abbot van Caloen were very hurtful:

He (Dom Adalbert) will give you all the necessary orders in my name. . . Be completely open with him and obey him as you would myself. He has the power to make decisions on my behalf. . . Be on your guard against the temptations of the enemy (Satan). . . Be

humble and you will be at peace. Your state of mind is not normal'
(SAZ, G.v.C. Papers).

Such a hurtful letter could not have pleased Dom Mayeul, and
only spurred him on to visit Dom Benoit d'Hondt in Maredsous.
Having received from Dom Adalbert, the necessary permission to
go to Belgium, Dom Mayeul left Bahia by boat for Ostend on 13
August 1901, and reached the abbey of St. Andre fifteen days later. Since Abbot van Caloen was still absent in Italy, Dom Mayeul
wrote to him on 28 August 1901, explaining his reasons for coming to Europe:

> *I enclose a letter from Dom Adalbert, with whom I spent several
> days in Bahia. This excellent religious told me that if he were in
> my place, he would have the same desire to go to Europe. He had
> no difficulty in giving me permission to make the journey. I will
> not go to Maredsous until I hear from you.... If you wish to see
> me in Rome, I will come there willingly. What I seek above all is a
> definitive solution to my situation. On my journey by boat to Eu-
> rope, I was accompanied by the Secretary to the Archbishop of Rio.
> He told me that the situation in our monastery in Rio was serious
> and the sooner it was resolved the better (SAZ, G.v.C. Papers).*

In spite of all their differences and difficulties, Abbot van Caloen
still had confidence in Dom Mayeul. Proof of this is the fact that,
as soon as the Dom Mayeul arrived in Belgium, Abbot van Caloen
appointed him novice master and librarian in St. Andre, the newly
established recruiting centre in Bruges for the Brazilian mission.
Dom Mayeul was happy to have some time in St. Andre, and occupied his time putting the two volumes on St. Alphonsus and
Probabilism through the press by publisher Desclee de Brouwer.
What was more disturbing, however, was the fact that Abbot van
Caloen was having second thoughts about proposing Dom Mayeul
for solemn profession. The latter could have known nothing of the
long memorandum, written by Abbot Gerard, under the title *"The
Case of Dom Mayeul"*, in the late summer of 1901. The memoran-
dum, addressed to Dom Benoit d'Hondt, was a frank assessment of
Dom Mayeul, and contained some very telling reflections:

> *I am forced to accept the decision of Dom Adalbert Surirsen, per-
> mitting Dom Mayeul to come to Europe, but while I may tolerate
> it, it runs contrary to my wishes....In all my decisions, I have to*

> *keep my dignity as abbot. . . . After all that has happened, I hesitate to admit him (i.e. Dom Mayeul) to Solemn Profession. He has a strong head and wishes to follow his own ideas. He shows an extraordinary stubbornness of mind and will, once he gets hold of some idea. He always gives the appearance of obeying, but he imposes his own will, for better or for worse! (SAZ, 'Memorandum: Le Cas de Dom Mayeul', G.v.C. Papers)*

In what seems to have been an accompanying letter to this memorandum, Abbot van Caloen wrote on 31 August 1901 to Dom Benoit d'Hondt, asking him to act as counsellor to Dom Mayeul:

> *He (Dom Mayeul) is passing through a crisis at this moment, and wishes to consult with you. I desire that you offer him whatever advice you think best, and then give me your opinion about his case. For my part, it is a matter of whether I dare admit him to Solemn Profession. He has an unusual turn of mind which frightens me. Please pray for our poor brother (SAZ, G.v.C. Papers).*

On 6 September 1901, Dom Mayeul wrote from his sister's house in Emelghem, acknowledging a letter from Abbot van Caloen, also dated 31 August. In this last letter, Abbot van Caloen expressed his annoyance with Dom Mayeul, for (i) visiting his family without permission; (ii) being over-excited; (iii) adopting a parti pris attitude, being opinionated without evidence; (iv) wishing to leave the Brazilian Congregation, and (v) lacking in humility. Dom Mayeul denied all of these accusations, saying that he would leave Emelghem immediately and go to Maredsous to consult with Dom Benoit d'Hondt. He wrote to Abbot van Caloen from the abbey of Maredsous on 16 September 1901, reporting on his several conversations with Dom Benoit d'Hondt:

> *His words have done me good. I pray you to hasten to give a solution to my situation, and if possible to grant me an interview to sort out all our differences. . . . Dom Benoit D'Hondt told me that I had a duty to make a full report to the Chapter of Beuron on the situation in Brazil. I have done this, desiring to put an end to the misunderstandings between the two Benedictine Congregations i.e. the Brazilian and Beuronese (SAZ, G.v.C. Papers).*

Writing again from Maredsous on 24 September, Dom Mayeul complained that it was more than two weeks since he last heard from Abbot van Caloen. He wished to end the dreadful period of uncertainty, especially as he was now happy with the advice he had received in Maredsous:

> *They have cleared up all my doubts, banished all my sorrows, and given me an assurance for the future. I have no reason for leaving the Brazilian Congregation. If your Lordship has not in conscience any grave reasons for dismissing me from this Congregation, I beg you to write without delay, and thus allow me to return to Brazil. . . . I wish to add that it would cost me dearly to be sent to Rio only after the death of the abbot. I still hope to meet you, either here in Belgium or in Italy, before my departure for Brazil (SAZ, G.v.C. Papers).*

Van Caloen wrote back to Dom Mayeul on 26 September, stating further reasons for being annoyed with the latter. It is difficult to understand the attitude of Abbot van Caloen. On paper, it seems that he was becoming paranoid. This time he accused Dom Mayeul of coming to Europe primarily to make formal complaints against him, and that the visit to Maredsous was a mere side issue, if not a blind. He certainly was testing, if not questioning, Dom Mayeul's loyalty. Once again, in a letter dated 28 September, written from Maredsous, Dom Mayeul denied these accusations:

> *I state on my honour that I did not come to Europe to make complaints against you, but simply to seek counsel regarding my vocation. I am sorry if some of my rather lively letters have annoyed you. Surely you realize that I have always adopted a frank attitude when writing to you. I now beg your Lordship to understand my situation. I would be so happy if these painful incidents could end, and be forgotten forever. Let us speak heart to heart on this matter, as I have desired for a long time (SAZ, van Caloen).*

Fortunately the storm was almost over. Word had come back from the archabbot of Beuron to both the abbot primate and Abbot van Caloen, saying how impressed he had been with the recent report on the Brazilian situation, in which Dom Mayeul defended the actions of Abbot van Caloen. The abbot primate, who was also abbot of Maredsous, decided at this stage to intervene on behalf of Dom Mayeul. Following on these negotiations, Abbot van Caloen decided that the time had come to draw a line over the past misunderstandings between himself and Dom Mayeul. There followed immediately a series of reconciliations, and Dom Mayeul found himself once again in Abbot van Caloen's good books.

Some time towards the beginning of October, 1901, Dom Maur van Emelen, the superior of the Recruiting House St. Andre, became ill, and asked for a replacement. Van Caloen, to show his goodwill, decided to appoint Dom Mayeul to succeed him temporarily, and at the same time appointing him novice master. However, still more wonderful news came, when Abbot van Caloen announced that he had accepted Dom Mayeul for solemn profession, setting the date for All Saints Day, 1 November 1901. What a great moment this was for Dom Mayeul. Incidentally it was a strange moment from the point of view of Benedictine history, in that Dom Mayeul made his solemn profession in the abbey of St. Andre in Bruges, while holding the office of novice master and prior of this same monastery! More importantly for Dom Mayeul, however, he was now a fully-fledged Benedictine, and could no longer be called "an aborted monk".

Within a month, Dom Mayeul was on the move again, this time to take up the post of prior in the monastery of Rio de Janeiro. He described the sequence of events in his memoirs:

> *Divine Providence had no plans to detain me in Belgium. Our Brazilian Congregation possessed a wealthy Abbey in Rio de Janeiro. Its patrimony was in danger of being confiscated by the Government in the event of the death of Abbot Ramos. The Holy See had ordered that another monk should reside permanently in the monastery, but this monk, feeling incapable of bearing the cross any longer, called for a change. Our Rev. Abbot van Caloen thought of me for that position of sacrifice, and offered it without imposing it on me. It was truly a zouave's posting; how could I have hesitated for an instant before accepting it?*
>
> *I visited the graves of my dear parents and my brother Medard. Once again I bid farewell to my brothers and sisters. Once again I boarded a German steamer at Antwerp. It was 12 December 1901. On 2 January the following year we entered the port of Rio de Janeiro, whose sweeping panorama I could only admire (Vol. II, 93-94).*

CHAPTER IV

Prior in Rio de Janeiro
(2 January 1902 - 23 July 1904)

AFTER a rather tedious three weeks journey by sea from Antwerp, which included a short stopover in Portugal, Dom Mayeul arrived in Rio de Janeiro on 2 January 1902. The ship was unable to make its way into port, as there were no docking piers built at the time. The passengers had, therefore, to transfer, with their luggage, to a small sailing boat, and endure a rather perilous journey into the harbour. In his memoirs, Dom Mayeul remarked that this stormy reception was a foretaste of the rather difficult time ahead of him in Rio *(Vol. I, 94-95)*. He was greatly disappointed to find no one on the quayside to meet him, especially as he had asked the purser of the ship the previous evening to telegraph the monastery to give them the time of his arrival. He described his reaction in a letter to Abbot van Caloen on 4 January 1902:

> *Through the negligence of the Lloyd's Company, nobody came to meet me. I eventually made my way to the Monastery of San Bento, to the great delight, but surprise, of Dom Ulric Sonntag, whom I had come to replace. The Abbot Frei Joao Ramos was absent, but appeared the following morning to greet me (SAZ, G.v.C. Papers).*

Dom Mayeul made a good impression on Abbot Ramos, especially by reminding him of the time he had sent money for the construction of the Santa Cruz monastery. While he was pleased to be appointed prior of the monastery of San Bento, he was somewhat taken aback, when told that his duties would be limited to presiding at table whenever the abbot was absent! Dom Mayeul had hoped to visit the nuncio, Mgr. Macchi, and the archbishop of Rio, but was strictly forbidden to do so by the abbot. He found life in the abbey in Rio very strange. There was only one public Mass each day, celebrated at 04.30 a.m. The abbot paid a number of so-called

ABBEY OF RIO DE JANEIRO

OLD MAP SHOWING THE LOCATION OF THE MAIN BRAZILIAN FOUNDATIONS

'chaplains' to offer this Mass. There were no liturgical celebrations, such as Lauds or Vespers. All the normal priestly functions, such as preaching and hearing confessions, had long been abandoned. He felt very isolated and frustrated, especially as his immediate superior, Abbot van Caloen, wrote to him very infrequently. On the other hand, Dom Mayeul wrote every month to van Caloen. These letters give a detailed picture of life in Rio throughout the year 1902.

Dom Mayeul had hardly settled into his new job when he was struck down with a bout of yellow fever, and forced to take to his bed. Abbot Ramos never once came to see him. This is not surprising, since the abbot led a rather strange life. He was married and lived outside the monastery with his wife, a son and two daughters. His son a medical doctor, was supposed to be treating Dom Mayeul, but hardly ever called. He records in his memoirs that a whole day passed without his being offered as much as a glass of water *(Vol. II, 95)*. On recovering from his illness, and availing of the absence of Abbot Ramos, he decided to visit the nuncio and the archbishop of Rio, to make them aware of the scandalous life of the abbot, who neglected his monastic duties, spending most of his day entertaining his relatives and so-called friends. There were lavish meals served in the monastery refectory, whenever Abbot Ramos was in residence, in which Dom Mayeul was forced to join, sitting on the right of the abbot. He wrote to Abbot van Caloen on 11 July 1902, giving details of his problem, proposing that Abbot van Caloen come to Rio to speak with the nuncio and the archbishop. He also expressed the hope that it might be possible to call in Rio a General Chapter, a meeting of all the abbots and superiors of the Brazilian Congregation, to deal with the situation. At the same time he expressed his longing for the restoration of full liturgical life in the monastery, and the companionship of some fervent confreres. This would, of course, require the influx of monks from elsewhere, and could not be done so long as Abbot Ramos was in office. Rome or Abbot van Caloen must act in the very near future, to depose the present abbot of Rio.

On 19 July 1902, Dom Mayeul wrote again to Abbot van Caloen, reporting the unacceptable rudeness of Abbot Ramos to a group of visiting monks from San Paolo. The offending remarks were made in front of some lay people (relatives and guests of the abbot), who were present in the refectory, much to the embarrassment of the said monks of San Paolo. This led Dom Mayeul to make the following recommendation:

I beg you, therefore, to kindly notify all the Brazilian Priors, not to send anyone to Rio, neither should they write to me, asking for a favour from the abbot of Rio. Please do not write anything about this to the Abbot, as he is sufficiently annoyed with me. Everything is "intrigue" here at the moment (SAZ, G.v.C. Papers).

Throughout the second half of 1902, life became very difficult for Dom Mayeul, since he was the only monk in permanent residence in the large abbey. He kept himself busy putting the well-stocked library in order, and doing some pastoral work, both inside and outside the monastery. He also took advantage of his free time to study the surrounding area of Rio de Janeiro. He never got used to the noise and bustle of the monastery, which was situated in the middle of the capital city. He expressed the hope that later on, the abbey of Rio might be moved into a new establishment in the country, while the old monastery would remain as a college. There was already a large day-school, under lay-management, functioning in most of the big halls and rooms of the abbey. He noted that the buildings themselves were in a sad state of disrepair, giving the appearance of an empty shell, bereft of monks and all the trappings of normal monastic life. One ray of sunshine came his way in the support he received from the abbot general of the Brazilian Congregation, Dom Domingo Machado, who wrote to him on 14 January 1903, offering encouragement and support:

I pray that your efficiency in performing the responsibility entrusted to you as prior of Rio, will result in the restoration of our beloved Congregation to its ancient splendour (ARJAN, Machado Papers).

Later that month, he received news that his sister, Leonie (religious name Sister Hilonia), had died in Belgium, on 18th January. She was only 35 years of age, and the third of his siblings to die young, the others being his brother Medard, and his sister Pharailde (Sister Alida). Dom Mayeul could not but reflect on his own fragile state of health, especially as he had fallen ill again, this time with gastric fever, caused by having to eat excessively rich food, when dining with the abbot of Rio. Having received permission from Abbot Ramos, he left Rio for nearby Petropolis, where the

Franciscans offered him hospitality and care. Once he was sufficiently recovered, he spent a month in the Benedictine abbey in San Paolo, to consult with his friend and former fellow novice, Prior Miguel Kruse. While there, he discovered that a campaign was already under way in the public press in San Paolo, directed against the foreign monks residing there, among who was Dom Miguel Kruse, a German. The monks were accused of planning to hand over the wealth of the abbey of San Paolo to the Kaiser in Germany. Evidence of the frustration, loneliness and impatience which Dom Mayeul felt at this time, is expressed in a long letter he wrote to Abbot van Caloen, then in Italy, on 24 March, 1903:

> *I would be only too happy to be able to thank you for sending Br. John, whose arrival here in Rio I have waited in vain for eight months. This formal violation of your promise is so much more cruel, in that my situation here is painful. This want of sincerity on your part only convinces me, that I cannot put any trust in your words, which are so often contradicted by your deeds. For my part, I will perform my duties here in Rio, until your arrival, giving witness in the same way I have already done in Olinda and Ceara. I hope to speak with you about a matter which has troubled me for more than two years. Indeed, your conduct towards me, for more than three years, has not been very helpful for my personal perfection/sanctification (SAZ, G.v.C. Papers).*

In this same letter, Dom Mayeul made a further plea to Abbot van Caloen to come to Rio, to speak with the nuncio, Mgr. Guiseppe Macchi, and convene a General Chapter of the Brazilian Congregation, at which the present abbot of Rio (Ramos) would be deposed. He insisted that the situation in the monastery could not be tolerated much longer, as the abbot's extravagances were gradually eating up the abbey's patrimony. The monastery had become nothing more than a social club, whose members were friends and relatives of Abbot Ramos.

Apparently, without consulting or notifying anyone in Brazil, Abbot van Caloen had, for some months, been in touch with the Roman authorities, asking their approval for a radical solution to the Rio situation. Resulting from these negotiations, Pope Leo XIII issued a decree *"Singulare Stadium"* on 22 November 1902, transferring the seat of the abbot general of the Brazilian Congregation from Bahia to Rio. This proposal required Abbot General Machado to relinquish his position as abbot of Bahia, and take up the post as abbot of Rio. In this way, the headquarters of the Brazilian Congregation was moved from Bahia to Rio, the capital of Brazil. Once installed, Abbot General Machado should call a meeting of the General Chapter of the Brazilian Congregation in Rio, and demand the resignation of Abbot Ramos.

When informed of these proposals, Abbot General Machado, who at this time was over 80 years of age, was evidently surprised, but nonetheless accepted the contents of the papal decree as coming from God Himself. He moved as soon as he could from Bahia to Rio, and set in motion the proposed plan. Dom Mayeul describes the immediate aftermath of these proceedings:

> At that time the Abbots in Brazil were elected for only three years. It was, therefore, only a matter of convening the General Chapter to have new elections and pension off the abbot of Rio (Ramos). The latter did not expect this measure, and as soon as he got wind of it, he qualified this plan as diabolical. Believing me to be conniving with its authors, he did not hide his animosity towards me. To maintain himself in his position, he summoned me to the Supreme Court, whose decision was far from favourable to him (SAZ, G.v.C. Papers).

Communication between Rome and Brazil was very slow at this time. It took several months before the papal decree of November 1902 reached Brazil and could be implemented by all those immediately concerned. The first indication that Dom Mayeul had of the new Roman proposals, reached him towards the end of April 1903, when he received an invitation from Abbot General Machado to attend a forthcoming General Chapter in Rio. As prior of the abbey in Rio, he was entitled to a seat and a vote at this important meeting. He could not help wondering how the Roman plan would develop, especially as he knew that there was a growing opposition among a certain group in Rio to the impending dismissal or resignation of Abbot Ramos. He could not have foreseen the possibility of some kind of demonstration by the latter's supporters, and was about to receive a rude awakening.

Apart from Dom Mayeul, who was already in Rio, all those who had a right to attend the General Chapter, arrived by boat at the capital city of Rio on 5 May 1903. They numbered six in all – Abbot General Dom Domingo Machado, Abbot van Caloen, Prior Miguel Kruse of San Paolo, Dom Ulric Sonntag and Dom Wandrille Herpierre. Before they disembarked, they received a message from Abbot Ramos, stating that he would only accommodate the abbot general and his secretary in the monastery. The others would have to find a hotel to stay in, though Abbot Ramos would pay their expenses. At the last minute they were saved from this clearly unacceptable arrangement, thanks to a representative of the archbishop of Rio, who met them at the boat, and invited Abbot van Caloen, and the members of the Chapter, to stay at his residence. Only then did they learn of the dangerous situation in the city, although they must have realized that something was wrong, when they saw the large military presence in the port of Rio, and were given a military escort from the ship to the archbishop's palace. Apparently several local newspapers had in recent days published an attack on the foreign monks, stating that they had been sent by the German Kaiser Wilhelm, to occupy the abbey of Rio. Due to its strategic position, being near a large naval base, it would become a focal point for a future invasion of Rio de Janeiro by the German navy. At the same time, the anti-German faction in Rio had circulated a rumour, stating that the foreign monks intended closing the abbey school. The school at this time had more than 800 pupils, was free, and contributed in no small way to the cultural life of the capital city. Its closure would amount to a national scandal.

Meanwhile, Dom Mayeul remained in the abbey of Rio, where Abbot Ramos still resided, carrying on his weekly extravagant entertainments, as if nothing had changed. On 11 May, a Sunday, Dom Mayeul was summoned by the abbot general to attend a meeting of the General Chapter of the Brazilian Congregation, in the archbishop's house. Following the correct legal proceedings, a vote was taken, and Abbot Domingo Machado was unanimously elected abbot of the monastery in Rio de Janeiro. This automatically meant the dismissal, or forced resignation, of Abbot Ramos. The next day, 12 May 1903, all the members of the Chapter entered the monastery of San Bento, for the solemn installation of Abbot Machado as the new abbot of Rio. This ceremony passed off without incident.

However, at four o'clock that same afternoon, while Abbot Machado, now the legitimate abbot of Rio, was having tea with the members of the Chapter in his room, loud noises were heard outside the monastery. Looking out the window of the room where they were gathered, they could see a large crowd of people, carrying machetes, guns and sticks, converging on the monastery. Dom Mayeul, as prior, was sent by Abbot Machado, to close the main door of the monastery. He left his fellow monks in the room and went to carry out the order. This took some time, as he had to make certain the door was securely locked. He then returned to the room where they were having tea, to discover that Abbot van Caloen and the other members of the Chapter, had disappeared. He learned later that one of the servants, Bonifacio, who had become aware of the dangers facing the "foreign monks", guided them to safety, using a secret passage under the garden. From there, because darkness had already fallen, they were able to make their way unobserved to the archbishop's house.

Meanwhile, Dom Mayeul found himself in a difficult situation, seeing that the monastery was about to be invaded by a hostile crowd. It was evident that there was no way of getting out of the monastery. The only solution was to find a safe place to hide inside the abbey. He made his way at once to his own, the prior's room, which, like most of the rooms in the monastery, was large, and had a stout wooden door. He proceeded to lock the door, putting a wooden beam across it on the inside. He then waited, not exactly in fear of his life, but anxious all the same for his safety.

We possess no less than three detailed accounts of what happened in the abbey of Rio that same evening. The first account, contained in Dom Mayeul's memoirs *(Vol. I, 105-109)*, is a very colourful version of the events, written more than twenty years later. Secondly, in *"Lumen Christi" (1980)*, the monks of San Bento, Rio, published a series of studies, in Portuguese, to commemorate the fifteenth centenary of the death of St. Benedict (480-1980). One of the essays is entitled: "Dramatica ocupacao do Mosteiro do Rio de Janeiro, 1903", *(pp. 133-147)*. This seems to be the most authentic, as well as the most detailed, version we possess. Thirdly, there is a full account in a French weekly newspaper, *"Le Pelerin"*, 25 October 1903, with illustrations by the famous Parisian artist,

ABBOT MACHADO, A WISE AND VENERATED ABBOT,
GREATLY ADMIRED BY DOM MAYEUL

Eugene Damblans. The affair hit the international headlines, and became a minor *cause célèbre*.

The main events of the evening are described as follow by Dom Mayeul:

I heard successive sounds of explosions, and the cries of the crowd, which left me in no doubt regarding the gravity of my situation. I knew nothing about my confreres, and thought that they might have been wounded, perhaps even killed. I was certain that I was about to be taken prisoner by a rioting mob, and began barricading myself into the room, realizing there was no escape. Already a mob had gathered outside my door, and they were trying to force their way into my cell. This door, built of Brazilian hard wood, known to be as strong as iron, was my only defence against the rioting mob, who continued to use every kind of instrument to break it down. Fortunately it withstood their onslaught. The rioters had been led to my room by some of the pupils of the school, who told them: "That is the cell of the prior, the tall, thin man, wearing glasses". The crowd became more and more furious, especially when they discovered that my confreres had fled the monastery. It was only at this moment that I learned about their escape, as I heard them cry out, after failing to break down my door: "It is useless! He (Dom Mayeul) is no longer there. He must have escaped with the others!" All I could do was to sit still in my chair and pray. I sat there for almost an hour, and was made more fearful when I heard the rioters say they were going to get an axe to open the door. However, at that very moment, I heard a loud cry from outside my window, repeating the same words over and over again: "In the name of humanity, do no harm to anybody. Get out of the monastery!" Immediately the banging on my door ceased. I then heard the voice of the chief of police, who had come to my rescue with a strong contingent of armed personnel, giving orders to the rioters to disperse or be arrested. Soon after this there was a quiet knocking on my door and a voice which said: "Father Prior, if you are there, you can open the door, we are the police and your friends!" I was then escorted to the archbishop's palace, where I rejoined Mgr. van Caloen and my confreres. Abbot Machado had remained in his room in the monastery of San Bento throughout the whole proceedings. He was too old to take any action. In any case, he felt safe, knowing that the crowd would never harm his person. Their actions were directed solely against the "foreigners" (Vol. I, 107-109).

This incident in the abbey of Rio remained in the memory of Dom Mayeul for the rest of his life. It is interesting to note that Dom Mayeul gave the following title to this chapter of his memoirs: "My Calvary in Rio de Janeiro". A close reading of these pages leads one to suspect that Dom Mayeul indulged in a fair amount of self-pity, as well as self-adulation, when writing about these events in Rio. The whole experience was apparently as much a test of his faith, as of his courage. He certainly emerged a stronger person, convinced that God had protected him from what seemed like certain death. He believed that by this saving act, God was preparing him for some future position of responsibility. And to add to his certainty of divine protection, he received a confirmation of this belief from Abbot Primate de Hemptinne, who wrote from Rome on 4 June 1903, congratulating him on his miraculous escape:

> *I have just been reading a number of Brazilian newspapers, giving details of the incidents surrounding the storming of Sao Bento. It must have been a very emotional moment for you. I bless God for having protected you, and for bringing peace and calm back to the Abbey in Rio.... I believe that, after a spell of profound inactivity, you will be given an important work to do. Divine Providence watches over us at every moment. In time we come to realize how all the phases of our lives eventually come together to complement each other (ASAR, de Hemptinne Papers).*

These were ominous words, which sounded almost prophetical to Dom Mayeul. Some months later, Abbot Primate de Hemptinne returned to this same incident in Rio, in a letter to Dom Mayeul dated Rome 9 December 1903, in which he sees an element of 'predestination' in what had happened, and asks:

> *Have you not felt this touch of God in the midst of the tragic events in Rio? Do you not acknowledge how good God has been to you, and how much I bless Him for it? I have personally thanked Him for saving your life. I pray that you will spend the rest of your life loving and serving Him, who has so admirably preserved you from danger (ASAR, de Hemptinne Papers).*

In the aftermath of the attack on the monastery, the head of the Brazilian army, General Hermes da Fonseca, and the minister of foreign affairs, Baron of Rio Branco, called on Abbot van Caloen, who was still in residence at the archbishop's house, offering their apologies for the recent riots. They assured him that it was now safe for all the monks, including Dom Mayeul, to return to the abbey in Rio. The Baron de Rio Branco explained his intervention as a matter of preserving the national honour. The monks received further encouragement in a personal message of sympathy and support from the president of the Brazilian republic, Dr. Rodrigues Alves. Undoubtedly, this official apology, and message of sympathy, helped to boost the morale of Dom Mayeul and his fellow Benedictines in Rio.

On returning to the abbey of San Bento, Rio, they found themselves facing an immediate problem: what to do with ex-abbot Ramos, who refused to leave the monastery, though under threat of excommunication. Eventually the minister for the interior, Dr. Seabra, intervened, and persuaded the ex-abbot to retire to one of the monastery's properties outside Rio. He was given a substantial pension, though he did not live long to enjoy it. He had been in poor health for some time, and died the following year (1904). There was some dispute over where he should be buried, considering his rather chequered career. However, Abbot Machado, always the perfect diplomat, decided that they would draw a curtain over the past. Thus they gave Abbot Ramos a full monastic funeral, and buried him in the abbots' section of the cloisters in San Bento, Rio, where he rests to this day.

Throughout the latter half of 1903 and the first half of 1904, Dom Mayeul was fully occupied in his double responsibility as prior of the abbey and rector of the abbey school. On his appointment as prior, he had accepted the post, but with one reservation, namely that he would not be asked to make his permanent monastic home in Rio. He found the monastery exposed on one side to city life, and on the other to a large naval base, which operated day and night. The site of the monastery was in no way conducive to the silence and recollection normally found in a Benedictine house for which he longed with all his heart.

One of his main concerns was to restore the recitation of the Divine Office i.e. the liturgical prayer of the church in Rio. Dom Mayeul had a beautiful singing voice, and missed the splendid liturgical celebrations, associated with a Benedictine monastery. It was a long time since any such services had been held in Rio. He, therefore, made a public announcement that there would be a solemn celebration on 23 June 1903, with the singing of first vespers for the Feast of St. John the Baptist. He was delighted and amazed at the number of people who attended. This was a historical day for the monastery, when full monastic life was restored. Very soon, more and more people started coming to the church for Mass and the other ceremonies. Dom Mayeul saw in this an opportunity to found an association of lay-supporters, called oblates, whose main object was to help the monks in various apostolic works, and also guarantee a good attendance on festive occasions in the monastery. He also founded the 'League of Frequent Communion', to encourage people to receive communion once a month. Through these associations he got to know a large number of people socially. He was thus able to build up a group of well-wishers, who provided the monks with much needed financial and moral support.

In the aftermath of the recent riots and disturbance, and the return of calm to the city, Dom Mayeul decided the time had come to re-open the school. He realized it was 'politically' desirable to dispel the rumour, that "the foreign monks" wished to close the school. He appointed himself the first rector of the refurbished school, which re-opened on 24 June 1903. Abbot van Caloen had provided him with the necessary funds to re-house the school in new and improved quarters, outside the monastic enclosure. He had the support of a loyal group of teachers, who cooperated with him in establishing good order and discipline. The school opened up another pastoral avenue for Dom Mayeul, offering him an opportunity to exercise both a social and religious influence on some of the most influential families of Rio.

It became obvious to all concerned, that the situation in the abbey of San Bento, Rio, had changed dramatically during the months following the riots. To begin with, Abbot General Machado, considering his age (81 years) and declining health, decided he could no longer hold the position as abbot of Rio. He resigned and returned to Bahia, where he spent his remaining years. Van Caloen became the new abbot of Rio, while Dom Mayeul continued as prior of the monastery and rector of the school. Slowly but surely, Abbot van Caloen had succeeded in getting more and more monks to come to Rio, and in 1904 made Rio the central novitiate house for the Brazilian Congregation. This brought new life into the monastery, assuring its future development.

In spite of all the positive aspects of life in Rio, Dom Mayeul became more and more convinced that he could never make his permanent home there. He had found a desirable property, outside Rio, for sale at a reasonable price. It consisted of 70 hectares, situated in the mountains of Tijuca, near Rio, and would make an excellent site for a monastery. Having acquired this property, Dom Mayeul proposed that the monks should move to Tijuca, and hand over the existing monastery in Rio, to be developed into a larger school or college. However, Abbot van Caloen considered Tijuca too isolated, and turned down the proposal. At the same time, Abbot van Caloen assured Dom Mayeul that he would arrange for his transfer elsewhere whenever the first opportunity presented itself. Eventually, in mid-July 1904, after spending more than two years as prior in Rio, Dom Mayeul was informed by Abbot van Caloen that he was being relieved of his post, and appointed prior in Bahia. He departed from Rio on 23 July, and arrived in Bahia on 25 July, where he was destined to face one of the greatest challenges of his life.

CHAPTER V

Prior in Salvador - Bahia
(25 July 1904 - 8 June 1907)

HAD DOM MAYEUL been given a choice of places to where he should be sent, the abbey of Bahia would hardly have been number one on his list. He would have preferred Santa Cruz, near Quixada, where he had spent a year and a half (Oct. 1899-June 1901) establishing a monastery, high up on a mountain-side, whose climate and clear air he had found so congenial. It was one of the few places where he felt he could belong, and even spend the rest of his life. But it was not to be. Obedience sent him to Bahia, where the monastery was situated in the heart of another big city. He expressed his inner feelings in his memoirs:

I felt all the horror of a man who has been enclosed in a prison, and deprived of the love of the countryside and the solitude for which I longed (Vol. I, 127).

As he took up his new post, he found himself facing a daunting task. The material state of the monastery was deplorable. From the ground floor to the roof, for almost a hundred years, nothing had been done to maintain the buildings. In some cases the walls had collapsed, leaving only rubble and debris. There was a dire need to plaster and paint every room in the monastery. The sacristy in the church was a complete ruin, and urgently in need of replacement. The same was true of the Chapter Room and the refectory, while the cells of the monks were hardly fit for human habitation. Time, money and patience would be needed to put the monastery into proper working order.

He discussed the matter with Abbot General Machado, who was sympathetic and supportive. However, since the financial situation of the abbey was rather precarious, the abbot counselled prudence, and a step-by-step approach. Dom Mayeul decided, therefore, to begin with the roofs of the monastery and church. The slates and

ABBEY OF BAHIA

Chapter Room of the Abbey of Bahia,
where the community council held their meetings.

the gutters needed immediate attention, as the rainwater flowed freely into rooms and corridors. He was fortunate in finding two excellent masons, who immediately set about doing all the necessary repairs. He then turned his attention to the church, where the side altars, including the Blessed Sacrament altar, had no protecting gates or iron grilles. This meant that the people could enter these sacred places, without supervision. Dom Mayeul arranged for new iron grilles and gates to be provided for the side chapels, and also in front of the main sanctuary. At one end of the church, he constructed a spacious sacristy, with a large room adjoining it. This latter room was intended as a meeting place for the various sodalities and other religious groups he planned to establish. One of Dom Mayeul's more enduring additions to the monastery buildings was a magnificent Chapter Room, with beautifully carved stalls. This doubled as a chapel, which, even to this day, is used by the monks for the singing of Compline each evening.

When the monastery was founded in 1582, few windows had been provided. Those that existed were very small, and allowed very little light into the rooms. Dom Mayeul judged that they were quite out of proportion with the large monastic buildings. After 300 years, not only the windows, but most of the mortar holding the sills, were in a sad state of decay. Thus a whole set of new windows, in the Roman style, were provided, and enhanced the appearance of the monastery. Dom Mayeul then turned his attention to the large cloister garden, which had become a virtual wilderness. New trees and shrubs were planted, and an area set aside for vegetables. Paths were set out and benches provided for seating during recreation. Since the monks hardly ever went outside the enclosure, and their places of recreation were so restricted, the garden had to be turned into a multi-purpose amenity. Of course, all this could not be done in one day or in one year, but the totality of improvements helped to make life more bearable for the monks, and more attractive to visitors and guests. Much of Dom Mayeul's work in these different areas has endured to this day. It is worth reflecting, that this spate of building in Bahia gave Dom Mayeul further experience in the art of construction, an art he had already practised with great success in Santa Cruz, and which he would practise to a greater degree in Trinidad. He believed he had a penchant for this kind of work.

At the same time as he was engaged in re-furbishing the monastic buildings, Dom Mayeul put his mind to examining the abbey's patrimony or financial situation. The monastery was, on paper, very wealthy. They owned property, mostly houses, in the city of Bahia, as well as considerable holdings in the countryside outside Bahia, and finally some properties in the state of Sergipe. However, owing to the shortage of monks over a long period of time, the administration of these properties had fallen into the hands of secular agents, while other properties had been alienated. Dom Mayeul decided that he had, first of all, to assess the size and value of the houses and other properties, and secondly, to investigate the honesty and reliability of the secular agents.

He discovered that more than half the houses belonging to the monastery were situated in the poorer quarters of Bahia. The people occupying these houses were often unable to pay the rent, and seldom undertook any maintenance or repair work. Other houses were in that area of the city which today would be called the "red-light" district. After much investigation, he decided to sell off all the houses which were unproductive, and with the money thus collected, set about restoring and modernizing the monastery's remaining houses in Bahia. Fortunately, the city was, at this time, expanding. Dom Mayeul found that many of the monastery's better houses, which he had restored, were situated in that part of the city designated for development, and would, therefore, attract a more affluent clientele. Finally, he decided to get rid of all the secular agents, believing that they had for years been lining their own pockets with money, which rightly belonged to the monastery. He appointed two reliable accountants, who set up a limited liability company, with responsibility for collecting rents. Several of the monks sat on the board of this company, and were thus in a position to monitor its proceedings.

As regards the properties in the rural areas, and especially in Sergipe, it had been found impossible to administer them properly from Bahia, on account of the lack of roads and other means of communication. Dom Mayeul made a preliminary journey to examine the situation in these rural places. He discovered that in many cases the original title deeds to the monastery's property had been lost, having been sent to Portugal nearly two hundred years previously, and apparently had disappeared in the famous earthquake in Lisbon, in 1755. What was worse, the greater part of the monastery's rural properties had been acquired over the centuries by the government or state, and seemed beyond reclaiming. Nonetheless, Dom Mayeul was determined to pursue the matter. Thus, on his return to Bahia, he hired an eminent lawyer to study the problem. After lengthy investigation, the latter discovered copies of the original deeds in the state archives in Bahia. It took a considerable sum of money to have the deeds copied, and eventually handed over to the monks of Bahia. It was only in 1906 that Dom Mayeul finally settled this important financial matter, and reclaimed most of the monastery's rural patrimony. In this way, he succeeded in laying a solid financial basis for the years ahead. He told the story of these negotiations in great detail in his memoirs:

> It was this transformation, with the accompanying growth and stabilisation, of the monastery's patrimony, that made it possible, later on in 1912, to undertake the foundation of a mission in the Antilles (Trinidad) (Vol. I, 135).

At the same time as he was occupied in all these material and financial negotiations, Dom Mayeul had not forgotten his responsibilities in the *spiritual* sphere, both inside and outside the monastery. On arrival in Bahia, he had been appalled at the low level of religious practice among the people, and felt he had to do something to draw them to the abbey church. Following his experience in Rio, he started by reorganizing the women oblates (associates of the monastery), who soon became his most zealous collaborators. In his memoirs he gave the list of similar organisations which he founded in Bahia during his time as prior:

> I managed to partly reform the Confraternity of Nossa Senhora das Augustia (Our Lady of Sorrows). I also established various new organisations: one of Frequent Communion, one of the Sacred Heart, one of the Souls in Purgatory, and another of Our Holy Father Benedict. I founded the organisation of St. Francis Regis for the conversion of unmarried couples, which were numerous in Bahia; also the Women's League for defending the Christian family and the interests of the Church, and re-established the League's monthly review "Paladina Do Lar". God helped me visibly, and for several years I maintained and developed these creations, as much through my sermons in our church as through my talks and

conversation, both public and private, in the meetings of all these associations (Vol. II, 121).

These early years in Bahia were not only fruitful in spiritual blessings for the people of the city, but they contributed greatly to the personal development of Dom Mayeul himself. As prior of the oldest Benedictine monastery in Brazil, he gained valuable experience in dealing with the pastoral needs of the people, and in organizing the daily life of a community of monks. He found an outlet for his many talents, as preacher, organiser, businessman, builder, spiritual director, innovator etc. There is no doubt that between 1904 and 1907 he left his mark on the abbey of Bahia. He was happy in his work, believing he had been chosen by Providence to help restore and build up the church in this large Brazilian city. He was especially pleased to witness the blossoming of faith and piety among people, who, through no apparent fault of their own, had neglected the practice of their religion for so long. His earlier training as a Redemptorist gave him an assurance, as well as some expertise, in coping with the challenges of religious life and practice in Bahia. There are few, if any, complaints in his memoirs dealing with these years. He had a happy, working relationship with Abbot General Machado, who supported him in all his undertakings, and gave him a free hand in organizing every aspect of work and life in the monastery.

Believing that he would spend the rest of his days in Bahia, Dom Mayeul steeped himself in Brazilian and Bahian history. As often as he could, he sought out the company of Abbot General Machado, relishing the many anecdotes and stories of former times recounted to him by this venerable old monk. He also visited a former abbot general, Frei Emmanuel de Santa Caesano Pinto, long since retired, who lived in the little monastery of Montserrat, on the outskirts of Bahia. It was during Frei Emmanuel's time, that the slaves owned by the monastery, about 700 in number, were given their freedom, several years before slavery was officially abolished in Brazil by the Emperor Pedro II. In recognition of his taking this initiative, the Emperor presented Frei Emmanuel with a golden snuff-box, which is still preserved in the abbey.

On top of all this, Dom Mayeul gave much of his time to the formation of the younger monks, who were arriving in batches each year from Europe and also from Brazil itself. Some of these were novices, requiring instruction in the Rule of St. Benedict, while others were studying either philosophy or theology. He personally supervised the studies of these young men. It has already been pointed out that he had received a rather patchy Benedictine formation. However, he seems to have rectified this by reading and studying the Rule of St. Benedict. One has only to browse through the three volumes of his memoirs, to see how much he had steeped himself in the monastic rule and spirituality. There is ample evidence of his interest in every aspect of monastic living and tradition. In later years he wrote a book on the Rule of St. Benedict, *"The Ascetical Method of the Teaching of St. Benedict"*. More important still, he made a deep study of the liturgy, i.e. the official daily prayer of the Church, as recited or sung by monks and priests all over the world. He was familiar with the multi-volume edition of Dom Gueranger's *"The Liturgical Year"*. Finally, one has to admit that he was a deeply religious person, with a great love for the things of God and of the Church. He combined these interests with a missionary spirit, which allowed him to reach out to everyone and bring them the message of Christ.

During his time as prior in Bahia, Dom Mayeul had one final ambition, namely, to start a school, which would be attached to the monastery. He had already gained some experience of a Benedictine school in Rio. The idea of the school was in accordance with the decree of Pope Leo XII, issued in 1827, by which the Benedictine monasteries in Brazil were formed into a separate autonomous Congregation. In this papal decree, Pope Leo XII had expressed the wish that the Brazilian monks should interest themselves in the education of young people. Slowly, but surely, he brought this idea to fruition, and succeeded in laying the foundations of an excellent secondary school in Bahia, which is one of the major activities of the monks today.

Abbot van Caloen was still, in principle, his superior. But Dom Mayeul hardly ever saw him, as the abbot was constantly on the move, travelling in Europe, seeking new recruits, on some fundraising campaign, or recuperating in his family's villa in the Cap d'Antibes, France. There is no doubt that Dom Mayeul felt more at ease when Abbot van Caloen was not breathing down his neck, as had happened in Olinda and in Rio. They were two strong characters, who only gradually came to tolerate each other. On the other hand, Dom Mayeul never lost his respect for Abbot van Caloen, whom he recognised as an essential contact person with the Roman authorities, and still officially responsible for the restoration of the Benedictine Order in Brazil.

Early in January 1906, Abbot van Caloen, being delayed in Europe, wrote to Dom Mayeul, instructing him to make a canonical visitation of the abbey in Olinda, in the North of Brazil. It was five years since Dom Mayeul had been there. He felt a certain nostalgia at the thought of visiting again this lovely abbey, where he had made his first profession. He was also flattered at being asked to undertake this delicate task, usually entrusted to someone holding the rank of abbot. Dom Mayeul's visit to Olinda ended to everyone's satisfaction, especially of Abbot van Caloen. This was the beginning of a new relationship between the two men, soon to be cemented by Abbot van Caloen proposing Dom Mayeul as successor to Abbot General Machado in Bahia.

There was one unexpected sequence to this Olinda visit, in that Dom Mayeul had an attack of malaria while there. He was brought to the Santa Casa de Misericordia near Recife, a hospital under the care of the German Benedictine Sisters of St. Ottilien, where he spent five weeks. The prioress, who attended to him, was a remarkable woman, a highly qualified nurse, who had studied hydrotherapy and homeopathology in Munich, and had practised her art on the African mission in Dar es Salaam, Tanzania. Throughout his life, Dom Mayeul had a problem when being nursed by a woman. This was a hangover from his sheltered upbringing, and led him to consider a woman, even a nun, as a danger to his vow of chastity. He describes in his memoirs his reaction to the nursing he received from the prioress in the hospital, and its happy outcome:

> *The treatment had the best results as much for my health, shown by my rapid recovery, as well as for a certain mental state I had acquired in my youth. In the past, my being treated during an illness by a woman, albeit a nun, had made me suffer considerable embarrassment and temptation. But now, even more than at Santa Agueda, when I had yellow fever, I learned to see in a woman's nursing only the goodness of God, without being troubled (Vol. II, 122).*

There seems little doubt that this was a turning point in his personal and psychological development. He was 44 years of age in

1906, and though very late in life, had at last come to terms with this side of his sexuality. One can only surmise that he returned to Bahia a changed man, having cast aside, during his five weeks in Recife, the phobias and scruples of half a lifetime. On this same subject of women, he wrote much later:

> *Above all, in my relations with people of the opposite sex, I have learned to maintain a perfect liberty of heart, without attaching myself to anyone. Another day, I heard one of my spiritual daughters say: "He (Dom Mayeul) loves everyone; therefore, he does not love anyone in particular". Furthermore, I have accustomed myself to see in every woman an image of Mary, who alone I love in every way, as the glory of her sex.(Vol. II, 129-130)*

The year 1907 brought a still more remarkable change into the life and status of the prior of Bahia. Dom Mayeul describes what happened in his memoirs:

> *In that same year, 1907, Mgr. van Caloen came to see our venerable Abbot General Machado in Bahia, to discuss his plans to present me to the Holy See as Coadjutor Abbot of the monastery of San Sebastian in Bahia, with the right of succession. Dom Machado was already a man of 83, and no longer performed any ecclesiastical functions. He made no objections to my appointment as his successor. Neither did any of the other members of the community who were all consulted. After Mgr. van Caloen's departure, I called together the members of the Chapter to inform them of what my style of government would be, so that if, perchance, it was not to their liking, they would still have time to inform the Holy See and suggest someone else for Abbot. ... Finally, I sought advice concerning the idea of my being appointed Abbot, and was told I should not oppose Mgr. van Caloen's plan, but leave everything in the hands of Divine Providence (Vol. II, 123).*

Apart from Bahia, where Dom Machado was abbot, and Rio, where van Caloen was abbot, none of the other monasteries in Brazil had an abbot. The other two monasteries, San Paolo and Olinda were governed by a prior. On 8 June 1907, Pius X nominated four monks, two as coadjutor abbots, respectively of Rio de Janeiro and Bahia, with right of succession, and two as abbots of San Paolo and Olinda. Dom Chrysostom de Saegher, a monk of Maredsous, was appointed coadjutor abbot of Rio, while Dom Mayeul became

THE 4 NEW ABBOTS AND ABBOT VAN CALOEN.
DOM MAYEUL, SEATED SECOND FROM RIGHT.

Vue de l'Abbaïe De Lobbes au bord de la Sambre.

ABBEY OF LOBBES

POPE PIUS X, WHO APPOINTED DOM MAYEUL AS ABBOT

coadjutor abbot of the monastery of San Sebastian in Bahia. At the same time Dom Mayeul was named titular abbot of the ancient abbey of Lobbes, in Belgium, and closed at the time of the French Revolution. Dom Miguel Kruse, formerly prior of San Paolo, was appointed abbot of this monastery, while Dom Pedro Roeser became abbot of Olinda.

The four new abbots had to wait until 24 November 1907 before being consecrated in Rio de Janeiro by Abbot van Caloen, whose return to Brazil was delayed for reason of ill-health. They thus had five months to prepare for this important occasion. Dom Mayeul used this time to take stock of his situation. He realized that he was being raised to a position that would bring him honour and prestige, but he knew, also, that most superiors lived in the shadow of the Cross, sooner or later. He had enough experience of life to know that there was no rose without thorns. His main fear was that this promotion would change him, or go to his head. He summed up his feelings in his memoirs:

> On receiving this news, I experienced a natural feeling of satisfaction, since all this was like a vindication for what had happened in the past. But at the same time I understood that heavier crosses were in store for me. However, I felt quite decided to do my best for God's glory and the good of our community. This was a good opportunity for remembering the following text of the Holy Bible: "Glory not in apparel at any time and be not exalted in the day of thy honour" (Eccl. xi, 4).

Dom Mayeul decided to take as his model Dom Domingo Machado, who, surrounded by a large number of Benedictine monks, celebrated his diamond jubilee of priesthood in Bahia, on 24 October 1907. This was a splendid occasion, and a moment of joy, especially for the old abbot, who had taken as his motto: "In God I trust". This trust was now reaping its reward, in the revival of monastic life throughout Brazil. Dom Mayeul felt honoured and privileged to have been part of that revival.

Dom Mayeul notified his brothers and sisters back in Belgium of his promotion. His brothers were clearly delighted with the good news, and offered him a beautiful pectoral cross of pure gold, wrought by Biais, in Paris. In Bahia itself, he received many tokens of goodwill and congratulations. The various Societies and Sodalities he had established in Bahia presented him with a rich mitre and a valuable ring, as well as all the other trappings he needed. Finally he had to choose a coat of arms and a motto. For his coat of arms, he chose that of a branch of his family, who were living in Ghent (Flanders) in the 18th century. The family coat of arms was sent to Dom Mayeul by count Verspeyen, whose mother Mary was a De Caigny. Dom Mayeul modified it in a religious sense, separating the four fields by a red cross. The other elements in the coat of arms were three stars, symbol of the light from above, and three oak acorns, pointing out the moral strength with which Dom Mayeul felt he had to arm himself. He had always liked the saying of Lacordaire that "monks are as immortal as oak trees". Lastly, he took as his motto the text of St. John "Peace in Truth and Charity" (II John, 3). Whether he was truly descended from a French aristocratic family or not is a matter of dispute, and in fact not important. The truth is that as abbot he had the right to a coat of arms, and was free to choose one from whatever source he wished. Thus any suggestion that he was being pretentious in this matter is not warranted and not really important. He rightly felt that his appointment as abbot was an honour, not just for himself, but also for his family and community.

Dom Mayeul, posing as the new Abbot

125

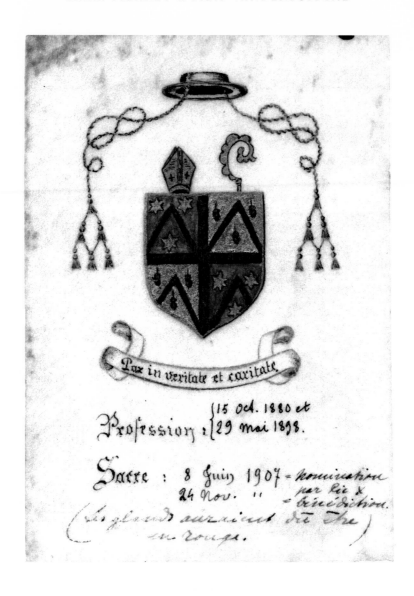

Pax in veritate et caritate.

COAT OF ARMS, CHOSEN BY DOM MAYEUL

CHAPTER VI

Coadjutor Abbot of
Salvador - Bahia

(24 November 1907 - 1 July 1908)

THE CHANGE of status, from prior to coadjutor abbot, un-doubtedly brought with it considerable changes in the way people treated Dom Mayeul. Henceforth he wore a ring on his finger, which, according to the custom of the time, the faithful would kiss reverently, each time they met him. He also wore a pectoral Cross, a still more noticeable appendage, which undoubtedly drew attention to the fact that he was a prelate. As regards his own situation, he could now make solid plans for the future, as he was virtually responsible for all the affairs of the monastery. Already at this stage of his life, he developed a penchant for making grandiose plans. It was an activity that pleased him greatly, despite the time-consuming element it involved. Throughout his life he had suffered from a certain contradiction or ambivalence in his attitude to various activities. On the one hand, he craved for stability, silence and a life of contemplation. But on the other hand, he experienced a kind of restlessness, which drove him to an almost frenetic activity of construction and renovation, which he hoped would be his personal legacy to posterity. In his heart, he probably longed to settle down, but he had to wait until the end of his life, when he retired to his hermitage in St. Leo Abbey, Florida, to find this long-sought solitude. Only then could he make his own the famous saying of General Charles de Gaulle, on retiring from public life into veritable solitude in 1968: "In the tumult of men and events, solitude was my temptation. Now it is my friend".

However, in the year 1907, solitude was far from his mind. He had to submit to all the elaborate ritual surrounding his blessing as

ABBEY OF BAHIA WITH THE CLOISTER GARDEN

a Benedictine abbot, which took place in the abbey of San Bento in Rio de Janeiro, on 24 November 1907. It was a splendid occasion, in a splendid setting. Mgr. van Caloen was the ordaining prelate, having been raised by Leo X to the episcopate, as titular bishop of Phocee, and also appointed archabbot (the title of abbot general was now dropped) of San Bento, Rio de Janeiro. The four new abbots: Dom J. Chrysostom de Saegher, Dom Mayeul De Caigny, Dom Miguel Kruse and Dom Peter Roeser, swore "to defend with all their strength the abbeys entrusted to their care". This oath was to ring in the ears of Dom Mayeul some years later, when he had to defend the abbey from spoliation. He describes in his memoirs, the meetings with Abbot van Caloen and the three other new abbots, immediately following the abbatial blessing:

> *After our abbatial blessing, Mgr. van Caloen held with us several meetings in our residence of Tijuca, in order that together we agreed on the measures that would be most advantageous for the development of our Brazilian Congregation. He urged us to see to it that our dignity should be respected, to ostensibly carry our pectoral cross in the presence of bishops, to abolish everywhere the use of the title "Frey" and replace it by "Dom". Some bishops had tried to oppose these measures but in vain; our perseverance, in the end, was successful (Vol. II, 127).*

Dom Mayeul returned to Bahia soon after this meeting. As co-adjutor abbot, he could now use what are called 'pontificals' (mitre and crosier, pastoral staff). Pontifical High Mass had not been seen in the church San Sebastian, for a long time. It proved an added attraction to those who attended the large abbey church, especially as Dom Mayeul presented a dignified figure, with a powerful and musical voice. There is no doubt that he enjoyed these splendid ceremonial occasions, which had a clear pastoral dimension. All his life, Dom Mayeul showed a love for, and appreciation of, the liturgy, and now, at long last, he found himself in his element. He had all the features and qualities of a prelate, to which one should add his eloquence as a preacher. He appeared as the perfect abbot, tall, distinguished-looking, and with an aura of authority on his brow.

But he had other horizons in view besides that of the city of Bahia. For a long time he had dreamed of founding a mission-house or monastery in the interior of the state of Bahia. This idea was shared by some of the younger monks in Bahia, who were anxious to extend their apostolate to the conversion of the pagan Indians in the vast rain forests of Brazil. Such a work was traditionally very Benedictine, when one remembered the names of monks who had evangelised Europe in the Middle Ages: Augustine of Canterbury, Boniface, Anscar, Willibrord, etc. Surely the Benedictine monks of the 20th century could do the same for South America. Dom Mayeul hoped that such a missionary commitment would prove an added attraction to those young men waiting in the recruiting house in St. Andre, Belgium. He had, of course, to ask permission for this missionary adventure from the bishop of Bahia, Mgr. Jerome Thome da Silva, in whose diocese the Indians lived, a permission which was readily given.

On 5 January 1908, Dom Mayeul, accompanied by Dom Sebastian Weber, left the abbey of Bahia, to undertake a journey of exploration to the Rio Pardo, a large river basin to the south of Bahia. They first took a steamship to the port of Canavieiras, situated at the mouth of the Rio Pardo, on the Atlantic Ocean. There they had a long wait, until their transport, a canoe, arrived at 2 o'clock in the morning, to bring them to their next destination, Jacaranda, 80 kilometres away. This leg of the journey took over 20 hours, without any hope of rest or sleep. The Rio Pardo is 660 Km in length and from 80 to 100 metres across. They arrived at Jacaranda late at night. No priest had visited this place for a very long time, though most of the local population were Catholics. They offered Dom Mayeul and Fr. Sebastian the use of a semi-abandoned building in which they could celebrate Mass the following morning. A considerable number of people attended, and Dom Mayeul took the opportunity to announce that he and Fr. Sebastian would begin a parish mission in Jacaranda on Wednesday of the following week. Neither monk had any difficulty in communicating with the people, who understood Brazilian-Portuguese, a language in which the two monks were fluent.

Jacaranda and Salobro marked the limits of what one could call 'civilization'. Beyond, in the distance, they could see the vast unchartered primeval forest, known as 'Indian country'. They were warned not to venture on their own into this territory, as they might be killed by the Indians. Not so long before this, a black man had been killed by poisonous arrows in this very area. In any case, the monks were not going to venture that far. They were fortunate in obtain-

ing the help of a wealthy Frenchman, Pedro Benazet, the owner of
a large tract of land around Salobro, and stretching as far as Serra
da Onca. He was the principal fazendeir or landowner, and a good
Catholic, being a cousin of Cardinal Andrieux, the archbishop of
Bordeaux, France. Dom Mayeul had already been in touch with him
and, just before leaving Bahia, received a very gracious letter, offering his full support:

> I wish to say how much I am ready to help you, so far as I can,
> in the generous initiative you are about to undertake. This will be
> a great victory for the Catholic religion, and a singular service for
> the advancement of the material and moral progress of the country.
> It would be wonderful if you could win for Christ the Indians,
> who are so numerous, and live in the thick forest between Cidade
> da Conquista and the coastal town of Canavieiras. You will meet
> with considerable difficulties. It will be necessary to open up new
> roads to reach the Indians, who have retreated far from the civilized
> population. These people, though ignorant and unlearned, possess
> many basic qualities, and are both honest and hospitable (Bull des
> Miss. Bresiliennes, SAZ 1908.p. 245).

When the two monks met Mr. Benazet, he invited them to stay at
his residence not far from Serra da Onca, and provided them with
the only practical form of transport, horses, as there were no roads.
They set out on the long journey through the forest. They were
somewhat hampered by a sudden heavy downpour, which turned
the paths into muddy rivulets. Dom Mayeul fell from his horse
into two inches of water, and found himself separated from his
two companions, Fr. Sebastian and Mr. Benazet. His greatest fear
was of being lost in the forest, but he was soon reunited with the
others. They eventually reached their guide's fazenda (residence),
where they were entertained to an excellent supper. They remained
there for two nights, during which time their host gave them a detailed account of the life and culture of the local people. They then
returned to open the mission in Jacaranda.

Word of the parish mission had got round to everyone living
within a twenty miles radius. On the opening day of the mission,
a Saturday, the area surrounding the little church was covered with
tents. The people had no intention of returning home until after
the mission, and were prepared to camp out for the two weeks. The
place was milling with people, both young and old. The priests

found themselves hearing confessions for hours on end, administering baptism to infants and adults alike, confirming many others. They had received permission for this from the archbishop of Bahia, in whose diocese Jacaranda and Salobro lay. Nearly one hundred couples, who had been living together, now had their unions blessed and regularized in the sacrament of matrimony.

One day, when emerging from the confessional, Dom Mayeul noticed a small black man in the shadows, who seemed almost ashamed to be in the church. He was dressed rather poorly, obviously trying not to draw attention to himself. When he saw Dom Mayeul he approached him and said, in a subdued voice: "Father, I am a man of the forest. I have come to be married!" Such humility was both moving and edifying. However, the most astonishing aspect of the mission was the large number of people who came to receive Holy Communion, with genuine, sincere devotion. Day by day the crowds grew, until it became necessary to preach the word of God in the open air. Each evening large fires were lit, to keep the mosquitoes away. The people sang songs, danced and enjoyed themselves. One particular night, a father, whose five sons had been baptised that day, offered a fireworks display in thanksgiving. Dom Mayeul admitted that the experience of this mission had been both a consolation and a joy to the monks. During the two weeks, they had taught these wonderful people to recite the Our Father, Hail Mary, and make the Sign of the Cross. Some said that they had never seen the shadow of a priest before. Dom Mayeul described in his memoirs the moving scene on 26 January 1908, as the monks said goodbye to these forgotten people:

> But the moment for our departure arrived. You would have to be there to see the mixture of joy and sadness of these good people. They were happy for having received the benefits of the mission, but sad at our departure, so much so that they did not know whether to laugh or cry. Some showed their joy by carrying our suitcases, kissing our scapulars, our hands, our feet, touching our canoe, helping us to go on board, asking for another medal, another holy picture. I had tears in my eyes. Willingly I would have stayed there with them, never to return to Bahia, so that I could help them, instruct them and lead them to God (Vol. I, 163-165, See also Bull. des Missions Bresiliennes, SAZ, Sept. 1908:"Voyage au Rio Pardo", pp. 166-168).

I was there in my true element, far from all superficiality and hypocrisy of so-called modern civilisation in large towns. Certainly one should not scorn the rich. I have even been for several of them the instrument of divine mercy. However, my preferences incline towards the poor and the most abandoned people. I find I am more at ease among them (Vol. II, 122).

On their journey back to Bahia the two monks made several stops, to visit a number of families they had contacted on the way to Jacaranda. They arrived back in Bahia early in the morning of 2 February 1908, in time to celebrate Mass for the Feast of the Purification of Our Lady in the abbey church.

Reflecting on the past month's missionary journey, Dom Mayeul was, first of all, filled with a desire to pursue this pastoral work among the Indians. However, this would not be possible until he had more monks at his disposal. Looking round his community in San Bento, Bahia, in 1908, he found he had only 10 priests and 4 lay brothers. It is interesting to note that four of these became members of the future community in Trinidad: Dom Sebastian Weber, Dom Paul Dobbert, Dom Charles Verbeke and Br. Joseph Kleinmann. While he never abandoned hope of getting more Brazilians to join the monastery, he decided there and then to go to Europe himself to seek more recruits.

Before leaving for Europe, Dom Mayeul approached the archbishop of Bahia, Mgr. Jerome Thome da Silva, to give him an account of the recent missionary journey to Jacaranda. The archbishop was very pleased to hear of the success of the parish mission in this remote part of his diocese, and gave Dom Mayeul an official letter supporting his future missionary work among the Indians. This letter, which Dom Mayeul took with him to Europe, showed the good relationship between Dom Mayeul and the archbishop at this point of time. The letter is dated 26 March 1908:

Rt. Rev. Dom Mayeul,

The journey that you are about to undertake in Europe prompts me to make the following remarks: The archdiocese of Bahia occupies a vast territory, and includes a population of more than two million inhabitants. These are found scattered in many places, sometimes at great distances from one another, and entrusted to a very limited number of priests, who find themselves overstretched and over-

*worked. I have the intention of founding a house of religious men,
in the interior and remote part of my diocese.*

*That is why I am now asking your Lordship, that profiting by
your stay in Europe, you may be able to recruit some young men,
who would be prepared to undertake the work of this foundation.
By doing this, the Archdiocese of Bahia will be much obliged to you
(Bull. Des Missions Bresiliennes, SAZ, 1908, p. 243).*

Dom Mayeul embarked for Europe at the beginning of March
1908. He had three reasons for making this journey: (i) To visit
Lourdes, and put his new responsibilities under the protection
of Our Lady of Lourdes; (ii) To recruit candidates from Belgium
and Germany for his monastery of San Bento, Bahia; (iii) To raise
funds for the missionary foundation to the Rio Pardo. He went
first to visit his family in Flanders. His eldest sister, Julie, who had
never married, told him that for some time she had been thinking
of entering a convent. However, her age (she would be 50 on 19
March 1908) was an impediment. Dom Mayeul discussed her case
with the bishop of Bruges, Mgr. Waffelaert, who granted her the
necessary dispensation. She entered the convent of the Missionary
Sisters of St. Augustine, and lived an exemplary religious life until
her death in 1929. He next went to Brussels, to pay an emotional
visit to his old Redemptorist friend and mentor, Fr. Dubois, who
had become almost totally blind. It says much for Dom Mayeul
that he retained such good relations with his former Redemptorist
confreres, while on their part, they rejoiced to see him so happy and
fulfilled in his present elevated office.

Dom Mayeul spent several months travelling round Belgium,
Germany and France, and succeeded in recruiting nine excellent
young men for his monastery in Bahia. He was in Lourdes when he
received word that Abbot General Machado of Bahia had died on 1
July 1908. The death of Abbot Machado meant that Dom Mayeul
automatically became the new abbot of Bahia. As it was his duty
and privilege to preside at the funeral rites of his predecessor, he
decided to return to Brazil immediately, bringing with him the nine
European candidates for monastic life.

On arrival in Bahia, Dom Mayeul was surprised at the unfortunate turn of events regarding the burial of the old abbot. The
centuries-long (since 1670) tradition in Brazil had been to bury

all monks, including abbots, in the monastery cloister, where deep caverns had been provided for this very purpose. However, the civil authorities in Bahia at this time, 1908, were ill-disposed towards the monks. A minor official in the department of health, perhaps seeking notoriety, refused the permission sought to bury Abbot Machado in the cloister of the abbey. The people of Bahia, as well as the monks, made a protest, but to no avail, as the decision of the health official received the backing of the governor of Bahia. It seemed, therefore, that the monks would have to bury Abbot Machado in the public city cemetery.

News of this debacle reached the ears of the monks of Rio, who had a great veneration for Abbot General Machado, the true restorer of the Brazilian Congregation. They proposed that the body of the old abbot be embalmed with care, brought to Rio where the civil authorities were well-disposed to the monks, and buried in the magnificent Chapter Room of the monastery. The embalming, which was performed in Bahia, caused some considerable trouble, as Dom Mayeul recounts in his memoirs:

The doctor who performed the embalming, and who we thought was a good friend, demanded an exorbitant sum of money for the job. I discovered that, instead of having money in the bank, we had nothing but debts. In vain, I knocked at the doors of my more fortunate confreres. However, help came in an unexpected way, in the form of a loan offered me by the Archbishop of Bahia, Mgr. Jerome da Silva. I made it quite clear to the doctor how much his demands would hurt us, even suggesting that St. Benedict might well punish him in some hidden way if he persisted. Unfortunately, love of money triumphed over his so-called friendship and fear of punishment. But it happened that, very soon after this, he lost his position as professor at the University of Bahia, fell ill and just before dying, begged me to pay him a visit. By his tears, more than by his words, he implored my forgiveness, which I gladly gave him, so that he could die in peace (Vol. II, 142).

Dom Mayeul was present at the funeral rights of Abbot Machado in Rio on 30 July 1908, which was attended by all the other Brazilian abbots and a large concourse of the faithful, from both Rio and Bahia. The abbey of Rio had, by the decree of Pope Pius X, dated 8 June 1907, become the headquarters of the abbot general of the

Brazilian Congregation. It was only fitting that this great Benedictine monk should have his final resting place in the beautiful abbey of San Bento, Rio, the capital city of Brazil at the time. The death of Abbot Machado marked the end of the old order, and ushered in the beginning of the new dispensation. His death, unfortunately, also removed from the scene an influential and steadying hand, whose presence might have helped to avert any future crises.

When he returned to Bahia after the funeral of Abbot Machado, Dom Mayeul felt very much on his own. He had to adapt to his changed situation, where he now had full authority and responsibility. Very soon he learned how to cope with the uncertainties and challenges of running a large abbey. His first move was to appoint as his prior a young Brazilian monk, Dom Benedict de Souza Leao Faro, who had been ordained a priest only a year previously. In this way, Dom Mayeul showed the people of Bahia that he intended administering the abbey to serve their interests, and not those of the foreign monks. He was fortunate in having the goodwill and support of most Catholics in Bahia.

CHAPTER VII

Abbot of Salvador - Bahia
(1 July 1908 – 16 February 1913)

ON RETURNING to the abbey of Bahia, his eyes rested on the vast structure of this almost four hundred year old building. While in Santa Cruz, he had developed the eye of a builder or contractor, and had gained further experience during his time as prior in Bahia (1904-1907), when he spent many long hours planning the restoration and painting of the abbey church, both inside and outside. The church, built in the renaissance style, with a magnificent dome, was a landmark in the city. Fully restored, it now presented a worthy appearance and was an ideal setting for the ceremonies which became a special feature of Dom Mayeul's abbacy. More and more people started coming to the abbey, especially on Sundays and feast-days, to join in the impressive celebrations over which Dom Mayeul presided. He revitalized the already established sodalities and associations, and, with the approval of the archbishop of Bahia, increased the number of apostolic and other pastoral works directed at the people of the neighbourhood. All this was not accomplished in a day. He gradually built up a large group of people who provided him with a regular congregation, and supported him in many ways during his time as abbot. Although he was Belgian by birth, he had renounced his Belgian nationality ten years earlier, and on 23 June, 1898, had taken out Brazilian nationality. By the time he became abbot in Bahia, he felt he was a fully-fledged Brazilian citizen, accepted as such by everyone. They respected him especially for the fact that he now held the same position, abbot of Bahia, as their late venerable Abbot Machado. However, he realized there were some, especially among the diocesan clergy, who still resented him for being a "foreigner", if not a usurper. Yet, in 1910, he had no reason to fear for the future of his abbey. The people of Bahia, whose ancestors had built the monastery, rejoiced at the sight of a growing and flourishing community. Twelve years previously (in

1898), there were only two monks in the monastery, and the buildings were in a sad state of disrepair. In 1910 there were twenty-four monks in residence, while the monastery was gradually being restored to its former glory. They acknowledged that all this was due to the hard work and organisational skills of Dom Mayeul

During the early months of 1910, Dom Mayeul gave his attention to one area of the monastery that was badly in need of a facelift, namely, the ground floor, which for two centuries had become the home of rats and bats. This was now transformed into classrooms for the growing number of students. In time, other disused buildings were refurbished to provide much needed accommodation for the oblate school. All this was made possible thanks to the fact that he now had sufficient funds at his disposal to undertake an extensive restoration programme. The houses and other property, situated in the better part of the city, owned by the abbey, which he had recently modernised, had tripled in value within a few years, and provided a steady income. Furthermore, a single overseer, a qualified accountant, now sufficed to look after the monastery's property in Bahia and elsewhere. Judging from the account books, and the reports of the Chapter meetings, the finances of the monastery were in good order. From every angle, the future looked bright and hopeful.

After dealing with the monastery building problems, he turned his attention to some unfinished business regarding his missionary project in the Rio Pardo. His first exploratory journey, to Serra da Onca and Salobro, in January 1908, convinced him that there was an urgent need to undertake a monastic foundation among the neglected people of this region. On 4 December, 1909, he set off once again for the Rio Pardo, accompanied by Dom Sebastian Weber, whom he appointed prior of the new foundation, Dom Bertin Dehaese, the chronicler of the mission, and Brother Isidore, a Brazilian, the link-person with the local people. After consultation with the archbishop of Bahia, he decided to make his foundation at a place called Angelim, situated not far from the river Rio Pardo, on a hill, surrounded by vast forests, but right in the middle of rich and fertile land. This was already holy ground, having a large and beautiful grotto, which Dom Mayeul succeeded in transforming into a church, and dedicating to Our Lady of Lourdes. The left bank of the river was inhabited by a tribe of Indians, whom he hoped to convert; the right bank was inhabited by small farmers, who lived by fishing and hunting. Some of these had never seen a priest before. This could be explained by the fact that the place was very difficult to approach, involving some considerable dangers to travellers, and was far from any centre of civilisation. On the other hand, the climate was cool and healthy. The missionaries were optimistic for the future of the foundation, which had a double purpose: the conversion of the Indians, and the sanctification of the Catholics who lived in the surrounding region.

Dom Mayeul wrote of this visit in his memoirs:

While there (in Angelim), I celebrated the feast of Christmas (1909), which was attended by a fairly large number of river people. Many of these showed their enthusiasm and joy, and performed Indian dances for us, by the light of the full moon. Indeed, the arrival of our missionaries seemed to augur well for a new era of prosperity for the district. The government of Bahia, as well as the municipality of Canavieiras, had, at my request, made some wonderful promises of material help, above all to open a viable roadway the length of the Rio Pardo. This was something long wished for by the people, who had, up to this, no other route but the river as a means of travel and communication. However, the work of constructing a road is still uncertain, owing to the sudden and heavy flooding during the rainy season. Only thus, by building a road, would it be possible for me to go ahead with my plan to build our new Abbey in this region (Vol. II, 144).

Soon after Christmas, Dom Mayeul left Angelim and returned to Bahia. On arriving he found a telegram summoning him to Rome, to attend a General Chapter of the Brazilian Congregation, under the presidency of Abbot Primate de Hemptinne. He thus had to leave Bahia almost immediately, going first to Rio and from there to Europe. He reached Naples on 10 February, 1910, after a journey of two weeks. The main purpose of the General Chapter was to draw up new Constitutions (regulations), adjusting the old ones to the present-day situation. In any case, the Constitutions of the old Brazilian Congregation had never been accepted by Dom van Caloen and the other European monks. At the suggestion of the abbot primate they took the Constitutions of the Beuronese (German) Congregation as a basis for the new Brazilian Constitutions, and worked at this throughout the month of March 1910.

While in Italy, Dom Mayeul took the opportunity to visit the shrine of our Lady of Pompeii, through whose intercession his life had been spared in 1899, when he had been struck down with yellow fever. He also went to Monte Cassino and Subiaco, two places associated with St. Benedict. When the General Chapter was over, Dom Mayeul spent some weeks visiting several countries in Europe, seeking out candidates for the Brazilian mission. He found six excellent young men, who, later that year, returned with him to Brazil. While passing through Belgium he had the pleasure of presiding, on 18 April, 1910, at the ceremony of the religious profession of his eldest sister, who had become, under the name of Dame Julienne, a missionary Canoness of St. Augustine. This happened at Roulers, where he also visited the minor seminary, the school he had attended from the age of eight to thirteen. His final stop was at Stanbrook Abbey, England, to see one of his spiritual daughters from Bahia, Maria da Consolacao, who later returned to San Paolo, as part of a foundation of Benedictine sisters in Brazil. He then embarked for Bahia.

On his return to Bahia in 1910, he took a long hard look at his situation. No one could deny that, up to the present, all his undertakings, whether internal or external, had been a success. Indeed, they had surpassed all human expectations. But what for the future? As he wrote later in his memoirs:

The years 1910-1911 were undoubtedly the highest moments of my career as an Abbot, being as it were, my Palm Sunday. Soon after that there was talk of persecution and exile — if not the destruction of the entire Abbey (Vol. II, 145).

Following the enactment of the Emile Combes laws in France in 1905, a veritable wave of anti-clericalism and anti-Catholicism ensued in that country, which led to the banishment of many religious orders, who were forced into exile in Belgium, England, Ireland and USA. This anti-clericalism spread from France into countries such as Portugal, and from Portugal into Brazil. At this time (1909-11), there was a strong freemason element in the Brazilian government, which now put into effect a series of attacks on the Catholic Church. Two particular incidents occurred in 1911, which caused Dom Mayeul to fear that the monks of Bahia might be the next in line for attack. The first was a fabricated story of a young girl, Idalina de Olivieira, an inmate of the Catholic orphanage of Chris-

THE SOURCE OF THE BENEDICTINE ORDER, THE ABBEY OF MONTE CASSINO IN ITALY, COMPLETELY DESTROYED BY BOMBARDMENTS DURING THE LIBERATION OF ITALY AND REBUILT TO ITS FULL GLORY IN THE 1950 AND 1960IES

tovao Colombo, in San Paolo, who was said to have been murdered by the religious in charge, and secretly buried in the grounds of the convent. There was a public outcry, and a call to bring the perpetrators to justice. The rabble offered to help the police find the body. Every corner of the house and outbuildings was minutely searched, while the religious women looked on in fear and trembling. The ring-leaders then started digging up the garden, determined to find the gruesome evidence of the crime. They eventually came across a secluded corner in the garden, where the ground had lately been dug up, but was smoothed down as if to conceal something. Their efforts were finally rewarded, for there was the corpse ... of a mule! When the case was called before the supreme court, it was revealed that the 'murdered' Idalina de Oliveira had been removed from the orphanage by her lawful guardians two years previously, and was still very much alive. In spite of this evidence, the papers offered a reward of $500 to anyone who brought evidence that would lead to the conviction of the culprits, i.e. the religious women who ran the orphanage.

The second incident, which occurred in Rio de Janeiro, was more disturbing. The federal government decided, without the least warning, to appropriate the Franciscan monastery of Santo Antonio, with all its furnishings and valuables. What made this move so much the more serious was the fact that the Guardian (superior) of Santo Antonio, Fr. Diego de Freitas, was a Brazilian by birth, and all the other friars were either born or naturalised Brazilians. The monastery was not rich, and the buildings were old and in a bad state of repair. Yet the Franciscans were ejected, and state officials began making an inventory of furnishings, etc. The people were furious, calling the whole affair a sacrilege, especially the inventory of the sacred vessels, chalices, ciboria, etc., which no layman was allowed to touch. The Franciscans had been the first Catholic missionaries to set foot on Brazilian soil, and were very popular with the people. The public outcry which followed made the headlines in all the national newspapers. The archbishop of San Paolo, Mgr. Duarte Leopoldo da Silva, came to the defence of the Franciscans, and a public debate ensued, which dragged on for months. Dom Mayeul certainly knew of these events in San Paolo and Rio, and had not long to wait before he came face to face with similar problems in his abbey.

The unfortunate incident, which occurred in the abbey in the summer of 1911, was rather bizarre, though nonetheless real. One evening the monks were in the church and heard a noise in one of the side chapels. They found a man asleep behind the altar. On being asked to leave he refused, so they informed the police. When the officers arrived they found a second man, and both were locked up in one of the monastery towers until such time as the prison van could come to collect them. The following morning one of the monks went to the temporary prison to bring the men some food. On opening the door they found one man fast asleep, but the other had hung himself. Again the monks informed the police, who took their time coming. One of the monks had cut the rope, in the hope of saving the man's life, and stretched the body on the ground. A rumour spread through the town, that the monks had caught a thief and murdered him. When, late in the afternoon, the police van came to remove the body, an angry crowd had already collected at the back gate of the monastery. Two policemen with clubs were posted at the gate to keep the people at bay, but were unable to prevent the crowd from entering the yard. The monks immediately closed all the doors and windows of the monastery, to keep the mob out. The police called for reinforcements, but were powerless to control the situation. Then the unexpected happened. Some members of the crowd, finding several large boxes, which were in fact beehives, and curious to know what they contained, quickly removed the cover of one. That same instant, hundreds of bees swarmed out and attacked the intruders, who in no time decided with prudence to make themselves scarce. The dead man was then removed in the police van, and peace once again restored to the monastery

Such agitations and anti-clerical feelings that flared up repeatedly at this time throughout Brazil set Dom Mayeul thinking. Personal attacks and anonymous letters addressed to Dom Mayeul began to appear in the press, with the result that a general atmosphere of fear reigned in the abbey. There was a genuine feeling that the government was about to close down all monasteries, and replenish the empty coffers of the state with the accumulated wealth of the monks. Under the circumstances, some of the monks proposed that they look for a temporary place of refuge, outside Brazil, until the storm passed over. Dom Mayeul decided to consult his Council, and found they advised immediate action. What they apparently wanted was not a new foundation, but a temporary abode, where they could salvage as much of the endangered patrimony and wealth of the abbey.

The big question was: "Where to go?" Dom Mayeul had for some time been gathering information on the West Indies. His eye rested on one such folder, promoting Trinidad as *"The island where East meets West" (Dom Odo van der Heydt, Hist. of MSB, Ch. IV)*. The population of Trinidad in 1911 was roughly 334000, of whom two-thirds were Christians (majority of Catholics), and one-third were Hindus, Muslim and other. A large part of the non-Christians came directly from East India, mainly Hindus, and that influx of Hindus continued for many years. After long discussion the monks of Bahia decided on Trinidad, one of the largest of the Caribbean islands. It had many advantages, firstly it was under British rule, which guaranteed religious freedom; secondly, it was not far from Brazil; and thirdly, it contained a colony of numerous Hindus, who might be the object of a missionary effort by the Benedictine monks.

At the same time as he was trying to ward off an impending freemason government attack on his monastery, Dom Mayeul was coping with some serious difficulties with the archbishop of Bahia, Mgr. Jerome Thome da Silva. The latter evidently resented the fact that the Dom Mayeul asserted his right, as an abbot, to celebrate Pontifical Mass, using crosier and mitre, as often as he liked. It is true that for well over a hundred years, the abbots in Brazil had ceased to use pontificals. However, Dom Mayeul believed he not only had the right according to Canon Law, but also the duty, to provide impressive and solemn liturgical celebrations in the abbey church in Bahia. According to a long-established Benedictine tradition in Europe, an abbot could celebrate Pontifical Mass on the major feasts of the Church. Dom Mayeul had witnessed such pontifical celebrations in Belgium, in the abbey of Maredsous, where he had been a novice, and in St. Andre, Bruges. However, the archbishop of Bahia, having no experience of European customs thought otherwise. Thus, finding himself in dispute with the authorities of Church and state, Dom Mayeul decided the time had come to act. Whether he gave himself and his community enough time to examine all their options is difficult to say. On the face of it, the action taken by Dom Mayeul seemed precipitous, though once he had committed himself to leading his community into exile, there seemed no way of turning back.

Dom Mayeul decided at once to write to the ecclesiastical authorities in Trinidad to find out whether a group of Benedictine monks would be welcome. His letter, dated 16 October 1911, was sent to Mgr. John Pius Dowling, archbishop of Port of Spain, Trinidad, and read as follows:

> As a religious persecution seems daily more imminent in Brazil, we are looking out for a place of refuge. To this end Trinidad appears to us most suitable: first, because it is not too far distant and within easy reach, the climate is similar and so is the language. Therefore, I wish, as soon as possible, to place my desires before you. I want to buy a house in a healthy locality, somewhere in the mountains, which could serve as a refuge for my monks in case of expulsion from Brazil. If my proposals are acceptable to you, I shall come to Trinidad to discuss the matter with you in person. I am the abbot of the Benedictine Monastery of San Sebastian of Bahia, of Belgian nationality (POS, Dowling Papers).

The archbishop replied favourably on 15 November, 1911:

> Your esteemed letter of 16 October reached me only this morning, for it came, I know not why, by way of New York. I thank you for that letter and wish to express my sorrow for the sad news of a threatening persecution... With regards to the Archdiocese of Port of Spain, I can assure you that I shall only be too glad to have you in the Archdiocese, or in Trinidad. Come then, and you can judge what locality is best suited (MSB, Dom Mayeul papers).

Dom Mayeul was not the man to sit back and do nothing when an opportunity for action presented itself. Believing there were serious threats hanging over his monastery in Bahia, Dom Mayeul decided to take up Archbishop Dowling's offer, and investigate the possibilities of finding a suitable site in Trinidad for a foundation. He set off by boat for Trinidad in December 1911 and gave a first-hand account of this venture in his memoirs:

> I brought with me a letter of recommendation from the Nuncio in Brazil, addressed to the bishops of Central America. If the foundation in Trinidad fell through, then I could look elsewhere in that region for a suitable place for my monks. I arrived in Trinidad on

27 December 1911. The Archbishop gave me permission to choose a suitable place for my foundation. The prior of the Dominicans offered me a great welcome and warm hospitality. I repaid him by advancing the financial help he needed to build a school. After three weeks of searching, my choice fell on a little property owned by an old Spaniard, situated in the mountains at about 17 kilometres from the capital. The place commanded a magnificent view and the climate was fresh and healthy. It had the advantage of possessing a ready source of good water, an abundance of woods, a stone quarry to provide material for building, and some good land which we could use for agricultural purposes. The Archbishop offered to buy this property in my name, if the Chapter of Bahia gave their consent (Vol. II, 146).

The Chapter of the abbey met on 15 March, 1912, when Dom Mayeul gave an account of what had taken place during his visit to Trinidad. He spoke so enthusiastically about the beautiful mountain site of the proposed monastery, and his plans for a temporary wooden house and chapel, that he got unanimous approval from his community for the foundation. In order to finance this adventure, a number of the monastery's houses in the city of Bahia were sold. The Chapter Book of the abbey, which relates the proceedings of the community meetings, mentions two houses sold for 3,500,000 Reales each, under this same day, 15 March 1912. Two weeks later, on 28 March 1912, three other houses were sold for the total sum of 15,000,000 Reales *(Livro do Capitulo, 1904-1914, pp. 24-25, A MOS. BAH).* Dom Mayeul was certainly providing a large fund of money for the Trinidadian foundation. He had no hesitation in selling these houses, convinced as he was that the government intended confiscating, sooner or later, most of the monastery's property. We have no way of knowing the exact amount of money set aside by Dom Mayeul for the Trinidadian foundation, but it was a very substantial sum.

In the meantime, there were signs of the coming storm. The members of the Masonic Lodge, the freemasons, who were militantly anti-Catholic, began a campaign against Dom Mayeul in the local newspaper, accusing him of master-minding the revival of the Catholic religion in the city of Bahia. At the same time, a number of the higher Catholic clergy in Bahia publicly objected to the very elaborate liturgical ceremonies performed by Dom Mayeul in the

THE WELL ATTENDED ABBEY CHURCH OF BAHIA. THE SUCCESS OF THE ABBEY
OF BAHIA CAUSED SOME FRICTION BY PULLING AWAY THE FAITHFUL FROM THE
OTHER CHURCHES.

DOM MAYEUL, ABBOT OF BAHIA

DOM MAYEUL (SEATED IN THE SECOND ROW, FIFTH FROM LEFT, NEXT TO MGR. VAN CALOEN), WITH THE COMMUNITY AT BAHIA.

abbey church, which were drawing the faithful away from their own parish churches. All the evidence points to an element of jealousy, on the part of the higher clergy, who resented the growing popularity of Dom Mayeul. He had good reason to believe there was a concerted conspiracy to force him out of Bahia.

Some time after the 15 August, 1912, the secretary of the state of Bahia, Orlando Fregose, one of the highest-ranking freemasons, made a secret agreement with a wealthy capitalist contractor, Signor Alencon, to demolish the ancient abbey church of Bahia. It was planned to use the site to construct a main arterial road across the city. The governor of Bahia, Signor Seabra, issued a decree on 27 August 1912, outlining the plans for this act of vandalism. That same day, 27 August, Dom Mayeul was presented with a copy of the official, government-controlled, *Gazette* of the state of Bahia, containing the draconian decree, ordering the closure of the monastery within six months. Dom Mayeul's immediate reaction was to issue a *"Notice to the people of Bahia (Aviso ao povo Bahiano)"*, asking them if they consented to the cold blooded destruction of the splendid abbey and church, which had been built by their ancestors, and which was one of the glories of Bahia. 5000 copies of this Notice were printed on a single sheet of paper, and distributed to all corners of the city. It caused an immediate public outcry. Dom Mayeul concluded his powerful piece of polemics as follows:

> At last, the final nail in the coffin of these proceedings, which I deem a violation of the norms of civilization, is the alleged motive for such a measure, which I do not now wish to describe: it is the necessity which the government claims to have over an area of 1200 square metres, as if in the vast area of Bahia there is not an alternative appropriate site for buildings! In view of this, though altruistically forgiving the authors of this decree, I am obliged in conscience to adopt all the legal and moral means at my disposal, and to legitimately defend the old monastery donated by the Bahian people, built and maintained by them to this day. It is to the Bahian people that I address myself, and ask them whether they want the monks to remain in the city of Salvador-Bahia, or whether they should go away to more hospitable lands, where the civil government, as much as the Church authorities, are eager to welcome us (Da Paladina Do Lar, Sept. 1912).

Da Paladina Do Lar 1912 with Abbot Mayeul on the cover

On reading this, there was utter dismay among the citizens of Bahia. They expressed their indignation at the proposed destruction of the monastery, in an article entitled, *"An Insult to the Benedictine Order (O insulto a Ordem Benedictina)"*, which was published in the daily newspaper: *Diario da Bahia, 30 August 1912*:

> *Signor Seabra, the Governor of Bahia, is igniting a very delicate situation. It is not right for His Excellency to issue such a virulent attack on an extremely respected religious Order, where there are distinguished citizens. Worthy and scholarly representatives hurl insults, scourging them (the monks) with unfounded epithets such as "exploiters", "plunderers of public property". Good judgment was completely ignored, when it was categorically stated that it was no longer possible to tolerate the likes of these friars, who have spirited away to foreign countries, the money from property bequeathed to the monastery by Bahians, who never suspected that the cunning monks would have done such a thing. . . .*

Lastly, the gravity of the situation increased with the threat printed at the end of an article in the *"Gazeta do Povo"*, which says:

> *The seditious and deceitful priest (Dom Mayeul) HAS TO SEE AND HAS TO KNOW that we are not afraid of the devil, even when he is dressed as the Abbot, and distributes bulletins (Notices) to the people of Bahia. The Order of St. Benedict has to know that the time of destruction (bombardment) has come. Any rights that the monks may have will be rescinded by the State. If the State really needs the land occupied by the monastery, it may resort to the relevant expropriation by juridical action.*

It seems that some people had not fully understood the content, or tone, of Dom Mayeul's original *Aviso*. He therefore decided to clarify certain points. He was given the opportunity of doing this in the columns of the *"Diario da Bahia"* on 30 August 1912, when he offered his readers a more detailed account of his position and that of the monks of the abbey. At the same time he replied to criticisms published in the *"Gazeta do Povo"*. Dom Mayeul approached his subject calmly and effectively. The following are the most important paragraphs:

> *Having read the demolition order which was to become effective within six months, I found this cruelty so incredible that literally*

speaking I had no other recourse should it be executed, but to retire graciously with most of the community, close the school of Brazilian oblates maintained by the monastery, and sell almost all the furniture, because there is no house in Bahia which could take all our furniture. Furthermore, if the decree were executed, I would have to send the majority of our monks to other countries. I stand by my expression "most hospitable lands" referring to Brazil. Over a period of some 15 years the Brazilian people extended warm hospitality to us, especially in our dear Bahia. In my judgment, Brazil is a hospitable country, and I can even elaborate and say it is a very hospitable country.

I am not a foreigner: the naturalization that I registered and received in 1898, guarantees me, with few exceptions, full benefits of all the rights of a Brazilian citizen. It is my adopted country, where often I was in danger of death, and which I will abandon only in the case of "force majeure" and unwillingly. I am a Brazilian, according to the law of the Constitution and, in my heart, prepared to make whatever sacrifice is required of me for the increase in religious, moral and intellectual values in Brazil and especially in Bahia. If I came to Brazil, it was at the urgent request of the old monks here, among whom are sons of Bahia (Diario da Bahia, 30 August 1912).

In several public pronouncements, Dom Mayeul had been wrongly accused of selling houses belonging to the monastery, and using the proceeds for his own use, and of planning to sell the monastery and church. Wishing to put the record straight in this matter, he explained his action as follows:

I sold many old and dilapidated houses, it is true, and I congratulate myself for so doing. Under the new Health laws, so badly needed in Bahia, Signor Pinto de Carvalho could easily have closed all these houses, and thus substantially reduced the patrimony of the monastery The proceeds of the sale and rents, as everyone can verify, were used, by special order of the Holy See, for augmenting the patrimony, construction of new houses and other profitable financial activities. Thus, the statement that I wanted to sell the church, and even the whole monastery, as the "Gazeta do Povo" asserts, is totally false (Diario da Bahia, 30 August 1912).

All classes of society in Bahia joined in supporting the cause of Dom Mayeul and the monastery, and took advantage of this occasion to attack the government. There appeared first of all an eloquent *Protesto* (protest) by a number of leading citizens:

> *We, the undersigned Brazilian citizens, who freely enjoy our civil and political rights, resolve solemnly to protest against the projected demolition of the historic monastery and the majestic Abbey church of San Sebastian in Bahia...The destruction of the ancient church is a crime against modern civilization. It is vital, patriotic and urgent for us to take action. Brazilians and Bahians! No, a thousand times no! The implementation of such a barbaric outrage against the historical, religious and social traditions of our beloved country would be absurd, monstrous and wicked! The Abbey represents the glorious stone pages of our tradition and is a solemn witness of the grandeur of the ancient city of Bahia (MSB, Dom Mayeul papers).*

However, it was the appeal to the *Governor Dr. Jose Joacquin Seabra,* written by Signora Amelia Rodrigues, which made the greatest impression on the governor, and forced him to revoke the decree. She used tact, powerful and colourful imagery, biblical examples, and womanly persuasion, to argue her case on behalf of those "Bahian Catholics crushed under the weight of such a distressing matter". It is worth quoting some of the more important sentences from her *Appeal*:

> *The monastery of San Sebastian is to be demolished. To what avail, Sir? To widen by a few metres a big arterial road, which will cross the city! You acquire some metres of land. Very good! But wait! How many sacrifices will it cost? At the cost of the honour of your government, the traditions of Bahia, of art, justice, religious feelings, yours, ours, and the people's! Eminent Bahian, should those few metres of land cost so much? Whatever amount is spent on the construction of a new road or buildings will not compensate for the loss of priceless and glorious antiquity, which represents capital accumulated during centuries of struggle and triumph, in the field of science, letters, learning and patriotism.*
>
> *The cathedrals of France are still standing; the monastery Batalha, in Portugal, was not even touched by the fury of profane soldiers. The one thing that can match the excellent art of other countries,*

is the dome of the church of San Sebastian, which can be seen from a distance, and, without doubt, lends a touch of noble elegance to the panorama of Bahia. It represents the soul of religion in Bahia, which rises up into the blue heaven of God's kingdom, where petty human squabbles have no relevance.

Oh, no! You are not going to destroy the monastery. This Bahian woman is begging you, with tears in her eyes. Yes! Innocent tears of hundreds of our fellow men today wet the aisle of that church, their sweat pours down on those stones which are going to be torn up. If your heart were as hard as those stones, if despite our plea you order their destruction, we want you to know, Dr. Seabra, that the hammer which strikes them, also wounds the heart of the Bahian Catholic women. These stones are soaked with the tears of our hearts.

If your magnanimity moves you to revoke the decree for our sake, you can be assured of our eternal gratitude. Bahian Catholics will throw open their hearts to crown your name with the choicest flow-ers, regardless of what is written about fickle politics, the justice or injustice of men. We hope to receive a favourable reply at your earliest convenience (MSB, Dom Mayeul papers).

Some days later, bowing to outraged public opinion, the gov-ernment capitulated. Dr. Seabra summoned Dom Mayeul to his palace, saying how much he had been pained by the *Aviso* (Notice) issued by Dom Mayeul. At the same time, the governor decided to bring the matter to a close, which he did by revoking the decree. One danger had been removed, but another loomed on the horizon. It appears that the triumph of the Benedictines over the governor, served to stroke the fires of jealousy in the hearts of some members of the higher clergy in Bahia. Dom Mayeul explains the situation in his memoirs:

Without any doubt, I had no illusions concerning the state of mind, in general, of the Brazilian clergy, in regard to the European reli-gious who come to Brazil in response to a call from the Holy See. A certain Brazilian bishop had not hesitated to say, in the presence of a Belgian Norbertine priest: "What a pity that we cannot dispense with their (i.e. the European religious) services!" At the time of my arrival in Bahia in 1904, I took the opportunity of paying my respects to the Vicar-General, at the same time asking him the fa-

vour of giving me a copy of the seal of the archdiocese. But, hardly had he heard the word "favour" than, cutting me short, he said in a brusque voice" "Favours! You foreign religious, you only think of favours and of privileges; you are never satisfied, and you want to draw everybody into your churches" (Vol. II, 148).

The words: "You want to draw everybody into your churches" is the key to the problem. The whole affair might well be called the *Battle of the Pews*. The Benedictine monks were attracting large crowds to their abbey church in Bahia, especially on the great feasts of the Church, which meant that the parish churches suffered a reduction in the number of faithful frequenting them. During the month of July 1912, a delegation, on behalf of the diocesan clergy, made complaints against Dom Mayeul and his community to the archbishop of Bahia. Up to this moment, the archbishop, Mgr. Jerome Jose da Silva, seemed to be well disposed towards Dom Mayeul, having supported the latter's many undertakings in the missionary and pastoral spheres. Now, there was a sudden volte-face. The first sign of this change of heart came, when the archbishop withdrew from the Benedictines the direction of the Confraternity of the Tabernacle in the cathedral. This was soon followed by an order, putting the control of the Catholic Ladies of Bahia under the control of the secular clergy. Previously this important and influential organisation had been centred on the abbey, and its monthly meetings held in the new conference hall built by Dom Mayeul

However, the breaking point between Dom Mayeul and the archbishop came as a result of Dom Mayeul's actions in trying to save his monastery from destruction. The archbishop followed the controversy between Dom Mayeul, the governor of Bahia, Dr. Seabra, and the secretary of state of Bahia, Orlando Fregose, all of which was conducted in public. Even before the decree was withdrawn, the archbishop summoned Dom Mayeul, by one of his canons, to appear at his palace, to give him an account of his conduct in this matter. This summons, in the form of an order from a superior to an inferior, came at a time of special anxiety for Dom Mayeul. The archbishop wanted Dom Mayeul to explain his conduct, especially in regard to the printed *Aviso* (Notice), in which Dom Mayeul challenged the governor's right to destroy the monastery. Dom Mayeul gave a detailed account of this matter in his memoirs:

I replied to the canon, who seemed very agitated, that under the circumstances, I could not acquiesce in the order, without violating the rights of the Holy See. I pointed out that our Abbey was exempt from the Archbishop's authority, and since this exemption was not a personal privilege, I could not renounce it without the authorization of the Pope. However, the canon and the Archbishop were not of this opinion. At the end of the day, I remained firm in my refusal.

In any case, even leaving aside the question of the exemption, what had I to gain by a visit to the Archbishop at this critical moment? Certainly, nothing positive would come of it. A seriously-minded person had declared to me some time earlier, under oath, that the Governor, who was a friend of the Archbishop, had consulted with this prelate regarding the decree to demolish the Abbey. I wondered if the whole matter centred on the fact that the beautiful liturgical ceremonies in our church were eclipsing those in the cathedral. But what was even more disconcerting, was the possibility that, in going to the Palace, the Archbishop would order or advise me to submit to the will of the Governor, and inevitably lead to my great embarrassment. Therefore, taking all things into consideration, I did not pay a visit to the Archbishop.

This was a most unfortunate turn of events, and one which led to Dom Mayeul becoming *persona non grata* with both the governor and the archbishop. In his determination to save his abbey from destruction, he failed to see that he was faced with a very delicate situation, in which his own reputation was at stake. The occasion called for the exercise of diplomatic skills, as well as the ability to compromise. It seems in retrospect, that Dom Mayeul was blind to the fact that he was acting somewhat high-handedly in refusing to meet the archbishop. It never occurred to him that he should make every effort to find a solution to his dilemma. This blindness is reflected in his account of the incident in his memoirs:

Taking all things into consideration, I did not pay a visit to the Archbishop. My conscience was clear....There is an old saying: "Do what you have to do, and don't count the consequences".

He refused to contemplate the consequences of his action. Yet, he must have known that he was treading on dangerous ground. It was almost as if he wished to provoke the archbishop, which in fact he did, as the archbishop took Dom Mayeul's refusal as a 'slap in the face', and a personal insult. In his memoirs Dom Mayeul admits that he never once consulted some wise person on the matter. When he wrote to Mgr. van Caloen on the matter, he was simply announcing the fait accompli, and certainly not seeking his advice. This had happened several times in his life, and happened again in 1923, though this latter case was not of his making. In this particular case – his difficulty with the archbishop of Bahia – there is undoubtedly an element of self-righteousness about it. Perhaps Dom Mayeul had already made up his mind that the time had come for him to leave Bahia, and go into exile in Trinidad with his monks. If that were truly his determined attitude, then he clearly did not care what the archbishop thought of him. On the other hand, it is hard to think that he had forgotten his many unfulfilled projects, such as the mission to the Rio Pardo. At the end of the day, he decided that, having fallen out with the governor, he could no longer count on the help of the government for his little colony in Angelim. It is true that only promises had been made in regard to government help for his missionary plans. On reflection, the vital link-road along the Rio Pardo now seemed like an impossible dream. Furthermore, it was almost certain that the archbishop would withdraw his backing for the mission venture in Rio Pardo. Having thus taken into consideration all these matters, Dom Mayeul reluctantly decided, there and then, to abandon his beloved mission to the Indians, and recalled the monks he had left in Angelim.

In all these sad confrontations, Dom Mayeul is not just offering excuses for his conduct and attitude, but rather a personal *justification*. This is evident from a long article he wrote: *"A new notice about the mission and raison d'être of the monks in Bahia"*, which appeared in *Da Paladina Do Lar* (Sept. 1912, pp. 9-10), commenting on the proposed destruction of his monastery:

> As I am being attacked, I want to end this exposé with a brief
> but honest personal justification. I included in my abbatial coat of
> arms, this inspiring motto: PAX IN VERITATE ET CARI-
> TATE (Peace in Truth and Charity). If I should fail in this noble
> combat in pursuit of truth and charity, the far-reaching vision of
> one of my ancestors who directed the very famous "Garde Wal-
> lone", so popular in military parades, would snatch away from me
> any flimsy attempt to escape death, which I faced bravely so often

CONSTANTIN DE CAIGNY,
PORTRAIT HANGING IN THE TOWN HALL OF THIELT

before. Even here in Brazil and in Bahia, people with the plague and yellow fever died in my arms, while friends and relatives withdrew in fear and horror.

If I allowed myself to be intimidated in any way, the very stones of the majestic ducal castle of the ancient Norman feudal lord (Le chateau de Coigny, France), whence my family got its name, would remind me of the number of my ancestors who died loving and serving the Catholic Church. If the physiological law of hereditary has any basis, I believe that I have been endowed with a passion for Art, and an uncompromising commitment to Truth and our Holy Religion. If I vacillated for a moment, all I had to do for inspiration was to remember one of my ancestors who built the Belfry in Thielt (Flanders). This resulted in my stance towards the plan to mutilate our Abbey Church, so alien to the rules of aesthetics (Da Paladina Do Lar — numero especial, Setembro, 1912, pp. 9-11).

This article gives us a clear insight to the almost make-believe world of Dom Mayeul who enjoyed playing at the game of heraldry. He used his ancestral background to boost his credibility with the governor and archbishop of Bahia. It is true however that General De Caigny who led the "Garde Wallone", a regiment of the Spanish army, is part of his family heritage and that Dom Mayeul is a descendant of the sixteenth century architect-builder De Caigny of Thielt. But all this suited his need for self-assertion, and provided him with real credentials, befitting someone who held the high office of abbot of Bahia.

Dom Mayeul had kept Archabbot van Caloen informed, albeit after the facts, on the whole affair. When the nuncio of Brazil made a formal complaint to Mgr. van Caloen, he immediately expressed his support to Dom Mayeul:

I have read everything about your case with great interest and sympathy. I thank God for having given you so much courage, and for having blessed your efforts. I admire your attitude, which is that of a good monk. God will reward you (30 Sept 1912, Vol. II, 151).

Before departing for Trinidad, he had to live one last moment of glory, namely the silver jubilee of his ordination to the priesthood, which was celebrated with great pomp and circumstance, in Bahia, on 13 October 1912. The occasion provided him with a kind of 'Swan Song or Last Hurrah', as he prepared to make his farewell to Brazil. He described his feelings during the jubilee celebrations as follows in his memoirs:

> *Mgr. van Caloen, with his Coadjutor, and the abbot of Olinda, were present for the occasion. The abbot of St. Paul sent a representative. The good people of Bahia were filled with joy, brought on by our recent triumph over the freemasons. Very few doubted that a secret storm was already brewing against the jubilarian! As for myself, I had the presentiment that this was the last time I would pontificate in our beautiful Abbey church. I received many precious gifts, and in the general reunion of the pious associations, which I had founded, many enthusiastic tributes were given in my honour. In replying to these ovations, I was filled with such emotion, that I could only utter a "Thanks", which stuck in my throat (Vol. II, 151-152).*

Not surprisingly, neither the governor nor the archbishop of Bahia took any part in this event. The Chronicles of the abbey give a detailed account of the proceedings, under the date 13 October 1912:

> *With rare pomp and splendour, pontifical High Mass was celebrated by Abbot Mayeul. His Excellency, Mgr. van Caloen, was in attendance in his great mantle, occupying a platform which was especially decorated for this occasion. ... Various faith groups from our church assembled in the new sacristy to congratulate our Rev. Abbot on his jubilee and present him with a most beautiful pectoral cross. After the Pontifical Mass there was a dinner in the elegantly decorated refectory. After dinner, the four voices of the traditional "Laudes Hincmari" were sung (Cronica abbadia de S.Seb. 1912, pp.13-14).*

In spite of all this adulation and celebration, as the weeks progressed, his sojourn in Bahia became more and more difficult. The final blow came when he failed to win the support of the new papal nuncio to Brazil, Mgr. Aversa, or any of the other high dignitaries in the Church. Mgr. van Caloen had invited Dom Mayeul to Rio, trying to mediate and to resolve the problem in an amicable way. However, the message from Mgr. Aversa was short: *"Comply with the wishes of His Grace, the Archbishop of Bahia; if not, I will be forced to bring the whole affair to the attention of the Holy See! "(Vol. II, 152)*

A last attempt was made when Dom Mayeul learned that Mgr. Da Silva Gomez, bishop of Fortaleza was on a visit in Bahia. He had formerly known Mgr. Gomez in Bahia and they had maintained an excellent relationship. Mgr. Gomez offered his help, by proposing to intervene with the archbishop on Dom Mayeul's behalf. In order to show his goodwill, Dom Mayeul accepted his offer to mediate. However, he soon realized that all the efforts were in vain. It is hard to say whether or not Dom Mayeul really wanted a solution whereby he had to give in on something. Did he accept the mediation efforts just for the sake of appearances? One thing is for sure; he definitely didn't want to bend down since he had Canon Law on his side.

The time had clearly come for him to leave Brazil. In his heart of hearts he must have found it hard to bow out so suddenly, and to admit that his apostolate in Bahia had definitely come to an end. He left Bahia for Trinidad on 16 February 1913, where he felt he was needed, close to his little colony of pioneering monks. He described these final moment in his memoirs as follows:

By leaving Bahia, I reached the great turning point in my life. I loved Brazil, and I loved Bahia. I had made a vow of stability for the Benedictine Congregation of that country, which I considered to be my new motherland. I loved the musical language, which is the eldest sister of the beautiful Latin idiom. I loved the people and their customs, especially the abandoned Indians in the interior of the country. Now it was necessary for me to leave this land of the Holy Cross (Santa Cruz). I have to admit that I felt sad at my departure, which implied so many renunciations and sacrifices. After all, I had given the best years of my life there, devoting my youthful energies to so many beautiful and noble causes for the good of the church, of our Holy Order, and of the Brazilian people. Yes, this was a very hard and sad adieu, which I had to make in the secret of my heart! And besides, what did the future hold for me? It was in the hands of the Trinity. In all silence, I left Brazil by boat, on 16 February 1913, for the island of Trinidad (Vol. II, 153-154).

CHAPTER VIII

The Foundation in Trinidad: The Beginnings
(17 January 1912 - 28 December 1913)

THE PROCEDURES for undertaking a Benedictine monastic foundation, especially in a foreign country, are complicated, and require much time and planning. Dom Mayeul had already taken the first practical steps, during his visit to Trinidad in December 1911. His meeting with the archbishop of Port of Spain – the capital of Trinidad – proved satisfactory to both parties, and they seem to have established a good rapport. Certainly, the enterprise started off in a spirit of mutual respect and an atmosphere of co-operation. Dom Mayeul deposited a large sum of money with Archbishop John Pius Dowling, to be banked by him, and held in trust for the monks. He then set out to explore the island, looking for a suitable site. Soon word travelled round the island that a rich Brazilian abbot was looking for a sizeable property on which to build a monastery. A number of people, with land to sell, came forward, but Dom Mayeul was not to be rushed. He realized it was a difficult, if not a tricky, business, and his resources were not limitless. He spent three weeks making a thorough examination of several places, having in mind the kind of place he wanted: situated high up on the hills, commanding a good view and having good clean air, with a ready supply of good drinking water, with fertile soil, and possessing stone and sand quarries with which to build. It seems that he had abandoned the idea of looking for a property with an already existing building, in which to house his monks. He decided it would be best for the monks to build their own monastery. They were to arrive as missionaries, prepared for hardships and all the trials of pioneers. This element of idealism was a constant factor from the very beginning, and proved one of the main features of the future Benedictine monastery in Trinidad.

The story of how Dom Mayeul finally decided on a property, some 700 feet above sea-level, belonging to Andrew Gomez, is told in his memoirs:

> On 17 January 1912, at an already agreed hour, outside the railway station at St. Joseph, I got into the carriage of Mr. Gomez, who proceeded to drive me towards his nearby property. Our journey took us to the top of a hill, about 200 metres above sea level, where Mr. Gomez's property was situated. The view was breathtaking, while the cool breeze refreshed us and the water from a near-by stream was delicious. We had reached the first stage in the climb of what turned out to be the highest mountain in Trinidad. I spent an hour looking round the place, which was neither considerable nor well-maintained, but it had potential and could be improved. The situation seemed ideal for a monastic foundation, being isolated, and I was determined to buy it. The soil seemed fertile, with much of the land cultivated as a cocoa plantation. There was a forest with beautiful trees, while the hillside of this mountain would provide plenty of stone for any future construction of roads and living quarters for the monks. A very important factor was the stream or river, which passed through a gorge, and was part of the property. I thought of the drought I had experienced in Ceara, in Brazil, and did not wish to risk a repetition. My guide assured me that even in the dry season, the water never ceased to flow. I remarked how the place looked somewhat abandoned, a fact which led me to believe that I might be able to purchase the place at a reasonable price.
>
> We partook of a little "lunch" in the cabin of the overseer. I noticed a horseshoe over the door of the cabin, and was told that this was a good-luck token and a guarantee of happiness! On the way down the hill, the price of the place was settled. However, I made two conditions: the purchase should not be made public for some weeks, and would be subject to the ratification of the community in Bahia. It was clear that by itself the property would not suffice for our needs. I had already made up my mind to buy several of the adjoining plots of land, whose owners would immediately raise their prices, if they knew of the contract I had made with Mr. Gomez. The latter kept our transaction to himself, for which I was always grateful.

And in any case, I was not an altogether free agent, as the Canon Law of the Church demanded that my community give their approval to the contract, though, I saw no difficulty in obtaining this approval (Vol. I, 211-213).

On returning to the capital, Port of Spain, Dom Mayeul called on the archbishop and received his approval of the terms of purchase. However, when he mentioned the matter to the Dominican Community, they were more sceptical. They pointed out that the real value of any property in Trinidad depended on its productivity. They saw no value in the beauty, the solitude, or the healthy atmosphere of the site. But Dom Mayeul knew his own mind, and remembered his experiences in Brazil, where he had faced similar conditions. He was determined not to fail this time, and was comforted by the fact that there was no 'van Caloen', or any other superior, to obstruct his plans. He had found a new assurance, at least in his own mind, that God was on his side.

On 26 January 1912, Dom Mayeul embarked from Port of Spain to New York, from where he visited the abbey of St. Vincent in Pennsylvania. There he hoped to find someone willing to come to Brazil, to teach English to the monks destined for the foundation in Trinidad. In spite of the very cosmopolitan population on the island, English was the official and predominant language. He succeeded in finding such a monk, who sailed with him to Brazil. When passing along the coast of the Carolinas, they ran into a ferocious storm, which turned into a minor hurricane. Fortunately their boat was new and had sufficient ballast to withstand the danger. One sometimes suspects that Dom Mayeul is exaggerating such events, but his account is verified, both as to the day and time, in a French (Parisian) scientific Journal *Cosmos*, which reported this unusual and life-threatening hurricane: "the worst in 40 years".

On returning safely to Bahia in March 1912, Dom Mayeul immediately called a meeting of all the professed members of his community, to report on his recent trip to Trinidad. He told them about his purchase of Mr. Gomez's property, and the terms set out by the archbishop of Port of Spain. These latter terms included the administration of the parish of Arouca, which was very close to the property chosen for the future monastery. The first batch of monks would consist of two fathers and one lay brother, and leave Brazil for Trinidad early in October 1912. In the meantime, there was much to do by way of preparation for the coming foundation: those chosen had to learn English, and study the geography, culture and life of the people in Trinidad, which at the time was an English colony. It says much for the persuasive powers of Dom Mayeul that he succeeded in getting his community behind the enterprise. The final decision on the Trinidad foundation rested in the hands of the Chapter (i.e. all the professed monks of the abbey of Bahia). The meeting was held in the splendid drawing-room of the episcopal quarters of the abbey. The official record of the event is given as follows in the *Chapter Book*:

> *On the 18th day of March 1912, Father Abbot, having convened the Chapter of the Community, communicated certain details of his trip to the island of Trinidad. He read a letter, received from His Grace, John Pius Dowling, Archbishop of Port of Spain, which was a reply to one written by the Abbot. The illustrious prelate invites, in terms replete with attention and courtesy, our Fr. Abbot to make a foundation wherever in his Archdiocese. This in provision of a religious persecution which threatened our Congregation (in Bahia) towards the end of 1911. During his sojourn in Trinidad, Fr. Abbot visited several estates, and found one which appeared to him very favourable, not only with regard to its topography, but also its climate. Nearby is a vacant parish, of which we could have the administration. Fr. Abbot intends to have a temporary chapel and a house erected there, all in wood, as is customary in the locality, and proposes to build later a church and monastery on the hillside of the property. All this was unanimously approved by the Chapter (Bahia, Chapter Bk, folio 24).*

However, a more detailed account of the arrangements for the foundation is given in a letter written, in French, by Dom Mayeul to Archbishop Dowling, dated 17th March 1912, the day before the Chapter meeting:

> *I desire that the three lots of land, bought from Mr. Gomez, be united into one unit by buying the land which separates them, and which belongs, I believe, to the Crown. I willingly authorize the buying of about 100 acres of government land, so that the future Priory may develop without the nuisance of having any neighbours encroaching upon it. I further wish that Mr. Gomez take a personal interest in our Mission, and plant banana trees, sweet potatoes,*

etc. which will be of great benefit to the monks. As regards the actual foundation, it has been decided that (1) The first group of monks should arrive in Trinidad during the month of August or September, 1912. The Superior will come from Southampton after his trip to Germany, where he will go after Easter, to recruit some vocations for Trinidad. We hope to have 3 or 4 priests, and an equal number of lay brothers; (2) Every month I will dispatch several packages, consisting of books, church ornaments etc., addressed to Fr. Casey, the Superior of the Presbytery. I count on him to get them through the Customs and keep them in the Presbytery for us. I hope that the government will dispense us from paying import duty, and in this way help our mission; (3) I ask Your Grace to allow the first monks to take up residence in the Presbytery of Arouca, simply on a provisional basis, until such time as we shall have built a house for our own use; (4) Finally, I wish to offer you some financial benefit for this work, allowing you 5% profit on all transactions (POS, Ben.).

Archbishop Dowling, having been authorized by Dom Mayeul to purchase the Gomez estate, proceeded to buy it for the agreed sum of $4,000. Many years later, he wrote the following account of this transaction:

By the 27th June 1912, the legal formalities had been fulfilled, the purchase price and incidental expenses paid, and thus the property became Benedictine. As I was merely an intermediary, I thought a visit to it unnecessary before its transfer. However, encouraged by Rev. James McDonnell, the parish priest of St. Joseph's, in whose parish the property lies, I took a walk to the railway station on 10th July following, and got a train to St. Joseph. There I was received by Fr. McDonnell and driven by him in his buggy to Saint Augustine, as far up the hill as we could drive. We climbed the hills till we got to the small dingy cocoa hut which the late Fr. Lehmann C.S.Sp. has immortalized. We rested there and also partook of some creole chocolate and milk which the Pastor had thoughtfully provided. Thus refreshed, we continued to climb till we reached the ravine, where the gentle murmur of running water again refreshed us, while indicating a very desirable asset for its Benedictine owners (Catholic News, 18 August, 1934).

By the middle of 1912, the people in Trinidad had become aware of the proposed Benedictine foundation. Thus, on 17 August, 1912, the Catholic News announced that *"the first Father of the Benedictine Community to be established in Trinidad will arrive by the next mail from England"*. However, some days later, the same newspaper announced that *"a change in movements became necessary, with the result that several monks will come here together at the end of November"* (C.N.31 August 1912). Such items of information gave evidence of the interest and good will shown on the island in regard to the forthcoming Benedictine foundation.

Dom Mayeul's greatest problem was finding a monk to lead the foundation, and the right team to form the first group. Looking at his community in Bahia, numbering 17, he knew he had some excellent monks, but he needed to ask himself if they were capable of handling the situation in Trinidad. In any case, he could not send them all to Trinidad. In a series of letters, written from Bahia to Archbishop Dowling between April and November 1912, we can follow the evolution of Dom Mayeul's thoughts on this matter:

> *17th April: I hope to come to Trinidad towards the end of October, with the Superior of the Mission, Dom Sebastian Weber, and a few monks. At the end of August, the monk who could be the Parish Priest of Arouca will arrive from Europe, if Your Grace accepts him. His assistant (curate) will come with me, as I wish to have two monks in the parish.*

> *19th July: My monks wish to celebrate my priestly Jubilee here in Bahia in October, thus the little colony cannot leave for Trinidad until 19 November, and no one will reach you before that. My monks are as committed as ever to the new foundation.*

> *4th August: If circumstances do not force me to alter my plans, the little group will depart for Trinidad on November 19th. The superior Dom Ambrose Vinckier is at present in a large cocoa estate to learn something about its cultivation. All are learning English.*

> *19th August: Five monks are destined for Trinidad, and their departure remains fixed for November 19th (POS. Benedictines).*

Some time after Easter, 1912, Dom Mayeul sent Dom Charles Verbeke to Belgium and Holland, and Dom Sebastian Weber to Germany, to seek candidates and financial aid for Trinidad. It is

clear from these letters, that Dom Sebastian Weber was Dom Mayeul's first choice of superior in Trinidad. However, because Dom
Sebastian was not available yet, he appointed Dom Ambrose Vinckier, who was in fact a cousin of Dom Mayeul, to that position. At
no time, in all these various communications, does Dom Mayeul
indicate the role which he himself might play in the actual foundation. He certainly did not see himself as part of the first group.
He was still abbot of Bahia, but committed to the foundation in
Trinidad. A considerable boost was given to the enterprise when,
on September 25, 1912, the two monks who had been sent to Europe returned to Bahia with 25 recruits, five Belgians, nine Dutch-
men and eleven Germans. Two days later, on September 27th, the
first monks set out for Trinidad, on board the "Vauban". They were
three in number: Dom Ambrose Vinckier, the superior, Dom Paul
Dobbert and Br. Anthony Feldner.

They arrived in Trinidad on 6th October, 1912, Rosary Sunday,
and were welcomed by a group of Dominican priests, led by the
vicar-provincial, Fr. Henry Vincent Casey, O.P. In the afternoon,
there was a grand procession around Marine Square. The archbishop walked at the end of the procession, with Fr. Ambrose on his
right and Fr. Paul on his left. Br. Anthony was also there, with his
rosary beads in his hands, just as if he were not in a strange place,
but in his far-away Austria. Indeed, all three felt immediately at
home, so warm was the welcome given them by the archbishop,
priests and people of Port of Spain. After Mass, Dom Ambrose
handed Archbishop Dowling a letter of introduction, dated September 27th 1912, signed by Abbot Mayeul De Caigny. It read
as follows:

> I have judged it prudent and in the interest of the Mission in Trini-
> dad itself, to send without further doing, two Fathers and one lay
> brother. It means a sacrifice from their part, but I love to see them
> ready for any sacrifice. A second batch follows in November. Dom
> Ambrose Vinckier is to be the superior of the Mission of Our Lady
> of Exile upon St. Benedict's Hill. He has full power to regulate
> everything with Your Grace and I hope he will give you satisfaction.
> I beg Your Grace to confirm his companion, Dom Paul Dobbert,
> as parish priest of Arouca, if you judge opportune; if not, he is to
> reside at St. Benedict's Hill. The lay brother Anthony Feldner, is
> to reside in Arouca as sacristan. The lay brothers, who are coming

in November, are destined for St. Benedict's Hill. It is not possible for me to accompany the Missionaries now, but I hope to arrive in Trinidad in the beginning of next year. Here in Bahia, we have just received 25 Postulants from Europe. I have to remain here to supervise their beginnings as monks. You will hear from our monks in Trinidad of the terrible persecution which the Brazilian government has inflicted upon us in Bahia. The diocesan clergy would be very happy if we were chased out of the country. I recommend my monks and their Mission to your charitable prayers. Mayeul OSB (POS. Benedictines)

There are a number of interesting factors relating to this letter and its contents, which were to prove breaking points in the years ahead:

(1) Dom Mayeul repeatedly calls the Benedictine foundation a 'Mission'. His monks were coming to Trinidad as missionaries, evidently with a view to converting some non-Christians to the true faith. Dom Mayeul had been told that there were some 100,000 Hindus in Trinidad; he hoped to make these the main object of his missionary work on the island. Archbishop Dowling took great offence at the idea of Trinidad being called a 'missionary territory'. Trinidad had been converted to Catholicism in the time of Christopher Columbus at the end of the 15th century.

(2) From the very beginning of the foundation, Dom Mayeul thought that he had the right to appoint a priest of his choice to any parish offered by the archbishop. In fact, the archbishop considered such appointments to be his prerogative. Dom Mayeul was free to propose a candidate, but he could not appoint anyone to a parish. Over and over again, in the years ahead, this led to much misunderstanding and even ill-will. Following on this was the fact that Dom Mayeul looked upon a parish as a mission-station, and not a well-established Church structure.

(3) It is difficult to understand how Dom Mayeul could have conceived the notion that Dom Ambrose should be given the title of superior of the 'mission' of our Lady of Exile on St. Benedict's Hill. Surely the foundation was to be a 'monastery', not a 'mission'.

(4) It is true that Dom Mayeul had the right, as the founder-abbot, to give an appropriate name to the foundation. Thinking of the reasons he and his monks had for leaving Bahia – they were fleeing from persecution – he decided to call the foundation *"The Monastery of Our Lady of Exile"*. It has retained this title ever since. However, wishing to give the actual property a more local name, he proposed at first to call it *"St. Benedict's Hill"*. In time, popular opinion changed this latter name to *"Mount St. Benedict"*. This name was, apparently, first suggested by Fr. Casey O.P. A short correspondence ensued between Dom Ambrose Vinckier and Dom Mayeul on this matter.

Finally, on 19th November, 1912, Dom Mayeul wrote to Archbishop Dowling as follows:

> *I have just received a letter from the Superior of "Mount St. Benedict", which causes me to add this P.S. before closing the mail. Dom Ambrose tells me that it is better to call our Mission "Mount St. Benedict" rather than "St. Benedict's Hill", and I see that the "Catholic News" speaks already in that sense. It is up to Your Grace to decide. I am not sufficiently acquainted with English to solve the problem. I leave the decision with Your Grace (POS. Benedictines).*

His Grace decided *"Mount St. Benedict shall be its name!"* In time, people often referred to the place by the shortened and more familiar name: "the Mount".

The ultimate question, which neither Dom Mayeul nor Mgr. Dowling asked at the time, was this: Who should control the multiple day-by-day activities of the monks *outside the monastery?* Dom Mayeul believed that he, or his delegate, Dom Ambrose, would have full authority in the allocation of any activity, parochial or otherwise, of his monks. Over the years, the abbot and the archbishop failed to find a modus vivendi in this matter. Dom Mayeul never accepted the fact that he had no canonical jurisdiction over the parochial work undertaken by his monks.

As already mentioned, Dom Mayeul excluded himself from joining the first group of monks who arrived in Trinidad on 6 October 1912, mainly because he was already committed to celebrating, in his abbey, the silver jubilee of his ordination to the priesthood, on 11 October. He thus missed the historical moment, when the three founding monks arrived in Trinidad on 6 October, 1912. The day after their arrival, the two missionary priests, Dom Ambrose and Dom Paul, paid an official visit to Archbishop Dowling, to take the required oath of allegiance or fealty, and to receive Faculties (i.e. permission) for exercising their priestly functions in the diocese. At the same time, Dom Paul was appointed parish priest of Arouca, while Dom Ambrose was left free to concentrate on organizing the new foundation. On Tuesday 8th October, the three monks made their first visit to Arouca, where they were enthusiastically received by the people of the parish. The Sisters of St. Joseph of Cluny had thoughtfully prepared the parochial house for the monks, as well as an evening meal. Dom Paul immediately became a popular figure, visiting the schools, teaching Plainchant and congregational singing. Dom Ambrose made frequent visits to the property on the hills above St. Joseph, but decided not to take up residence there for the moment. They awaited the arrival of the next group of monks, before committing themselves to any structural work on the already existing *ajoupa* and its surroundings.

On 27th November 1912, Brs. Joseph Kleinmann and Donatian Marcus arrived in Trinidad. Br. Joseph was an "all-rounder", i.e. carpenter and builder, and immediately began work adapting the one-room *ajoupa* (hut) into two small rooms, one as an oratory, and the other a dormitory for the community. All furniture was of a primitive kind, empty packing-cases serving as table, chairs, bed and even cupboard. Meals were cooked and taken in the open air, under a mango tree. Not surprisingly, they immediately became an object of curiosity for the local people, who had never before seen a monk. However, there was an immediate problem regarding language, as, between them, they possessed a strong mixture of French, German, Portuguese and English. In spite of this, they succeeded in winning the friendship and support of many. The innate kind-heartedness of the Trinidadian people was further evidenced when they brought fowl, eggs, rice, coffee and even pieces of furniture and kitchen utensils. It was a happy beginning, and gave great heart to the three monks, who immediately settled down to leading a very simple monastic life on this remote hillside. They spent their first Christmas (1912) on the island, with a simple liturgical celebration in the little oratory, and a meal in the open air, under the mango tree. Their thoughts were mainly on the future, wondering what the New Year (1913) would bring by way of change and improvement.

BR. ANTHONY AND BR. JOSEPH CUTTING DOWN THE HILL ON THE NORTHERN
SIDE OF THE MONASTERY

THE FIRST CHURCH ON THE BARREN HILL IN 1913

During the early days of 1913, the monks had to concentrate on two important matters: how to guarantee a constant supply of good fresh water, and how to secure some of the surrounding lands, so that they could make a private road, and have a better access to the place. In fact, these two matters were interrelated. It would be necessary to acquire the adjoining Crown Lands, not only in order to secure a permanent water supply, but also to consolidate their holding and protect their privacy. Dom Mayeul had already authorised the purchase of some one hundred acres of land, either from the Crown or from private owners. By January 9, 1913, the monks had acquired three more parcels of land, which meant that the separate parts of the Gomez estate were now united into one whole, while at the same time the water rights were secure.

However, there were as yet no pipes to act as conduits for the water. The monks had to go down the ravine to fetch water, and it was no easy job to carry it along the unbeaten tracks of the estate. Br. Joseph immediately set about solving the problem. He bought a few thousand feet of pipes, which he laid down at strategic places, and thus brought the water from the ravine to the monastery. This feat of engineering was an object of interest to the reporter of the Port of Spain Gazette, who wrote on 25 May 1913:

> By a well laid out scheme, water was brought up with fairly heavy force from the river some hundreds of feet below, in a pipe laid in a somewhat circuitous route, some 1500 feet, very often the forks of the trees being utilized to support the pipe. Water of excellent quality and delightfully cool can thus be obtained throughout the day, at the rate of five gallons per minute.

February 1913 saw the arrival of reinforcements, with three clerics and two lay brothers, bringing the total number in the community to eleven. One of the lay brothers, Everard Mokveld, the future Br. Gabriel, proved to be a most valuable asset to the young community. In time he became a master-builder and architect, and along with Br. Joseph Kleinmann, was the force behind most of the building programmes in Mount St. Benedict over the coming years.

On 23 February 1913, Dom Mayeul arrived from Bahia, and remained in Trinidad for a month. He immediately drew up plans for a series of buildings, which he considered essential for the develop-

THE FIRST CHURCH AND REFECTORY, 1913 -1914

PAINTING OF THE FIRST CHURCH, 1913

THE FIRST ORATORY IN 1912 - EARLY 1913
UNTIL THE NEW CHURCH WAS FINISHED.

ment of the foundation. First of all, he believed that no serious work could be undertaken until the monks had a large workshop, as well as an engine room, both of which he intended equipping with suitable and modern machinery. There was no possibility of getting these things in Trinidad, and he already planned to buy this heavy machinery and equipment in New York. Secondly, he chose the spot where a temporary wooden chapel should be erected, considering this the most important building in the future monastery. Work should begin on this as soon as possible. Thirdly, he studied the plans for a wider and better road, capable of taking carriages and cars up to the monastery. This latter undertaking was beyond the expertise of the monks. It was decided to commission a local engineer, Mr. McLean, of the Tacarigua local road board, to provide a suitable plan. The agreement was signed on 24 July 1913, between the monks and the contractor, A.D. Degazon of St. John's village, for the construction of a road which provided a safe and solid passage from the bottom of the hill to the building site. Much of the heavy work of building this road was done by the monks themselves. The cost of this main road came to $1,304. It was completed by November 1913.

Although the property gave the appearance of being little more than a wilderness, Dom Mayeul remembered his experience in Ceara, Brazil, and was quite undaunted at the task ahead of his monks. He seemed in his element, providing the necessary incentive and enthusiasm for the hard work of clearing the bush and scrubs, cutting hardwood posts in the neighbouring forest, buying imported flooring boards of pitch-pine and wall-boards of white-pine, and rafters for the roof, etc. The total structure of the chapel measured 68 by 21 feet, and contained under one roof the sacristy, situated behind the high altar. Below the church there was a small shop for the sale of religious articles, and a room for the father superior, while above the sacristy, at the west-end, was a small bell-tower. The building was completed in the first days of August, 1913, and the first Mass celebrated on August 10th. By any standards, this was a remarkable feat, and a credit to the dedication of the monks. The blessing of the church, by Archbishop Dowling, was fixed for August 15th, but had to be postponed until December 28th 1913, owing to the golden jubilee celebrations of St. Mary's College, Port of Spain. During his sermon on that day, the archbishop spoke highly of the Benedictines and their work in Trinidad.

Two monks, both priests, joined the group on November 1, 1913: Dom Sebastian Weber and Dom Bertin Dehaese. The former now took over as parish priest of Arouca, devoting his spare time to the study of English and Hindustani. Dom Bertin, who spoke French and Portuguese fluently, though stationed in the monastery, was constantly in demand as the visiting preacher for great occasions in the Rosary Church, where French sermons were then in vogue. Finally, on November 29, two novice lay brothers arrived in Trinidad: Joachim Schuler and Carloman Eckert. There were now fifteen monks attached to the monastery, with Dom Ambrose Vinckier as superior. It was a sizable community by any standards.

Dom Mayeul was absent from Trinidad between the end of April and the end of November 1913. He was still officially abbot of Bahia, and as such, was invited to Rome, in March 1913, to take part in the election of a coadjutor (assistant) to the ailing Abbot Primate de Hemptinne. His visit also coincided with the solemn inauguration of the newly restored tombs of St. Benedict and his sister, St. Scholastica, at Monte Cassino. Finally, he had some personal unfinished business to attend to, relating to his problems in Bahia, with the governor and the archbishop.

It is difficult to understand Dom Mayeul's state of mind as he sailed for Europe soon after celebrating Holy Week and Easter in Arouca in 1913. To some of his community in Trinidad, it seemed that he was abandoning them, just when they needed his leadership and advice. They felt that the proposed trip was motivated by a desire to advance his personal aggrandizement as abbot of Bahia, by attending a splendid celebration in Rome, along with hundreds of other Benedictine abbots, whereas he should be giving all his time and energy to the Trinidad foundation. There was certainly an element of prestige and self-glory in his decision to accept the invitation. But, as happened so often in the story of his life, there were mixed motives. Never for a moment did he imagine that he was abandoning his community in Trinidad, but believed that he carried them with him. At the same time, he could not overlook his responsibilities to his brethren in Bahia either. One of his reasons for going to Europe was to find young men prepared to volunteer for work either in Brazil or Trinidad. He took with him a large sum of money, all part of the Trinidad Foundation Fund, which he spent, buying machinery, items of artistic value, visiting Benedic-

BR. GABRIEL, BR. JOSEPH AND BR. RAPHAEL IN THE FIRST WORKSHOP

THE SECOND WORKSHOP, BR. GABRIEL AND BR. JOSEPH

tine monasteries in different countries looking for candidates, etc., all to promote the foundation in Trinidad and to strengthen his home base, i.e. in Bahia.

He sailed first for New York, where he spent three weeks, mostly on a shopping spree, buying a selection of the latest machinery and equipment for the newly constructed workshops in Trinidad. One such item was a powerful motor-driven unit, capable of generating electricity. Another machine, also automated, was for cutting and preparing wood. These, and other items, proved of inestimable value over the coming years, allowing the monks to undertake many and varied building programmes. The German and Austrian lay brothers soon mastered the intricacies of the new machinery, and produced some wonderful work; for example, the carved wooden choir-stall for the new chapel, as well as floors and roofs for the many buildings etc. One might be tempted to call Dom Mayeul "a big spender", but he certainly knew what he was doing. New York, at this time, was one of the most advanced centres of engineering in the world, and there was a regular, reasonably cheap shipping service direct to Trinidad. The workshops/sawmills became the future centre of much monastic activity and enterprise. Without this modernised work-centre, it would have been impossible to undertake the buildings which gradually appeared on the Mount during the coming years.

Dom Mayeul sailed from New York to Italy mid-May 1913. Among the passengers on board the ship crossing the Atlantic was Father Lemieur C.SS.R, who had been rector of the Beauplateau house of studies in Belgium at the time Dom Mayeul left the Redemptorists. They had remained friends, and this meeting helped to cement their relationship, as well as to shorten the journey. On arriving in Italy, Dom Mayeul immediately made his way to Monte Cassino, to take part in the splendid ceremonies to mark the opening of the newly adorned crypt of St. Benedict and his sister St. Scholastica. Cardinal Gasquet, the papal legate for the occasion, presided over the celebrations, attended by several bishops and hundreds of Benedictine abbots. Dom Mayeul was in his element, enjoying the splendid ceremonies and the beautiful singing. The festivities continued until 8 June, when the abbots assembled in Sant'Anselmo, Rome, for the election of the coadjutor to Abbot Primate de Hemptinne. The choice fell on Dom Fidelis von

Stotzingen, the abbot of Maria Laach, Germany, of the Congregation of Beuron. Little did the new abbot primate, Dom Fidelis, know at that time that in the future he was destined to hear and read too often about Dom Mayeul. Dom Mayeul had now fulfilled the two main events of his visit to Italy, in Monte Cassino and in Sant'Anselmo. The third reason for his coming to Rome, namely to deal with his recent problems in Bahia, suddenly surfaced, as he explained in his memoirs:

> *In the middle of all these happy events, I received an official notice, asking me to remain in Rome, at the behest of the Holy See, to answer the complaints made against me by the Nuncio of Brazil and the Archbishop of Bahia. I was hardly surprised at this, and went without delay to the church of St. Alphonsus, to ask God, through the intercession of St. Alphonsus, for the grace to be able to imitate him in the ordeal which had fallen upon me. At the same time, I renewed my offering as a victim, if it pleased God to accept this, for the needs of his Holy Church (Vol. II, 155).*

Dom Mayeul seemed oblivious of the fact that all the big guns in the Church in Brazil were against him: the primate, the nuncio and the archbishop of Bahia. He consulted the newly elected coadjutor abbot primate, as well as Mgr. Gerard van Caloen, on his situation. Both apparently showed themselves sympathetic to his cause, but, of course, they had no real say in the matter. Mgr. van Caloen, however, encouraged him to prepare his defence, and to seek an audience with the Pope Pius X. Dom Mayeul describes this audience which took place on 27th May 1913:

> *I brought with me a written report of my case, which the Pope now read carefully. He then looked at me with great kindness and said: "Even if it is necessary to suffer much from a representative of the Church, still, one must have patience, constancy and faith, and in time you will receive much light and understanding." I then told him that I found myself between the hammer and the anvil, and the Holy Father laughed; then gave me his blessing and dismissed me. I left the audience strengthened and consoled. But what had Pius X meant by the words: "Exinde multa solamina percipies" (You will experience many joys). Would I experience these consolations here below or in heaven? He did not specify the point and I left without asking him. The essential thing, however, seemed to be, that sooner*

STATUE OF ST BENEDICT,
BOUGHT BY DOM MAYEUL IN GERMANY IN 1913

THE PLAQUE OF OUR LADY OF EXILE, BOUGHT IN GERMANY IN 1913

or later, whether in this world or the next, I would be happy one day (Vol. II, 155-6).

Dom Mayeul decided at this moment to leave Rome and travel in Europe. In Belgium, he went to the Cistercian abbey of Westmalle, near Antwerp, where he had his *Defence* printed. This was a precise exposition, in Latin, of his quarrel with the governor and archbishop of Bahia. However, he had another, personal problem to resolve, namely his deteriorating health. He thus took the occasion to consult the celebrated Dr. Verriers, of the University of Louvain, a leading heart specialist. He was advised to take the waters of Nauheim in Germany, but decided it would be an unnecessary expense, though he agreed to follow a regime set out for him by Dr. Verriers. In Germany, he visited several religious centres, mostly seminaries, with a view to recruiting some candidates for Trinidad and Bahia. Also in Germany, in Munich, he bought a plaque of Our Lady of Exile, the patroness of the new church in Trinidad, and a large statue of St. Benedict. In the future, this purchase would prove to be of utmost importance for the survival of the foundation. He also visited the abbey of Beuron, where Dom Hildebrand de Hemptinne, the Primate, was in retirement.

During this time (June-September, 1913) he corresponded regularly with Dom Theodore Neve, the abbot of St. Andre, Belgium, giving a frank account of his personal situation. In a letter to Abbot Neve, dated 21 June 1913, which accompanied a copy of his *Defence*, he mentions the matter of 'exemption', which was the breaking point in his dispute with the Brazilian Church authorities. According to Dom Mayeul, quoting a decree of 1890, the Brazilian Benedictines enjoyed complete 'exemption' from episcopal authority or supervision, though this 'exemption' was denied by the current Brazilian hierarchy. He concluded this letter with the ominous words: *"Without this exemption I shall not remain in Brazil, and shall ask for my demission as abbot of Bahia"* (*Zevenkerken, T.N. no. 4*). In another letter to Abbot Neve, Dom Mayeul showed himself highly critical of the attitude of the Roman authorities towards the Brazilian Benedictines, and regretted their decision to appoint Dom Laurent Zeller, abbot of Seccau, an Austrian, (and, therefore, a complete outsider) as apostolic visitator of the Brazilian monasteries: *"It is a humiliation for our Congregation"*.

Looking realistically at the situation in Bahia, and the many problems which faced Dom Mayeul, one could be led to believe that he was the architect of his own downfall. However, his case was not unique. Though he was the only Brazilian abbot who thought it wise to seek a safe refuge outside that country, it must not be imagined that he was the only one to find himself in difficulties. Practically the entire Brazilian Congregation at this time (1912-14) was passing through a severe crisis. The abbey in Rio de Janeiro had recently undertaken an extensive building programme, and found itself unable to raise the required money. The abbey in Olinda was in dispute with the archbishop of Recife, who wished to close their agricultural high school. The monks of Santa Cruz, whose monastery had only recently been elevated into an abbey, found themselves without any means of subsistence for their small community. Undoubtedly, the most serious problem was the fact that none of the abbots of the Congregation were Brazilian. There were Germans abbots in San Paolo, Santa Cruz and Olinda, while in Rio and Bahia there were Belgians, Abbot van Caloen and Dom Mayeul. It was generally felt that the time had come to appoint Brazilian abbots to these monasteries, especially as the shadow of the Great War was beginning to show itself everywhere, even in South America. Under the circumstances, it was no wonder that Rome decided to obtain first-hand information from an independent source, and ordered an extraordinary visitation of the Brazilian monasteries. However, it is not quite clear why they appointed Dom Laurent Zeller, the abbot of Seckau, a German-speaking Austrian, as apostolic visitator, in July 1913. At the time, no one, of course, seems to have foreseen the outbreak of the Great War a year later, on 4 August 1914.

In June 1913, in an explicit way of support for Dom Mayeul, the Chapter from Bahia sent a telegraph to the abbot primate. It is not possible to find out who exactly took the initiative but this is definite evidence that Dom Mayeul had the support of his community:

Chapter (Capitulum) from Bahia unanimously request to maintain Abbot Mayeul (APR 613).

In the month of September, 1913, Dom Mayeul was summoned back to Rome. He had brought with him the printed copies of his "Defence" (entitled *De Conflictu inter Exmum Archiepiscopum Bahiensem et Abbatem Majolum De Caigny*), which he now distributed

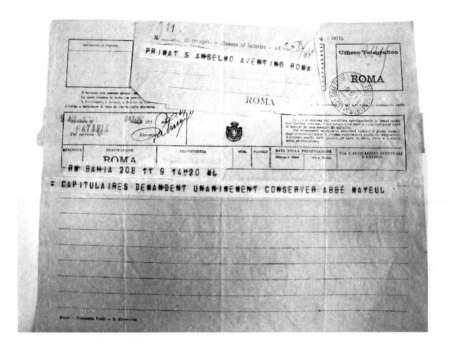

Telegraph sent by the Chapter of Bahia on 9 June 1913,
expressing support for Dom Mayeul

DOM MAYEUL IN 1913, PICTURE TAKEN IN SANT'ANSELMO IN ROME.
SANT'ANSELMO IS THE HOME OF THE ABBOT PRIMATE OF THE BENEDICTINES AND
SEAT OF THE BENEDICTINE CONFEDERATION. IT IS A BEAUTIFUL 19TH CENTURY
MONASTERY, BUILT IN A CLASSICAL STYLE, ON TOP OF ROMAN RUINS WHICH DATE
FROM THE 1ST CENTURY BC TO THE 4TH CENTURY AD.

to the relevant Roman authorities. This impressive piece of writing was couched in the style of a philosophical dissertation. Despite the help he obtained from Dom Paul Delatte (abbot of Solesmes, then in exile in Quarr Abbey, Isle of Wight), Dom Mayeul's *Defence* failed to convince the Roman authorities of the justice of his cause. One critic said of the document that its author was either "a saint or an imposter". Thanks to the good services of Mgr. Bresson, one the secretaries of Pius X, Dom Mayeul succeeded in getting a copy of his *Defence* to the Pope, but without any positive effect. He sent another copy to the prefect of the Congregation for Religious, Cardinal van Rossum, a Dutchman and Redemptorist, who acknowledged it with a note on his visiting card saying: *"With my wishes for the success of a just cause" (Vol. II, 156).* Cardinal van Rossum was the most high-ranking Dutchman, attached to the Roman Curia. In 1918 he became prefect of the Congregation of Propaganda Fide, and as the prefect, his name frequently came up during the Dom Mayeul saga in Trinidad. But more on that in following chapters.

Reading between the lines of the case, including the lengthy correspondence on both sides, and not least Dom Mayeul's own memoirs, one has to conclude that there could be only one outcome, namely, victory for the Brazilian episcopate. Both the primate of Brazil and the archbishop of Bahia made it clear that only the banishment of Dom Mayeul from Bahia would satisfy them. The Primate went so far as to say he would offer his resignation unless this happened. Mgr. Cherubini, the sub-secretary of the Congregation for Religious, had the job of breaking the news to Dom Mayeul that the case had gone against him. He advised him to return to Trinidad immediately, and occupy himself with the new foundation there.

> *On 11 October, after the departure of the Archbishop, Mgr. Cherubini, the sub-secretary of the Congregation for Religious, as the secretary was absent, said to me: "This whole affair is nothing more than a question of jealousy". And since there did not seem any immediate possibility of a solution, he gave me permission to return to Trinidad, to occupy myself with the new foundation there. Thus, the Primate of Brazil obtained his first success, in that he was keeping me away from Bahia. The final success, here on earth, was never in doubt: the Primate won his case, all because of the desire for peace (Vol. II, 157-158).*

Dom Mayeul was very disappointed when he learned that a good compromise allowing him to stay in Brazil failed. Foreseeing the difficulties to resolve this conflict, the abbot primate and Abbot van Caloen, had conceived the idea of creating for Dom Mayeul an abbey "Nullius" in the region of Porto Sequro, in the south of the state of Bahia. But this project was rejected, mainly because Cardinal Scipione Tecchi was strongly opposed to it. In fact he had refused to see Dom Mayeul. Dom Mayeul reflects on this in his memoirs:

> *This systematic opposition will not surprise anyone who is in touch with ecclesiastical history. One has always seen evidence of the human element at every level of the Hierarchy. It would be naïve to ignore it and folly to deny it. Also, the single fact of the permanence of the Church, despite the human elements contained therein, is undoubtedly proof of its divinity. It seems to me that a Papal zouave should be prepared to accept suffering from the Church and for Her, in whatever form and measure it may please God (Vol. II, 157).*

Undoubtedly, Dom Mayeul was deeply hurt by the whole affair, believing in his own heart that he had been treated unjustly. He wrote about his sorrow in his memoirs and made this remarkable reference to one of the rules of St. Benedict; "one should pray for his enemies":

> *Father Faber wrote some lines which I could well apply to my own situation: "Our sorrow must be our own. We must not expect anyone else to understand it. It is one of the conditions of true sorrow, that it should be misunderstood. Sorrow is the most individual thing in the world. We must not expect to get sympathy at all sufficient to what we are suffering. It is best, therefore, to keep our sorrow as secret as we can (F.W. Faber, The Foot of the Cross, pp. 99-100).*

> *Faithful to this motto, I wished for and sought in utter sincerity "peace in truth and charity". Having told the truth, I was happy henceforth to keep silence. Up to what point the Archbishop was in good faith, only God is the judge. St. Benedict tells his monks that they "should pray for their enemies in the love of Christ" (RB, Ch.4). I did this, especially when, later on, I learned the Archbishop had died. It was with such sentiments in my heart that I left Rome (Vol. II, 158-159).*

Dom Mayeul left Rome on 14 October 1913 and went immediately to the Benedictine monastery of St. Guiliano d'Albaro, near Genoa. Here he spent the next ten days on retreat, and found that the atmosphere of this delightful place brought him peace and calm. He finally embarked at Genoa on 6 November 1913, on an Italian steamship, and arrived in Port of Spain, Trinidad on 23 November.

On his arrival, little did Dom Mayeul expect that he would be in a similar situation when ten years later (1923), he was again prepared to take on the Roman authorities and the archbishop of Port of Spain, with more disastrous results for himself.

CHAPTER IX

Dom Mayeul takes up residence at Mount St. Benedict

(23 November 1913 - 30 May 1915)

ON HIS ARRIVAL in Trinidad, Dom Mayeul immediately took up residence in the refurbished small hut at the top of the hill. The hut once belonged to the guardian of the Gomez estate, bought by Dom Mayeul in 1912. He seemed happy with this, though he hardly considered it as a permanent arrangement. Soon after he moved to the cabin built near the newly constructed wooden church. He wrote to Archbishop Dowling on 26 November, explaining why he had not yet visited him on his return from Europe, as he had difficulty in walking. He was also fully occupied studying the developments on the Mount, and preaching the annual retreat to his community. In conclusion, he assured the archbishop he was satisfied with the general state of things in the monastery *(POS, Ben. Dom Mayeul to Abp Dowling, 26 Nov. 1913)*. It seems he had much to admire in what he saw around him. The main road to the monastery had been completed and this was a truly remarkable piece of work, done by the monks. The road, some two kilometres in length, rose, in graceful zigzags, from the lower plain right up to the monastery. In this way, access to the monastery was made considerably easier: people could now arrive on foot, in carriages or in cars.

Equally important was the fact that the church and the engine shop were now operational, while the property was clearly becoming habitable. When the archbishop visited them on 28 December, to bless the wooden church and the engine shop, there was a general atmosphere of achievement, and even pride, felt by all the monks. Some people criticised Dom Mayeul for choosing such a narrow

The small hut on the hill, in which Dom Mayeul took residence when he arrived in Trinidad

Postcard showing Dom Mayeul's hut
sent to the Abbot Primate on 25 XI 1913

A view of Mt. St. Benedict looking North East

THE WINDING, ZIGZAG, FINISHED ROAD

194

terrain on which to build a monastery. One of the Dominican Fathers had remarked that the place was of no real value and *"no one would visit the monastery on account of having to climb such a height; the whole undertaking was bound to be a complete failure" (Vol. II, 159)*. Time would prove them very wrong.

Dom Mayeul spent the first week in January 1914 reviewing the overall situation. He came to the conclusion that the money he had brought from Brazil would only give them a modest income, hardly sufficient to maintain his community, which was growing all the time. He would have to accept some parishes in order to subsist in any degree of comfort. However, his main concern was the actual organisation of the foundation. He had reasons to feel some doubts about the internal running of the monastery, as he wrote in his memoirs:

> *The Superior, Dom Ambrose Vinckier, had, during my absence, acted against my orders and committed some serious indiscretions. I had to dismiss him, a fact which caused him great displeasure. He would never forgive me and he immediately began a campaign of defamation against me. With the agreement of the Archbishop he was given charge of the parish, since his continued presence in the monastery would not have contributed of the peace of the place. This was my first trial in Trinidad. I had another problem with one of the lay brothers, who I sent away for serious reasons. In the end, I nominated as prior the excellent Dom Sebastian Weber, who had already given proof of his worthiness, when Superior of our mission in Angelim (Brazil) (Vol. II, 159-160).*

Dom Mayeul received a letter from Archbishop Dowling, dated 3 January 1914, granting the Benedictines the right to erect the 'Stations of the Cross' in their church. At the same time, the archbishop indicated he would like to revise the financial arrangements already existing between him and the monks. Now that Dom Mayeul was back in residence in Mount St. Benedict, the monks should be able to manage their own affairs. Replying to Dr. Dowling on 9 January 1914, Dom Mayeul calculated that the capital sum still existing amounted to US$67,000. He would like to retain a reserve capital of $60,000, to be invested at a good rate of interest. The remaining $7,000 would be needed to pay for on-going works. He had already started building a new wing, consisting of twelve

THE FIRST CELLS FOR THE MONKS BUILT IN 1914

THE FIRST CELLS FOR THE MONKS BUILT IN 1914

cells, with a balcony in front, and a library in the middle. It also contained the new refectory. This was a great improvement on the earlier arrangement, when the monks took their meals in the shade of a mango tree *(POS, Ben. Dom Mayeul to Abp Dowling, 9 Jan. 1914)*. Life was becoming more and more bearable for everyone. They still felt somewhat isolated and hoped in time to entice more pilgrims to visit the monastery. Early in 1914 an event occurred which changed everything for the better.

During his recent trip to Europe, Dom Mayeul had visited Munich, where he bought a magnificent statue of St. Benedict, and arranged for it to be shipped directly to Trinidad. It arrived towards the end of January 1914. The monks decided to mark its actual reception at Mount St. Benedict with a public festival. The statue, mounted on a large decorated stretcher, was brought in a triumphant procession, from the bottom of the hill, all the way to the monastery church. A large crowd of pilgrims joined the procession on foot, forming an impressive cortege, which was preceded by more than forty cars. The people sang hymns and recited the rosary, as they led the statue of St. Benedict up to his permanent sanctuary. It seemed to everyone that St. Benedict was at this moment taking possession of the mountain. The place could now, in truth, be called "Mount St. Benedict". The occasion proved to be a turning point in the history of the foundation. The day's proceedings were reported in the newspapers, and appealed to the imagination of many people on the island. The inhabitants of Trinidad suddenly found they had a powerful protector in St. Benedict. Today, the statue stands in the new church, and has become a much visited shrine, a place of pilgrimage and prayer.

A few weeks later, another occasion for promoting devotion to St. Benedict presented itself, namely the Saint's official Feast Day, 21 March 1914. *The Port of Spain Gazette* reported the proceedings as follows:

> *From an early hour and by various means of conveyance, large numbers of people were to be seen, yesterday morning, wending their way on to Mount St. Benedict to take part in the first solemn celebration of the Feast of the Founder of the Order of monks who now inhabit that locality. Shortly after half-past nine o'clock, the Lord Abbot, Dom Mayeul De Caigny, entered the church, and proceeded to the throne. Having put on his mitre, and with crosier*

in his hand, Solemn Mass was celebrated by Dom Sebastian Weber,
the prior. After the Mass, the Abbot imparted the Pope's blessing to
the kneeling crowd. In the afternoon at 4.30, there was Pontifical
Vespers, followed by the "Te Deum" and Solemn Benediction of the
Most Blessed Sacrament. Thus, the first solemn celebration of St.
Benedict's day in Trinidad was brought happily to a close (POS
Gazette, 22 March 1914).

There were a number of important consequences following on
these two public manifestations of support for the monks. The first
was the financial advantage brought to the monastery by the number
of pilgrims. The shrine of St. Benedict became a focal point for the
people of the island to come and pray for favours. At each visit they
made whatever pecuniary offerings they could afford. Dom Mayeul
realized immediately, that this would ease the monastery's financial burden, and make them less dependent on the money they got
from their parishes. Very soon the numbers of pilgrims had risen to
such an extent that extra facilities for coping with the crowds were
needed. Secondly, the pilgrims soon began to seek out the monks
for confession and counselling. This eventually became one of the
major pastoral works of the community. Rooms, called parlours,
for receiving the pilgrims, were soon provided, and a rota of monks
allotted certain hours for attending to the needs of the people. One
hundred years later, the parlours of Mount St. Benedict are filled
seven days a week, with long lines of pilgrims seeking counselling.
Thirdly, such reporting of their activities, as quoted above, gave the
monks more publicity than they probably needed. Both the *Catholic*
News and the *Port of Spain Gazette* reported regularly any important
event in the life of the Benedictine monks. This had one unfortunate result, namely, it aroused the jealousy of some of the local
clergy, both diocesan and religious. These latter felt that the monks
were getting more than their share of the limited financial resources
of the Catholic population on the island. This became a recurring
problem in the years ahead. Some suggested that the Benedictines
wanted to take over the whole island of Trinidad. The monks appeared unaware that they were creating trouble for themselves. They
continued to hold celebration after celebration under the public
gaze, and all the while the crowds of pilgrims increased beyond
anything they could have imagined.

The situation might have been different, if the monks had simply become a 'seven-day-wonder' for the people of Trinidad. But that was not the case. The people continued to be fascinated by the sight of monks, who were undertaking all kinds of difficult manual work, and at the same time providing spiritual benefits and services to the pilgrims, who came every day to the monastery. To some observers, the monks were super-human beings, creating a multi-purpose monastery out of waste-land on the hillside above Tunapuna. Traditionally monks lived behind stone walls and within cloisters. But here they were in the open, constructing roads and bridges, building a monastery with their own hands, supporting the great heat of the day, and at the same time celebrating Mass and the Divine Office, hearing confessions, counselling hundreds of pilgrims each day, and happy in all their endeavours.

1914 continued to be a year of development and public acclaim for the monks. In the afternoon of 14 May 1914, an impressive ceremony of the blessing of bells was held on the Mount. During his recent European trip, Dom Mayeul had bought three bells in the famous Tellin foundry in Belgium, and had them transported by ship to Trinidad. The largest bell weighed 780 lbs., the second 540 lbs., and the third 375 lbs. Archbishop Dowling was invited to perform this ceremony, but had to decline, owing to another engagement that day. The bells were consecrated by Dom Mayeul on 14 May 1914, in the presence of many friends of the monastery. The sermon for the occasion was preached by Rev. Bernard Carey, C.S.Sp., and parish priest of Diego Martin. The daily ringing of these bells was a further reminder to the people of the region that the monks had come to stay, and were already committed to a regular round of public Masses and liturgical prayers. The monks were, indeed, fulfilling the injunction of the Rule of St. Benedict, which stipulated that they should spend their time between PRAYER and WORK (Ora et Labora).

On 29 May 1914, Abbot Laurent Zeller of Seckau, Austria, arrived in Trinidad to undertake a canonical visitation of Mount St. Benedict. This was a routine affair, to gather information about the progress and working of the recent foundation. He was accompanied by Mgr. Gerard van Caloen, at this time abbot of Rio de Janeiro and President of the Brazilian Congregation. Mgr. van Caloen was very impressed by all that he saw, the exceptional loca-

ONE OF THE BELLS PURCHASED IN BELGIUM, AT THE WELL-KNOWN TELLIN
FOUNDRY. THE BELLS WERE DONATED BY A BELGIAN LADY,
VISCOUNTESS DE COETLOSQUET.

tion on the hill as well as the new road and the buildings. Abbot Zeller was equally impressed, but noticed that there was no accommodation for the large number of pilgrims who visited the monastery every day. He proposed that the monks construct two guest houses: one, to be called "the rest house" for the poor, who would be housed free of charge, and the other, more elaborate, to be called "the guest house", for those who could pay. These two buildings were contracted out, the guest house to Nicholas Sedeño of St. John's Village, and the rest house to a Mr. Lamy of Tunapuna. They proved very helpful, especially during the wet season, when the roads were often flooded, and the distance from the monastery to the railway station in Tunapuna some five kilometres. The two houses, each about 25 metres long, were completed in record time. Both were well-supplied with water, and had sufficient accommodation for those who wished to stay. In front of the guest houses, a large esplanade was built, where the pilgrims could sit and admire the view of the surrounding countryside.

Prior to his arrival in Trinidad, Abbot Laurent Zeller had been to Bahia, where he tried unsuccessfully to sort out the long-standing dispute between Dom Mayeul and the archbishop of Bahia. Once in Trinidad, he asked Dom Mayeul if he wished to take legal action against the archbishop of Bahia, in order to assert his right of residence in Bahia. After all he had acquired in 1898 the Brazilian citizenship. It was a delicate and difficult situation, which needed a speedy solution, seeing that Dom Mayeul was still officially abbot of Bahia, but no longer resident there. In his memoirs, Dom Mayeul gave an account of his response to Abbot Zeller's question:

> I told him that if the Major Superiors (i.e. all the abbots in Brazil), or the chapter of Bahia, wished to pursue the process, that I would not oppose them. However, personally I was not in favour of such a move, believing with the Apostle: "The servant of God should not involve himself in litigation (II Trin., II.24)". Realizing also that besides the annoyance and upset which always accompanied such a process, it would lead to an endless waste of time and money. I added that I naturally wished for a victory of our cause, but, in the event of my obtaining this, I would immediately ask for my resignation as abbot of Bahia. I was aware of the moral impossibility of my undertaking a fruitful apostolate in Bahia, knowing the

CANONICAL VISITATION 1914,
ABBOT ZELLER, ARCHABBOT VAN CALOEN AND ABBOT MAYEUL

203

1914: THE COMMUNITY MEMBERS PRESENT AT THE MOUNT, AT THE TIME OF
THE CANONICAL VISITATION

unyielding opposition of the Primate (i.e. the archbishop) and the higher clergy. Finally, I told him that I would abide by the solution proposed by the Holy See, no matter what it entailed. This attitude left me in peace. The Major Superiors in Brazil followed the policy of abstention adopted by the Abbot Visitor. My chapter in Trinidad adopted my point of view. As a result, there was no process initiated by me (Vol. II, 163).

Evidently it was during this canonical visitation of the Mount, in the early summer of 1914, that Dom Mayeul decided his days as abbot of Bahia were ended, and that his future now lay in Trinidad. He hoped he would be allowed to retire as abbot of Bahia with honour, which, in fact, happened the following year, 1915.

The visitation ended on 2 June 1914, without any radical changes in the running of the foundation being proposed. Dom Mayeul was given the green light to proceed with the various buildings which were needed. Having completed the guest and rest houses, Dom Mayeul decided to construct a larger gift shop, to cater for the growing crowds of people, who wished to purchase candles and oil, to burn in front of the statue of St. Benedict, as well as other religious objects. It became necessary to have two brothers serving in the shop, selling rosary beads, scapulars, medals, holy pictures, prayer-books, etc. One little book, *"A Novena in Honour of St. Benedict"*, became a best-seller overnight. Thanks to the large sale of oil for the votive lamps in front of the statue of St. Benedict, lighting was provided for the church throughout most of the day and even into the night, thus saving the community considerable expense in this department. However, most edifying of all was the fact that many poor people, who had no money, brought gifts of eggs, chickens, fish, vegetables, rice and coffee, for the monks. The generosity of the pilgrims has been a feature of life in Mount St. Benedict since the very beginning. In return, the monks have been able to share their good fortune with others, by dispensing alms to those who come to the monastery seeking help.

During the wet season (July–October) of 1914, Dom Mayeul became dissatisfied with the accommodation provided for him in the tiny hut near the church. He felt that his position as superior of the Mount warranted something more suitable. He thus looked around for a new site, on which to build something more worthy. His decision was influenced by a number of factors. The first was

THE FIRST GUEST AND REST HOUSE BUILT BY LOCAL CONTRACTORS, ALSO SHOWING
THE FIRST FORD AUTOMOBILE

PILGRIMS VISITING THE MOUNT

a long-standing project, the brain-child of the governor, Sir Alfred Malouney, to build a sanatorium at the summit of Mount El Tucuche, the second highest mountain in Trinidad, and situated to the north of Mount St. Benedict. The idea was supported by the distinguished Dr. Marry, who had studied medicine in Paris, and was now resident in Trinidad. However, it never came to fruition. Early in 1914, Dr. Marry, having made the acquaintance of Dom Mayeul, suggested that the monks establish a sanatorium on the summit of their own property, some 600 metres above sea-level. Dom Mayeul was impressed by the arguments put forward, being especially taken by the "healthy" aspect of the proposed site. It seems that he made up his mind on the matter without seeking expert opinion, and also without consulting his community. He simply decided there and then to build a magnificent multi-purpose structure (monastery/sanatorium), which he later called "Mount Thabor", and referred to also as "the upper monastery". The site he chose commanded a magnificent view of three sides of the island. Its most appealing feature was the pure air and a fresh and constant breeze. Furthermore, it was seldom covered by clouds, as was the case of Mount El Tucuche. Dom Mayeul already decided at this early stage (1914), that his sanatorium would not be a public amenity, but limited to the monks and the local clergy, and those who came to spend some time on retreat in the monastery. It would provide a very healthy place for older or infirm monks, as well as bone-fide priests and friends of the monastery, who wished to make a retreat, or whose health demanded some kind of recuperation.

A second factor which led Dom Mayeul to build this structure on a higher level was the need to provide a peaceful place for his student-monks, where they could study in peace. In this way they would avoid the noise and bustle of the crowds of pilgrims, who visited the lower monastery throughout the day. And finally, the upper monastery would provide a suitable residence for Dom Mayeul. He thus set about making detailed drawings and plans for his so-called "Sanatorium", but which turned out to be a minor Windsor castle. There were to be two towers, one of which was to be set aside for the use of Dom Mayeul. It was a magnificent idea, but one which in the end became a liability and an embarrassment. First of all, it was built in Tapia, the local building material, which was not long-lasting, and could hardly be expected to resist the winds and rains during the wet season. It became impossible, or perhaps too expensive, to install electricity on Mount Thabor. A more serious problem was the distance to be travelled between the upper and lower monasteries, which involved climbing a steep path, often in the dark. This was the only supply line for food and other necessities for those living in the upper monastery. In the long run, the most serious drawback of the Mount Thabor venture was the strain it put on the community's financial resources. Dom Mayeul chose Brother Joseph Kleinmann as the monk in charge of building this structure, which took five years to complete. Though a brilliant handyman and a self-taught engineer, he was not an architect, and had no experience in building such a large and ambitious structure.

The monastery came face to face with its first real crisis within a matter of weeks of the departure of Abbot Zeller and Mgr. van Caloen. On 14 August 1914, the Great War broke out in Europe, and its repercussions spread across the Atlantic. Since Trinidad was an English colony, the island was officially at war with Germany. This created a problem for the monks on the Mount, because several members of the community, including the prior, were German. In fact, only a few days before the declaration of war, a new batch of monk-recruits arrived from Germany. Some of these young men were full of the German national pride of the time, which became inflated, when news reached Trinidad of successive German victories over the Allies on the Western front, especially the invasion and fall of Belgium. Pro-German sympathies were expressed in different quarters, and it was said that Archbishop Dowling, an Irishman, let everyone know that his sympathies lay with the Germans. What further aggravated the situation was the fact that the local clergy, being for the most either Irish or Spanish, did not hide their hostility towards the Allies.

Dom Mayeul, a Belgian by birth, was clearly on the side of the Allies. He showed where his sympathies lay, when, on 14 September 1914, he wrote a personal letter to the King of the Belgians, King Albert, assuring him of the prayers of his community, and praising the noble cause of Belgium. He received a reply, dated 2 October 1914, from one of the King's Secretaries, written from the Royal palace, Palais d'Anvers, which said:

The King read your letter of 14 September last with much emotion, and thanks you sincerely for the very cordial sentiments expressed

*therein. Your expression of sympathy to Him has been greatly ap-
preciated. Our country fought to the end for the defence of honour
and justice.*

*Assuring you, Reverend Father, of my deepest appreciation of your
kind thoughts.*

The Secretary of the King (signed)
(F.A., F. De Caigny, Belgium)

Soon after the declaration of war, the chief of police visited the
monastery, and took the names of all the members of the community, who belonged to any country at war with the British Empire.
However, instead of interning them in military camps, as happened
in the cases of other people, the governor allowed them to stay
in the monastery, taking the word of honour of Dom Mayeul,
a Belgian ally. At the same time, they were forbidden to leave the
monastery without the permission of the police. Thus no one, who
was considered as "civilly undesirable", could leave the monastery
without a special pass. In the case of anyone disobeying this order,
a word from Dom Mayeul was enough to have the culprit interned.
A notable exception to this was Dom Sebastian Weber, a German,
who was allowed to keep his parish (Arouca), together with his two
companions, both German.

Dom Mayeul soon had a delicate situation on his hands, which
he described in his memoirs:

*I presumed that everyone would be satisfied, and conform to the
arrangements. However, I failed to anticipate the attitude of the
younger monks, who had joined us recently from Germany, and
did not as yet wear the habit of our Order. I had forbidden the
two most excitable of the young German monks, who lived in the
parish with our German parish priest (Dom Sebastian Weber), to
visit the monastery, where they would sow dissension. But, they
only laughed at my prohibition, and came to the monastery to call
my bluff, as it were. I made it clear to them, that if they visited
again, they would be interned. Stubborn and proud, they presented
themselves again in the monastery, and caused excitement among the
other German monks. That same evening, the government authorities, having been notified of the situation, took the two into custody,
and the others, with one exception, wishing to show their solidarity,*

followed them into captivity. In one sense, this was a good thing, because of the relative peace which thereafter reigned in the monastery, (Vol. II, 164-5)

There was a growing suspicion in the minds of some on the island, that the Benedictine monks were sympathetic to the German cause, especially as the prior of the monastery, Dom Sebastian Weber, was a German. As a result, many English and French people, who had visited the monastery regularly, ceased to do so. It was said publicly that the monks were sending signals at night to German warships from the upper monastery (Mount Thabor) then under construction. One of these mysterious German warships was called the "Karlsruhe". A further suspicion fell on the newly built esplanade in front of the two guest houses, which, it was said, the monks intended using as a site for a cannon, as part of their defensive system favouring the Germans. The government authorities sent someone to investigate these two suspected danger-zones, but found no proof of any pro-German activity on the part of the monks. All these matters caused much distress to Dom Mayeul, who feared they might compromise the good name of the monastery. They cast a dark cloud over the young foundation, but in no way prevented the community going from strength to strength. Thanks mainly to the extraordinary success of the pilgrimage in honour of St. Benedict, and the support of the local people, Mount St. Benedict survived the war years.

There was one final matter which Dom Mayeul hoped to address as soon as possible, namely, the raising of Mount St. Benedict from being a priory to that of an abbey. He found himself in an unusual situation, being called "abbot", but, in fact, ruling over a priory. The numbers of monks in the community by 1915 had grown sufficiently to warrant it becoming an abbey. Early in September 1915, Dom Mayeul approached Archbishop Dowling, requesting that the monastery be raised to the status of an abbey. He received a categorical refusal in a letter from the archbishop, dated 11 September 1915, which ended with these words: *"I am not disposed to give my support to the establishment of an Abbey in my diocese"* (POS. Ben.). To which Dom Mayeul replied on 14 September: *"It seems to me that your letter of 11 Sept. 1915 left me with a rather painful impression"* (POS. Benedictines).

From this moment on, Dom Mayeul realized that Archbishop Dowling would never tolerate another "prelate" in his diocese, and that the monks would therefore have to wait until he either died or retired before opening up this question again. In fact, they had to wait more than thirty years, until 1947, before the Mount became an abbey. This was a very sore point in the mind of Dom Mayeul, who felt offended by Archbishop Dowling, as it deprived both the Mount, and himself (Dom Mayeul), of all the privileges and status associated with being an abbey. It showed both the intransigence and undisputed power of an archbishop at this time, with no hope of referring the matter to any outside arbitration. This matter proved a serious breaking-point between the archbishop and Dom Mayeul, and soured their personal relationship. How far this decision of Archbishop Dowling was harmful to the development of the monastery in the long run, is a disputed point. One can only suspect that it proved a serious handicap, and put an obstacle in its way towards developing in a normal way.

CHAPTER X

Events and Problems
of the Mid-war Years
(30 May 1915 - 16 November 1916)

ALTHOUGH the Great War was still in progress, and political feelings high in both Trinidad and Brazil, in June 1915, a General Chapter of the Brazilian Congregation was convened in Rio de Janeiro, to which Dom Mayeul was invited. Mount St. Benedict was still part of the Brazilian Congregation, and was expected to send its highest ranking member to represent it. Before leaving Trinidad, Dom Mayeul made one final adjustment to those in charge of the monastery during his absence. While retaining Dom Sebastian Weber, a German, as prior, he appointed another monk, a Dutchman, Brother Willibrord Luiten, as his replacement in all things civil, to liaise with the governor, who would hardly deal with a German in such matters. This latter appointment caused a major incident in the community, as Dom Mayeul mentions in his memoirs:

> *When I communicated this necessary measure to the community chapter, it caused an outburst of rage, such as I had never previously experienced, on the part of three Germans. They rose in their seats, and with fury, raised their fists towards me. This was an unheard of scandal, and, for me, a true, but sad, revelation. I did not have time to remedy the situation, as the boat was about to leave. In haste, I went to the Archbishop to say goodbye, at the same time asking him to help the prior in calming the agitated members of our community (Vol. II, 166-7).*

Fortunately, the archbishop took up this last request, and used his influence to defuse the situation in the Mount. Evidence of this comes from a letter addressed to him by Dom Sebastian Weber, the prior of Mount St. Benedict, on 3 June 1915:

> *The protest which had been made by a few of the members of our Community with regards to the appointment of our Brother Willibrord as a civil representative of the Community, was for me very great pain. However, owing in a large measure to Your Grace's firm and wise attitude supporting our Rt. Rev. Lord Abbot as to the said appointment, I am glad to inform Your Grace that the storm is over and that peace and calm reign again in our Community (Archdiocese POS, Ben.).*

It is difficult to understand Dom Mayeul's apparent lack of firmness and diplomacy in dealing with this German crisis in his community. He failed to realize that, from the moment war broke out, there would be serious tensions and dissensions amongst his Germans monks, who found they were treated as enemies in a British colony. Perhaps his experience in Brazil had not helped. There he had seen the Germans fit in very well in the various Benedictine monasteries, while two abbots of Brazilian monasteries, Dom Miguel Kruse (San Paolo) and Dom Peter Roeser (Olinda) were also Germans. But Brazil was not a British colony like Trinidad. Once the war started, many Brazilians showed a clear sympathy towards Germany, whereas in Trinidad, the prevailing mood among the general population was that of being pro-British.

As he boarded the ship *Minas Geraes* in Barbados for Rio, there being no direct link between Trinidad and Brazil, owing to the war, Dom Mayeul's mind was filled with many things. He was returning to his beloved Brazil, but this time without any official status. He had only recently heard the news that Pope Benedict XV had resolved Dom Mayeul's long-standing dispute with the archbishop of Bahia and the primate of Brazil. The matter had been brought to a conclusion by a decree of the Sacred Congregation for Religious, dated 6 March 1915, by which Dom Mayeul was released from his charge as abbot of Bahia, and regained his title, that he got in June 1907, of Titular Abbot of Lobbes, a former Benedictine monastery in Belgium, closed at the time of the French Revolution. By this same decree, Mount St. Benedict was raised to the dignity of conventual priory, and Dom Mayeul nominated its superior. As a conventual priory, the Mount became autonomous and not dependent any longer from another abbey. A final clause put in place an arrangement, whereby the personnel and patrimony of the ancient abbey of Bahia should be divided between the monastery in Bahia and the new priory in Trinidad. Abbot Laurent Zeller was charged with overseeing these arrangements (MSB, Box 10. iii). This decree broke the last link that Dom Mayeul had with Bahia. It also meant that he had lost his case against the archbishop of Bahia, and there could be no appeal.

After a sea journey of 16 days, during which they called at Para, Pernambuco and Bahia, Dom Mayeul arrived at Rio, in time for the General Chapter, presided over by Dom Laurent Zeller. One of the principal aims of the General Chapter was to promulgate the Roman decree of 6 March 1915. All the members were German, except Dom Mayeul and Mgr. van Caloen, who were Belgian. Mgr van Caloen took the occasion of the General Chapter to resign his position both as archabbot of the Brazilian Congregation and abbot of San Bento, Rio. He felt that after twenty-two years (1893-1915), it was time he handed over the responsibility for the Brazilian Congregation to someone else. Secondly, his health had deteriorated in the last year or two, and he found it difficult to deal with the day-to-day affairs of the Brazilian Congregation. There was a third reason why Mgr. van Caloen offered to resign, namely, a financial one. Up to the beginning of the war, the van Caloen family had been the main benefactors of the restored Brazilian Congregation. But the war changed all that. Belgium became one of the main centres of fighting between the Germans and the Allies, with the result that the country's economic basis collapsed completely. The van Caloen family, who lived in Bruges (Belgium), suffered a serious financial setback, and could no longer offer any help to Brazil.

Finally, the war also brought a great change in the thinking of Dom Gerard van Caloen. All his life he had been pro-German, but after the invasion of Belgium in 1914, he became anti-German. In his farewell circular letter (Monita Paterna No. 10) dated 16 July 1915, he wrote of the war as having "ruined the whole world". To him, it seemed liked the end of the world, certainly the end of the world as he had known it. What further aggravated the situation was the fact that many of the Brazilian monasteries were in serious financial difficulties, resulting from over-spending and the partial collapse in the country's economic base. He concluded this circular letter by expressing his one regret, namely, that of leaving (abandoning) his beloved Indians in the Amazonian district (*MSB, Box 10, viii, Circular Letters, nos. 5-10*). He told the members of the General Chapter that he intended retiring to Belgium and joining the community of St. Andre, Belgium. With the resignation of Mgr. van Caloen as abbot of Rio, a successor had to be found to take over the government of this important monastery. Dom Peter Eggerath, a monk of San Paolo, was eventually elected abbot of Rio de Janeiro on 14 October 1915, and blessed on 13 February 1916.

Resulting from the resignation of Mgr. van Caloen, Dom Laurent Zeller was nominated by the Holy See as president of the Brazilian Congregation, while at the same time he retained his position as administrator of the abbey of Bahia. It was a rather strange arrangement, seeing that he hardly spoke a word of Portuguese. Indeed, his present stay in Brazil was limited, as he was expected to return in the near future to Austria, where he held the position of abbot of Seckau.

Throughout the last months of 1914, there had been some lobbying by the president of the Benedictine oblates of Bahia, on behalf of Dom Mayeul, hoping to influence the Roman authorities and have Dom Mayeul restored to his position as abbot of Bahia. A series of letters passed between the president of the oblates, Ritta A. Cunha, and a certain Dom Leler, which reveal the depth of feeling among the oblates, now deprived of their spiritual director, Dom Mayeul:

> *We would like to say how anxious we are because of the protracted absence of our Spiritual Director Dom Mayolo De Caigny, who was such a source of inspiration to us... We respectfully and urgently ask Your Excellency, if he would try to arrange his return from Trinidad and send him to his Abbey (Bahia) where he is really missed (St. Leo, XII, C-8).*

It is unlikely that Abbot Zeller knew anything about the lobbying, but it is most likely a coincidence that, before departing from Rio, he made a grand gesture towards Dom Mayeul, by inviting the latter to visit Bahia on his way back to Trinidad. This visit was in fact necessary to allow Dom Mayeul to renounce all the civil rights he had over his former abbey. It turned out to be a nostalgic experience. Dom Mayeul found to his surprise that, on entering the vast church of San Sebastian, the large crowd burst into clapping, and threw flowers from every side in front of their former abbot, as he made his way up the church. He had always been a great favourite with a certain section of the people of Bahia, especially his beloved 'oblates', and those who acknowledged his role in saving the monastery and church from destruction during the recent political disturbances. However, Dom Mayeul must have realized that this belated celebration in his honour was but a passing moment of exaltation. More ominously, his re-appearance in Bahia had not gone unnoticed among certain member of the higher clergy, who could not hide their outward resentment at his present popularity, while inwardly rejoicing at his being deprived of his abbacy (*Vol. II, 167-8*).

One final event needs to be mentioned regarding this visit of Dom Mayeul to his former abbey. On 23 July 1915 Dom Laurent Zeller called a Chapter meeting of the community of Bahia, to which Dom Mayeul was invited. In his address, the abbot president outlined the decree of the Holy See (i) concerning the 'dismissal' of Dom Mayeul as abbot of Bahia, (ii) determining the canonical status of Mount St. Benedict, now raised to the status of conventual priory, and (iii) arranging for dividing the goods of the abbey at Bahia between Trinidad and Bahia. He promised that, after getting the required information regarding the needs of both monasteries, he would "make sound judgments in the interests of both houses". In the course of his address, he made two references to Dom Mayeul:

(i) *The Holy See requires Dom Mayeul to leave the governance of this Abbey, and at the same time appoints him prior of Mount St. Benedict, conferring on him the title of Abbot of Lobbes. The Holy See does not explain specifically the motives that governed this decision, but expresses only, in general terms, the circumstances that caused this decision, after pondering diligently and prudently.*

(ii) *I cannot end this meeting without expressing to you, Dom Mayeul, how much we appreciate your efforts in working for the good of this Abbey. It is eight years since Your Excellency arrived in Bahia. I don't particularly wish to speak of all that Your Excellency endured over this period of time, but my only prayer is that God will reward you in His own magnificent way (MSB, original in Portuguese).*

Dom Mayeul's situation, as abbot of Bahia, had become difficult, if not impossible. He had become *persona non grata* with the archbishop of Bahia and the primate of Brazil, as well as the nuncio, and was a serious cause of division in the city of Bahia. One wonders what Rome would have done with Dom Mayeul, had he not already provided an escape hatch for himself, by making the foundation in Trinidad. One suspects that the Roman authorities took the easy way out, by appointing him superior of Mount St. Benedict and reinstating him as titular abbot of Lobbes, a title which he got in 1907 before being appointed abbot of Bahia. There was no reprimand, no recrimination. On the other hand, Rome kept a record of the 1912 case in the archives of the Congregation for Religious. Years later, in 1923, evidence from this file would resurface when Dom Mayeul resigned, again under a cloud, from his position as superior of Mount St. Benedict. He apparently learned nothing from his Bahian experience, and continued to govern his monastery in Trinidad, with the same principles and the same self-assurance.

According to Dom Odo van der Heydt, who became later on the archivist of Mount St. Benedict, Dom Mayeul returned from Bahia a humiliated, broken and embittered man. He had suffered a crushing blow, a terrible humiliation. His grand vision, to make the abbey at Bahia the centre of missionary foundations would remain a dream. He would never be able to accept his loss.

Dom Mayeul could not understand why Rome had ruled against him. He had proven to be a most loyal zouave, who had not only prevented the demolition of the abbey but had restored it to its previous glory. By all means he had respected and executed the rules from the Holy See, especially with respect to the exemption and he had successfully fulfilled the oath he had taken as an abbot to protect the assets of the abbey. He lost heavy morally; he lost his dignity and the presence of the Bahian community who had shown such a great affection for him. Between Dom Mayeul's return from Rome in Nov 1913, where he made his defence against the archbishop, and this very last visit to Bahia almost two years later, Dom Mayeul wrote numerous letters expressing his frustration and moral pain. These letters addressed to the abbot primate are currently in the archives of the abbot primate in Rome. This is an extract from one of the letters:

> *The greatest regret I have since my childhood is that I was too young to become a zouave in the army of Pope Pius X and to shed my blood for the Holy See. Since then I made an oath to always be a champion of the Holy See. I defended our exemption and our Abbey, all in obedience to the decrees of the Holy See. I succeeded in both cases. However what did I get as a result? I suffer profoundly from the injustice done to me by the Holy See. And for what motive? To keep the peace with the Archbishop and out of fear for a schism (a rift between Rome and the Brazilian Archdiocese)! The Holy See forgets my utmost inner love I have for the Church, a love that I sucked in with the milk of my pious mother. My condemnation by the Church has merely increased my faith in the divine aspect of the Church, since the human aspect within the Church is not able to destroy Her (Rome, APR, #5 1915).*

However Dom Mayeul realized later on that, for the future of the foundation in Trinidad, he had to accept with some good grace the decision of the Holy See, as he explained in a letter to the Holy See, through the abbot primate:

> *I accept the decision of the Holy See in all simplicity of faith, with full confidence and in conformity to the Will of God. Regarding anything that I find difficult, I offer it up for the triumph of the Holy Church and the happiness of the Holy Father. For those things that I find consoling, I thank the Pope and the members of the Sacred Congregation for Religious. I shall henceforth devote myself, body and soul, to the new foundation in Trinidad, which has been confided to me by the Holy See (Vol. II, 165-6 and APR #5 DM to Abbot Primate).*

The year 1915 saw a considerable increase in the numbers of monks who joined the new foundation in Trinidad, bringing the community up to 26 members. Ever since its foundation in 1912, there had been a steady stream of new members from Bahia to Mount St. Benedict. It may be helpful to give the names of all the monks who joined the community during its first three years of existence, with the dates of their arrival in Trinidad:

1912:

Oct 6th   1. Dom Ambrose Vinckier (Priest)

2. Dom Paul Dobbert (Priest)

3. Br. Anthony Feldner, (Professed lay brother)

Nov. 27th   4. Br. Joseph Kleinmann (Professed lay brother)

5. Br. Donatian Marcus (Professed lay brother)

1913:

Febr. 11th   6. Dom Urich Frommherz (Solemn professed cleric)

7. Dom Fridolin Frommherz (Solemn professed cleric)

8. Gustave Frommherz (Postulant oblate)

Febr.23rd   9. Dom Maur Barreira de Alencar (Solemn professed cleric)

10. Adrian van Tongeren (Postulant lay brother)

11. Everard Mokveld (Postulant lay brother)

Nov 1st   12. Dom Sebastian Weber (Priest)

13. Dom Bertin Dehaese (Priest)

Nov. 23rd   14. Dom Mayeul De Caigny (Abbot)

Nov. 29th   15. Br. Joachim Schuler (Novice lay brother)

16. Br. Carloman Eckert (Novice lay brother)

1914:

March 20th   17. Br. Raphael Goemaere (Professed lay brother)

June 14th   18. Br. Ludger Nauer (Novice lay brother)

1915:

Jan. 1st	19. Br. Willibrord Luiten (Simple professed cleric)
	20. Br. Odo van der Heydt (Simple professed cleric)
May 30th	21. Br. Odilo van Tongeren (Simple professed cleric)
	22. Robert Boxruth (Choir postulant)
Aug. 10th	23. Dom Charles Verbeke (Priest)
	24. Br. Hugh van der Sanden (Simple professed cleric)
	25. Anthony Callaghan (Choir postulant)
Sept. 10th	26. Dom Anselm Romano (Priest)
	27. Br. Wilfrid Broens (Simple professed cleric)

All the above monks came from Bahia. However, at the same time, there was a high rate of withdrawals. Within a very short time, two returned to Bahia, six left, while three joined other Congregations. Such statistics tell a sorry story, indicating that life in Mount St. Benedict was proving difficult, if not impossible, for some. This was to remain a constant pattern for many years. The material structure of any monastery is built with bricks and mortar, but the spiritual, inner structure consists of its personnel. The founder of a monastery has to guarantee a solid structure at both levels. It is true that every monastery has its teething problems. Often these are of a financial or material kind, and, given time, can generally be overcome. But when the problem centres round the monks themselves, the solution is not so easy to find. Mount St. Benedict seems to have had more than its share of these latter problems. One of the biggest obstacles facing the early monks in Trinidad was that of language. Trinidad was an English colony, and English the predominant language spoken on the island. However, the monks who came from Bahia and elsewhere were for the most part non-English speaking. Even Dom Mayeul himself had to learn to speak this language. It is significant that the annals of the Mount, i.e. the official record of daily events in the monastery, from 1915 to 1921, are written in Portuguese. It is very likely that Portuguese was the language commonly spoken in the monastery during its first ten years of existence. One gets the impression that teaching English to the newly arrived monks was not a priority. There was so much else to fill their day, such as manual work and study. Without a common language in the community there could be no bonding and no unity. During these early days, one probably heard more German and Portuguese than English spoken on the Mount.

Another underlying problem was the climate of Trinidad. This was before the days of air-conditioning. Unlike in Bahia where most of their work happened inside, the monks were expected to do hard manual work on the various building projects, but also in the fields, under a boiling sun, while wearing their heavy black monastic habits. There is very little evidence of recreation or holiday breaks, while the daily time-table was quite severe by modern standards. All the evidence points to the fact that the monks, especially the younger ones, were sorely tested during these early days of Mount St. Benedict. It is no wonder there was such a high fall-out rate.

In spite of all the above-mentioned problems, the year 1915 saw increased activity in all areas of the monastery. While the contractors were busying themselves with erecting the guest and rest house, the monks were building a larger refectory and a Chapter Room, all running parallel to the church. This was a two-storied construction, with a number of parlours and a row of very small cells for the brothers and oblates, on the ground floor. During the construction of the refectory, Br. Joseph had an accident, falling from the roof and sustaining a fractured leg. He was taken unconscious in a buggy to the colonial hospital in Port of Spain, a journey of nearly two hours. Fortunately he recovered quickly, and was able to resume work within a few weeks. No sooner was the refectory completed than Dom Mayeul decided to enlarge the church, by joining the church with the refectory. This work was carried out by the lay brothers, helped by the clerics. One observer gave the following description of all this activity:

> *The young clerics were most of the time employed in some kind of manual labour, especially during the holiday time. Nearly all were competent painters, planters of cashew-nuts, makers of roads, etc. and all took part in the various works in progress. They could*

THE BRIDGE, SUPPORTING THE NEW WATER SUPPLY SYSTEM.
FIRST FROM LEFT IS DOM HUGH VAN DER SANDEN, APPOINTED IN 1923 BY DOM
MAYEUL AS HIS SUCCESSOR.
DOM HUGH WILL PLAY A VITAL ROLE IN THE FUTURE OF THE MONASTERY.

THE BRIDGE, HOW IT LOOKS NOW

be seen on the roof of the newly constructed buildings with a tar-brush, or along the main road with a pickaxe and wheelbarrow to open canals after rainfall. The year 1915 saw the erection of yet another kitchen with pantry and storeroom alongside the refectory, also the stables were built and a carriage house with cocoa drying roof.

However, the most important work for the year 1915 was the great water scheme. It is not easy to realize the amount of labour and outlay which was involved in this scheme. The pipe-line, which Br. Joseph had laid in the beginning of 1913, was fastened for the great part to the roots of trees, which provided a very primitive support. For the new water-scheme it was absolutely required to have independent supports and of greater durability. For this purpose second-hand rails were bought at three pounds sterling per ton. The pipes themselves were imported from U.S.A. The work of embedding the pipes involved some blasting of the rock, which was usually done at midday, when the community was at lunch. It happened one day that the community was assembled in the refectory, and Br. Willi-brord had gone out, as usual, to sound the bugle, so that everyone could take cover. That particular day it was a "lusty call to arms", and soon heavy explosions rebounded through the ravine with roll-ing echoes, soon followed by more explosions of similar strength, twelve of them in succession. The Abbot at the head table looked rather uneasy, but the greater part of the community thoroughly en-joyed the treat (Referring to the explosions as a cannon salute, Dom Odo added jokingly). It was January 27th, 1915, the birthday of Kaiser William II. The pipeline reached the monastery on June 1 1916, and the bridge was completed and blessed on November 16 of that same year. St. Maurus was chosen as its patron saint (Dom Odo, Early History of MSB, p.38-40).

Throughout 1915, three of the German monks (Dom Paul Dobbert, Bros. Ulric and Fridolin Frommherz) remained in the military internment camp of St. James. Their life was so unhappy and restricted, that they sought every means of finding a way out of their difficult situation. They were not helped by a very strict, in-deed, insensitive, letter, dated 19 September 1915, written by Dom Sebastian Weber, the prior, reminding them that they were monks, and were bound to live by the Rule of St. Benedict at all times:

Owing to the special circumstances in which you are living at present, as well as to your actual conduct in the confinement, our Rt. Rev. Lord Abbot Mayeul De Caigny, has thought proper to remind you, through my mediation, of some principles and rules by which you ought to guide yourselves in your recent condition (POS, Ben.).

The prior detailed, under six headings, how the monks were to conduct themselves in the prison camp. The German monks were so upset by this letter that they forwarded it to Archbishop Dowling, seeking his advice and help. There followed a lengthy correspondence between the archbishop and the German monks throughout November-December 1915. It seems that the archbishop was prepared to help Dom Paul Dobbert, and pay his passage to Bahia, but Dom Mayeul intervened to prevent this happening. In a letter to Archbishop Dowling, dated 26 November 1915, Dom Paul thanks him for *"the certificate of my leaving this archdiocese which I loved so very much"*. A week later, on 3 December 1915, Dom Paul tells the archbishop that Dom Mayeul has intervened to prevent him leaving the colony (Trinidad).

On 29th of last month I should leave the Colony. All was ready, but in the last moment I got a letter from the American Consul telling me that Dom Sebastian Weber came to his office and by order of the Lord Abbot, cancelled and nullified all arrangements I had made. It is the 4th time I am disappointed. Now I am in a worse position because the prior took away the money for my passage. I cannot understand why the Lord Abbot is doing so. I received his formal permission, and even an order from the Abbot Primate and another from the Abbot Visitator. I do not know why the Lord Abbot is putting these difficulties in my way. He always speaks to us about obedience, and he himself is not practising it towards his highest Superiors. I beg Your Grace's prayer for me, because I am badly touched by all that (POS, Ben.).

One cannot but feel sorry for Dom Paul. He had come to Trinidad from Bahia with the first group of monks. He soon became fluent in English and was a popular figure in the colony. For several years he served in the parishes of both Arouca and Caura, during which time he formed a close relationship with Archbishop Dowling. But once the war began, he found himself *persona non grata* with

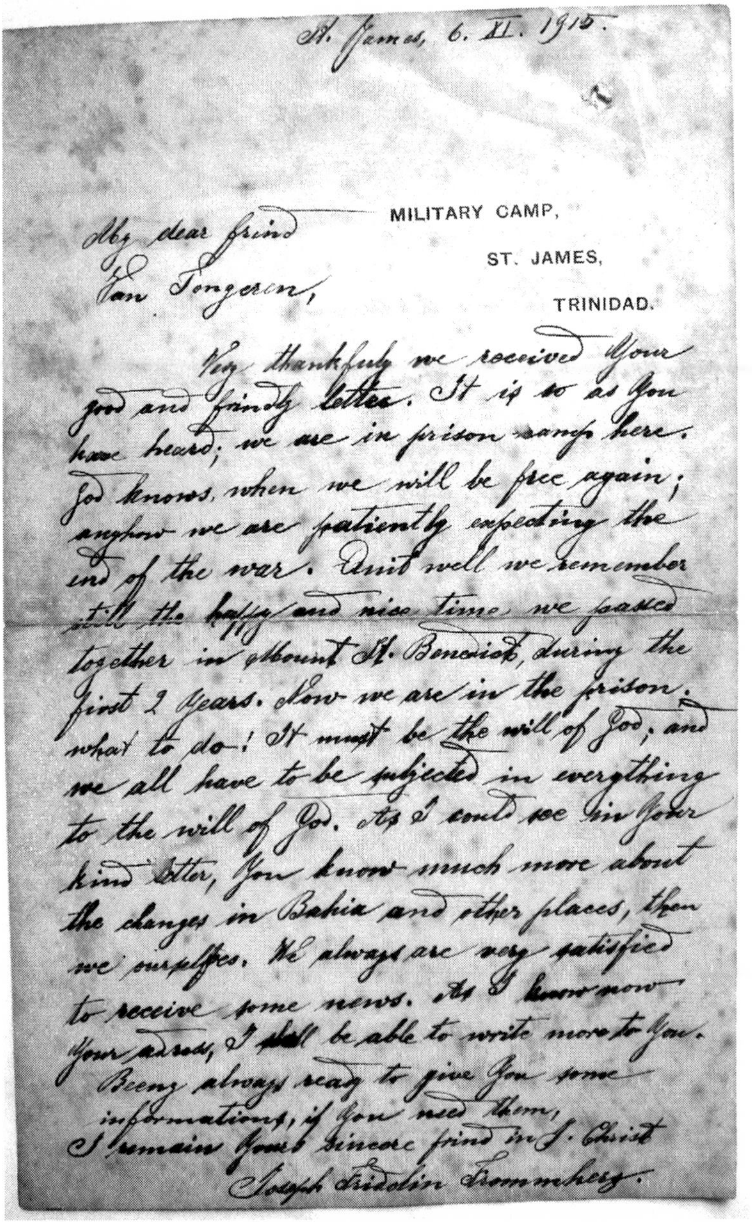

St. James, 6. XI. 1915.

MILITARY CAMP,
ST. JAMES,
TRINIDAD.

My dear friend
Van Tongeren,

Very thankfully we received Your good and friendly letter. It is so as You have heard; we are in prison camp here. God knows, when we will be free again; anyhow we are patiently expecting the end of the war. And well we remember still the happy and nice time we passed together in Mount St. Benedict, during the first 2 Years. Now we are in the prison; what to do! It must be the will of God; and we all have to be subjected in everything to the will of God. As I could see in Your kind letter, You know much more about the changes in Bahia and other places, then we ourselves. We always are very satisfied to receive some news. As I know now Your address; I shall be able to write more to You. Being always ready to give You some informations, if You need them, I remain Your sincere friend in J. Christ

Joseph Fridolin Frommherz.

LETTER FROM DOM FRIDOLIN FROMMHERZ,
WRITTEN FROM THE MILITARY CAMP ST JAMES

227

the colonial authorities. This meant he had to retire from active ministry, and subsequently was sent to the internment camp at St. James. The archbishop was very critical of Dom Mayeul's treatment of Dom Paul and found himself in a difficult situation. However, he succeeded eventually in getting Dom Paul his passage to La Vega, Caracas, Venezuela. In a long letter to Archbishop Dowling, dated 17 March 1916, Dom Paul thanks him for his certificate of good conduct, which guaranteed Dom Paul the protection of the Bishop of Caracas, who gave him a parish as soon as he arrived. Dom Paul had enough Spanish to take up his duties at once. He told the archbishop that:

> The Government grants me a small salary of 15 pesos (60 francs,) and so I am living here now in poverty, but satisfied to work again in the vineyard of the Lord, expecting an occasion to return to Brazil to my dearly beloved monastery of Bahia. If the two companions of mine (the two Frommherz brothers, still in the internment camp in Trinidad) could obtain their liberty, I would be too glad to receive them here in my house. I fear they will lose their vocation if they stay there at St. James for any longer time. I am here satisfied, but at every moment I remember the happy days I spent there in Trinidad in my parishes, first at Arouca and then at Caura. I loved that island and the people very much. And the monastery was so nearby, for any necessity, whereas here I am very isolated. How is Dom Ambrose and Dom Bertin and Dom Anselm and Mount St. Benedict? How many happy and also sad days all these names recall to mind! Thank you again and again, Most Rev. Lord Archbishop, for your kindness in coming so many times to see us, when I was interned, and where we were abandoned even by our own companions and Superiors (POS, Ben.).

Archbishop Dowling was likewise successful in arranging for the two Frommherz brothers to leave the internment camp in Trinidad and go to Caracas, where they were well received by the apostolic delegate. Dom Fridolin Frommherz was ordained to the priesthood in Caracas, on 23 September 1916, by the Internuncio (Cf. Letters of Dom Fridolin Frommherz to Dowling, Caracas 19 April 1916 and 24 September 1916, POS, Ben.).

All these arrangements by the archbishop were looked upon by Dom Mayeul as nothing more than a blatant interference into the affairs of the Mount.

On 25 April, 1916, another rather startling letter, making some very damaging accusations against Dom Mayeul, reached Archbishop Dowling. It was written by a monk of the Mount, Dom Bertin Dehaese, who at the time was working in the parish of Caura:

As for Abbot De Caigny, his conduct in our (i.e. Dom Ambrose and Dom Bertin) regard is incomprehensible. The letters we receive from him are contradictory. We have to be very prudent with Fr. Abbot, because sincerity hardly ever enters into his actions. The Church authorities in Brazil (Bahia) called him "the fabricating Abbot". Indeed, our supposedly diplomatic Abbot resorts to telling lies when such appears to serve his purpose. It is for this grave reason that I am unable to accept the orders of our Abbot, because I no longer have any confidence in him. Everywhere Abbot De Caigny is known as a liar. Your Grace can easily understand how painful it is for a young religious monk to live under an abbot of this temperament, and how we have to be very prudent in our dealings with him (POS, Ben.).

In general such accusations could be very damning. These calumnies about Dom Mayeul were addressed to Archbishop Dowling and show clearly the intrigues that were going on. In Rome however, the sad story of Dom Ambrose and Dom Bertin was already well known by the abbot primate and the abbot visitator. Soon after this, the Congregation for Religious, at the request of Abbot Primate von Stotzingen, released Dom Bertin and Dom Ambrose from their vows as Benedictines. The 'Rescript', the legal answer of a Pope to an inquiry, granting Dom Ambrose and Dom Bertin secularization status is dated 15 September 1916 (*Cf. S.C. De Religiosis, No. 1643/15*). Secularization is not considered and granted easily. Over the years many attempts had been made to convince Dom Ambrose and Dom Bertin to comply with the rules of the Benedictine Order. In vain, however, and only after many deliberations and considerations by the Roman authorities, was the secularisation granted. It was a sad day for the young foundation in Trinidad. Dom Ambrose, the first to arrive in Trinidad from Bahia in October 1912, had been the first superior of the Mount. In fact Dom Sebastian Weber, who had been superior of the mission in Angelim, south of Bahia, was slated to become the first superior of the Mount. When the first monks left for Trinidad Dom Sebastian was still occupied finishing some important tasks at Bahia. Dom

Sebastian, who had just recently returned to Bahia from Europe, where he had been quite successful in the recruitment of vocations, was still too involved with the new postulants. It was impossible for Dom Sebastian to join at that time the first monks in Trinidad. Hence Dom Ambrose was appointed as superior and given a chance to prove himself. Shortly after Dom Mayeul arrived in Trinidad (28 Nov 1913), a long letter dated 8 Dec 1913 from Dom Mayeul to the abbot primate explains in detail all the reasons and consider- ations why Dom Ambrose had not been retained as superior and replaced by Dom Sebastian who had also arrived in Trinidad in Nov 1913. It must not have been an easy decision for Dom May- eul considering that Dom Ambrose Vinckier was his direct cousin. Dom Mayeul left however the final decision in the hands of the abbot visitator as he wrote in his letter to the abbot primate:

> *In a very delicate way I appointed Dom Sebastian as prior and Dom Ambrose as subprior. He appreciated the fact that it was done in a open and delicate way but yet he (Dom Ambrose) became very angry, he wanted to leave immediately, he was going to ask for his dispensation,.... He was going to accuse me in Rome. Perhaps it would have been better in the given circumstances and considering good sense, to leave Dom Ambrose in the position of prior to avoid any vengeance. But I would have felt guilty for not having taken the right decision. I proposed Dom Ambrose to wait taking further actions and to wait for the visit of the Apostolic Abbot Visitator. I promised that I would submit to any final decision made by the Abbot Visitator (APR B1, 8 Dec 13).*

The fear for vengeance, as expressed in this letter, would unfor- tunately be proven to be warranted. This was the beginning of a long stressful and damaging period leading to the secularisation of Dom Ambrose. It is difficult to make a very good judgment on this matter, which may have been for a part a clash of strong personalities. The case of Dom Bertin is equally sad. He was a highly educated monk, who spoke fluent French, Portuguese and English. He had become a well-known figure, as well as a popular preacher, on the island of Trinidad, during the first two years of the foundation. The loss of these two monks to the community of the Mount was heavy. They were subsequently accepted into the diocese of Port of Spain by Archbishop Dowling. This was also the beginning of a long, very deplorable period. The secularized monks would use every occasion to make the life of Dom Mayeul more complicated and contribute to the disastrous year for Dom Mayeul in 1923. Dom Bertin would eventually be expelled from his parish by the parishioners and, being French, leave for Martinique, where he died.

Considering the frequent correspondence the abbot primate received, the Mount could have easily been perceived by Rome as a centre of tension. The majority of the monks however were quietly enhancing their spiritual life and contributing positively to the future of the Mount. One of these monks, Dom Odo, couldn't sit on the sideline any longer and watch silently. In 1915 he wrote a long letter to the abbot primate in Rome, explaining the moral pain Dom Mayeul was suffering. Here are a few extracts:

I only recently arrived in Trinidad at Mount St. Benedict. For two years and a half I was at San Sebastian Abbey at Bahia where I completed my novitiate and one year of religious study. I was happy there in the shadow of the old monastery among my Benedictine brethren. In Bahia they are holding Dom Mayeul in high regard. They always talk about him, always with a fraternal love. And if it would be permitted for a monk to have a wish, it would be the desire to be with Dom Mayeul. I was happy to arrive here and to see our Abbot and my community. I noticed immediately in how much pain our Abbot was. It is normal that there are difficulties in a new foundation but after a couple of days I had seen too much. It is because I don't want to lose my peace of mind and soul that I am writing you. I don't want to accuse my brothers but I can not tolerate any longer the attitude of a few of our members. They are in constant breach of the Benedictine rules. I know that all they wish to do is to make it difficult for our Abbot Dom Mayeul in and outside the monastery. Day by day we see their mysterious behaviour. I am writing you, our Rev Abbot Primate, also on behalf of Dom Willibrord, to put in your hands a just cause. Things can not continue as they are. We are convinced of your power by your word and your prayer (APR6 Dom Odo to Abbot Primate Feb 1915).

So thanks to the good spirit of the majority of the monks, in spite of the defections and misunderstandings, the monastery continued to flourish and grow. On 10 April 1916, the community acquired 37 acres of land at Guaico, in the ward of Turure. This place was soon afterwards christened "St. Placid's Farm". From the original 67 acres, the monastery grew within a few years to 600 acres, comprising 70000 cocoa bushes, 15000 coffee bushes, more than 1000 banana trees, without counting the innumerable fruit trees. By this time (1916) the monks had also developed a profit-making honey-business. Sometimes a single extraction brought in $2000 of excellent honey. The apiculture soon become famous and over the years proved to be a useful source of income. Another sign of activity was the construction of Mount Thabor, which was sufficiently advanced by 13 May 1916, making it possible for the first Mass to be said at an elevation of 1800 feet above sea-level. On 16 November 1916 the iron bridge, crossing the ravine at the back of the monastery was completed and blessed. It survives to this day (2012).

CHAPTER XI

Mission to the Hindus
& Other Pastoral Involvements

ONE OF THE PRINCIPAL reasons Dom Mayeul had chosen Trinidad, when the threatening persecution in Brazil led him to consider making a foundation on that island, was the thought of evangelising the 100,000 Hindus, who were said to reside there. From the very beginning of the foundation in Trinidad there was a strong missionary thrust, directed towards the Hindus. In his memoirs, Dom Mayeul often refers to the Hindus as "coolies", which is a term that is no longer acceptable, and used to describe the indentured 'workers', who came mostly from India to Trinidad in the second half of the 19th century. 30 May 1845 is reckoned as the date of the first arrival of these indentured 'workers' from India. The East Indians who came to Trinidad in the mid-19th century were treated as quasi-slaves by the planters. It took more than a century-and-a-half before the Hindus in Trinidad obtained full civil rights, and could claim their own cultural identity. On 30 May 1996, mainly under pressure from the United National Congress government, the first national holiday was celebrated in Trinidad, under the heading *Indian Arrival Day.*

The majority of Hindus, both men and women, left India for employment in Trinidad, under a five-year contract. They were guaranteed a free return passage when they had completed ten years of industrial residence in the colony, though they could also return to India at their own expense after five. The people who emigrated from India were essentially illiterate labourers and petty cultivators, who came from depressed rural areas and were looking for employment. The government in India insisted that 40 women would accompany every 100 men on each shipment. This last stipulation was important, not only to allow some Hindu men to marry Hindu women, but the presence of women on the plantation helped the community to retain a semblance of its cultural and social identity (*Cf. The Construction of an Indo-Caribbean Diaspora, Eds. Samaroo and Bissessar, U.W.I. 2004, pp. 6-7*). The system was state-sponsored and regulated, and well-documented. On paper, it seemed reasonable and good, but, unfortunately, the promises were seldom fulfilled.

Although slavery as such had been abolished throughout the British Empire in the early 19th century, the Indian indentured "workers" were in practice treated as slaves, especially by the planters. They were denied all political or social rights, could not vote and were treated as inferior beings by most of the people on the island. Their marriages were not recognized by the state for nearly a hundred years. As long as they were prepared to provide a settled pool of cheap labour, especially in the valuable and intensive sugar economy in Trinidad, it was difficult for them to improve their situation. It has been calculated that nearly 1.3 million Indian people were transported, under the indenture system, to the colonies of Natal, Mauritius, Guyana, Trinidad, Surinam and Fiji, between 1845 and 1916, when all such emigration ceased.

Life was very difficult for these immigrants, with very low pay and poor living conditions. They were forced to live in the countryside, where the infrastructure was either primitive or non-existent. The planters were determined to keep the Indians in the labour force at any cost, living apart from the other people on the island and forming their own ethnic ghettos. Their only consolation, or life-line, was the practice of their religion and fidelity to their cultural heritage. In the early days, they were too poor to build temples or places of worship, and in any case, they had not brought with them any priests or religious leaders, who would have provided some cultural support. Trinidad at this time was very English and very Protestant. The Hindus were looked upon as 'pagans', and deprived of the basic rights to education and civil liberties. One of their most serious restrictions was the refusal by government agents to allow the Hindus to cremate their dead. This was against all their religious instincts and traditions. They were forced to continue burying their dead until cremation was made legal in the 1930s. Any attempt on their part to break out of their mould was looked upon with suspicion by their masters. The Indians were often referred to as 'a people in-between', having no place in Trinidadian society.

Yet, in spite of, or because of, all these limitations, the Indians succeeded in maintaining much of their cultural heritage and identity. In the alien environment of Trinidad, they had no choice but to hold on to their traditional way of life. In any case, during those early days, no serious attempt was made, either by the government or the planters, to integrate the Indians into the already divided society on the island. They were treated everywhere as intruders and outsiders, while their language, religion, dress, food and social values were ridiculed *(Cf. Calcutta to Caroni and the Indian Diaspora. Eds. J.G. La Guerre & A.M. Bissessar, 25-6).*

Given the fact of human nature, this situation could not last forever. The first step towards granting Indians the possibility of settling in Trinidad came in 1859, when the Colonial Office offered the indentured Indians a grant of land, if they renounced their right to a free return passage home. This system of commuting return passages got under way in 1869, when the governor, Sir Arthur Gordon, offered 10 acres of Crown land as an alternative to every return passage. The earliest land grants in lieu of return passages were made at Couva and Pointe-a-Pierre. Gradually, with more and more Indians opting for either a land grant or a money payment, East Indian villages or settlements soon developed. The Indians immediately began farming their lands, growing rice, cocoa, maize, peas, etc., which they were able to sell in the open market. To begin with, they faced certain difficulties, such as the lack of proper medical facilities, the absence of proper transport, the poor conditions of the roads, and the fact that much of the land was swampy. Yet, by means of hard work, and by combining plots or lots of land, the East Indians succeeded in producing large quantities of cocoa, so that by the 1890s, the total value of the island's cocoa crop came to 23 million pounds. They then moved into sugar-cane planting, which proved even more profitable *(Cf. K.O. Laurence: "Indians as permanent Settlers in Trinidad before 1900", in Calcutta to Caroni, pp. 134-136).*

A further improvement in their economic situation came in the early 20th century, when many East Indians opted out of the agricultural business, and took up such skilled jobs as jewellers, chemists, shop-keepers, barbers, tailors etc. This diversity of economic activity meant that some individuals achieved considerable wealth, and gradually began to assert their right to enter into public life. By the year 1912, when the Benedictines arrived, the majority of the 130,000 Hindus in Trinidad had decided to stay on, encouraged by new opportunities for work and for improving their situation. From being temporary sojourners, they had become permanent settlers, and were accepted as part of the Trinidadian scene. The majority still followed their traditional Hindu religion, but were beginning to reach out to new ways of expressing and fulfilling their spiritual needs.

Following on his experience in Brazil with the mission in Angelim, which proved a complete failure, Dom Mayeul was determined to avoid making the same mistakes a second time. One of the principal difficulties the Benedictine monks faced in the Brazilian situation was that of communicating with the native people, who spoke their own language. After investigating the situation in Trinidad, Dom Mayeul discovered that while some Hindus spoke English, the majority normally conversed in their own language, Hindi. Therefore, in order to make a serious approach to the Hindus, the monk chosen for this mission would have to learn to speak Hindi. Dom Mayeul decided that he himself was too old to start learning Hindi, and chose Dom Sebastian Weber, the prior of the Mount from 1913-15, who had led the mission in Angelim, Brazil, to begin studying Hindi, and dedicate himself to making contact with the Hindu people.

The Hindus were by nature very religious, being drawn towards places which had an obvious spiritual association or appeal. Such a place was Mount St. Benedict, which soon attracted crowds of Hindus, who came there to pray or to talk with the monks. The brother porter, whose principal job was to welcome pilgrims to the monastery, had converted some time previously from Hinduism. He acted as a bridge between the Hindus and the monks, being happy to explain the rudiments of Catholicism to the pilgrims, before handing them over to Dom Sebastian for further instruction. After some time, these Hindus, who had come to know the monastery, invited Dom Sebastian to visit their homes. Many of them lived in the hamlet just below Mount St. Benedict, so that this became a convenient apostolate for the monks. Archbishop Dowling, who had always taken an interest in converting the Hindus, though without any great success, having heard of Dom Sebastian's work, nominated him "The Apostle of the Hindus" for the whole

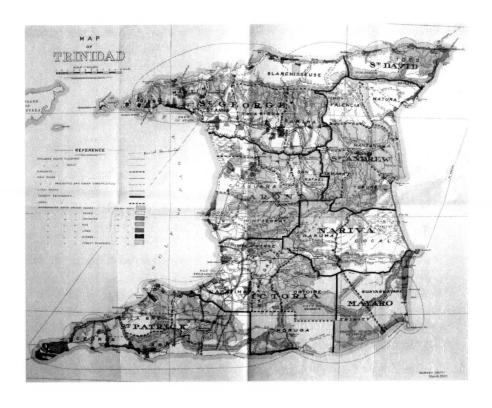

MAP OF TRINIDAD, SHOWING THE PARISHES, SENT TO THE ABBOT PRIMATE IN
ROME. CEDROS IS LOCATED IN THE LOWER LEFT CORNER.

island of Trinidad. Dom Sebastian was soon able to extend his attention to the Hindus who lived in Cedros, a parish served by the Benedictine monks, and at Chaguanas, where there were thousands of Hindus.

For his part, Dom Mayeul continued to take a personal interest in this mission to the Hindus, mainly through the parlour ministry, i.e., counselling and speaking with those who visited the monastery. He found that the Hindus showed considerable affiliation with the Christian religion, seeing many parallels with their own beliefs. But what gave the Mount a special appeal to them was the sanctuary to St. Benedict in the church. Some claimed that they had received favours by praying to St. Benedict, and looked upon his statue as having miraculous powers. Certainly the shrine to St. Benedict became a focal point for many Hindus who visited the monastery. Within a short time, some Hindu parents and grandparents were asking to have their children baptised. Traditionally they had a sincere belief in the powers of water to purify from sin, as is witnessed by the annual ritual bathing in the river Ganges, in India. Dom Mayeul explains the situation as follows in his memoirs:

Our Hindu pilgrims showed considerable sympathy towards our religion, and some parents were not opposed to their children being baptized. The reason for this, they said, was that the children, not born in India, were not strictly held to follow the Hindu religion. One old grandmother allowed her grand-children to be baptized, and ended by being baptised herself. Others of her extended family followed her example, and a total of some 40 Hindus were converted to Christianity. During and after the ceremony of baptism, which was performed in the monastery, the Hindus sang their own songs and danced with joy. The monks provided some delicacies and sweets, which added to the festivities. One day I received a visit from a Hindu priest, who said to me: "I wish to enter into your society. I do not practise usury, neither do I smoke or drink. Thus, there is no obstacle to my joining you and realizing my wish". He was surprised to hear me say that these conditions were not enough to grant him full acceptance into our religion (Vol. I, 257-8).

Dom Mayeul noted that Holy Week was a special time for the Hindus to come to Mount St. Benedict. They found Good Friday very attractive, and the Adoration of the Cross a moment to relish. However, one wonders how much of the Catholic religion they actually understood. Nonetheless, during these early days of Mount

St. Benedict, the monastery held some kind of appeal for them, mainly as a place of worship. They had not yet built their own temples in the Tunapuna, St. Augustine area, and being religious by nature, needed some holy place in which to worship. Over the coming years, Dom Sebastian continued his mission to the Hindus, though the number of Hindus who became Catholics was never very high. Dom Mayeul calculated that out of some 130,000 Hindus in Trinidad in 1920, only 5000 had become Catholic

There was one problem which the monks had to deal with, when faced with crowds of Hindu pilgrims, who visited the monastery and especially the church. This related to the valuable objects in the church, such as the precious reliquary in front of the statue of St. Benedict, or other rich ornaments, donated by some wealthy people. The Hindu women were greatly attracted to anything made of gold or silver, with a view to adorning their arms, necks and legs. Some of them apparently found it difficult to resist taking any valuable objects they came across, whether in a church or on someone's person, believing there was nothing wrong in this. Dom Mayeul writes in his memoirs of a certain Hindu woman, who tried to snatch his pectoral cross, and was quite surprised when he resisted. Resulting from such experiences, the monks had to take certain precautions to protect their valuables. It must be said, however, that the vast majority of Hindu pilgrims behaved themselves admirably, and only brought honour to themselves and the monastery.

Another area of ministry, to which the Benedictines were forced to give their attention, was dealing with real or supposed possession by the Devil. A cross-section of Trinidadians, not just Hindus, came to the Mount and spoke of their experiences with the 'powers of darkness', of a spiritual world beyond the grave. Archbishop Dowling appointed Dom Sebastian Weber as the diocesan exorcist, the priest who could be called on by those who believed they were possessed by evil spirits. It took some time for the monks to familiarize themselves with this situation, and to accept the fact that Trinidad was a country where superstition and folk magic were part of everyday life. The word used to describe the use of sorcery and witchcraft was *Obeah*, a long-standing tradition for healing, helping, and bringing people luck in love and money. There were various levels of *Obeah*, ranging from voodoo to belief in ghosts. Almost from the first moment he became involved in pastoral work on the island, Dom Mayeul was confronted with the ever-present reality of witchcraft, superstition and sorcery. He wrote as follows in his memoirs about his own experience in this domain:

From the first moment of my arrival on this island, I was amazed to hear people speaking frequently of these matters, which they commonly called "Obeah". The newspapers reported cases, which had come to the notice of the police, or were brought before the courts. It was evident that these practices of "Obeah" were usually done secretly by people interested in making money, who played on the simple beliefs, or gullibility, of the people. In all my life, outside of Trinidad, I had never heard anyone speak of "spirits" under the names of 'Jumbies", "Douens" etc., and of their supposed relationships with human beings. For me, it was beyond belief. Yet, so many people did in fact live under the constant fear of evil spirits (Vol. I, 261).

Dom Mayeul then cites several cases of diabolical possession he had personally experienced, and how it had been necessary to call on the services of Dom Sebastian Weber. Apparently, each time Dom Sebastian was thus involved, he had first to contact the archbishop and obtain his approval. In several letters to Archbishop Dowling, Dom Sebastian describes his experiences at exorcising the devil *(Arch. POS)*.

Dom Mayeul had to deal personally with several cases of diabolical manifestation. Those who came to the monastery seeking relief from their diabolical experiences were mostly the so-called 'pagans'. It was these very pagans, mostly Hindus, who came to the monastery in their dire need, believing that the monks had some hidden powers over the forces of evil. None of the founding monks of the Mount had anticipated such pastoral encounters, which became a constant factor in their lives during those early years. They found this work of helping people with their problems very tiring, if not exhausting. Dom Mayeul wrote in his memoirs about the long hours he had to spend in the parlour:

In spite of all the obstacles, the people visited our shrine in ever growing numbers. Soon, it became necessary to organise special trains, and from every corner of the island, buses brought large contingents of pilgrims to the foot of our mountain. People came from neighbouring islands, and even from the continent (South America), and often without distinction of their beliefs or faith. Catholics came to the "Mount", along with Protestants, Moslems, Buddhists and pagans. These long sessions lasted each day from 7.00 a.m. to midday, and again from 1.00 p.m. until 6.00. Over time, I began to suffer from bad headaches, as well as migraine and vertigo, to such an extent that I feared I might be getting Meningitis. At other times, I became paralysed in my legs, and was forced to retire to bed. Still, I had to soldier on as bravely as I could, until such time as the number of priests increased. Eventually, I was able to reduce my work load with pilgrims in the parlour to four days a week. This left me free to deal with my correspondence, which was increasing day by day, and eventually led to my employing 2 or 3 monks as secretaries to reply to the great number of letters we receive constantly (Vol. II, 175).

This is one of the first clear indications we have of Dom Mayeul suffering health problems while at the Mount. Life at the Mount during these early years (1915-19) was physically exhausting for everyone. The monks had to endure a climate, which fluctuated between great heat and high humidity. There was too much work to be done and too few hands to help. It was truly heroic. None of the monks was allowed to remain idle during these early days. Apart from his parlour work, Dom Mayeul had to give a weekly spiritual conference to the community, and daily instructions on the monastic rule to the novices and clerics. Then he had the oblates, mostly women, whose spiritual welfare he had to care for.

Our oblates held a monthly reunion in the "Mount", and made their spiritual exercises (Retreat) there. I was responsible for giving them their ascetical conferences, which helped many to lead a more intense spiritual life, while for others it proved the stirring of a religious vocation. Some of these latter were to join the Benedictine sisters in the Abbey of Jouarre, in France. "Mount St. Benedict" thus became, by a double title, a veritable sanatorium, where the needs of body and soul found their respective needs and satisfaction (Vol. II, 176).

On top of all these activities, he shouldered the day-to-day responsibilities of organising the monastery, with its daily round of choir-work (Opus Dei), the parishes, the pilgrimage to St. Benedict, the different building programmes etc. Along with every other member of the community, he never had a moment to relax. There is reason to believe that he drove others as hard as he drove himself. He saw every situation from the viewpoint of a superior, and showed little or no empathy with the problems of those monks, who bore the heat of the day and the fatigue of hard manual work.

His attitude towards his monks bordered on that of aloofness, and it made others believe that he was insensitive to their feelings. There is good reason to think that he remained somewhat on the fringe of his community, excepting, of course, the times he joined the monks for prayer in choir and meals in the refectory. Later (1918-1923), when he took up residence in Mount Thabor, he became more and more cut off from his community.

CHAPTER XII

The Last Years of the War and After

THE WAR YEARS brought many unforeseen problems to the Mount. Apart from the embarrassing question of the internment of the German-born monks as prisoners of war, the community was virtually cut off from the rest of the world, especially from Europe. Travel to Europe was suspended between 1914 and 1918, although there was an erratic postal service to non war-zones in Europe. All this forced the monks to adopt an inward-looking attitude to their various problems. It also led Dom Mayeul to take a more independent approach to his decision-making. Even when he could write to, or receive letters from the abbot primate, there was always a lengthy delay in getting a reply. There were no telephones available for transatlantic calls. This forced him to consult more than previously his immediate local superior, Archbishop Dowling, as is evidenced by their extensive correspondence at this time. This was very unfortunate, as their relationship was often strained. At no time did they become intimate or on first name terms. The two burning questions: the German prisoners, and the servicing of the parishes, proved breaking points on more than one occasion.

These four years (1914-1918) were pivotal, if not vital, for the new foundation. It was a time of consolidation and expansion, and of making hard decisions. However, the shadow of the war, and the uncertainty of how long it would last, hung over these pioneering years of the Mount. The monks had to live within the limits of their small island, depending on their own resources and initiatives. They were forced to use local material for their building needs, which explains why some of the additions to the monastery at this time were of poor quality. Their financial resources were also limited. Any further subsidies they might have expected from their mother-house, Bahia, had been postponed by virtue of the agreement made by the General Chapter in 1915, which declared the Mount to be autonomous, i.e. self-supporting, and that any further payments made to Trinidad by Bahia would be decided by Rome. It would take until 1920 before this issue on the payments was put to rest. Matters were made all the more complicated, in that the monks themselves remained a divided community, especially in language and in ethnic (national) groupings. Another cause of division was the fact that half the community spent their time outside the monastery in the parishes, while the other half remained at home, holding the fort, as it were, and waiting for a better day.

Given the difficult conditions under which they were forced to operate, there is no doubt that they faced many personal problems as they adjusted to life in Trinidad. Most of them had spent their formative monastic years in Bahia, a city of a hundred churches, where the abbey buildings, and especially the church, were large and magnificent. In Bahia they had a splendid Chapter Room, a large refectory and other such common rooms, while the monastic cells were unusually spacious. These cells had originally been designed to accommodate not just one monk, but also his slave, who had an alcove in the same room. Although slavery had been abolished in Brazil at the end of the 19th century, the monks of Bahia inherited these large rooms. No such luxury existed in Trinidad, where the monks had either to share rooms, or to occupy tiny and almost unfurnished cells. In practice, it meant they were forced to resign themselves to a life of poverty and deprivation. Some of the monks became discouraged, and asked to be allowed to return to Bahia, or to be secularized. This proved to be another serious breaking point for the community, and one which Dom Mayeul found difficult to resolve. It may also explain the almost frenetic building programme, which continued at the Mount throughout the war years and after. Dom Mayeul hoped that he might save the situation, by keeping his monks busy. He set in motion a programme of building, with a view to providing better accommodation, while the property was continually in a state of expansion. Thus, in November 1917, he bought the neighbouring San Miguel estate, consisting of 422 acres, from M. J. de Silva. This doubled the size of the monastic holding. Within a short time of purchasing the San Miguel estate, the monks started keeping bees. They discovered that their hillside property could produce excellent honey. The enterprise became a commercial success overnight, and helped to swell the coffers of the community. In time, the monks became famous all over the island for their honey.

Dom Mayeul was aware that the lay brothers were the backbone in the community, being happily employed in diverse and worthwhile occupations. Any grumbling or complaint came from a small number of clerics and priests, and continued for several years. At one point (in October 1915) Dom Mayeul made a flying visit to Panama, to investigate the possibility of making a Benedictine foundation there, to house some of his disaffected monks. He wrote at length of this Panama venture in his memoirs *(Vol. I, 244-248)*, but his narrative only serves to prove how he could get sidetracked at times, when dealing with the growing problems at the Mount. The Panama idea came to nothing, although Dom Mayeul enjoyed his trip by boat to Puerto Rico, Colombia, and Panama. Throughout the early months of 1916, he spent much of his time developing Mount Thabor, the upper monastery. This ambitious project took four years to complete, starting with a chapel and the abbot's wing, and followed by the rest of the large castellated structure. During this time, work stopped on the buildings in the lower monastery. The decision to build this immense structure was an unfortunate and ill-advised one, which in the long run proved to be the undoing of Dom Mayeul.

From August 1916 to February 1918, Dom Mayeul found himself facing a new, and more personal, experience. It concerned a young Jewish Russian lady, Edith Dunaew (nee Donnerberg) who became infatuated with him *(Vol. I, 272-276)*. She was the wife of Nicholas Dunaew, a Russian aristocrat, born in Moscow on 26 May 1884, who had fled Russia under Czar Nicholas II. He was also Jewish, and a future play-wright and movie-star. Edith was born in St. Petersburg in 1893, of a German father and Russian mother. She lost both her parents before she was five years old, and was then adopted by an uncle, who took her to Germany, where she received an excellent education, though without any religious input. She was a brilliant linguist, speaking fluent Russian, German, French and English, and she also had the elements of Greek and Latin. But her main talent was writing. Before she was 21, she had published three novels and two books of poetry. However, her personal life was rather bohemian, and she spent much of her time travelling.

She met Nicholas Dunaew in Paris, and soon afterwards they were married in London. They decided to emigrate to the United States, and by early 1914 had settled in New York. While Edith attended Columbia University and graduated in philosophy, Nicholas studied art and the cinema. Within a short time, Nicholas found himself offered work as a film-producer and actor, which brought him to Hollywood. Edith, however, remained in New York. During the winter of 1915-1916, she took a long vacation in Barbados, hoping to do some writing. She lodged in a boarding-house, where she met the Wharton family, from Trinidad. This was the beginning of a deep friendship between Edith and one of the Wharton girls, Agnes, who was of the same age. The Whartons were frequent visitors to the Mount, and Dom Mayeul had become Agnes' spiritual director. It is not surprising that Edith soon decided to bring Edith into contact with Dom Mayeul. The first time Dom Mayeul heard about Edith Dunaew was in a letter he received from Agnes Wharton, written from Barbados, dated 9 August 1916:

> *There is a Russian lady staying in a boarding-house close to us Madame Dunaew is an author, and is quite young, twenty-five; but it seems such a pity that she has no religion, because some of her theories are grand. I am very fond of her, and she is, I think, a lot fond of me. From the very first instant I have felt that I would like her to come into touch with you. What is still stranger is that it is not at all unlikely to happen, as she hopes to visit Trinidad shortly. She belongs to what is known as the artistic world and writes about it. Why I should speak so much to you of this lady I scarcely know myself. Perhaps it is that some good will come of it (St. Leo, Dom Mayeul Papers).*

By mid-October 1916, Edith had moved to Trinidad and was staying with the Whartons. Agnes wrote again to Dom Mayeul on 22 October, saying that Edith had arrived in Trinidad, and would like to accompany her (Agnes) to the Mount, to meet Dom Mayeul. At what stage, if ever, Dom Mayeul learnt that Edith was Jewish, we do not know, as the fact is never mentioned in any of the extant correspondence.

On 26 October, Agnes and Edith went to see Dom Mayeul and stayed in the guest house. Edith was fascinated by the monastery, the monks and the scenery, but especially by Dom Mayeul, who took time off from parlour work to speak with her. On returning home after this visit, Agnes Wharton wrote to Dom Mayeul saying:

> *Your extreme kindness to ma chere grande petite Russe and my-self during our visit was delightful and most enjoyable. Madame Dunaew likes you very much, and has already talked frequently of her future visits to the Mount. Father Abbot, you must be storming heaven with your prayers, for there is a strange attraction drawing Madame to the Mount and especially to Thabor. We would both be much obliged if you would let us know what arrangements are to be made for our board and occupation of a bedroom in the guest house for a fortnight. Madame Dunaew seems anxious for the quiet, free life of your dear Mountain home. She has asked me to enclose her letter to you as well* (St. Leo, A. Wharton to Dom Mayeul, 27 Oct. 27, 1916).

Dom Mayeul was thrilled with Edith's letter, and replied to her, in French, on 29th October 1916:

> *Madame, Your letter, which I read with great pleasure and interest, is the first, which will be followed by a thousand others! I am so happy to be able to add a little drop of happiness, which God has in store for you, and of which your visit to our Thabor is but the dawn. The calm you found here of which you speak, after all your restlessness and anxieties, can only lead to peace of soul and happiness. As regards your coming visit, I have already spoken about it to your dear and good friend (Agnes). Believe me, my home is your home. Thus, come and enjoy the pure air of our Mountains as much as you like. It will give me great pleasure to speak with you and have an exchange of ideas. Later, I will read with pleasure your novels and your other writings* (St. Leo, Dom Mayeul Papers).

From the first moment of their meeting, Dom Mayeul became infatuated with his Russian visitor, finding in her a kind of soul sister, with whom he could discuss so many things. They were both interested in philosophy and literature. They continued to write to each other, and whenever Edith visited the Mount, they had long discussions about literature and religion. On 15 December, 1916, Dom Mayeul wrote a long letter to Edith, and jokingly ended the last paragraph with these words:

For the life of me, I just don't know what kind of fairy you are, to make me write four large pages; something I have never done before for anyone (St. Leo, Dom Mayeul Papers).

He continued to write long letters to Edith throughout 1917, while she spent more and more time in the Mount. By then, he had dropped the more formal "Madame" and addressed her as "Edith". She began reading some of the books in the monastery library, one of which Dom Mayeul mentions in his memoirs, namely the four volumes of Auguste Nicolas: *"The Essence of the philosophy of Christianity" (Vol. I, 273).* It seems that, under the guidance of Dom Mayeul, she began a very extensive and demanding programme of reading in Catholic theology, as well as some of the Fathers of the Church, such as St. Augustine. She also succeeded in reading the *"Epistles of St. Paul"* in Latin. Whether she was able to digest all this is another matter. One gets the impression that she overworked herself intellectually. Between 1916 and 1917, while in Trinidad, she wrote a 500-page novel in German, entitled *"Modern Pagans".* The heroine of the book is called Tamara. Dom Mayeul believed this book was based on her personal experiences of life in Russia, Germany and the United States. As no copies of this book, or any other written by Edith, seem to have survived in the archives of either St. Leo Abbey or the Mount, it is interesting to get Dom Mayeul's views of the novel in question. He wrote as follows to Edith on 2 May 1917:

I have just finished reading some pages of the manuscript of your novel. If I am not mistaken, Tamara is none other than you Edith, who no doubt you recognize better than I can. Poor child, she has suffered so much. Her beautiful soul was worthy of a more honourable destiny. Her faults are the result of her having been raised in a particular milieu. She deserves a happier future, in keeping with her own worth. I have no idea how the novel ends, if, indeed, you give it a conclusion. But I hope it will be as morally uplifting as it will be logical and literary, given your own particular talent for such things. In short, during your next visit to "the Mount", we will discuss your novel, and the Philosophy of Christianity. This twofold study will be completed by another, because all true psychology leads to Christ. You speak to me of your melancholic ideas, but I implore you, please do not entertain such things. You are not living

under the Russian skies, which you describe so well, but in the trop-
ics: Heaven is here, clear, brilliant and joyful. Don't forget the little
prayer I taught you, and the other things you promised. If Tamara
had had other parents, she would have become a little saint. It is still
not too late to become one (St. Leo, Dom Mayeul Papers).

Edith was a complex character, an intellectual, and somewhat out of place in Trinidad. Considering that she spoke German, she had spent most of her life in Germany, and that her stay in Trinidad co-incided with the 1914-18 war, some people took her for a German spy. They blamed the Wharton family for introducing her to the monastery. Such a suggestion was contradicted by the fact that she was travelling on an American passport, and that she had turned her back on Germany before the war. It was said by others that she only took an interest in the Catholic religion in order to ridicule it in her books. But, as her books were written in German, no one could understand them anyway. Others frowned on the relationship between Agnes Wharton and Edith Dunaew, and intimated that they were lesbians. Edith certainly presented an enigma to many on the Mount. There may have been an element of jealousy among the other women (oblates) living on the Mount, who resented Dom Mayeul giving so much of his time and attention to her. There was also the question of the monastic enclosure, from which women should have been excluded. Edith visited Dom Mayeul in Mount Thabor many times, which suggests that Thabor was not part of the enclosure at this time. However, in the light of the action taken by Archbishop Dowling some years later (in 1923), when he ac-cused Dom Mayeul of allowing women there and violating the en-closure, the visits of Edith and Agnes to Thabor, in 1916-18, left much to be desired, and were, to say the least, indiscreet.

In order to get a full picture of the relationship between Edith, Agnes and Dom Mayeul we would need to have the complete three-way correspondence, during the years 1916-18. Unfortunately, there are some gaps. We have most of the letters written by Agnes to Dom Mayeul, and also the letters from Edith to Agnes. We have some of the letters written by Dom Mayeul to Edith, and five let-ters written by Edith to Dom Mayeul between 14 December 1916 and 1 March 1917. But many questions have to go unanswered. One important piece of information we get from the letters of Edith to Agnes, relates to Edith's deteriorating health throughout

1917. She writes regularly for supplies of pills and medication. She complains, in letter after letter, of not sleeping, having headaches and being tired. This condition continued for a long time, and suggests either she was suffering from meningitis, or had some serious brain problem. Dom Mayeul encouraged her to work as hard as ever, and only came to realize the true situation when it was too late. Another strange fact that emerges from the existing correspondence is Edith's constant demand for supplies of food. In many of her letters, written from the guest house at the Mount, she speaks of being hungry, and asks Agnes to send her butter, bars of chocolate and tins of biscuits. It seems that these delicacies were not only for herself, but also for Dom Mayeul. Several times she mentions that the biscuits were intended as a present for Dom Mayeul, which she would bring up to Thabor at her next visit. During most of the latter half of 1917, and up to February 1918, Edith seems to have been on her own at the Mount, as Agnes was forced to remain at home in Port of Spain, nursing her mother and sister Ruth, both of whom were ill for several months.

Throughout the final nine months Edith was staying at the Mount (May 1917-February 1918), the question of her becoming a Catholic must have arisen. However, her case was a difficult one, seeing that she had no religion when she arrived at the Mount. Dom Mayeul undoubtedly used their time together to speak of God, while at the same time he prompted her to read some religious books, including the Bible. But it was a slow process, and Edith had many things on her mind, especially her own writings. At no time did Dom Mayeul give up on her becoming a Catholic. He could only wait and hope. However, there was one side of Edith which he never discusses or discloses, namely the fact that she was manic depressive. This becomes evident from the few of her poems, written in German, which have survived. One such poem is entitled "Karma", another "Mondlicht", and the most revealing of all, "Finale". They speak of death and suicide, using very morbid language. While the extant poems are not dated, one feels that they were written during her time at the Mount. As they were found among the Papers of Dom Mayeul one has to presume that he had seen them, though he does not seem to taken them seriously. Had he suspected she was so obsessed with death, he surely would have taken steps to save her from herself. Perhaps he only read her poem

"Finale" after her death. It is a long poem, but the last five lines will give some idea of its message:

> *I played with sensual highs, love and duty and morals.*
> *I played with loyalty, with dreams and death.*
> *I was so tired, so tired like a sick tortured child.*
> *All I wanted was death, death now and only death,*
> *As the last and deepest pleasure (MSB, Dom Mayeul Papers).*

Throughout her time in Mount St. Benedict, Edith seems to have hidden these gloomy thoughts of death from Dom Mayeul, and continued to read the books on the Catholic faith and philosophy recommended to her. What brought her round to taking a more serious look at the Catholic faith was her interest in the liturgy. She found the religious ceremonies at the Mount, especially on solemn Feast Days, both moving and inspiring. She may have remembered some of the splendid Russian Orthodox ceremonies when she was very young. This experience led her to discover prayer, which in turn brought her into touch with God. How far she discovered all this by herself it is difficult to say, but the climax came in September 1917, when she wrote on the back of a holy picture-card, in her own blood, the following words in French: *"Mon Dieu, je veux vous aimer toujours "* (*My God, I always wish to love you*). She signed it *"E.D"* and added the date; *"20. IX. 17"*. Some years later, Agnes Wharton wrote the same words in French, and also in her own blood, on the same card, and signed it: *"A.W."* adding the date: *"26.3.19"*. Dom Mayeul kept this particular card, inserting it in his memoirs (*Vol. II, 175*).

Dom Mayeul gives a detailed account of Edith's final days in his memoirs:

> *What gave me encouragement was her deep sincerity, her serious study of our religion, her love of our holy ceremonies, and the spirit of prayer which she finally attained. Her health declined little by little, which surprised me, and one day she told me that her days were numbered. There were ominous signs of her deterioration, which came to a head in February 1918. At that moment, I asked her if she had any doubts concerning our faith. When she replied that she had no doubts, I suggested she should not postpone her decision. I also told her that she should not become a Catholic to please me, but rather to please God. I feared lest some human*

EDITH DUNAEW,
HER PICTURE IN THE MEMOIRS VOLUME II

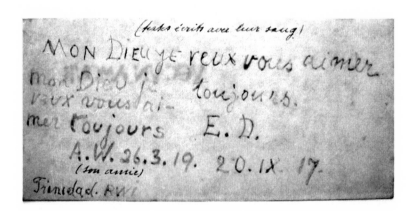

THE LITTLE CARD WITH THE TEXT WRITTEN IN HER BLOOD

consideration would mar the purity of her conversion. Then, with great seriousness, she looked at me with her beautiful eyes, and said to me after a few moments of reflection: "I have decided".

I prepared her for her abjuration, and the date for her reception into the Catholic faith was fixed for Holy Week. But, during the night of 18 February, she suddenly fell very ill, and asked the housekeeper of the guest house to call me immediately, so that she could receive baptism. "I wish to die a Catholic", she repeated several times. When I arrived, she seemed to have lost consciousness. I immediately called the doctor, and then proceeded to baptise her. At that moment she became calm. During her last moments, I recited acts of faith, hope and love, of contrition and conformity to the Will of God. The doctor came, but he could do nothing. She died the following morning (Vol. I, 275-6).

For reasons which we can only guess, in January 1917 Dom Mayeul applied to the government for permission to have a private burial ground at the Mount. Was it a coincidence, or did he have some premonition of Edith's pending death? In any case, a suitable site was chosen and the cemetery blessed by Dom Mayeul on 2 November 1917. Thus, when on 19 February 1918 Edith died, Dom Mayeul approached the local authorities, who gave him permission to bury her in the new monastery cemetery. According to Dom Mayeul, Edith had already chosen a plot for her own grave and had indicated the spot to Agnes Wharton *(Vol. I, 276)*. We have a photograph of her grave, taken soon after she was buried. Unfortunately, in the years after, her tomb and grave have been overbuilt by another tomb. Her funeral was a large affair, attended by the entire monastic community, and also many pilgrims. These latter had come to know and admire Edith, especially during Lent, when she showed such reverence and prayerful recollection, at the daily recitation of the Stations of the Cross. Edith's husband was not in attendance at the funeral, but Dom Mayeul composed a memorial card, in Latin, which he sent to the family. This gave a short account of her life, with quotations from the Bible and the Rule of St. Benedict. Also quoted in the memorial card, in red print, were the same words, which she had written in her blood. In concluding his account of Edith's time in the monastery and her death, Dom Mayeul wrote: *"Such is the history of the First Flower in our cemetery"(Vol. I, 276).*

It is only right that the last word on Edith should come from one of the Whartons. On 21 February 1918, two days after Edith's death, Mrs. Emma Wharton wrote to Dom Mayeul as follows:

It will seem strange for me to write to you about Edith, you, who knew her better than I did perhaps, for to you she poured out her soul and waited for your verdict. Poor Edith! How she loved and believed in you. Let me thank you for all you have done for her. She has no one here but us, to do so, and I know that she would have liked to thank you, for you have saved her. Who would have thought that Edith, brought up as she was, mixed in society of the artistic world as she had been, would some day find herself on Mount St. Benedict, learning to disdain the world every day more and more, and end her days there so peacefully. She often used to say that she wished to know no one but the Abbot and ourselves. Poor child, how she must have suffered. Her end has been the subject of meditation to me. After the funeral, I wanted to say a few words to you, but it was too late and you must have been so tired. Today is another sad day for us. Mr. Baker, the American Consul, is coming in a few minutes to take an inventory of her things; poor Agnes is in such a state. God willed everything to be so and we thank Him (St. Leo, Dom Mayeul Papers).

On the very day that the war ended, 11 November 1918, Dom Mayeul was received in audience by Archbishop Dowling. The latter commented on the result of the war by saying: *"I would never have expected it, or thought it possible!" (Vol. II, 175).* This remark implied that he had expected the Germans to win. In Ireland, many were pro-German during the war. Clearly the archbishop, being Irish, was also pro-German, a fact which would not have appealed to Dom Mayeul, who supported the Allies. Nonetheless, on this same occasion the archbishop made Dom Mayeul a member of his private council, though he continued his policy of remaining aloof. Whenever he was invited to a religious celebration on the Mount, the archbishop declined to attend. There was much dismay, indeed, consternation, in the monastery on 3 June 1917, when the first two Benedictine monks were ordained priests. It was taken for granted that they would be ordained in Mount St. Benedict, following an old Benedictine tradition. However, the archbishop insisted that the ceremony be held in the cathedral in Port of Spain. This decision of the archbishop was evidence of a noticeable lack of cordiality in all his dealings with the monks of Mount St. Benedict. Sadly for the Benedictine monks, this remained a very disturbing factor throughout Dom Mayeul's time as superior. It would seem, on the face of it, to have been a personal thing between Dom Mayeul and the archbishop, and neither party was prepared to meet the other halfway.

On another level, the success of the Benedictines in attracting such crowds to the Mount, caused some jealousy among the clergy in general in Trinidad. Whether the archbishop was reflecting this 'envy', or exercising his genuine pastoral duty, it is hard to say. It is certain, however, that Archbishop Dowling, during these early days of the Mount, failed to understand or appreciate the Benedictine traditions, or their way of life. This was evident in his refusal to grant faculties (permission) for hearing confessions to all the monk-priests at the Mount, as was the custom in other European monasteries. He maintained that two or three priest-monks could cope with the pastoral needs of all the pilgrims visiting the Mount. Likewise, his attitude towards the appointment and management of parishes, entrusted to the Benedictine monks, ran contrary to all monastic traditions, and blatantly contravened the Constitutions of the Brazilian Congregation. Even when Rome ordered him to respect the Benedictine traditions in this matter, he refused to comply.

Throughout the last years of the war, Dom Mayeul indicated that he was anxious to visit Europe as soon as hostilities ceased. He had, however, to wait until 29 June 1919, before he could realize this wish, mainly because of travelling restrictions. He had several reasons for making a journey to Europe: (i) to meet the new Pope, Benedict XV, and obtain from him some privileges in favour of the Mount and its pilgrims; (ii) to recruit some candidates from Holland; (iii) to visit Buckfast Abbey, in Devonshire, England, whose monks were building, with their own hands, the abbey church. He planned to send one of his monks, Br. Gabriel, to Buckfast, to study the practical side of architecture, in view of their own building needs. The abbot of Buckfast (Dom Anschar Vonier), readily agreed to his request, and Br. Gabriel spent a very fruitful year in Buckfast.

Dom Mayeul arrived in France at the beginning of July, 1919, and went first to Lourdes, thus fulfilling his wish to pray at the grotto where Our Lady had appeared to Bernadette in 1858. He then visited Holland, and succeeded in obtaining several candidates for Trinidad. After that he travelled to Belgium, but was appalled at the widespread destruction of villages and towns, caused by the war, especially in Flanders, his home province. His family suffered much from the material point of view. He was relieved to find that his youngest brother, Alois, survived unharmed, being simply thrown on the ground, when shells fell in his proximity. However, one of his nieces had not been so lucky. She was killed by an exploding shell during one of the last battles with the retreating Germans, while distributing apples to the allied soldiers who were advancing. The destruction scenes Dom Mayeul witnessed at this time in Belgium remained with him for the rest of his life, and deepened his attachment to his native Flanders. Apparently Dom Mayeul was well aware of the importance of using the press for the sake of the monastery's public relations. In Oct 1919, The Port-of-Spain Gazette reported extensively on Dom Mayeul's visit in Europe: *"Lord Abbot De Caigny in Europe. What he is doing for the monastery"*. The article expanded on the fact that Br. Raphael was studying cheese and butter making at a Trappist monastery near Ypres, the purchase in Holland of a new state of the art cooking stove, and much more:

> *He (Dom Mayeul) was more than grieved to witness the wanton destruction (of the war) on all sides of the country, but more so of his native village, half of the extent of which he was absolutely unaware, and the facts which were withheld from him. The Flemish question of language has become, more than ever acute, especially in the Universities as well as in the government circles. As is fully known, there is a Liege-Brussels line, dividing Belgium into Flemish and Walloon populations, expressing themselves in Flemish and French respectively. This language question, as in Canada, is likely to produce great difficulties.*

Then Dom Mayeul made a short visit to Switzerland, to meet Abbot Primate Fidelis von Stotzingen, a German, who resided in Einsiedeln, Switzerland. He next went to Rome, where he was received in audience by Benedict XV at the end of October, 1919. In those days it was fairly easy for a prelate to arrange such a private meeting with the Pope. The following is an account of this audience:

> *Indeed, Benedict XV received me with great kindness, and showed himself very interested in the great pilgrimage in honour of our*

October 30, 1919.

THE PORT-OF-SPAIN GAZETTE, THURSDAY,

Lord Abbot de Caigny in Europe

WHAT HE IS DOING FOR THE LOCAL MONASTERY.

BRO. RAPHAEL STUDYING FARM-
ING AND CHEESE AND
BUTTER MAKING.

WILL BE COMING BACK TO
TRINIDAD SOON.

BELGIUM.

Writing from Belgium, his native land, the Right Rev. Dom Mayeul de Caigny, Lord Abbot of Mount St. Benedict, expresses the sad opinion that conditions in the tight little kingdom are far from satisfactory, and the approaching elections are looked forward to with anxiety. The gallant Patriot, King Albert, it is said, while entering the city of Bruges made certain concessions to the Socialists, which it is feared, may prove pernicious to the practice of religion in general. The high cost of living is alarming and there is no sign of any immediate improvement. He was more than grieved to witness the wanton destruction, on all sides of the country, but more so of his native village—half of the extent of which he was absolutely unaware, and the facts of which were withheld from him. The Flemish question of language has become, more than ever, acute, especially in the Universities and other teaching bodies as well as in the Government circles [As is fully known, there is the Liège-Brussels line ; Ostend dividing Belgium into Flemish and Walloon populations, expressing themselves in Flemish and French respectively]. This language question, as in Canada, is likely to produce great difficulty.

FRANCE.

His Lordship, following a short stay in Paris, proceeded to Lourdes, after having visited Chateauroux, where there are immense American Military Baracks. At this centre soldiers are to be everywhere seen. Here a soldier from Mains addressing some friends, in the hearing of Dom de Caigny, remaked : "Germany is quickly recovering, while there is so much permission in France!" His Lordship remained in the town of the famous grotto for three days. While at Lourdes he observed how fine an impression the the British and French soldiers created; so many of them approaching Holy Communion. The trains are in very bad order and delays are the order of the day. There are, apparently no available materials and nobody to repair the vast ruins.

FOR MOUNT ST BENEDICT.

His Lordship has placed Brother Raphael (so well known by pilgrims and others visiting Mount St Benedict) at a Trappist Monastery, near Ypres to learn some details of farming and cheese and butter making, especially.

The esteemed lay brother hopes to be returning soon to take charge of these new departments at Mount St Benedict.

His Lordship has also acquired a beautiful set of vestments for Pontifical High Mass, the golden ornaments of which was donated some sixty or seventy years ago by the Duchess of Angonleme to the Princess Louise de Condé, foundress of the Monastery of the Rue Monsieur, in Paris. He has also secured several valuable volumes for the library, including Migné's Patrology, etc.

A FINE STOVE FOR THE MONASTERY.

His Lordship has sent out, from Holland, one of the latest makes of stoves, capable of accomplishing the cookery for a community of sixty or eighty members. Supplied by the well-known firm of Meijs, of Scheveningen, near the Hague,—it is giving the greatest satisfaction. There is one single hole for the supply of fuel, and by a clever device heated air and smoke circulates round the big oven—the heat and air travelling over a distance of 2 x 68 inches (length) and 33 inches width, and 24 inches height ; and there is a heavy galvanised hotwater basin of 10 gallons capacity. It is a lovely stove, some of the many advantages being ; no soot under the pots, equal heat all over the plate, and all space being utilized. The Lord Abbot also visited the renowned Buckfast Abbey, in England, and many of its features will be introduced in the Monastery of Mount St. Benedict.

His Lordship hopes, Deovolente, to be back here before the end of the year. A most hearty welcome awaits him.

POS GAZETTE REPORTED ON THE TRIP OF DOM MAYEUL TO EUROPE,
OCTOBER 1919

THIS LIFE-SIZE STATUE OF OUR LADY OF FATIMA IN THE ABBEY CHURCH
AT MOUNT ST. BENEDICT WAS A GIFT FROM AN ANONYMOUS PORTUGUESE
BUSINESSMAN IN 1953 IN FULFILMENT OF A PROMISE. IT IS CARVED BY TWO
BROTHER SCULPTORS FROM CEDAR WOOD AND TOOK NINE MONTHS TO COMPLETE.
THE SCULPTORS WORKED ALONG THE DIRECTIONS GIVEN BY FR. NEVES, THE
PARISH PRIEST OF OUR LADY OF MERCY AT LISBON, PORTUGAL, WHO EXPRESSED
THE WISH THAT THE STATUE SHOULD COME AS CLOSELY AS POSSIBLE TO THE
DESCRIPTIONS OF THE THREE VISIONARIES OF FATIMA TO WHOM OUR LADY
APPEARED IN 1917.

Holy Patriarch in Trinidad. Willingly he accorded me a plenary indulgence four times a year, in favour of the pilgrims: 4 February, the Feast of Our Lady of Exile, 21 March, the Feast of St. Benedict, 11 July, the Feast of his Patronage, and 15 August, the Feast of the Assumption of Our Lady, which is venerated by the Portuguese under the title of "Our Lady of the Mount" (Vol. II, 175-6).

Dom Mayeul obtained a final concession from Benedict XV, granting indulgences to those who recited the Petrine Prayer, 'You are Christ, the Son of the Living God', while in front of the Tabernacle of the Blessed Sacrament in the Church of Mount St. Benedict, Trinidad. This concession was confirmed by a papal brief, dated 9 June 1920, signed by Cardinal Gasparri, addressed to Dom Mayeul. The full text of this papal brief, in Latin, is given in his memoirs *(Vol. I, 281).*

From Rome, Dom Mayeul made his way by train to Paris, where he spent several weeks trying to obtain a direct passage by boat to Trinidad. As it was less than a year since the war ended, passenger links across the Atlantic had not yet been fully established. In the end, he had to travel first to Para, in Brazil, and from there take a boat to Trinidad, via Barbados. He arrived back at the Mount in time to celebrate Christmas 1919, having been absent from Trinidad for almost six months. We have no idea what the community at the Mount thought about Dom Mayeul at this time, and whether they were convinced that his absence in Europe had been really necessary. All we know is that he was becoming more and more a distant figure, less and less involved in the day-to-day life on the Mount. Many of the monks felt that he had neglected their best interests, by putting on hold for several years the much-needed building programme for the lower monastery. Instead, from 1916 to 1920, he had channelled most of the monastery's resources, men and money, into the development of the upper monastery, which he had called Mount Thabor.

CHAPTER XIII

Vital Issues at Stake in Mount St. Benedict
(1919-1921)

DOM MAYEUL would need to have been a professional juggler to cope with all the challenges he faced on his return to the Mount at the end of 1919. The list of matters demanding his attention included the following: (i) How to increase the number of priests in the community, to deal with the growing demands for parlour work within the monastery, and to fill the positions in the parishes offered them by the archbishop; (ii) How to prepare for the canonical visitation of the Mount, by Abbot Laurent Zeller, announced for mid-1920; (iii) How best to control and use the increased income accruing from the pilgrims to the shrine of St. Benedict, in the monastery church; (iv) Which building projects should be started or completed, before the return of their master-builder and architect, Br. Gabriel from Buckfast, England.

Writing to Archbishop Dowling on 18 January 1920, Dom Mayeul raised a number of questions relating to the need for more priests at the Mount. He had three candidates: Odo van der Heydt, Wilfrid Broens and Hugh van der Sanden, who were completing their theological studies. While their studies had been somewhat disrupted during his recent absence in Europe, they had now completed the full course as required by Canon Law. He offered as an extenuating factor a recent injunction from Benedict XV, which stated that "virtue" was more important that "science" in future priests. As soon as they were ordained, it would be possible to send some of them to help in the parishes. Dom Mayeul requested that the ceremony of ordination be performed at the Mount by the archbishop. However, such an arrangement did not meet with the latter's approval, and the ordination took place in the Dominican

Convent in the Port of Spain on 13 May 1920. In view of the future role played by these three candidates in the history of the Mount, it is interesting to note what Dom Mayeul says of them in his letter to the archbishop, on 7 May 1920:

> *Brother Hugh van der Sanden is a good student. I hope to send him to Rome to improve himself, so that he may become the Prefect of Clerics. Br. Wilfrid is a late vocation. He is 40 years of age, and has found study rather difficult, though he is very practical. Br. Odo is an excellent Master of Ceremonies, but has poor health, and therefore is unable to study too much. They will begin their 6-day retreat this morning, 6th May, and will arrive on Wednesday next in town, to be ready for the great ceremony on 13 May (POS, Ben.).*

All three were excellent monks, and their ordination augured well for the future of the monastery. Dom Mayeul realized that the training of the other younger members of the community for the priesthood, had to be one of his priorities. It was in order to provide a suitable place and atmosphere for such studies that he moved the student monks to Mount Thabor. As far as we know, this arrangement worked well for all concerned. One gets the impression that the Mount – with its upper and lower monasteries – was a hive of activity. On paper, it looked as if the foundation had come of age, and that its future prosperity was assured. It was also the moment when the monastery should have been raised from being a priory to that of an abbey. This would have provided Dom Mayeul with the extra authority and prestige he needed to carry out all his ambitions for the future consolidation of the Mount. However, such a move was impossible, considering the views of Archbishop Dowling.

Reading between the lines of his correspondence with the archbishop, one can see the frustration which Dom Mayeul continually experienced. Sadly, they both lacked the diplomatic skills to proffer a solution. If the two men had met face to face more often, and not relied on a correspondence, conducted in French over a long number of years, the situation might have been different. As matters stood, they never really got to know each other. They remained more on the level of strangers, instead of two adults responsible for the well-being of the Catholic Church in Trinidad. Why they never wrote to each other in English is a mystery. Perhaps Dom Mayeul had not yet mastered English, although he must have used English in his parlour work at the Mount. This was another example of how language played a major role in forging, or obstructing, the future progress of the Benedictine foundation in Trinidad.

Abbot Laurent Zeller, the Administrator of the Brazilian Congregation, arrived in Trinidad in August 1920, to conduct the canonical visitation of the Mount. Two important matters had to be dealt with. First there was the question of regularizing the vows of stability (or permanent allegiance/commitment) for those monks who had originally made vows of stability for the abbey of Bahia, and over the years had come to Trinidad. As a result of the arrangements made during the General Chapter of the Brazilian Congregation in 1915, the Mount had become an independent conventual priory, though remaining within the Brazilian Congregation. As a result the monks had to renew their vow of stability which had been delayed until now, on account of the war. Up to this moment, the Mount was still a dependent priory of Bahia and their vow of stability was still with the abbey of Bahia. They were now given the choice of returning to Bahia, or opting to change their stability from Bahia to Trinidad. All the monks, except one, decided to offer themselves in the service of Mount St. Benedict. This was an important step in the history of the Foundation, giving it a more solid basis, and allowing for a more ordered organisation in the future. In the Ordo, the official handbook of the Brazilian Congregation, for 1921, the Mount is called: "The Conventual Priory of Our Lady of Exile". Dom Mayeul is listed as titular abbot of Lobbes and superior. The following were members of the community at this moment: Choir monks: Dom Sebastian Weber, prior, Dom Odo v. d. Heydt, subprior, Dom Charles Verbeke, Dom Anselm Romanus, Dom Wilfrid Broens, Dom Hugh van der Sanden, Dom Odilo van Tongeren, Br. Augustine Callaghan, Br. Maur Maingot, Br. Placid Ganteaume. Lay brothers: Anthony Feldner, Joseph Kleinmann, Raphael Goemaere, Gabriel Molkveld, and Landelinus Acqui. Altogether, there were 17 monks at the Mount in 1921. Two years later, according to the Ordo for 1923, the community had increased to 28. From the point of view of personnel, the monastery seemed to be in a healthy and stable situation.

Also on account of the war another important issue was still pending. Abbot Laurent Zeller, who had been appointed in 1915

DOM MAYEUL IN 1920

to carry out the decree of the Holy See relating to the split, of personnel and patrimony, between Bahia and Trinidad, made his findings known to Dom Mayeul. Dom Laurent announced the retention of the status quo in regard to the personnel and in regard to the patrimony, i.e. the sums of money advanced by the abbey of Bahia to the foundation in Trinidad. Meaning that no more monks from Bahia could leave for Trinidad and the capital taken by Dom Mayeul in 1912-1913 to Trinidad could remain in Trinidad. But no more money would flow from Bahia to Trinidad except for a further 50 Contos to be given in annuities of 5 Contos for a period of 10 years (5 Contos = 5 million Real). Based on 1933 official conversion rates, 5 Contos was about 400 US$. Before 1933 the Conto was pegged to the price of gold: 1 Conto was 180 grams of gold. In 1922, 5 Contos was worth about 1000 US$ (US dollars of 1922). So over a ten-year timeframe, the devaluation of the Brazilian Real was approximately 60%. Considering the total capital that Dom Mayeul transferred to the foundation in Trinidad, it is obvious that from a financial point of view, this was an outstanding decision. In the years 1930 and 1940 the Brazilian Real would further decline in value at an astonishing pace.

Abbot Laurent Zeller then had to deal with the question of the parishes, which was not so easily resolved. According to the Constitutions (regulations) of the Brazilian Congregation, isolated parishes, i.e. parishes at a considerable distance from the monastery, were not permitted, unless there were at least three monks serving there. Up to the moment of the canonical visitation in 1920, this mandate had never been observed, principally because the archbishop would not permit it. Dom Mayeul hoped that Abbot Zeller would be able to find a solution, or at least twist the arm of the archbishop and find some compromise. But it was not to be. The archbishop, who was a man of independent character, and believed that he alone was responsible for running the diocese, refused to listen to the arguments put forward by the abbot visitator. There was a serious shortage of priests in his diocese, with more parishes to be served than priests available. Thus, when arranging for monks to take up parishes, the archbishop demanded that each monk-priest have his own parish. The problem might have been overcome, if Dom Mayeul had enough non-priests (brothers) or regular oblates, to make up the numbers in each parish. But this was not the case. It seems that the archbishop was incapable of understanding the Benedictine demands in this matter. He was a member of the Dominican Order. No such restriction was demanded by the Dominican superiors in the case of appointing Dominican priests to parishes. The Holy Ghost Fathers, who had several houses and schools in Trinidad, likewise had no problem with the appointment of one of their members to a parish. The Benedictines, in the mind of the archbishop, were making unreasonable demands on him, especially as he saw the problem mainly from the economic point of view. Every priest in a parish had to be supported by the diocese, or from the revenues of the said parish. Many of the parishes were very poor, and unable to support even one priest. It was certainly beyond the means of the archbishop to support three monks in any one parish, a fact which he upheld, even when Rome ordered him to accept the Benedictine demands. Throughout Dom Mayeul's time at the Mount, this question of the parishes was never resolved. It was undoubtedly one of the reasons why the archbishop took such a dislike to Dom Mayeul. From 1920 on, there is a gradual hardening of attitudes on both sides of their correspondence. Indeed, it would not be an exaggeration to suggest that from then on, the archbishop began looking for some means of having the abbot removed from his position as superior of the monastery. He just could not cope with the latter's intransigence, and had become weary of the endless negotiations.

Early in 1921, Dom Laurent Zeller, the apostolic visitator, sent a detailed report of his findings in Trinidad to Pope Benedict XV, to the prefects of the Congregation of Propaganda Fide and the Congregation for Religious, and also to the abbot primate. He made special reference to the difficulties arising from Archbishop Dowling's refusal to accept the clauses in the Constitutions of the Brazilian Congregation, forbidding a monk to work alone in a parish, which was at a distance from the monastery. Mgr. Dowling, however, had anticipated such a report, and wrote on 1 February 1921 to Cardinal van Rossum, the prefect of Propaganda Fide, explaining his point of view (*C.P.F. 777/21, Dowling to van Rossum, 1 Feb. 1921*). The diocese of Port of Spain had more parishes than priests, and many parishes were so poor they could hardly support even one priest. There was no way they could support three monks in a cella, as demanded by the Brazilian Constitutions. He was happy to have the Benedictines take charge of certain parishes, but they should fall in with the practice followed in the diocese by the Dominicans and the Holy Ghost Fathers, i.e. one priest per parish.

The archbishop's letter took some six weeks to reach Rome. Cardinal van Rossum eventually replied on 9 June 1921 *(C P.F.1488/21)*, regretting the difficulty over the question of parishes, while expressing his hope that a solution could be found to everyone's satisfaction. On the same day, Cardinal van Rossum wrote to the abbot primate, giving his views on the dispute between the Benedictines and the archbishop over the parishes' issue. It was clear they had reached an impasse, and no immediate solution seemed possible under the circumstances.

In the meantime Dom Mayeul knew that Rome was studying the situation, and informed the archbishop in a letter dated 25 March 1921:

> *I have not yet received any news from Rome; I have the impression that the Abbot Primate is not satisfied with the arrangement for our parishes, and that the report of the Abbot Visitator will be critical of the present system. I have confidence in the Holy See, which will have due regard for the needs of the diocese (POS, Dom Mayeul to Abp Dowling, 23 Mar. 1921).*

But, to the great surprise of the archbishop, the Congregation of Propaganda Fide, on whom Trinidad depended, upheld the decision of Dom Laurence Zeller. But Mgr. Dowling, always obstinate in his manner of viewing any situation, refused to be beaten, and sent another appeal to Rome. Owing to this turn of events, the status quo was maintained. Rome eventually confirmed its original decision, which Dom Mayeul only heard about in September 1921, in a letter from our abbot primate, dated 26 August 1921. Dom Mayeul immediately implemented the decision by the Holy See:

> *As for myself, I could not hesitate any longer in carrying out the decision of the Holy See. The Abbot Primate had told me that this decision had been taken after a mature examination of the case and had been officially communicated by Propaganda Fide to the Archbishop of Port of Spain. Therefore, it must be <u>absolutely</u> followed. I called a meeting of our Chapter, and everything was put in order, although not without some difficulty. In fact, more than one of the monks, accustomed to live alone in a parish, showed himself clearly averse to having his conduct controlled by the presence of a confrere,*

let alone live in a situation where he depended on another monk
(Vol. II, 178).

But ultimately Dom Mayeul found himself caught up in a no-win situation. Some of the monks, who preferred to be alone and independent at the parish, as they had been until now, favoured the ideas of the archbishop. In addition the archbishop would never forgive Dom Mayeul his loss. Hence, Dom Mayeul should have realized that the only way to have been in a winning position with everyone, was by having negotiated a working compromise for the parishes' issue. It was a repetition of his experience in Bahia, when he showed that he had a blind spot when dealing with his ecclesiastical superiors. It is true that Archbishop Dowling showed a definite rigidity in his treatment of the monks, but Dom Mayeul was equally unbending in his refusal to even meet the archbishop half-way. The parishes' issue was becoming 'a recipe for disaster', which, in the long run, meant that Dom Mayeul became the victim of his own intransigence. But there were other difficulties hovering on the horizon, much more serious than the parishes' issue. One such difficulty was the construction and composition of Mount Thabor.

CHAPTER XIV

Mount Thabor:
A Trinidadian Shangri-La
(13 May 1916 - 31 July 1922)

THERE ARE references to Mount Thabor in previous chapters on how the idea of building a monastery cum sanatorium, on a higher level above the existing monastery, was proposed to Dom Mayeul by an eminent Trinidadian doctor as early as 1915. Because Mount Thabor played such an important role in the life of Dom Mayeul it is necessary to analyse the thinking behind this extraordinary venture, and try to understand how it could ever have been conceived, let alone built. Unfortunately, the structure was completely destroyed between 1925 and 1926, by persons unknown. All that remains are some photographs and the abandoned site. There is a considerable mystery surrounding the demise of this magnificent structure, suggesting as it does an element of tragedy if not a personal vendetta. Mount Thabor symbolized everything that Dom Mayeul had dreamed of, when he embarked on the Trinidadian foundation. It was as personal to him as if it were a monument to him. One gets the impression that the people who destroyed it were trying to wipe out his memory, in much the same way as the Russians destroyed the statues of Stalin, and the Iraqis the statues of Saddam Hussein. The whole episode is a sad affair. Had Mount Thabor remained in its splendour, though from the very beginning there were certain question marks about its durability, it might have become a thing of wonder, one of the seven wonders of the island of Trinidad! Instead, it is now only a memory, or rather, a legend.

At certain stages of his career, Dom Mayeul hankered after the life of a hermit or solitary. His namesake, St. Mayeul, abbot of Cluny, had retired to a hermitage at the end of his life, and one gets the feeling that Dom Mayeul cherished similar thoughts from time to time. Indeed, one of his reasons for becoming a Benedictine monk had been to find peace and quiet in a monastery, something he felt he could never hope for as a Redemptorist priest. But it was not to be. Even as a novice in Maredsous, he had been uprooted from Belgium and sent to Brazil. Once in Brazil, his life was a constant series of moves from one monastery to another, with no hope of anything resembling the ideal of Benedictine stability, except perhaps in Santa Cruz (Ceara). When he stood on the hill above Tunapuna, Trinidad, in 1911, he probably allowed himself a moment of reflection, and dared to hope that he had at last found the place of his dreams. It was only some years later, when he decided to build Mount Thabor, that his dream became a reality, albeit a very short-lived one.

It is possible to offer some explanation of the grandiose ideas which came into his mind, as he set about planning his monastery on the hill above Tunapuna. He loved architecture and grandiose buildings. In his memoirs, he explained to have inherited this passion and love for building and construction from his ancestors who, in the 17th and 18th century, were architects, church, town hall and belfry builders *(Vol. II, 286-287)*. He was very interested in his ancestors who may have had aristocratic French family roots, hence the De Caigny. Dom Mayeul liked to do things on a grand scale. When it came to planning the various buildings that would constitute Mount St. Benedict, he wanted above all to leave behind him a "Monument for Posterity". Whenever he was in residence, he insisted on supervising the building of the monastery on the site he had chosen in 1912, 600 feet above sea-level. Between 1912 and 1916, a great number of buildings were constructed at the lower monastery, including living quarters for the monks, a temporary church, a guest house, a rest house, workshops, kitchen, etc.

Dom Mayeul waited until 1916 to begin the construction of Mount Thabor, a thousand feet above the lower monastery, though the idea had been gestating in his mind since 1915. Certainly the building was sufficiently advanced when, on 13 May 1916, Mass was celebrated in the "Villa Coeli", the first section of the future Mount Thabor to be completed. While the 'healthy' sanatorium aspect of Mount Thabor was one of the principal reasons for its being built, there was another reason, which became more and more obvious as time went on. By 1916, the daily crowds of visitors to the Mount had increased to such an extent, that they were beginning to intrude on the peace of the monks. The ordinary silence one associates with a monastery hardly existed throughout the day. Furthermore, Dom Mayeul, when planning the lower monastery, seems to have neglected to set out a designated area reserved to the monks, known as the 'enclosure'. A constant flow of people walked, talked and wandered around the hillside, waiting their turn to speak with a monk in one of the parlours, or to visit the shrine to St. Benedict in the church. It became almost impossible for the younger monks to study in such an atmosphere, while the noise of the crowds was distracting, if not annoying, to the community in general. Dom Mayeul decided that he needed a more secluded place for his student monks, and also for the novices. With this in mind, he proceeded to draw up plans for a large building – indeed, a veritable castle – on a site some 1,800 feet above sea level. According to the Ground Plan, it was to consist of a chapel, a grand entrance hall, a library, two refectories, one for the monks and another for guests, sixteen cells for the novices and clerics, three guest rooms, and last, but not least, two magnificent towers, one of which would provide accommodation for Dom Mayeul

The actual building took four years to complete, mainly under the supervision of Br. Joseph Kleinmann, during which time very little work was done on the lower level monastery. By any standard, Mount Thabor was a magnificent structure, which might well have come from the imagination of King Ludwig II of Bavaria. One immediately thinks of a similar structure on Caldey Island, Wales, where Abbot Aelred Carlyle built an exotic monastery for his Church of England Benedictine community, prior to their conversion to Roman Catholicism in 1913.

In order to forestall any criticism of Mount Thabor, Dom Mayeul, on 10 April 1922, put down on paper his ideas and intentions regarding the building. His reflections came under four headings:

I.   The place to be called the "upper monastery", to provide accommodation for the novitiate and the clericate (i.e. those young monks studying philosophy and theology). It is ideally suited for contemplation, and provides a very beautiful solitude, combined with cool air. It is meant to complement the "lower monastery", which will cater for the more active apostolate, such as pilgrims and visitors.

2. The new Canon Law, which was published in 1917, lays down a regulation (Canon 554.5) about novices, whose quarters should be separate from that of the rest of the professed community. Mount Thabor provides such a setting for the junior monks, who would thus be saved from all the comings and goings of the monks working in the parishes and in the parlours.

3. On big Feast Days, all the community could come together to Mount Thabor for liturgical celebrations. However, even on weekdays, the liturgy on Mount Thabor would be more solemn, whereas the monks in the lower monastery could have a simple liturgy to suit their external obligations.

4. Mount Thabor can also serve as a sanatorium or health centre for older monks, or monks who are convalescing. It will provide an asylum for those who would otherwise have to go into hospital or a rest house in Port of Spain *(MSB, Box I, File ix)*.

Although when he conceived the idea of Mount Thabor, Dom Mayeul could not have read James Hilton's novel *"Lost Horizon"*, which only appeared in 1933, he was, unwittingly looking for the kind of place to which Hilton gave the fictional name of "Shangri-La". This was a mystical, harmonious place, isolated from the outside. The dictionary definition of "Shangri-La" is "a distant and secluded hideaway, usually of great beauty and peacefulness". That is exactly what Dom Mayeul was seeking all his life, and Mount Thabor came closest to his ideal.

The only first-hand description of Mount Thabor we possess was written by a well-known journalist and traveller, A.E. Murray, who visited the place on 31 July 1922 and called it *"a triumph of modern architectural genius"*. The following is an edited version of his account:

> *Mount Thabor, which is situated on the Northern part of the island, is 1,851 feet above sea-level. Arriving there, after a long and exhausting climb, one felt transported to another sphere, so rarified was the atmosphere, so imposing the grandeur of the surrounding scenery. I was so engrossed by what I saw and seemed to feel, that for some time I remained oblivious to the imposing building that stood before me, a building representing a perfect picture of archi-*

MOUNT THABOR,
BUILT BY BR. JOSEPH KLEINMANN

tectural skill and design, a triumph of modern architectural genius. Standing on an almost level plain, surrounded by lovely hibiscus trees, is the building Mount Thabor, which can be seen several miles off. It measures 80 feet, while the northern facade has a full length of 40 feet. It contains fifteen rooms, a chapel and large hall. There are two towers, 40 feet high on either side. On the right tower, which is reserved for the Lord Abbot, the Papal Flag is flown, and on the left, which contains three large guest rooms, the Union Jack.

The chapel, being only semi-public, is not open to the public at large, but only to the community and its guests. The building is actually occupied by a happy set of young students, preparing themselves in this enchanting solitude and quiet for the Holy Priesthood. Rooms are kept in readiness for such of the monks as require either spiritual or corporal rest. In order not to disturb the quietness of the place, visitors can only be admitted on Mondays, and must be provided with a written permit. Guests will find themselves at home in one of the three large guest rooms (Port of Spain Gazette, 1 August 1922).

One might well ask: how did Dom Mayeul get the necessary permission to build Mount Thabor? The truth is that Dom Mayeul never considered it necessary to seek permission from anyone to build such a magnificent mansion. He acted on his own impulse, without asking the community to vote on the matter. And it seems, he was completely within his rights. Between 1912 and 1915, there was no Chapter (i.e. Community Council) at the Mount, as the monastery still depended on Bahia, and Dom Mayeul remained throughout that time abbot of Bahia, as well as the superior at the Mount. When approving the foundation in Trinidad, the Chapter of Bahia had voted for the erection of a temporary chapel and a monastery, with no actual specifics. Dom Mayeul thus felt free to do as he liked. The entire enterprise was symptomatic of his independent outlook, and an example of his failure to consult others in a matter which concerned them on a personal level.

On several occasions Dom Mayeul invited the archbishop to come to bless Mount Thabor, but without success. As we shall see, the archbishop had his own reservations about the place. The matter came up again in April 1922, when an article appeared in the *Catholic News*, on the subject of "A Retreat" with special reference to the importance of having a suitable place for retreats for priests in Trinidad. Taking this article as his cue, Dom Mayeul wrote to the archbishop on 5 April 1922 *(POS. BEN.)*, hoping to awaken some interest and enthusiasm for Mount Thabor in his mind. But it all seems to have been in vain. In any case, Dom Mayeul had to admit that he was having some serious structural problems with Mount Thabor. They were not quite ready for the archbishop. He wrote as follows to the archbishop:

> *Indeed, our residence on Mount Thabor is very favourably situated for Retreats. Previously I have invited Your Grace to come to bless this establishment for this very purpose. Unfortunately, the moment has not yet come for this, as we have had a great disappointment in regard to its construction. This may have been caused by the use of inferior cement, or else on account of the violence of the wind, which allowed the rain to penetrate the plaster. Up to this moment we had never built at such a high altitude and in such an exposed place. We are hastening to re-plaster the building before the rainy season comes. After that, I hope that Your Grace will come to bless the Retreat House, which is intended above all for priests (POS. Ben.).*

We know that the archbishop had observed the erection of Mount Thabor from his own fine palace in Port of Spain, which was likewise a castellated structure, and much admired in its own right. Mount Thabor could be seen from miles around, dominating the skyline, and was, undoubtedly the most spectacular building on the island of Trinidad. It would be too much to say that Archbishop Dowling looked upon Mount Thabor with a jealous eye, but it certainly gave him cause for thought. He considered it in bad taste, and another example of Dom Mayeul overstepping himself in an effort to assert the ascendancy (or the superiority) of the Benedictines. He had made it clear to Dom Mayeul that he resented the presence of another prelate in his diocese, and had shown his disapproval of Dom Mayeul's habit of celebrating Pontifical High Mass in Mount St. Benedict on big Feast Days.

The final story of Mount Thabor will be told in a later chapter. Suffice to say here that the project was ill-conceived and built with the wrong material (tapia). The entire structure was unsound, and unable to withstand the gales and winds which blew with great force at the height of nearly 2,000 feet. Brother Joseph Kleinmann, who was in charge of the whole operation, lacked the skills of an architect. Had Dom Mayeul waited a few years, and put the building in the hands of Br. Gabriel Mokveld, the outcome might well have been different. Mount Thabor was destined to become an 'Achilles Heel' for Dom Mayeul and the remote cause of his having to leave Trinidad in 1923.

CHAPTER XV

Signs of the Gathering Storm
(1921 – 1922)

THROUGHOUT the years 1921 and 1922, there were many signs of trouble on the horizon for Dom Mayeul, which must have indicated that time was running out for him as superior of Mount St. Benedict. Reading between the lines of his letters to the abbot primate, one gets an insight into the many difficulties facing him. He faced so many obstacles and difficulties that he imagined himself to be a Job-like figure, surrounded by enemies and heading for disaster.

As already mentioned, in the beginning of 1921, Dom Laurent Zeller, the apostolic visitator, had sent a detailed report of his visitation of the Mount, in 1920, to the abbot primate. The abbot primate summarized on 26 August 1921, in a letter to Dom Mayeul, the findings and outstanding issues, as reported by Dom Laurent Zeller. In two letters, dated 10 October and 27 November 1921, replying to the abbot primate, Dom Mayeul attempted to offer explanations and excuses. He detailed the incidents and circumstances which had led him to a state of desperation (*APR, 613.* *#2*). It is also quite obvious from all the correspondence that Dom Laurent and Dom Mayeul were not at all, to say the least, on good terms with one another. Not surprisingly, Dom Mayeul couldn't stand the moralizing and dogmatizing attitude of Dom Laurent, who always had his finger in the air when speaking.

At the head of the list of difficulties was the question of the parishes allocated to the monks. By 1921, the matter had reached a crisis point, despite recommendations and instructions from the Holy See on the matter. As already mentioned, Archbishop Dowling refused to accept the terms of reference laid down by the Constitutions of the Brazilian Congregation relating to parishes run by monks, whereby each parish was to be turned into a *cella*, a community of 3 monks, in which they could lead some kind of regular life. The archbishop felt encouraged in his opinion by the fact that 2 monks of the Mount, Dom Paul Dobbert and Dom Ludger Nauer, both German, publicly sided with him on the issue of the parishes. Both monks had never really adopted the Benedictine spirit and they had always been a thorn in the side of Dom Mayeul by their negative attitude at the Mount.

Dom Paul, who was part of the first 3 monks leaving Bahia in 1912 for Trinidad, never forgot how, during the war, he was forced to go to a camp. With the help of the archbishop, but against the will of Dom Mayeul, he left Trinidad in 1916 for Venezuela. It didn't work out as planned and after some time he left Venezuela, and returned to Bahia. In Bahia he found himself without a monastic base and caused some tensions. In 1922, Dom Mayeul attended in Rio the General Chapter meeting, where he met with Dom Paul. The latter convinced Dom Mayeul that he was a changed person. Dom Mayeul, probably too eager to get more monks at Trinidad, allowed him to return to Trinidad. The case of Dom Ludger Nauer is equally sad. He had been prepared for ordination in 1921, but that had been postponed by Dom Mayeul owing to severe immoral conduct. Showing great remorse, Dom Ludger convinced Dom Mayeul not to report this incident to Rome, and to give him a second chance. Dom Mayeul agreed, but this would also prove to be an unwise decision. Dom Paul and Dom Ludger would soon forget their promise of being changed people, and they would play an important indirect role in the resignation of Dom Mayeul in 1923. Dom Paul eventually ended up asking for and obtaining secularization – the cancelation of the monastic vows. Dom Ludger would remain an unhappy monk, and would leave for the USA. In 1925, Dom Paul died of thyroid fever and this made a great impression on the community of the Mount since, of the 3 secularized monks, 2 had died (Dom Ambrose in 1922 and Dom Paul in 1925) and Dom Bertin was forced out by his parishioners and left for Martinique, where he died. Dom Hugh van der Sanden wrote about this to Dom Mayeul: *"Dom Paul Dobbert died last week; the sad event made a great impression. It is indeed a very striking thing, which makes one reflect. All three disappeared in such a short time"* (MSB, letter HVS to Dom Mayeul Dec 1925).

The situation was made all the more difficult when the archbishop chose to give the monks three parishes situated at great distances from Mount St. Benedict. Two of these, Erin and Cedros, were at the other end of the island, while the third was St. Vincent, an island many hundreds of miles away. This meant that the monk, or monks, in the two Trinidadian parishes, would be cut off entirely from their community in Mount St. Benedict, especially during the rainy season, when roads were often impassable. Both Erin and Cedros were very poor parishes, and could hardly support one priest, let alone three monks. Dom Mayeul had asked over and over again for the monks to be given a parish near the monastery, but this request was repeatedly turned down by the archbishop. Thus, it became evident that as long as Mount St. Benedict was affiliated to the Brazilian Congregation, there would be a constant state of conflict over parishes. What is interesting to note is that to the surprise of the prior of the Mount, when the monastery became affiliated in 1927 to the Belgian Congregation, he learned that the same requirements on monks working in parishes applied.

> *The Lord Abbot Visitor brought forward first the question of the parish centres. He told us that Rome had obliged us to accept the Constitutions of the Belgian Congregation and that according to these, no monk was allowed to dwell alone in a parish (APR 613, #6, Dom Hugh to Abbot Primate 20 Oct 27).*

It took three more years to resolve the issue with the archbishop. In 1930 Dom Hugh, superior of the Mount, wrote to the abbot primate that the problem had been resolved: *"It is a great consolation for me of having obtained a good settlement with the Archbishop after so many years of disagreement. We agreed in keeping two centres: St. Vincent and the town of San Fernando. The fathers have habitually to live together in each centre"* (APR 613 #7 13 March 1930). Thereafter the parish question ceased to be a subject of contention between the superior of the Mount and the archbishop.

Dom Laurent Zeller's report, as summarized in the letter of the abbot primate to Dom Mayeul on 26 August 1921, contained a number of issues that the abbot visitor had found troublesome. The first one was the financial situation of the Mount. Over a number of years, Dom Mayeul had undertaken extensive building programmes, both in the lower monastery and, more recently, in Mount Thabor, which made serious inroads on the monastery's resources. There seemed to be no attempt at budgeting. Questions were being asked as to how much money the monastery actually had, and what the relation was between the annual income and expenditure. There was even a suggestion that the monastery's patrimony had been squandered, thus putting the future of the monastery in jeopardy. The war years had necessarily brought some privations, especially in the living standards of the community. But this did not stop Dom Mayeul going ahead with his ambitious plans for Mount Thabor, oblivious to the fact that he was building a "Castle of Cards", which would one day fall around his ears.

From the very beginning, the monastery had depended on its agricultural resources to provide most of the day-to-day needs of the community, with the sale of surplus crops bringing in a tidy sum of money most years. St. Benedict modelled his monastery on a Roman Villa, which was a self-contained unit, having all essential facilities, living quarters for the monks, a church, its own water supply, farm, vineyard, etc. Dom Mayeul was determined to make the Mount as complete and independent as possible. Over time Dom Mayeul increased the monastery's holdings, so that by 1921 the so-called "farm" consisted of some 600 acres. However, farming was a hazardous business in Trinidad, with weather conditions playing a very large part in deciding good or bad harvests. The year 1921 proved a disastrous one for the monastery farm, owing to a continued drought and the consequent failure of crops. It was a nightmare especially for the lay brothers, who could only stand by and see all their hard work going for nothing. The situation was not only a financial, but also a psychological, disaster for many in the community. Over the coming years, this would be a continual problem for the monks. There was never any question of selling or disposing of the lands, even when conditions became almost desperate, as happened after the Wall Street Crash of 1929. All the same, it is necessary to remember that the monks of the Mount faced great hardships from time to time, and were called upon to make great personal sacrifices. Fortunately, they were not on their own. The people of the surrounding area proved most supportive, and came to the help of the monks during any crisis. By 1921, the monks had become part of the local and island scene. They were there to stay.

Throughout 1921, the number of pilgrims coming to the monastery increased substantially, with most of them making a financial offering. The pilgrimage to St. Benedict was the main attraction, but the numbers coming for counselling to the parlours was also on the increase. The monks were amazed at the generosity of the people, especially as both rich and poor often put their hands deep into their pockets. This windfall proved a welcome relief for Dom Mayeul and the monks of the Mount, as it removed one of their greatest worries, i.e. the inability to meet their day-to-day financial needs. The income provided by the pilgrims kept on increasing year by year, a situation which thankfully continues to this day.

The accounting records show the following totals for 1921 and 1922: on the revenue side, for 1921, $13039 and for 1922, $12252. On the expenses' side: for 1921, $13076 and for 1922, $11858. Revenue had decreased by $800, but the expenses also decreased with $1200. The most import conclusion is that there was no capital drain as some had suggested. The monastery finances broke even but there was no money for the needed improvement, expansion or ambitious construction plans at the lower monastery. The second major conclusion from looking in detail at the numbers is that without the income from the pilgrims, as mentioned earlier, it would be impossible to break even. The revenue from everything related to the pilgrims (donations, mass intentions, sales of religious items, candles,..) accounted for 58% of the revenue. So without the pilgrims there would be no way of surviving. Interest on capital deposits accounted for 25%. The patrimony of the monastery included 657 acres (260 hectares), machinery, buildings, living quarters, furniture,.. valued at about $56700. In addition there was the capital deposited at various banks totalling $51600 and earning good interest. The hard work of the whole community was at the basis of all this. But one cannot but appreciate the vision Dom Mayeul had, making the Mount a missionary centre and shrine for pilgrims. Without the pilgrimage, the Mount could never have survived. Looking at the total amount he brought over from Bahia, Dom Mayeul managed to increase its value even under wartime conditions and in generally very tough conditions. However the investment made in Mount Thabor worked out to be a very bad decision. His vision of Mount Thabor as a centre of religious education and spiritual retreats was well-merited but for practical reasons not at all feasible. The money would have been much better spent improving and expanding the lower monastery.

Obviously in 1912 and 1913, Dom Mayeul didn't have a crystal ball to predict the future but he must have had a hunch and notion of what the future held in store for Brazil. Based on the economic analysis of that time, great inflation and constant devaluations, the assets of Bahia were under great danger even without considering for a moment the government's hunger to take over the monasteries and their belongings. Dom Mayeul, being a European with a great sense of history, must have compared the Brazilian situation with the French Revolution during which all Church assets, including schools, were either destroyed or sold. France was after the Revolution a wasteland at the intellectual, cultural and economic level. We would need to make a complete analysis of Brazil in those days but we can say almost with certainty that it was a very wise decision to take part of the assets of Bahia and bring them to safety in a country where the British Empire guaranteed law and order.

Yet in his reply to the abbot primate, Dom Mayeul could not resist challenging the way the division of the patrimony of Bahia had been handled. According to Dom Mayeul the Roman decree stipulated a split between Bahia and Trinidad. However he claimed that the share Trinidad got was far from being in compliance with the decree.

> *From the ten thousand volumes in the library we got eight sets of which several were incomplete. With respect to the split of the capital, Trinidad got only 50 Contos payable over ten years, and this out of the one thousand Contos. No further comment! During my 49 years as a religious I've never before experienced a similar Canonical Visitation. I would lie if I said otherwise (APR 613, #2 Letter Dom Mayeul to Abbot Primate 10 Oct 1921).*

With respect to the capital, Dom Mayeul was perhaps not correct or not completely honest with this statement. The capital he brought over to Trinidad in 1912 and 1913 and the 50 Contos payable over 10 years equal to 500 Contos or 50% of the one thousand Contos he referred to. However if the one thousand Contos was the amount of financial assets still available at Bahia in 1921, then Dom Mayeul had a point. Hard to say who was right but it suffices to say that once again Dom Mayeul was not in agreement.

The second topic listed by the abbot primate was his failure to provide a tight enclosure for the monastery. The buildings were all heaped together, with guest house and retreat house on the same level as the living quarters of the monks. The Canon Law of the Church legislated for a distinct area of a religious house to be cordoned off and reserved for the sole use of the community. It is true that Dom Mayeul had provided a make-shift enclosure, in the form of a hedge, but according to the abbot primate, the hedge failed to keep the people out. It was a common sight to see men and women wandering all over the monastery area, disturbing the normal silence of the place. The Mount needed a walled-in area, with clear-cut signs, indicating it was reserved for the monks. This never happened as long as Dom Mayeul was in charge. Dom Mayeul made the argument that the cost for building a wall or fence was prohibitive and that the steep hillsides and the ravine formed a good natural barrier. In fact Dom Hugh, the successor of Dom Mayeul, has been of the same opinion during his term as superior.

The third question related to the lack of new professions and the lack of discipline to comply with the Constitutions. According to Dom Mayeul this point was strongly contested by his Chapter to the point that they felt surprised and offended by this accusation from the abbot visitator. Then the list ended with questions relating to the ongoing construction at Mount Thabor instead of at the lower monastery.

On top of all these difficulties, the abbot primate was also displeased by the serious complaint against Dom Mayeul, made by Dom Charles Verbeke in a long letter to the abbot primate, dated 1 June 1921 *(APR 613, No. 6)*. Among other things, Dom Charles accused Dom Mayeul of being "severe, indiscreet and cruel". According to Dom Charles, Dom Mayeul was so intolerant that several members of the community of the Mount had been driven to seek secularization (to leave the monastery and become secular priests). Dom Mayeul seems to have been blind to the real situation, probably as a result of his adopting an attitude of aloofness for far too long, which led to his being out of touch with some of his monks. On the other hand, the monks who had made the complaints to the abbot primate about Dom Mayeul's attitude remained a source of unending discussions, even after Dom Mayeul had left Trinidad. Dom Hugh, the superior, wrote that: *"For the un-*

happy monks it was always the fault of the Lord Abbot Mayeul. When Dom Mayeul had left Trinidad it was practically the whole community that was at fault" (APR 613 #7 6 Dec 1926). After Dom Mayeul had left Trinidad, Dom Charles Verbeke was frequently in conflict with the new superior of the Mount and the abbot visitor. Dom Charles remained an unhappy monk and eventually obtained secularisation. On 20 Oct 1927 Dom Hugh, prior at the Mount, wrote to the abbot primate:

> *There is still sad news I have to communicate to you. Fr Charles Verbeke in his last letter manifested to me his intention of secularizing. This intention however was not exactly against all expectations. Some years ago, the Lord Abbot Dom Mayeul, said already that he would do so one day. Dom Charles has come so far that he can't agree with anything, any contradiction acts on his nerves. Your Lordship, you will find out his character and the state of his spirituality. It is indeed very sad to see monks, after some twenty years of religion, having failed completely in spiritual life. Dom Charles is always the victim of misunderstanding and persecution and therefore I think unsuitable for community life. He is a man to be pitied (APR 613 #6 and #7).*

Although Dom Mayeul was the superior of Mount St. Benedict, and free to organize the day-to-day affairs of the monastery, there were other areas in which he had little or no control. The Mount was affiliated to the Brazilian Congregation, and had to accept the decisions made by the General Chapter, consisting of delegates from all the monasteries in the Brazilian Congregation, which met at regular intervals. The General Chapter of 8 September 1922, presided over by Abbot Primate von Stotzingen, was held in Rio de Janeiro. Dom Mayeul attended in his capacity as superior of the Mount. The members of the General Chapter passed a number of important resolutions, which changed the entire scene in Mount St. Benedict. The most important decision was the one which excluded, or rather 'expelled', Mount St. Benedict from the Brazilian Congregation. The reason given was a geographical one, namely, that Trinidad was situated at too great a distance from Brazil, and direct communications between both countries, by sea and post, were for all practical purposes, non-existent. It was proposed that Trinidad be put under the direct jurisdiction of the abbot primate, until such time as the monks could find another Congregation to accept them. Dom Mayeul had a problem in regard to this exclusion from the Brazilian Congregation. As far back as 1897, he had made a personal commitment to Brazil, when he took out Brazilian citizenship, and he had no wish to renounce this allegiance after twenty-five years. He made it quite clear to all concerned that he personally, according to his vow of stability, wished to remain in the Brazilian Congregation, even if this meant saying good-bye to the Trinidad foundation.

It is no coincidence that on 8 September 1922 the "Presidente das Oblates", Mrs. Ritta S de A. Cunha, wrote a strong letter of support for Dom Mayeul to the abbot primate. The confidential letter may have been hand delivered, personally to the abbot visitator, since the letter is dated on the day of General Chapter. Mrs. Cuna must have met the abbot primate since in her letter she refers to his facial features, his physiognomy. In the most elegant handwriting Mrs. Cunha wrote on behalf of all the oblates the four page letter outlining not only all the good Dom Mayeul had done for the abbey of Bahia, but also giving an impressive list of all the religious foundations, associations and publications that were initiated by Dom Mayeul. In addition she asked the abbot primate for a special favour:

> *Allow me, Monsignor, on behalf of all the oblates, to ask for an important favour. When Dom Mayeul took over at Bahia, the monastery was in a decadent and disastrous state. The Abbey was almost in ruins. It is Dom Mayeul who brought back the splendour of the Abbey and all the religious societies and publications that are currently much alive.... Dom Mayeul has been the victim of his devotion and his energy,...we are begging you, Mgr. Abbot Primate, to be his powerful defender and guardian when needed....We rely on your justice, your kindness and goodness because, before God I confirm that what I say is the truth which you will see as well at the day of the Last Judgment. Please excuse me for my audacity which is based on the trust I gathered from your soft physiognomy; the reflection of your grandeur and the goodness of your heart (APR 613, B1, 8 Sept 1922).*

However, there was one other important matter raised at this Rio de Janeiro General Chapter, which affected Dom Mayeul personally. At one of the final sessions, he made a formal request to the delegates of the Brazilian Congregation that they should approve of the Mount being raised to the status of an abbey, with himself as the first abbot. The Trinidadian foundation had the required number of monks and its buildings, while not ideal, were sufficient for the moment. It was in the power of the General Chapter of the Brazilian Congregation to initiate and approve this step. His proposal regarding the Mount becoming an abbey was received coldly by the delegates, and turned down categorically. He considered this refusal a personal affront to him, ending his hope of seeing the Mount raised to the status of an abbey during his time there (*APR., 613, #6, Dom Mayeul to Abbot Primate*). This hope had now been shattered, and caused him to become totally disillusioned. In addition Mount St. Benedict had been expelled from the Brazilian Congregation. This was the second time he returned from Brazil a humiliated, broken and embittered man. Dom Mayeul had suffered again a crushing blow, a terrible humiliation.

However he had no wish to abandon his foundation in Trinidad, which he knew was now well established, and a going concern. He had done everything to bring it to its present successful development, but he suddenly found himself up against insuperable obstacles. The year 1922 thus marks a turning-point in the life and career of Dom Mayeul He made up his mind there and then (in December 1922) to retire as superior of Mount St. Benedict, and seek some suitable place where he could spend his remaining days in peace and solitude, praying and writing. He summed up his situation as follows in his memoirs:

> *By the fact of the separation of Mount St. Benedict from the Brazilian Congregation, passed by the General Chapter in September 1922, and my wish to remain in this Congregation, my stay in Trinidad was inevitably coming to an end. Thus, on returning to the Mount from Rio, I began to take all necessary steps to prepare for my final departure. Contrary to my usual custom, I advanced the date of appointing the annual officers of the monastery. To the surprise of all, I now named as prior, a young Dutch monk (Dom Hugo van der Sanden), who I had for some time been forming to be my successor. He responded perfectly to my wishes, and later I had the satisfaction of seeing my choice ratified by the Holy See (Vol. I, 292).*

In any case, Dom Mayeul was by this time becoming tired of being superior, a position he had held since 1907, when he was appointed abbot of Bahia. It seems that along with the Brazilian Congregation difficulty, he had other reasons for resigning as superior of the Mount. Top of his list was his relationship with Archbishop Dowling, which by the end of 1922 had become almost impossible. There was not only the parishes' issue, but also several other matters, such as the ongoing problem of the archbishop refusing to ordain monks who had completed three years theology, and his withholding faculties for all the priest-monks to hear confessions. Finally there was the letter of 4 July 1922 from the Archbishop to Dom Mayeul about the rumours of immoral conduct that had happened at the Mount, rumours that would further escalate the tensions between the Archbishop and Dom Mayeul. They would fight as two knights in full jousting armour, a fight that Dom Mayeul would lose. But more about this in the next chapter. As if all these problems were not enough, Dom Mayeul had to deal, on a day-to-day basis, with a number of his monks, who had ceased to communicate with, or obey, him, and who were seeking, or had already sought, release from their monastic vows.

On a more personal level, in recent times he had experienced some worrying health problems, mostly headaches and general fatigue, which had forced him to reduce his workload in the parlours. In other words, he was beginning to feel his age, although he was only sixty. While he had no wish to rush his resignation, he hoped to retire as superior of the Mount, in a dignified manner, sooner rather than later. As the year 1922 ended, his mind was filled with all these problems and difficulties. Many of the letters he wrote over the last two years to the abbot primate reflect his desperation and show clearly to have been a cry for help. Everything had gone against him.

One cannot but have a lot of respect for Abbot Primate von Stotzingen. He was in charge of the hundreds of Benedictine foundations worldwide and yet he found the time and patience to read and to reply to all the letters from the Mount and Dom Mayeul. Dom Mayeul must have realized that the abbot primate's patience was not endless. He wrote to the abbot primate:

I hope this is the last time I have to distress you. Our relation has been tense and strained for some time. It was the uncertainty

ABBOT PRIMATE FIDELIS VON STOTZINGEN

and insecurity that bothered me. In the future I will be a changed person. I beg you to forgive me and to forget the past (APR 613, B1, 21 Feb 1922).

Dom Mayeul's wish to live a more normal life would prove to be impossible. He must have faced the new year of 1923 with forebodings and uncertainty. Although it began auspiciously enough, it eventually turned out to be one of the most difficult years of his life. Unfortunately, Dom Mayeul would not be able to keep his promises made in his letter to the abbot primate. The abbot primate would have to wait until 1924 to see the light at the end of the tunnel.

CHAPTER XVI

Annus Horribilis

(1923)

DOM MAYEUL spent the first three months of 1923 on various pastoral and apostolic matters. To begin with, he was involved in converting two people to Catholicism, one a Scottish Presbyterian gentleman, and the other an Anglo-Catholic lady. The first was a member of the Hunter-Blair family, then living in Trinidad, a cousin of Dom Oswald Hunter-Blair, abbot of Fort Augustus. Dom Mayeul received Mr. Hunter-Blair into the Church in February 1923. The second case was not so easy, as the lady firmly believed that the liturgy of the Anglo-Catholic Church was authentic. Dom Mayeul spent many hours discussing the matter with her, and finally succeeded in bringing her round to accepting the truth of the Roman Catholic Church's liturgy. We have no way of calculating how many people Dom Mayeul brought into the Church in this way, but all the evidence suggests that they were quite numerous.

During the month of March, he paid an official visit to the monastery's outlying missionary centre at Erin, to offer his monks support and encouragement. On his way back to the Mount he passed through San Fernando, the second largest city on the island. While there he paid his respects to an old friend, Canon Cantwell, the parish priest, who was delighted to see him. Then, much to Dom Mayeul's surprise, the Canon invited him to preach a mission in San Fernando, scheduled to begin the following Sunday – it was already Friday. Dom Mayeul was taken aback, thinking it was all a joke. When the Canon repeated his request, the abbot hesitated, mainly on the grounds that he had never before preached a mission in English. However, it was the kind of challenge Dom Mayeul could hardly refuse, and for which he had been trained during his Redemptorist days. He returned to the Mount and asked the prayers of his community for the success of this parish mission. He travelled to San Fernando on the Saturday evening, and on the

Sunday preached in the morning and evening, to an overflowing crowd in the large church. For eight days, he was fully occupied, preaching twice daily and spending long hours in the confessional. This was to be his last pastoral function in a Trinidad parish. On returning to the Mount, he spent the first three days of Holy Week in Mount Thabor, preparing to preside at the celebrations of Holy Thursday, Good Friday and Easter Sunday.

While there, he received a letter from the archbishop with the request to give Dom Paul charge of a parish. This was clearly on the request of Dom Paul himself since Dom Paul's desire to be alone in a parish was financially motivated. In fact Dom Mayeul had no monk to spare to accompany Dom Paul at the parish to be compliant with the instructions. Dom Mayeul gave the following account in his memoirs:

> *This request was clearly contrary to our Constitutions, and to the decision of the Holy See. My duty was quite clear. I should give a firm and polite refusal. I did not ignore the fact that my attitude would be extremely displeasing to his Grace. But, zouave of the Pope and of the Church that I was, I said to myself: "Do what you have to do, come what may"! (Vol. II, 182)*

On 2 March 1923 Dom Mayeul wrote the abbot primate about the pending crisis with the archbishop on the issue of the parishes. He begged the abbot primate to personally come over to resolve the issue. The abbot primate had recently written a letter to the archbishop but to no avail. Dom Mayeul told the abbot primate "the future depends on it". Little did Dom Mayeul know then that indeed his future would soon be at stake and something would 'come his way'.

Easter Sunday fell on 1 April in 1923. As there was no Easter Saturday Night Vigil at this time, Sunday was celebrated as the climax of the Holy Week liturgy. Soon after midnight on Saturday, crowds of people began to arrive at Mount St. Benedict, to assist at the Pontifical High Mass of Easter Day, which began at 3 a.m. The Mass, which included a sermon preached by Dom Mayeul, lasted until 5 a.m. This was followed immediately by a solemn procession of the Blessed Sacrament at dawn, a Brazilian custom which the Benedictines had introduced to Trinidad. The Gospel account of the Resurrection, as related by St. John (Ch.xx.1), stated that Jesus rose from the tomb during the early hours of Easter Sunday morning. The monks and the people re-lived the original moment of the resurrection, by processing though the scenic hillside of Mount St. Benedict, the atmosphere made all the more meaningful with the fading darkness of the night and the first rays of light. As soon as the rising sun – representing the Risen Christ – appeared on the horizon, the bells of the church rang out. This was the signal for the monks to sing a solemn "Alleluia", announcing to the people of the surrounding district that it was Easter Day. One final touch was added to this splendid occasion: the re-enactment of the meeting of Jesus and His Blessed Mother, which took place just before the procession arrived back at the entrance to the church. Altogether it was a most impressive liturgical celebration, with Dom Mayeul dressed in full pontifical vestments, including mitre and crosier, and the people in their colourful Sunday best. On returning to the church, Dom Mayeul gave the people the solemn Blessing of the Blessed Sacrament. Many said they had been given a view of "a corner of heaven" that Easter Day. Dom Mayeul could hardly have known that this would be his last Easter Sunday celebration in Mount St. Benedict. Twenty-five years had to go by before the Mount saw another such pontifical Easter celebration. In less than a week after the moving ceremonies of Easter Sunday, Dom Mayeul was forced to leave this "corner of heaven", never to see it again. The blow, which virtually banished him from Mount St. Benedict, came suddenly and unexpectedly, and was delivered by no less a person than Archbishop John Pius Dowling.

Whether Dom Mayeul had any premonitions of the pending thunderbolt from the archbishop it is difficult to say, but he could hardly have foreseen the actual way in which he was forced to leave Trinidad. Indeed, the manner of his leaving the Mount was nothing more than the proverbial blow from a bishop's crosier, implying all sorts of censures, and even excommunication. A careful study of the relevant documents, and they are, indeed, very numerous, provides insights, as well as some explanation, into the situation which led to the expulsion of Dom Mayeul from Trinidad. It is a long and complicated story, with many twists and turns. For both the archbishop and Dom Mayeul, it was a clear question of right or wrong. All one can do is to present the evidence from the relevant documents, and let them speak for themselves.

As has already been mentioned, Easter Sunday 1923 fell on 1 April. On the following Thursday, 5 April, Archbishop Dowling wrote an official letter to Dom Mayeul in Latin, withdrawing Dom Mayeul's faculties for hearing confessions in the diocese for two years, and at the same time forbidding any woman to be admitted to Mount Thabor. He concluded by advising Dom Mayeul to consult the Holy See and his superiors in Rome "as soon as possible", implying that Dom Mayeul could no longer continue as superior of the Mount with this censure hanging over his head. The letter was delivered to Dom Mayeul the following day, 6 April, and came both as a surprise and a shock. Its contents, especially the clause forbidding him to hear confessions, meant a complete upheaval in Dom Mayeul's life, putting an end to all his pastoral work in the parlour, with would-be converts, parish missions etc. A rough English translation of the archbishop's letter is as follows:

> For reasons known to both of us, and in virtue of the decree of the Council of Trent. S. XXIV, I hereby withdraw from you, all faculties to hear confessions of both sexes in this diocese, for the next two years. Furthermore, I strictly prohibit you to allow any woman to be admitted to the place called "Mount Thabor". I advise you, as soon as possible, to get in touch with the Holy See and your Superiors in Rome, to discuss the state of your soul (MSB, Dowling to Dom Mayeul 5 April, 1923, in Latin).

The archbishop added a note to this letter: *Posted it myself, 5 April 1923*, and signed it +*J. P.*

Dom Mayeul replied calmly to this letter on 7 April 1923 acknowledging receipt of the archbishop's letter, assuring the latter that he was prepared to submit to his decision, although he stated that he was unaware of having ever committed a grave fault:

> I wish to acknowledge receipt of your letter of 5th, and to say that I submit to your decision. Your Grace advises me "to consult with the Holy See and my Superiors as soon as possible". I hope to leave on Tuesday next by the "Stuyvesant", or by the first steamboat that I can get. In departing, I promise to pray for Your Grace. I dare to add that by the grace of God I am unaware in my conscience of ever committing any grave fault (APOS, Dom Mayeul to Dowling, 7 April 1923, in French).

He concluded his letter by asking if the exclusion of women from Mount Thabor applied to his two domestics, a cook and a housekeeper, both over 60 years of age. The archbishop replied eventually, not to Dom Mayeul but to Prior Hugh van der Sanden, saying that both women came under his ban (*MSB, Archb. Dowling to Dom Hugh*).

For some considerable time before he wrote the suspension letter, the archbishop had reason to cast a critical eye on certain activities in Mount Thabor, which were reported to him. Stories were being banded about regarding the number of women visiting the place, and even living within its precincts. We have seen how Edith Dunaew, the young Russian lady, was a regular visitor to Mount Thabor, as far back as the years 1916-18. But there were other women who had access to Mount Thabor. From a reading of Dom Mayeul's extensive correspondence, one can count at least nine women who either lived permanently at the Mount or visited frequently. First of all, there was Magdelena Salvedra, a Brazilian woman, whom Dom Mayeul claimed to have saved from a life of prostitution, by bringing her with him to Trinidad in 1913. She remained at the Mount until early 1924, when Prior Hugh van der Sanden had to send her back to Brazil. She was a very difficult character, highly strung, though Dom Mayeul always maintained that he was able to control her. Some of the other women resented her presence, and were jealous of the favouritism shown her by Dom Mayeul. Then there was Norah O'Rourke, who continued to correspond with Dom Mayeul after he left the Mount. Her letters, dated from 17 June 1931 – 26 October 1934, provide us with useful information about life in Mount Thabor during the years 1917-23. She mentions two of the young women who were her contemporaries in the monastery: Laura and Alice, calling them "vipers", as they were always causing trouble, through jealousy, story-telling and petty-mindedness (*St. Leo, N.O'Rourke to Dom Mayeul 17 June 1931*). The names of the other women were: Agnes Wharton, Rowena Lamy, Camilla Waters, Clara, Stella, Georgie, Minnie, Miss Nellie de Verteuil and Mrs. Muriel Evans. They all came under the title of "oblates" (lay associates) of the Mount, and as such were given privileged status. Considering that there was no official enclosure in the monastery at this time, these women were free to wander round, engaged in various duties, but clearly out of place in a religious house of men. Not all of them resided permanently at the Mount. Agnes Wharton lived with her mother in Port of Spain, Mrs. Evans and Miss de Verteuil also lived in Port of Spain, though all three visited the monastery frequently.

It was inevitable that the presence of so many women at the Mount gave rise to rumours of misconduct, which came eventually to the ears of the archbishop. He blamed Dom Mayeul for the problem, and had it in mind to bring the matter up with the latter at a convenient moment. The opportunity came in the summer of 1922. In June 1922, Dom Mayeul informed the archbishop of the accusations, made by an oblate of the Mount, that on a regular basis she suffered serious sexual misconduct by 2 Dominican brothers. At first, Dom Mayeul had advised her, not willing to be involved personally, to bring the matter to the attention of the prior of the 2 Dominican brothers. The prior disregarded the accusations and even reprimanded heavily the oblate woman, also because he knew that Dom Mayeul had been informed. By a slip of the tongue, she had told the prior that it was Dom Mayeul, who had advised her to discuss the matter with the prior first. Dom Mayeul took matters in his own hands. However, by informing the archbishop in writing, he launched a boomerang that came right back, hitting him in the face. On 4 July 1922, the archbishop replied as follows to Dom Mayeul:

> *People are telling me so much about these matters that I am not always ready to listen to them. Even you, high up there at Mount Thabor, are not spared from these accusations. However, if the rumours you mentioned are true, and concern grave sin, then I need to know the truth, so that I can act upon it (APR. 613, #2, Report, p 6).*

One has to admit that the archbishop's letter of July 1922 was fair in the sense that he wanted to resolve the issue, first by finding out the truth and then to act on it. However, considering the fact that the archbishop also belonged to the Dominican order and considering the strained relation between the two of them, it would have been wiser for Dom Mayeul, if he had not directly confronted the archbishop. But as we already know, Dom Mayeul could not spell the word 'diplomacy'. It is possible that the archbishop was so furious and upset with Dom Mayeul, who had dared to confront the archbishop with immoralities, that may have happened in his Dominican order, that he vowed to take the first opportunity to react the same way. The opportunity would come in March 1923, with far reaching results. But for now, in his reply, he could not resist including; *"Even you, high up there at Mount Thabor, are not spared from these accusations".*

In addition, Dom Mayeul must have known that Archbishop Dowling had already cast a critical eye on Mount Thabor, which he considered ill-conceived and ostentatious. He had his suspicions about its real purpose and value, in spite of its name: the upper monastery. Though invited several times, he had never visited the place, which he could see from his own splendid castellated house in Port of Spain. His letter to Dom Mayeul remained unanswered for several months, a fact which obviously surprised him. Apparently Dom Mayeul had failed to let the archbishop know that he would be absent from the Mount for nearly three months, from mid-July to mid-October 1922, attending a General Chapter of the Brazilian Congregation in Rio de Janeiro. Thus it was only on 15 October 1922, that Dom Mayeul got round to answering the archbishop's letter. He assured him that the accusations were nothing more than rumours and calumnies, and brushed aside the whole matter, saying that:

> *Throughout my long life as priest and Superior, I have learnt to be very circumspect in believing everything I am told; and especially when it is a case of calumnies, I take very little notice of them at all (POS. BEN. Dom Mayeul to Dowling 15 Oct, 1922).*

In spite of this rather nonchalant reply to the archbishop, Dom Mayeul confided later, in his extensive report and defence for the Roman Church authorities, that he had been greatly shaken by the archbishop's letter of 4 July 1922: *Since this moment, I felt as if a Sword of Damocles was hanging over my head (APR., 613, #2, Report, p 6, 7-8 May 1923).*

He certainly had good reason to be worried. One suspects that in his heart of hearts, he knew that his whole world was crumbling around him. Why he failed, at this early stage (Oct.1922), to defend himself more vigorously against the insinuation and accusation, made by the archbishop, is a mystery. Perhaps he had become blind to the seriousness of the situation. Within two months Dom Mayeul had put the archbishop's letter right out of his mind, as is evident from the former's very friendly Christmas message, sent to the archbishop on 22 December 1922 *(POS. BEN., Dom Mayeul to Dowling, 22 Dec. 1922).*

But the matter was not allowed to rest there. At the end of March 1923, a serious accusation against Dom Mayeul was brought to the notice of Archbishop Dowling, which he could hardly ignore. Whether he rushed to judgment and acted without due investigation, we cannot say. In any case, he was presented with what he considered to be a damning indictment of Dom Mayeul, in written and oral testimonies, the truth of which he had no reason to doubt. He thus felt compelled to act, and bring the law of the Church down on the head of Dom Mayeul.

The damning letter was written on 27 March 1923, and addressed to Archbishop Dowling by a Jesuit priest, giving explicit details of the case of a lady penitent, who claimed to have had illicit relations with a monk of Mount St. Benedict. The name of the monk is not mentioned in the letter, though the writer adds a note to the effect that "the name of the monk is in the envelope". Unfortunately, the envelope, with the name, no longer exists in the archives of the archbishop of Port of Spain. This same Jesuit priest advised the lady to tell her story directly to the archbishop, which she did on 29 March. The archbishop took notes during this interview, and later sent a full report of the matter to Rome. On the strength of the information he had thus received, the archbishop decided to impose an immediate suspension on Dom Mayeul *(POS, BEN. Rev. E.D. to Dowling, 27 March, 1923. The letter of the Jesuit is in English; the report of the Archbishop is in Latin).*

In his memoirs, Dom Mayeul is very brief, hardly one page, on what happened during that week. However, he is not leaving out the crucial information, clearly indicating that something very serious, unknown to him, had happened. But what exactly? Obviously all this was damaging in every aspect, but how to defend himself without having the facts? He accuses the archbishop of giving in to unprovoked anger against him, in the aftermath of their disagreement over the parishes' issue, and, more seriously, of believing unconfirmed accusations of immoral conduct by unnamed persons. He regretted that this trouble had come upon him at the very moment when he was on the point of offering his resignation as superior of the Mount, a move which would have allowed him to depart with dignity and with his reputation untarnished. However, the die had been cast, and he was forced to take immediate action to safeguard his own reputation, and the future of Mount St. Benedict.

> *Indeed, I had not foreseen such an explosion of anger on the part of the prelate, though God allowed me to read these lines with a calm mind. Had not Pius X said to me: "You will have to suffer much from your fellow clerics", while at my Profession I promised to support every indignity and insult (Rule, ch. 7). I had intended handing in my resignation as Superior of Mount St. Benedict, within the next few months, but God evidently wished that this be done sooner (Vol. II, 182).*

Had the relationship between Dom Mayeul and the archbishop been on any kind of normal human footing, they could have sorted out their previous differences over a cup of tea. But they had drifted so far apart, corresponding in French rather than English, that they never got round to knowing or appreciating each other. There was no way Dom Mayeul could call on the archbishop to seek a direct explanation of the offending letter. His only resort was to leave Trinidad as soon as possible and consult the abbot primate in Rome. Dom Mayeul's mind must have been in a kind of whirl, as he set about booking a passage to Europe on the steamer Stuyvesant, which was due to sail from Port of Spain on the following Tuesday 11 April. He gave his reasons for leaving Trinidad at this moment in his lengthy report to the abbot primate:

> *Firstly, to give a complete and truthful statement to my Superiors in Rome, and listen to and follow their advice and their orders; secondly, to try to prevent a serious scandal, which would result in a lessening of the respect due to the Archbishop of Port of Spain. Before leaving the Mount, I took only two members of my Council (Fr. Hugh and Sebastian) into my confidence, putting them under strict secrecy, adding that if my suspension should become public they should tell the women, who were friends of the monastery, to say and do nothing, without first hearing from Rome (APR, 613, #1: Report of Dom Mayeul to Abbot Primate, p. 13, 8 May 1923).*

He decided it would not be necessary to give any details to his community. His monks were so used to his frequent departures to Europe and Brazil, that they would presume he had been summoned to Rome on urgent business and would ask no questions. In any case, Dom Mayeul was so convinced he would be exonerated, i.e. Rome would overturn the decision of the archbishop, that he saw his present trip as nothing more than a short one. He would be back in Trinidad within a few months. He seems to have completely forgotten his experience in 1913, when he went to Rome on a similar mission, to vindicate his reputation following his dispute with the archbishop of Bahia, only to find that Rome ruled against him. As he set sail on 11 April, he was in buoyant mood.

Writing that same day to his prior, Fr. Hugh, he noted that Mount Thabor looked very well from Port of Spain and the harbour. He also wished to remind Br. Raphael to plant a hibiscus hedge round the orchard in Mount Thabor, and ended the letter with the ominous phrase: *"I hope to see everything going on all right when I come back" (MSB, Dom Mayeul to D.H. 11 April 1923)*. This last statement is clear evidence that he intended returning to the Mount after his visit to Europe. He spent much of his time on board the *Stuyvesant* writing two lengthy "Reports" to the abbot primate, one on the suspension, and the other on the question of the parishes. Both reports give a detailed overview on how the relation with the archbishop escalated to the current situation. In addition, he explains in detail, including sources and facts, the 1922 calumnies. With respect to the March 1923 accusations and the suspension, Dom Mayeul gives a full account. He expands also on the severe consequences of his suspension for the community, the pilgrims and the Mount. The well structured report, and defence, contains many references to what Canon Law dictates, and the overall argumentation and explanation could not have been improved by a trial lawyer, not even the best one. For Dom Mayeul it was obvious that the archbishop had acted too hastily, without respecting Canon Law. However he realized also that in this case, there could be no real winner *(APR, 613, #1: Report of Dom Mayeul to Abbot Primate, 8 May 1923)*.

Dom Mayeul arrived at Le Havre, on 27 April, and thence took a train to Paris. After celebrating Mass in the cathedral of Notre Dame, he went to the convent of the Benedictine nuns in Paris, Rue Monsieur. There he met one of his former spiritual daughters from Trinidad, Dorothy Wharton, related to Agnus Wharton, who was having personal problems adapting to life in that particular convent. He promised he would find somewhere more suitable for her as soon as possible. He had planned to stay a few days in Paris, but instead headed for Rome immediately. The parish priest of Notre Dame had told him that, on the following Sunday evening, 29 April, Pope Benedict XV would beatify Sr. Thérèse of the Child Jesus.

> *Arriving at Le Havre, I learned that the following Sunday, 29 April, there would take place in Rome, the Beatification of the Venerable Thérèse of the Infant Jesus, about whom I knew very little at this time. However, in Paris, the Reverend Mother of the Benedictines offered me a copy of her autobiography to read on the journey to Rome. This book so enchanted me that I forgot all about my own cross, for I read there the following words: "Let us be convinced that we shall never find love, without suffering" (Life of Thérèse of Lisieux, p.321) (Vol. II).*

He thus took the overnight train from Paris to Rome, in order to be in time for the ceremony. Arriving there, he booked into Sant'Anselmo, the international Benedictine University in Rome, where the abbot primate resided. However, the abbot primate was in Germany at the bedside of his brother, who was seriously ill, and was not expected back in Rome for at least ten days. In the evening of his first day in Rome, Dom Mayeul joined a group of abbots who had places reserved in St. Peter's cathedral for the beatification ceremony. He was so captivated by the enthusiasm for the newly declared Blessed Thérèse, that he decided to put his future into her hands, and vowed to visit Lisieux as soon as he could. Blessed Thérèse would become the patroness of his old age. He also continued reading her autobiography, or *Life*, a copy of which had been given to him by the Mother Abbess of rue Monsieur, Paris.

Owing to the absence from Rome of the abbot primate, and anxious to consult with someone in authority, Dom Mayeul decided on 3 May to pay a visit to Cardinal van Rossum, the prefect of Propaganda Fide, the Roman Congregation with responsibility for the Church's missionary territories, which included Trinidad. Cardinal van Rossum was already aware of the problems facing the Benedictines, having been in direct contact with Archbishop Dowling in 1921 over the parishes' issue *(Prop.Fide. 777/21, 8 Marzo 1921)*. However, he was evidently surprised at the latest developments, especially the accusations of sexual misconduct made against the person of Dom Mayeul. On this visit, Dom Mayeul brought with him a document, signed by two members of the Mount's Council, under oath, declaring Dom Mayeul innocent of the charges made against him. At the same time, Dom Mayeul stated categorically to Cardinal van Rossum that he had never committed a fault of this kind *(APR, 613, #1, Report to Primate, p.4)*. The cardinal was evidently convinced, and confirmed this by a note to Dom Mayeul on his Visiting Card, which said simply: *"I wish your Lordship the best of success in a just cause" (Vol. III, Original Visiting Card)*.

It seems, however, that Cardinal van Rossum had a purely advisory role. Dom Mayeul had yet to put his case before the three authorities who could make the necessary decisions: firstly, the abbot primate, secondly, the Congregation for Religious, and thirdly, Pope Benedict XV. The abbot primate returned to Rome on 11 May. Dom Mayeul met with him the following day.

It appears that, already before the suspension of Dom Mayeul, the abbot primate had been in touch with the Congregation for Religious as far back as March 1923, regarding the Mount. Following on the visitation of the Mount in 1920 by Abbot Laurent Zeller, there was some unfinished business to be attended to, such as the separation of the Mount from the Brazilian Congregation. Cardinal Laurenti, the prefect of the Congregation for Religious, which had the responsibility for all the religious Orders in Trinidad, wrote to the abbot primate on 12 March 1923, proposing a canonical visitation of the Mount. The secretary of this same Congregation, Abbot Mauro Serafini, wrote the same day to the abbot primate, suggesting the name of Abbot Maurus Etcheverry, as the person Rome had chosen to undertake the visitation of the Mount. At that time, the main point on the agenda was the separation of the Mount from the Brazilian Congregation *(S. Cong. Relig. N. 501/13)*.

However, by 14 May 1923, there were now three other matters requiring an immediate resolution: (i) How to deal with the suspension of Dom Mayeul by Archbishop Dowling; (ii) What to do about Mount Thabor; and (iii) How to find a solution to the problem of the parishes *(MSB, Dom Mayeul to Dom Hugh, 14 May 1923)*. All the parties concerned agreed that a solution to the first matter, that is the suspension of Dom Mayeul, should be given priority. The other items could wait until the visitation of Abbot Etcheverry, scheduled for August-September 1923. His findings and report will be dealt with in the next chapter.

Dom Mayeul had several discussions with the abbot primate, during which the latter suggested that Dom Mayeul make a formal approach to the Holy See, stating his innocence. Dom Mayeul explained his own views on this, when writing to the prior of the Mount on 26 May 1923:

As for myself, for some time I have made a vow to put into practice the saying of Holy Scripture: Bonum est praestolari cum silentio salutare Dei (It is good to await in silence the saving power of God). Indeed, for nearly 30 years now I have been a superior, and I am getting tired of the responsibility. To give in one's resignation is not a sin, and was not a sin in St. Mayeul's case (the abbot of Cluny, his patron), although it may have caused some suffering to others. To take my case to Rome, with all its implications, accusations and complications may well be the occasion of many sins. No doubt, it could lead to a great humiliation, if I were not to be exonerated after making an official appeal or complaint to Rome. I realize that I have been the victim of a serious calumny. All will be revealed on the final Day of Judgment. If the Cardinal Prefect insists that I make an appeal to Rome, I suppose I will have to do so, but it may not be necessary. In the meantime, the Archbishop of Port of Spain has to provide proof of his accusations (MSB, Dom Mayeul to Dom Hugh, 26 May 1923).

Over the following week, Dom Mayeul did a lot of deep thinking. Although advised by the secretary of the Congregation for Religious, Abbot Mauro Serafini, that he should make a formal reply to the archbishop, rebutting the accusations, he decided to remain silent. The abbot primate, while critical of the highhanded action of the archbishop, convinced Dom Mayeul that his position in Trinidad was now an impossible one. There was no way he could return to Trinidad and take up where he had left off. Some time between 28 May and 9 June 1923, Dom Mayeul decided that he had no other choice but to offer his resignation as superior of the Mount to the Roman authorities. A constant theme in many of his letters, at this time, is his desire to start a new life away from Trinidad, in order to do some writing. He made up his mind on 9 June 1923, announcing his decision to resign as superior of the Mount to his prior, Dom Hugh van der Sanden:

I dreamed the other night that they wanted me to take up again the government of Mount St. Benedict, and that I fought strongly against this imposition. For some time now, I had dreamed of imitating my Patron Saint Mayeul, to better prepare myself for death. It is now 30 years that I have been Superior, and I am very tired of giving orders. In short, I have given in my dismissal, and as there may well be some criticism, I hasten to add that my retirement was not imposed upon me. For the rest, in making my request to the Holy See, and obtaining a positive response, I also realized that my life in Trinidad would become very difficult. There would have been further resentments, and further letters would have been written against me. In thus retiring, I feel I am serving the best interests of our dear monastery. If you hear any other versions, you will at least know which one is the true one.

The Abbot Primate believes that the Archbishop has exceeded his rights in the case of Mount Thabor, and in regard to the suspension, the calumniator will have to render an account to God, and likewise the Archbishop, who has believed the calumny without proper enquiry. I cannot understand why the Archbishop took such measures against me. I can only presume that it all was on account of the problems I had in upholding the Constitutions of our Congregation, which clashed with the wishes of the Archbishop, over the allocation of parishes to monks of Mount St. Benedict. However, I hesitate to make any judgment about the Archbishop's motive. I pardon everyone with a full heart, for the love of Jesus Crucified (MSB, Dom Mayeul to Dom Hugh, 9 June 1923).

The same day he wrote a farewell to all of the monks of Mount St. Benedict:

It is the last time that I write to you in common. As Saint Elizabeth of Shonau said before her death: "If I have offended anyone, I ask forgiveness, and for my part I forgive all those who may have caused me any offence or hurt". I hope you will have a better superior, who shall succeed in bringing dear Mount St. Benedict to the highest degree of spiritual and material prosperity. I often told you that I intended, sooner or later, to follow the example of my Holy Patron, St. Mayeul. It is now 30 years that I have been superior, and that burden is very, very heavy and dangerous.

I will never forget to pray for you; and those who will pray for me, will be rewarded in Heaven. God bless you all, and our good

Father St. Benedict also. P.S. In my audience I asked the Apos-
tolic blessing for all of you (MSB, Dom Mayeul to Dom Hugh,
9 June 1923).

On the face of it, the decision of the Roman authorities left a
lot of things unresolved. It seems that they were unwilling to take
on the archbishop of Port of Spain. In those far-off days, bishops,
and especially archbishops, were laws unto themselves, especially if
they lived as far away from Rome as Trinidad. Communication was
slow and unreliable. There is no doubt that the Roman authorities
believed Dom Mayeul to be innocent of the charges made against
him, and offered him the possibility of retiring with honour. This
is evident from the official letters, addressed to both Dom Mayeul
and the abbot primate, on 26 June 1923, and signed by Cardinal
Laurenti, prefect of the Congregation for Religious, and his secretary, Abbot Mauro Serafini, accepting Dom Mayeul's resignation
(Congreg. for Relig., N. 3459/23). Dom Mayeul was completely
exonerated, allowed to retain his titular abbacy of Lobbes, and put
under no restrictions in regard to any future ministry. If Rome had
found any suggestion of improper conduct on the part of Dom
Mayeul, he would have been deprived of his priestly faculties. He
had, in fact, been given a clean bill of health by the Roman authorities. The matter was, in fact, buried, and never surfaced again. Included in the final arrangements for the retirement of Dom Mayeul
were two clauses, which stated (i) that the Mount should, in the
future, provide for the sustenance and support of Dom Mayeul,
and (ii) that the latter be received, on a permanent basis, into a
monastery nominated by the abbot primate. It meant a total and
final break with Trinidad.

On receiving official word of Dom Mayeul's resignation, the pri-
or Dom Hugh and the subprior, Dom Weber, wrote immediately
to the abbot primate in Rome:

> *The resignation of our Father is a severe test and a great loss for our*
> *community, which is his work thanks to his relentless effort.... The*
> *news is very sad for all the community. When I read it to them, you*
> *could see on their faces that they were full of sadness and surprise. It*
> *is, indeed, a great cross to lose the Father of the monastery, who knew*
> *so well how to guide and lead us to eternal life. He suffered much*
> *criticism but always from people who had a lot to correct at themselves*
> *first (APR, 613, #7, 23 July 1923 and APR, 613, # 6).*

The prior, Dom Hugh, wrote to Dom Mayeul expressing his great shock at the news:

> It was with great sorrow that I received the news of your Lordship's resignation. Greater trial for our foundation we cannot imagine. How much we all shall miss you in every detail of our daily life, and especially in our spiritual training.
>
> How much I would have liked to have you still for a good many years, to be imbibed of the sweet, solid and prudent doctrine. On the other hand, I thank Our Lord that He has given us the privilege to have had such a great MASTER of the spiritual life in my beginning of religious life, and that at least I was able to obtain some sound and safe principles, which will be a guide for my whole life.
>
> During your Lordship's absence, I was craving the whole time for your return. You may imagine the shock I got after the news. But if the grief of your children is great, I quite understand also your suffering. I especially shall never be able to show enough thanks for all you have done for me, particularly for the great confidence you had in me. I only understood that during your absence. I have tried my best to correspond to it. For all that I have done that has pained or hurt your good heart, I beg your paternity's humble pardon. Need I say that I shall pray always for your Lordship? Everything around me speaks about you, and even my internal life is your work.
>
> Although you are no more our superior, you will always be our FOUNDER, and you may be assured, you will always hear about your dear Mount St. Benedict.
>
> All the friends of the monastery are very sorry over your Lordship's demission. Many commentaries, of course, were made. Everything was explained by telegram. Mount Thabor was closed by telegram from Rome. Naturally we were at a loss sometimes to explain things, because we rightly understood that there was something very grave in the matter. Yesterday I was so happy to receive your letters, because your silence was even badly interpreted, as if you would not be allowed to write (MSB, Dom Hugh to Dom Mayeul 6 August 1923).

Some reactions to the news of Dom Mayeul's resignation were very emotional. Dom Odilo van Tongeren's letter to Dom Mayeul was the most moving:

My dearest Father in St. Benedict, You will never realize the sadness which repeatedly comes over me, by calling you "Father" alone – not more my Lord and my Guardian – and even the word "Father" makes me feel as one standing at your grave, for you are dead for me. However hard it is for me to miss you in the future, yet I look back at the past and kiss your frozen hand most tenderly, bent over your coffin, and thank God for whatever you did for me, and farewell forever! On Saturdays, I'll pray the 'Exaudiat' for you as long as I live, and kindly say an occasional prayer for me also, who remains with the fondest love (MSB, Dom Odilo to Dom Mayeul, 5 August, 1923).

In spite of not being a native English speaker, Dom Odilo ends his letter with a quotation from Shakespeare's "Measure for Measure", an apt reference to the calumnies made against Dom Mayeul:

O Right Reverend Lord Abbot
O place and greatness, Millions of false eyes
Are stuck upon thee – volumes of report
Run with these false and most contrarious quests
Upon thy doings
(Shakespeare: Measure for Measure, Act IV, Sc. i)

Finally, in a long letter to Dom Mayeul, Dom Jean Gualbert van de Plas, gave a detailed account of the Chapter meeting at the Mount, when the prior announced to the community Dom Mayeul's resignation:

When Fr. Prior, with downcast eyes and a mournful face said: "Today, my dear brethren, I have to communicate to you the sad news from the Abbot Primate that our dear Lord Abbot has resigned". It was really pitiful to see all those anxious and nervous movements of those present. I myself did not know what was going on. I did not see anything, the light from my eyes had gone. I felt sad, sorry and giddy, that I was rather glad that Fr. Prior shortened the conference. God only knows what we have lost! I cannot be grateful enough for all Your Lordship has done for me. The only way I can show my gratitude is to pray daily for your Paternity. I thank Your Lordship, in a special way, for all good and favours bestowed on me. I shall always keep in grateful memory, the many

> *spiritual lessons, conferences, so practical and beautiful, given in*
> *the course of our unions in community life at Mount St. Benedict*
> *(MSB, Dom Gualbert to Dom Mayeul 6 August 1923).*

These letters give a totally different picture to the long-held tradition, or hearsay, that when Prior Hugh announced the resignation of Dom Mayeul, the majority of the community clapped their hands and banged the floor with their feet, openly rejoicing at the news. The above-quoted letters must have given Dom Mayeul some consolation, showing, as they did, that he was still held in high regard by the majority of the monks of the Mount. He undoubtedly felt sad at the thought of never seeing his beloved Mount St. Benedict again, and only gradually became reconciled to the reality of the situation.

In his memoirs, he gives very little information about himself at this time, except to say that before leaving Rome he got the blessing of Pope Pius XI. Immediately afterwards, he went to St. Peter's basilica and deposited his pectoral cross at the feet of the statue of St. Peter. From St. Peter's, he went to the church of St. Alphonsus in Rome, where he obtained a copy of the miraculous painting of Our Lady of Perpetual Succour, to whom he had a deep devotion. After making this purchase, he reflected that he would need Our Lady's help to overcome his many rebuffs, and to sanctify his old age *(Vol. II, 184-5)*.

At the end of June 1923, Dom Mayeul left Rome travelling first to Belgium and then to France, looking for a suitable Benedictine convent for Dorothy Wharton. She had left Trinidad in 1918 to join the Benedictine community of rue Monsieur, Paris, but was not happy there. He eventually arranged for her to be accepted into the Convent of Jouarre, situated outside Paris, where there was a flourishing community of some 85 nuns. Dom Mayeul was so impressed by the fervent atmosphere of this Benedictine convent that he offered himself as an honorary chaplain to the nuns. His general situation was still uncertain. He was a misplaced person, unattached to any monastery, awaiting the final decision by the abbot primate regarding his permanent acceptance into a monastery willing to have him.

Evidently, the most traumatic moment in his life occurred during that time in 1923 when he experienced a serious temptation to give in to despair and bitterness. He suffered from a terrible depression and was contemplating suicide. He explained his feelings in his memoirs:

But still the demon was not asleep, and I was afflicted with a terrible temptation to despair. I had before my mind a picture of horror, as I contemplated my moral situation in the eyes of the world. This temptation became almost an obsession (Vol. II, 184).

Although, in his heart of hearts, he knew he was innocent of the accusations made against him, he feared that if these calumnies entered the public domain, his reputation would be seriously tarnished. In this frame of mind, he wrote as follows to Abbot Primate von Stotzingen on 9 July 1923:

I received, with sadness, the document from the Holy See, dated 26 June 1923, accepting my resignation as Superior of Mount St. Benedict, which you sent me I fully accept your words of sympathy. For my part, I received this document with a certain joy, mixed with sadness. In the very depths of my being, my soul felt on the brink of death, at least to the point of desiring or causing it, if such a thing was permitted. I also had a temptation against faith, when I saw how sins of adultery, fornications etc. went unpunished. This temptation became almost an obsession, and in the end, in order to rid myself of it, I decided to make a pilgrimage to Lisieux, where Blessed Thérèse filled me with her caresses.

On 23 Oct. 1923 Dom Mayeul wrote in the same words to Dom Hugh van der Sanden, his successor at Mount St. Benedict:

At the time of the Beatification of Blessed Thérèse, I asked her to win for me the grace of dying in a state of happiness. This favour was denied me. So I asked for the grace of a moral death, i.e. the complete detachment from material things. It was thanks to this, that I was able to offer my resignation with complete detachment. It did not cost me any regrets. And so I live free from all responsibility, hidden away in a tiny corner, in order to pray, to study and to write. This is the last stage of my life, and I think it will be the best, the sweetest and the most meritorious.

Such reflections show the mindset of Dom Mayeul in 1923, but fortunately his pilgrimage to Lisieux and the years to come in Florida would soon help him to overcome this.

On the first day in Lisieux, he celebrated Mass in the chapel of the Benedictine sisters, where Blessed Thérèse made her First Holy Communion, using the same missal as she had, when renewing her baptismal promises. The following day he offered Mass at the Carmel, at an altar beside her shrine. One of the highlights of his visit was a conversation in the parlour with the Mother Prioress, a blood sister of Blessed Thérèse, who gave him a lock of hair of Blessed Thérèse. He also obtained permission to dedicate his first book, *"Twenty-Five Years as a Missionary in the Tropics"*, to the Blessed Thérèse. This was the first of many such visits he made to Lisieux over the coming years. On his way back to Paris, he visited some of the places in Normandy, where he believed his family roots lay.

Since all the authorities in Rome, including the abbot primate, were on their summer holidays, he had to wait until September before getting any definite news. In the meantime, he needed a temporary *'pied a terre'*, where he could leave his luggage and books, and have a forwarding address, until his future home was decided. The abbey of Jouarre proved an ideal choice. He was destined to remain there until April 1924, when he finally left Europe for St. Leo Abbey, Florida.

Some time in the late summer of 1923, Dom Mayeul seems to have turned his back for good on the Mount, and became reconciled to spending the rest of his life elsewhere. The circumstances of his departure left him open to the accusation of abandoning his newly established monastery in Trinidad, and of walking away from an enterprise to which he had dedicated ten years of his life (1913-23). The unbending attitude of Archbishop Dowling left the abbot primate and the Roman authorities with no other solution to the impasse than the resignation of Dom Mayeul. Was the future of Mount St. Benedict at stake because of this crisis? It is true that Rome had ordered an extraordinary visitation of the Mount by Abbot Maurus Etcheverry, a French Benedictine monk, who was fluent in several languages, including English, which was necessary in the case of Trinidad. The abbot primate briefed him on the main issues facing the monks of the Mount: (i) that of the parishes, i.e. how the monks involved in this apostolate should maintain some kind of monastic life at the same time; (ii) how to arrange that the Mount, having been expelled from the Brazilian Congregation in 1922, should be affiliated to some other well-established Benedictine Congregation, preferably a European one.

ABBEY OF JOUARRE IN FRANCE, A FAMOUS BENEDICTINE CONVENT WHICH HAD
A LOT TO SUFFER UNDER THE FRENCH REVOLUTION OF 1793. THE ENORMOUS
LIBRARY, WITH ANCIENT DOCUMENTS, WAS SET ON FIRE AND DESTROYED.

309

All eyes were now directed towards Dom Etcheverry, on whose mission, depended the future of the Mount. He met Dom Mayeul in France just before taking a ship for Trinidad at the end of July 1923. Their meeting, in the French monastery, Abbey d'En Calcat, was friendly, and according to Dom Etcheverry, "helpful". In fact, he reported to the abbot primate on 19 July:

> *He seemed to me to be very reasonable, making no complaints or recriminations, and ready to cooperate in every way, in the handing over of power and property rights to his successor at the Mount. He said nothing about his difficulties with the Archbishop, and I made no allusion to this matter either. He was obviously very much preoccupied with his own future, which he hoped would be in the tropics, though not in Brazil, for his health's sake (APR, 613, #4, Etcheverry to Abbot Primate, 19 July 1923).*

CHAPTER XVII

The Mission of Abbot Etcheverry to the Mount

(1923)

THE PRIOR and the monks of the Mount awaited with a certain anxiety the arrival of Abbot Maur Etcheverry. He had been appointed by the Roman Congregation for Religious to undertake an extraordinary visitation of the monastery, in the aftermath of the resignation of Dom Mayeul. The terms of reference of his mission are listed in a document from the abbot primate to Dom Maur Etcheverry dated 14 6 1923 (APR 613, #3):

> *First, should we abandon the Mount and liquidate everything and make restitution to Bahia? Or should we maintain the Mount and if yes, keep the Mount under the Brazilian Congregation or look for another Congregation? Perhaps Buckfast? Second, is there someone at the Mount that we can consider capable of taking the responsibility as Superior? Third, on the assets: detailed analysis of the financial situation. Some say the Mount is poor, other sources say this is not the case. What are the facts? Who owns the title of ownership? If Dom Mayeul is the official owner, how can we transfer ownership? Does the Mount really need the 5 Contos that Bahia has to pay on an annual basis? The Bahia finances are not very good. Fourth, what are the exact accusations from the Archbishop against Dom Mayeul? Fifth, make it clear to the Archbishop that the decision of Propaganda Fide on the parishes' issue must be implemented.*

Prior Hugh van der Sanden and his Council realized that their situation was under scrutiny by Rome, but life in the monastery continued unchanged during the four months following the departure of Dom Mayeul in April, and they held out good hope for the future of the place. According to a long-standing tradition – still retained as part of the folk memory of the monastery – Dom Etcheverry was sent to Trinidad to close down the Mount. Abbot Etcheverry was, in fact, a very mild man, kind and thoroughly honest, determined to help the monks of the Mount adapt to their present situation, and to sort out any problems they might be facing at the moment or in the future. The extraordinary treatment of the Mount can be explained by the fact that it was so far away from Rome, and communication was slow and difficult. Furthermore, its Brazilian origin and background had been a mixed blessing, bringing with it certain tensions and difficulties. By 1923, the Mount had broken away from the Brazilian Congregation, and been put under the immediate jurisdiction of the abbot primate. In many ways it was considered by Rome to be something of an anomaly. So part of the mission of Abbot Etcheverry was to examine how the monastery could be kept within the Benedictine fold, put on a firm footing, and its future development and prosperity guaranteed. It was mainly due to this positive state of mind that his mission turned out to be such a success.

Dom Etcheverry left Bordeaux on 26 July 1923 and arrived in Trinidad during the second week of August. The prior and community received him with the usual liturgical honours, and accorded him every facility for conducting his visitation in an atmosphere of friendliness and cordiality. He was clearly impressed by the general situation in the monastery. His first task was to conduct individual talks with the prior and the community, and to listen to their personal stories. These interviews were done orally, except in the case of Dom Charles Verbeke, who, being stationed on the island of St. Vincent, was unable to come to the Mount for the visitation and had to give his evidence in writing. It appears that Dom Charles was not a very happy man, and for years had been something of a thorn in the side of Dom Mayeul. At the time of Abbot Etcheverry's visitation he had the pastoral charge of this remote island (St. Vincent), where he was out of reach of his monastic superiors, and able very much to do his own thing. His 4-page 'Memorandum' to Abbot Etcheverry, dated August 1923, while giving a fairly reliable summary of his monastic life since 1906, is very critical of Dom Mayeul's role as superior of both Bahia and the Mount. He accuses Dom Mayeul of deception, indiscretion, annoyances, etc. which had made his (Dom Charles') life very difficult, and caused him serious health problems. He had already expressed these same allegations to the previous abbot visitor, Dom Laurent Zeller, in 1920, and to the abbot primate in 1921, accusing Dom Mayeul of allowing abuses to creep in, and asking quite bluntly that Dom Mayeul be removed from his position as superior of the Mount. However, Dom Charles got quite a surprise when Abbot Etcheverry decided to visit St. Vincent, and study the situation there first hand. He found Dom Charles' lifestyle very unsatisfactory, and in his final report to Rome, is very critical of Dom Charles, as will be seen later in this chapter.

Since Dom Charles is such an important player in the anti-Dom Mayeul camp, it is worthwhile quoting some lines from a letter which he wrote to Archbishop Dowling on 5 October 1923:

> *Regarding the Lord Abbot Dom Mayeul De Caigny, the Visitator has questioned me concerning him, and I have given him such information as corresponded with the truth. He asked me whether I would affirm certain of my communications sub jurejurando (under oath), and I have done so in writing. Now it has come to my knowledge that in the Port of Spain it is the general belief that I am the cause of Dom Mayeul's resignation. The rumour is that I have written to Rome, calumniating the Lord Abbot. What is worse is that even my friends are believing this, and that I am losing the moral and physical impossibility of defending myself.... And what I am wondering at is, that Mount St. Benedict does not seem to take my defence at all (POS, BEN. Verbeke to Dowling, 5 October, 1923).*

Dom Etcheverry had hardly arrived in Trinidad when he wrote his first impression to the abbot primate:

> *My impressions so far? It looks to me that it would be regrettable to abandon Mount St. Benedict. The material aspect is not bad at all, but with respect to the spiritual, religious and discipline aspect, I suspect many shortcomings (APR 613, #4, 13 8 1923).*

It is clear from Dom Etcheverry's two reports, both dated September 1923, (i) to the prefect of the Sacred Congregation for Religious and (ii) to the abbot primate that he kept strictly to his mandate summarized as: (a) whether the Mount could be maintained as a truly Benedictine house, giving hopes of fulfilling the conditions, including the financial aspect, for the normal development as a monastery; and (b) the measures that should be taken to assure its future. His answers to these were mostly positive, interspersed with some criticisms. Contrary to his first impressions, the day after he had arrived in Trinidad, that he suspected many shortcomings, he found the Mount in good working order, both as regards the spiritual and material spheres, though needing some adjustments and improvements in certain areas. *(Cong. Relig. 501/23) and (APR, 613, #3)*

The report to the abbot primate was thorough and well-structured, looking at the situation from the material and monastic point of view. He gave a detailed survey of the buildings, noting the absence of any real enclosure, like a wall, but that other measures had been taken to prevent unauthorized access. He suggested that the galvanized roofs be replaced with something more lasting and solid. On the economic front, he noted that the monastery had no debts, and that there was a considerable reserve of money in the bank. Dom Etcheverry included in his report a very detailed financial picture on the assets (capital, property, land, furniture,...) and on the revenues and expenditures of the last years. The property was extensive (600 acres), mostly consisting of cocoa and coffee plantations. He confirmed that the pilgrimage to the shrine of St. Benedict brought in substantial revenue, as well as many Mass intentions and that a sum of money should be set aside for new buildings at the level of the lower monastery. He was also worried about the long-term threat to the cocoa plantation, owing to cocoa imports from Africa and elsewhere.

At this stage in his report, Dom Etcheverry gave also a detailed pen-portrait, with frank comments, of each of the monks. The majority met with his approval. There were 20 monks in the monastery, consisting of 8 priests, 8 professed, 4 lay brothers and 3 male oblates. Some of the monks were dispersed in outlying parishes, at the behest of the archbishop, and this had brought some serious problems and misunderstandings.

His first conclusion on the question whether the Mount could be maintained didn't leave any room for ambiguity. Notwithstanding the problems, he concluded that it would be disastrous to think of closing down the monastery and selling the property. He added that in addition it would have been impossible to recoup the money already invested in the enterprise. The buildings were not suitable for any other purpose than a monastery.

He continued that, to assure the future of the monastery, something ought to be done about recruitment, with emphasis on encouraging local people to join the community. On the present superior, Dom Hugh van der Sanden, he noted that while it is true that Dom Hugh is an excellent monk and the best candidate for the function of superior, he was very young and lacking in experience and that he should be supported by frequent visits from either the abbot primate or someone delegated by him. The report also indicated that one had been too tolerant when admitting postulants. According to Dom Etcheverry there was no good selection process in place, in order to have a good rate of success. He was also critical about the follow-up and discipline among new postulants. He wrote that they have been abandoned and on their own and the monastery needed a very strong superior.

As mentioned, the majority of the monks met with his approval, except for Dom Charles Verbeke and Dom Ludger Nauer. The latter was not spared from serious criticism confirming the same reservations Dom Mayeul had expressed before about Dom Ludger. Dom Etcheverry accused him of *having a false mindset, never satisfied, always accusing, lacking monastic discipline, came from a seminary where he already had problems and at the Mount, Dom Ludger has not been blameless with respect to morality and ethics (APR 613, #4, 13 8 1923).*

The abbot visitator had spent some time in St. Vincent, where Dom Charles Verbeke was pastor. Occupying more than forty lines in the typed report about Dom Charles, Dom Etcheverry made a lot of reservations and concluded that he had a very independent character. Also that he had a lifestyle which was not compatible with that of a monk and would find it difficult to adapt to community life at the Mount. Yet, he was doing good work; he was hard working and had a lot of talents and should be allowed to remain as pastor of the island of St. Vincent.

Dom Etcheverry was both surprised and appalled when he first set eyes on Mount Thabor. He questioned each of the monks and found that not one approved of this venture, which had cost a lot, perhaps up to US$15,000. Considering that it was some 1000 ft. above the lower monastery, and accessible only on foot, it required a strong heart and stronger legs to make the journey. He didn't consider Mount Thabor to be of any use considering the number of monks. But he mentioned that perhaps in the future Mount Thabor could be used, though on a smaller scale. He thought the structure too vast, and its appearance bizarre. More particularly, he was worried about the maintenance costs, and suggested that the building should be reduced in size, and only essential repairs undertaken, to prevent it becoming a ruin. Anyway, destruction would be its fate within a few years.

As regards the parishes, the abbot visitor believed that they provided a useful and even necessary occupation for some of the monks, though a more suitable arrangement for staffing the parishes needed to be made. The only alternative to the parishes, as an occupational outlet for the monks, would be the establishment of a college or boarding school, at the Mount. However, on enquiry, Dom Etcheverry found that the idea of starting a college was not viable, owing to the great number of such institutions already on the island. The parishes should, therefore, be maintained as the most acceptable work outlet for the monks. Moreover, they guaranteed an element of good standing with Archbishop Dowling, and brought the monks into closer contact with the general population of the island.

The last item on Dom Etcheverry's report to the abbot primate came under the title "Relations with the world of women". He reckoned that the number of women in and around the monastery was a disturbing factor, which needed to be dealt with urgently, and blamed Dom Mayeul for having allowed the so-called apostolate of the oblates to get out of hand. These women had eventually developed into a kind of 'coterie', with consequent jealousies and rivalries. He recommended that, in order to maintain the peace and good reputation of the Mount, women should be kept severely at a distance from the monastery *(APR., 613, # 3, Appendix, p.6, in French)*.

In his report sent to Cardinal Laurenti, the prefect of the Sacred Congregation for Religious, Dom Etcheverry deals at length with the question of affiliating the Mount to a European Benedictine Congregation, preferably the Belgian Congregation. He outlined the history of the Mount and its previous relationship with the Brazilian Congregation, from which it was expelled in 1922. Already some contact had been made between the Mount and the Belgian Congregation, and the signs of a possible rapport were very positive. These negotiations should continue, and hopefully would bear fruit in time. The fact that many of the monks at the Mount come from either Belgium or Holland, was a further reason for pursuing this matter *(S.C. Relig., 501/23)*. Negotiations concerning this matter lasted for several years, in fact until 1927, when the Mount was finally accepted as a member of the Belgian Congregation, today known under the title: 'The Congregation of the Annunciation'.

On his return to Europe from Trinidad at the end of September 1923, Dom Etcheverry continued to correspond with the abbot primate on the subject of the Mount. However, he was a very busy man, involved in a number of other pressing matters, such as congresses, conferences, etc., which took up much to his time. Thus, as late as December 1923, he had not yet finalised his report on his visitation of the Mount, though he promised to reserve his first moments of leisure in the new year to this work *(APR, 613. #4, Etcheverry to Abbot Primate, 21 Dec.1923)*. He seems to have had Dom Mayeul very much on his mind, asking the abbot primate if any solution had yet been found regarding Dom Mayeul's final place of residence. He was also critical of Dom Mayeul's lengthy stay in the Benedictine abbey of Jouarre, near Paris, and the fact that he was pontificating (i.e. celebrating Mass with full abbatial regalia) in convents and churches throughout France. He noted that Dom Mayeul was writing his memoirs, and requested the abbot primate to discourage Dom Mayeul from publishing them. Dom Etcheverry sent his final report on his visitation of the Mount on 4 April 1924. In his covering letter, he states that he has refrained from saying anything 'directly' about Dom Mayeul, realizing that the abbot primate was already sufficiently informed of this matter *(APR,613, #4, Etcheverry to Abbot Primate, 4 April 1924)*. One suspects that there was an agreement between Dom Etcheverry and the abbot primate that the conclusions on the subject of Dom Mayeul's resignation, was a matter for the abbot primate himself. Certainly the matter never came up for discussion in their correspondence. It is more than likely that the abbot primate had reserved the details of Dom Mayeul's case, the accusations, for himself.

For his part, Dom Mayeul never forgot how Archbishop Dowling had treated him unjustly, in withdrawing faculties to hear confessions in the diocese of Port of Spain, and believing the calumnies made against him by unnamed parties. He made the following reflection on the harsh treatment he had received from the archbishop:

As for myself, I am absolutely convinced that if I had given in to him on the question of the parishes, he would never have taken these measures against me. This conviction is based on a psychological understanding of his character, applied over a period of nine years by personal experience, and confirmed by other people who are competent to make a judgment in such a case. The final judgment of this question rests with God, who uses men, with all their faults, as instruments of his designs on each one of us (Vol. II, 185).

A surprising witness to the truth of this comes from an unlikely source, namely Dom Charles Verbeke. He had similar experiences, as Dom Mayeul with Archbishop Dowling, which he reported in a testimonial written in 1927 to Abbot Visitor Robert de Kerchove:

As regards the Archbishop, he is not easy to get along with, indeed, the opposite. He makes pastoral life very difficult. In 1925 I paid a visit to the Archbishop in Trinidad. After an interview of half-an-hour, during which everything went well, I was on the point of leaving, when I mentioned a parish mission to be preached by the Redemptorist Fathers of San Dominique in St. Vincent in May 1926. At the mention of the word 'mission', the Archbishop became furious. St. Vincent had no need of a parish mission and he started criticising everything I had done there since becoming pastor. I was so upset, that I went immediately afterwards to discuss my situation with Father English, the head of the Holy Ghost Fathers in Trinidad, asking him what line of judgment the Archbishop took in such matters. Fr. English cried out loud: "Follow a line of judgment. Never! He is a most unreliable, most revengeful, person... He is nasty" (Dom Charles Verbeke to Abbot de Kerchove, 1927).

Dom Charles' testimonial is quoted here by way of backing up the opinion that Archbishop Dowling was undoubtedly a difficult person, who had to be handled with kid gloves. Dom Mayeul was the last person in the world to adopt a kid-glove attitude with anyone. However, late in 1923, he felt that he had to vindicate himself, having waited several months before making a final statement of his case to the archbishop. At the end of December 1923, he penned a long letter to the archbishop, wishing him a Happy New Year for 1924, and at the same time saying "goodbye" to the diocese of Port of Spain. This letter is missing from the archbishop's archives, and may well have been destroyed by the archbishop. However, Dom Mayeul, made a copy of it, which he inserted into his memoirs. Since it is his final word on his relationship with the archbishop it is worth quoting. It is a moving letter. The archbishop never replied to it:

> *Indeed, I leave your diocese, Monsignor, with a serious doubt in my mind, which I feel I have to mention in all simplicity. Speaking of the relations, which his monks ought to have with their bishop, St. Benedict underlines the two conditions which should inspire and accompany his (the bishop's) intervention: (i) he must act with 'a chaste mind' and (ii) be motivated by 'a godly zeal' (Rule of St. Benedict, Ch. 64). In regard to the 'chaste mind', this implies that he acts without passion or prejudice, but with courtesy. In regard to "godly zeal", the bishop should act without partiality, but look at everything from God's point of view.*

> *Now, I ask myself how these two conditions were fulfilled in my case. From the very first moment of my arrival on the island of Trinidad, I asked that you frankly tell me if anything, I said or did, displeased you. My only concern was to do everything for the glory of God and the good of souls. Yet, it had come to my ears how you were lenient and forgiving in the case of several priests who had committed fornication, whereas for my part, having done nothing of the kind, I had to bear the weight of your rigorous condemnation. It seems to me that there is a partiality in your way of dealing with different people, two different weights and two different measures, which is contrary to the injunction of Sacred Scripture. And where can I see any "godly zeal" in your dealing with me?*

> *I hope to see you in Heaven, where, recognizing your error, you will offer me your excuses. In any case, you may be sure that I have forgiven you long ago, and that I pray each day for you at Holy Mass (Vol. II, 186-7, Dom Mayeul to Dowling, December 1923).*

Archbishop Dowling, having read this letter, must have realized that he had dealt unjustly, or at least harshly, with Dom Mayeul. But it was too late now to do anything. As far as we know, he never considered offering Dom Mayeul an apology, although that would have been the correct thing to do. He had a number of options open to him. Firstly, he could have made a further complaint against Dom Mayeul to Rome, but decided, on second thoughts, against taking this step. Secondly, he could ignore the letter, destroy it, and make no acknowledgement of it to Dom Mayeul, which is what he did. At the end of the day, it seems that Archbishop Dowling decided to erase all memory of Dom Mayeul from his mind. He was greatly relieved that Dom Mayeul had left Trinidad for good, and would never darken the door of his house again.

One would have hoped that the problems with the parishes would have ended after Dom Mayeul left Trinidad. On the contrary, the archbishop remained inflexible and stubborn and over the years the same conflicts were all too frequent between the archbishop and the prior of Mount St. Benedict, Dom Hugh van der Sanden. At one point, Abbot Visitor Chrysostom de Saegher and Dom Hugh were shown the door at the archbishop's palace. Dom Hugh wrote about this to the abbot primate on 20 Oct 1927:

> The canonical visitation was a great blessing to the monastery. All the members of the community were very pleased with the visit of Dom Chrysostom. However with the Archbishop he was not so happy; as I anticipated he obtained nothing. ... During the meeting when Dom Chrysostom finally realized that the Archbishop obstinately held to his opinion, he declared that he was obliged to report this to the General Chapter and to Rome. It is very strange that the Archbishop can disregard orders from Rome to such an extent. It really is a great pity because, with a little bit of goodwill from his part, the matter could be resolved. On the other issue of having monks ordained after they fulfilled the requirements, he neither gave in. When he (the Archbishop) could not answer any longer to the arguments of Dom Chrysostom, the Archbishop stood up in a fury and said 'cela suffit' (that's enough) forcing us to leave. Dom Chrysostom will report the actions of the Archbishop to Rome but I know I will be the target of his (the Archbishop's) wrath but I trust in God since I did nothing but my duty.

In late December 1927, Dom Hugh informed Dom Mayeul at St. Leo Abbey of these events. The news came as no surprise to Dom Mayeul, he had seen it all before. In fact, it confirmed that, in the past, he had not been the source of the conflict with the archbishop on the matter of the parishes.

FR. HUGH VAN DER SANDEN, APPOINTED BY DOM MAYEUL IN 1923 AS HIS
SUCCESSOR AND CONFIRMED BY THE ABBOT PRIMATE AFTER THE CANONICAL
VISITATION OF DOM ETCHEVERRY. DOM HUGH LIVED HIS FAITH AND HE
PERSONIFIED THE "MOUNT" SINCE HE WAS A 'MOUNTAIN' FOR THE MONKS, THE
PILGRIMS AND FOR THE MONASTIC LIFE.

CHAPTER XVIII

The Road to St. Leo Abbey, Florida

THROUGHOUT the summer (July-August) of 1923, despite having a roof over his head in the Benedictine abbey of Jouarre, Paris, Dom Mayeul felt uneasy and insecure. He was anxious to find a permanent place of residence as soon as possible, where he could settle down to write his memoirs. He had accumulated a great number of personal manuscripts, diaries, letters and notes over the years, which were stored in his room in Mount Thabor. These were essential sources for his biography. He wrote on 10 July to Prior Hugh of the Mount, proposing that he (Dom Mayeul) should come to Trinidad to collect his manuscripts and papers *(MSB, Dom Mayeul to Dom Hugh, 10 July 1923)*. But as time went on, and he realized that he was never going to return to Trinidad, he asked Dom Hugh to send these personal papers to him in Paris. Dom Hugh, however, pointed out that the cost of sending them from Trinidad to France would be very high. It seemed more practical, to leave the bulk of his papers in Trinidad until he had moved to his final destination. There followed a long correspondence between Dom Mayeul and Dom Hugh on this matter. At the end of the day, some of the more important manuscripts were sent to Paris, but the bulk of his papers and personal belongings remained in Trinidad for the moment.

In the meantime, the abbot primate was doing his best to find a permanent home for Dom Mayeul in some monastery, with options reaching as far as Italy, Congo, Brazil and USA. Europe was ruled out, mainly for health reasons. Dom Mayeul, having spent some twenty-five years in the tropics, would find it difficult to survive the cold winters, on account of his rheumatism. One cannot but admire the patience and goodwill of Abbot Primate von Stotzingen, who at this time, carried the responsibility for the whole

Benedictine Order on his shoulders. Gathering from the number of letters written by Dom Mayeul to the abbot primate, the former seemed to think that he was the only monk occupying the abbot primate's time. But then, it is possible that he was now almost desperate. In any case, all his life he had been an impatient person, demanding instant answers, and having his own opinion accepted, today rather than tomorrow. Fortunately, he had not very long to wait, on 4 August 1923, the abbot primate wrote to Dom Mayeul laying out the various options. Among these was a monastery in Florida, USA, St. Leo Abbey. Dom Mayeul thought this proposal worthwhile examining and wrote to the abbot primate: *"Your proposal that I go to Florida seems to me the most appealing. . . . I would be obliged if you could pursue this project"* (APR, 613, #6, Dom Mayeul to A.P. 17 & 30 August 1923).

The abbot primate wrote immediately to Abbot Charles Mohr of St. Leo Abbey, Florida, asking if he was willing to accept Dom Mayeul in his monastery for a prolonged stay. Abbot Charles replied, on 15 October 1923, stating rather bluntly that he would be happy to accept Dom Mayeul, though under certain conditions:

> *Now regarding the resigned Abbot, he is welcome. But as I generally have many guests during the winter, I want him to put off his visit until after Easter. He is welcome under the following conditions:*
>
> *(1) I want no pay from him.*
>
> *(2) I will supply him with Mass Intentions every day.*
>
> *(3) He will have to furnish his own clothing.*
>
> *(4) In the event of sickness he will pay the doctor.*
>
> *(5) I will furnish him all the paper and postage he needs.*
>
> *(6) He will have to be satisfied to take things as they come.*
>
> *I cannot furnish him with any special attendants, nor furnish all the attention he is used to getting in South America. If he will be just one of us, we will get along. It's not going to cost him anything whilst with us. Of course, if at any time I would feel that his presence among us was not pleasant for us, I would not hesitate to tell him so. We are a very democratic people, and he will have to get used to our ways.*

With all this understood and agreed upon, he is welcome (APR, 613, #6, Abbot Charles to Abbot Primate, 15 October 1923).

Dom Mayeul's first reaction to this letter was to have a good laugh, and then to accept the conditions laid down by Abbot Charles. He told the abbot primate that he was happy to wait until Easter 1924, before going to Florida. He then wrote personally to Abbot Charles of St. Leo Abbey, accepting his conditions, and saying how much he looked forward to going to Florida in April 1924 *(St. Leo, Dom Mayeul to Abbot Charles, 12 November 1923).* He added a postscript, saying that while he had originally planned to leave Paris before the winter of 1923-24 set in, a number of factors had emerged to make him change his mind. Firstly, the problem of surviving the cold winter in Paris had been solved by the installation of a new central heating system in the abbey of Jouarre. Secondly, as he settled down in Paris to begin writing his memoirs, he decided that he would write them in French. However, he soon discovered that his French had become rusty. He needed, therefore, to spend some more time in Paris, improving his knowledge of French, and developing a good style of writing in that language *(APR, 613, # 6, Dom Mayeul to Abbot Primate, 5 November 1923).* Thus he was quite happy to postpone his journey to Florida until after Easter. In the meantime, he would avail himself of the excellent library in the abbey of Jouarre to do some reading in French, while he hoped to discuss his project with some of the Benedictine sisters, who were prepared to help him with his linguistic problems. These months in Paris were not wasted, but gave him the opportunity to undertake a serious apprenticeship in the art of writing in French. On Oct 16 1923 he wrote from Paris to his nephew Gerard De Caigny:

> *I still have a lot to write and still more to compose; I am taking notes preparing my publications. I am so happy to be able to consecrate myself to this work, at the evening of my life. Pray to God that I may still live a number of years to finish my work (F.A., F. De Caigny, Belgium).*

Dom Mayeul spent the feast of Christmas 1923 with the Benedictine nuns of rue Monsieur, Paris, singing a pontifical High Mass and presiding at all their ceremonies. Early in January 1924, he travelled to the south of France, to spend a week with Mgr. Gerard van Caloen, who was living in retirement in his family's villa in the Cap d'Antibes. They spent most of the time discussing their experiences in Brazil. Former differences were now forgotten, allowing their relationship to rise to a new level of mutual appreciation and understanding. Considering all the disagreements and misunderstandings in Dom Mayeul's life, it was good that he had this happy reconciliation with Mgr. van Caloen. After all, he owed more to his fellow-Belgian monk than he ever admitted in writing. Mgr. van Caloen had been the prime mover in bringing him to Brazil in 1897. This led to his becoming the abbot of Bahia in 1907, and eventually the founder of Mount St. Benedict, Trinidad, in 1912.

When he returned to Jouarre mid-January 1924, Dom Mayeul settled down to write his memoirs. Over the following three months he made such good progress, that he already discussed with the abbot primate the possibility of publishing the first volume. He pointed out that the book was not a biography ('a life'), but his personal 'souvenirs' of the missions in Brazil and Trinidad. He left it to others to decide whether it should be made public. Above all, he had no intention of offending his confreres in Brazil or Trinidad, and, for this reason, had avoided writing on difficult or delicate matters *(APR, 613, # 2, Dom Mayeul to AP, 14 February 1924)*.

The only other matter which exercised his mind during these final months in Paris was money. He had still to finalise the details regarding his pension, to be paid by Mount St. Benedict, at the rate of one-dollar a day. He hoped he would not be a financial burden on the community in Trinidad. Yet, he had no choice in this matter, as the Roman authorities had already laid down certain principles which had to be followed. Dom Mayeul was glad that there was some agreed arrangement. This allowed him a degree of independence and security during his twilight years. However, his more immediate need was money to pay for his passage to Florida, which he had to book well in advance. He intended travelling second-class on the boat, which was due to sail from Le Havre on 26 April (APR, 613, # 6, Dom Mayeul to AP, 29 February 1924). At the end of the day, the abbot primate sent him enough money to pay for this journey.

During the final weeks before leaving Paris at the end of April 1924, Dom Mayeul put the finishing touches to the first volume of his memoirs. Both the abbot primate and Abbot Etcheverry knew that Dom Mayeul was engaged in this particular work, and were hoping to stop its publication there and then. Dom Etcheverry wrote to the abbot primate on 1 April 1924: *"You have told me about his memoirs. I think that the best moment to stop him publishing them will be when he asks for an imprimatur"* (i.e. an official license to publish a book, given by a bishop or abbot) (*APR, 613,#4, Etcheverry to AP, 1 April 1924*). They feared that Dom Mayeul would speak of matters which were delicate or personal, and cause embarrassment to some people in Brazil and Trinidad.

As he embarked on the final phase of his life, Dom Mayeul intended turning his back on the past and making a new start, though this did not imply forgetting all that had happened to him, especially during his twenty-five years in Brazil and Trinidad. His memoirs were not so much an apologia for his life, as a detailed record of his achievements. Among these latter, he chose two particular events of which he was clearly proud: (i) the saving from destruction of the abbey of Bahia in 1911, and (ii) the inauguration of the pilgrimage in honour of St. Benedict, in Mount St. Benedict, Trinidad, in 1913 (*Vol. I, 188*).

There was another dimension to his move to Florida. Throughout his life, he had sought some place in which he could sink his roots, settle down and find a permanent home, yet such a place had always eluded him. Now, in his twilight years, he dared to hope that he could find a permanent home. He was looking for a quiet place, preferably in the countryside, in which he could spend his days in contemplation, study and writing. He summarized his ideas when writing to Abbot Charles Mohr of St. Leo Abbey on 10 November 1923: *"My only wish is to find a place of rest, in a suitable climate for my health, to enable me to write some books, four if possible"* (*St. Leo, Dom Mayeul to Abbot Charles, 10 Nov. 1923*). He had no idea, of course, what awaited him in St. Leo Abbey, Florida. In one way, it was a jump into the dark. Providentially for Dom Mayeul it turned out to be an idyllic place, something beyond his wildest dreams. In St. Leo Abbey he found that peace and happiness he had been longing for all his life. Although it was not high up on a mountain, and the buildings were nowhere as grand as Mount Thabor, yet in its own way it turned out to be his Shangri-La. At the eleventh hour, he had found a place where he could feel at home. All that now remained was for him to adapt to his new life and new surroundings.

Dom Mayeul sailed from Le Havre to New York on Saturday 26 April 1924, arriving in New York on 7 May. From New York

St. Leo Abbey

he travelled by train to Florida, and reached St. Leo Abbey on the evening of 10 May. The abbot welcomed him warmly, and then asked if Dom Mayeul would like to take up residence in one of the abbey's outlying parishes. When Dom Mayeul turned down this offer, the abbot seemed pleased, and said he would show his visitor the following morning, the place he had in mind for his stay with them. The next day they drove out to a place called the 'college farm', about 7 km from St. Leo Abbey. It was, in fact, the abbey's hermitage, very isolated, and occupied by two lay brothers, who looked after the extensive orange groves. The buildings, all in wood, were quite extensive. One of the houses had been prepared for Dom Mayeul. It consisted of several large rooms, one of which served as an oratory, a kitchen, then a dining room, a bedroom, a study, etc. It was ideal, just what Dom Mayeul had hoped for. The abbot asked if Dom Mayeul would like to live there, and received an immediate reply "certainly". Apparently, the abbot had, up to then, found it impossible to get any of the priest-monks to reside there, which meant that the two brothers had to make a daily trip to the abbey for Mass. Now, with Dom Mayeul in residence, the brothers would be able to have Mass every day, an arrangement that pleased them no end. The hermitage was an independent unit, and the brothers, one of whom was a German from Bavaria, were excellent cooks. The abbot, evidently a practical kind of person, said he would give Dom Mayeul three days to decide if he wished to stay. He hinted that his visitor would have changed his mind by then. It was a week before the abbot returned, and expressed his surprise when Dom Mayeul told him he was very happy in his new home. As a result, Dom Mayeul became a kind of seven-day wonder to most of the community in St. Leo, but after a month or two they realized he had settled into his hermitage, and from then on, he was left very much to himself. The only exception was the abbot, who during these early days, often invited Dom Mayeul to accompany him on various journeys by car, mostly to visit the monastery's outlying parishes. But even these trips soon ceased. From then on Dom Mayeul was left very much to himself by both abbot and community.

Dom Mayeul's first concern was to put his two lay brother companions at ease in his presence. Hearing that he had been abbot of a large monastery in Brazil, they expected him to be demanding and fastidious. In order to win their approval, Dom Mayeul dispensed with his pectoral cross and other such insignia of office. Within a very short time relations were on a friendly footing, helped by the fact that Dom Mayeul was able to give the correct German name for a particular dish served up for dinner one evening. He remembered how he had eaten this same dish when in Bavaria, during his final days as a Redemptorist. But it was the prayerful, spiritual attitude of the abbot that won over the two brothers more than anything else. They were grateful for his fervent celebration of Mass every morning, and his regular recitation of the Divine Office in the oratory. It proved to be a good start for Dom Mayeul, allowing him to settle in to his hermitage without any hiccups.

While Dom Mayeul brought a fairly extensive amount of luggage with him to Florida, he hoped that Prior Hugh of the Mount would send him the remainder of his personal belongings, including some precious manuscripts and notes, which he had left behind in Trinidad. However, there was no hurry. Time was on his side. First of all he needed to get his bearings, adapt to the climate of his new home, and work out some kind of daily schedule or timetable. He found the climate of Florida suited him admirably, allowing him to enjoy good health over the coming years. He was 62 years of age in 1924, and destined to spend the next fifteen years (1924-39) in his hermitage in St. Leo, writing spiritual books, attending to his extensive correspondence, praying, preaching retreats, and travelling.

Evidently, his main interest was in writing, an activity he called "the apostolate of the pen". He had somehow managed to salvage several literary works, composed during his student days as a Redemptorist, which he now proceeded to revise and correct. These consisted mainly of two works: (i) *"Meditations on the liturgical texts for the Sundays and Feasts of the year"*; and (ii) *"Florilegium Biblicum"*. At the same time he put the finishing touches to his work, *"Twenty-Five Years as a Missionary in the Tropics"*. After that he hoped to write a three-volume life of St. Thérèse of Lisieux, to be followed by a study (a commentary) of "The Magnificat", and finally a work on St. Benedict. These last three books were published some years later, but the two earlier works, as far as we know, were never published. All were written in French, and as such unsuitable for the American market. The *"Commentaire ascetique du Magnificat"* and the *"Trilogie St. Thérèse de l'Enfent Jesus"* were published in 1934 by

Charles Beyaert, Bruges (Belgium), and the *"Methode Ascetique de St. Benoit"* also by Beyaert in 1938. His only other literary output during these years in St. Leo consisted of his extensive correspondence. All his so-called official letters, such as those to the abbot primate in Rome, and to the prior of the Mount, have been preserved. As regards his personal correspondence, he seems to have kept most of the incoming letters, which are now preserved in the archives of St. Leo Abbey, Florida.

Dom Mayeul took some months to settle in to life in his hermitage, which meant a delay in completing his memoirs and starting his other literary projects. He was greatly worried, if not annoyed, at the delay in sending his personal belongings to Florida, and in paying his pension regularly and in time. There were several heated exchanges between himself and Fr. Hugh over the question of the 'dollar'. Fr. Hugh understood that the dollar in question was the Trinidadian one, whereas Dom Mayeul insisted that the arrangement was for an American dollar a day, worth nearly six times the Trinidadian dollar. In all of these cases, Dom Mayeul proved quite unbending and always insisted on having the last word. Although he had severed all connection with the Mount, Dom Mayeul continued to comment on some of Fr. Hugh's decisions, especially in appointing personnel in the monastery, as when Fr. Sebastian Weber was sent to work in one of the parishes. He also reported to the prior some rumours he had heard in regard to the guest house being infested with bugs. The prior of the Mount had to bear the brunt of Dom Mayeul's occasional interferences. For example Dom Mayeul was very surprised when he heard that Fr. Hugh had been forced to send Magdelena, one of Dom Mayeul's oblates, away from the Mount. Dom Mayeul refused to accept the prior's reasons for doing so, and on 21 May 1924, he wrote the following harsh words to Fr. Hugh:

> I have waited in vain for you to explain to me the reasons for sending Magdelena away. You were excused in your last letter on account of the boat; but this reason, valid at the time, was no longer upheld in your next letter. I just cannot believe that you would use this rather common subterfuge in order to put me off. This is not a very nice way to act, especially considering my age (MSB, Dom Mayeul to Dom Hugh, 21 May 1924).

On the other hand, in other instances the prior, Fr. Hugh, really appreciated the feedback from Dom Mayeul. Dom Hugh kept Dom Mayeul well informed about what was going on at the Mount. In some of his letters to Dom Mayeul he was directly asking for his advice. Fr. Hugh sent, on the occasion of Dom Mayeul's feast day (the Feast of St. Mayeul on 29 April), the following respectful letter, telling him how much they were missing him, wishing him many peaceful years to come at St. Leo and informing him about the work and repairs that were going on at the monastery.

I am sorry having delayed so long in wishing you a happy Feast. The busy Holy Week and your travelling on sea are two matters of apology for me. Nevertheless, your have been nonetheless remembered in my prayers on the day itself, and more than on other days I felt Your Lordship's Paternity was missing. May God grant you still many happy and peaceful years of contemplation here on earth. What precious gift of God, after having born all the heat of the day, to enjoy its well merited refreshing evening at St. Leo.

In the years gone by, you have strongly fought as a true soldier in the first ranks of God's army; now He has called you nearer to Him in order to taste a little of sweetness, which He has stored up for you from all eternity. The enemies tried to embitter your life, but they paid the greatest service they ever could have thought of.

In the monastery everything is going on quietly. The brethren are still making repairs. The kitchen is finished, and nearly also the front of the chapel. The other buildings need only slight repairs, but the buggy-house must be built over, on account of the new tank and store-room for provisions. At the same time it will be transferred to behind the house of the brethren, where we have started already to dig the hill, in order to have a good plain level. Later on, there will come, at the same place, a workshop and stables. Our main reason for doing so was to have as much as possible of the buildings at the same level, and thus spare a great deal of climbing, and according to calculation it will be cheaper to cut than to build a high concrete wall on the slope of the hill. For the rest, everything is going on as before (St. Leo, Dom Hugh to Dom Mayeul, 6 May 24).

Dom Mayeul wrote regularly to Dom Hugh, exchanging confidences and giving his opinion on the information provided to him by the prior, Fr Hugh, and by the many correspondents he still had in Trinidad.

Strangely enough, in his correspondence with the prior of the Mount, Dom Mayeul never once mentions the question, or fate, of Mount Thabor, which was one of the central factors leading to his resignation as superior of the Mount. Soon after 1923 the building was condemned because of the inferior material (tapia) used in its construction, and the fact that it was built at such a great height, which left it exposed to strong winds and heavy rains. An inspection of Mount Thabor was made by the local authority. Their report was highly critical of the building and recommended that it be knocked down (*County of St. George, A.S. 16 Oct. 1925*). In any case, the prior and Council of the Mount had decided that the cost of maintaining Mount Thabor was prohibitive. They recommended that their financial resources should be put into improving the buildings of the lower monastery, which had been neglected for many years (*MSB, Record of resolutions*). A final judgment on Mount Thabor is given in a lengthy document, written in Latin by Dom Sebastian Weber and subtitled: *"About the building of Mount Thabor"* (*MSB, Box I, ix*). Dom Sebastian's arguments centred round two points: (i) The community had never voted for the construction of Mount Thabor in the first place and (ii) its original *raison d'etre* could no longer be upheld: namely that it would serve as a sanatorium or health centre for the monks. He wrote this report for the abbot visitator, Dom Etcheverry, in 1923. All the evidence suggests that based on all these reports, the demolition of Mount Thabor, was just a matter of time. Apparently, there were no tears shed by any members of the community of the Mount at the final demolition of Mount Thabor. The same brother who was responsible for building Mount Thabor, Br. Joseph Kleinmann, had to supervise the demolition project. Today, only a few water cisterns remain of this once impressive building.

Immediately after his arrival at St. Leo Abbey, Dom Mayeul sent a postcard to the abbot primate showing the St Leo abbey buildings. What is more revealing are a couple of his letters sent in June and the autumn of 1924. He was very happy being at the abbey farm but at the same time he could not resist coming back on the injustice done to him by the archbishop in Trinidad:

More than once I felt the curiosity to find out who accused me and of what. Without a doubt in the eyes of the archbishop I am a great sinner. But all that doesn't interest me any longer. I am happy in the situation I am in. I don't want to change it for anything else. I am to stay here! In the farm house, when saying mass, I feel in heaven. The good Lord, after having allowed my suffering, He is now spoiling me. Again thank you Rev. Abbot Primate (APR #B1, 9 June 1924).

SAINT LEO, FLORIDA

ST. LEO ABBEY AND COLLEGE, SAINT LEO, FLORIDA.

POSTCARD OF THE ABBEY BUILDINGS SENT TO THE ABBOT PRIMATE SHORTLY
AFTER DOM MAYEUL ARRIVED AT ST. LEO IN 1924.

334

CHAPTER XIX

The Hermit in St. Leo Abbey,
Part I

ONE WONDERS how much the change of residence to a remote farmhouse in Florida proved to be a culture shock for Dom
Mayeul. Certainly, it took him some time to adapt and settle in,
but he was determined to make a go of it. He did not want another
'failure'. Given his age, 62 years, this was his last chance to find a
place he could call home. We know that during most of his time in
St. Leo, he never succeeded in getting the Mount out of his mind,
as can be seen in his correspondence with both the abbot primate
and Prior Hugh.

Mount St. Benedict's was undergoing an important change of
status during the years 1924-27, in that the monastery was making
a definitive break with the Brazilian Congregation, and becoming
affiliated to the Belgian Congregation. It would affect Dom Mayeul both directly and indirectly, especially in regard to his vow of
stability. He had made it clear to all concerned, that he wished to
remain attached to the Brazilian Congregation, and even though he
was Belgian by birth, he had no intention of changing his stability to the Belgian Congregation. In any case, he had no personal
involvement in these negotiations. All he could do was to look on
and await the results. The process for Mount St. Benedict of changing Congregations involved three people: Prior Hugh van der Sand-
en, Abbot Primate von Stotzingen, and the president of the Belgian
Congregation, Abbot Robert de Kerchove. Already in 1924, the abbot primate, acting on behalf of the Cardinal Prefect of the Congregation for Religious, had invited Fr. Hugh to come to Rome to
discuss this matter, which required official Roman approval (*MSB,
APR to Dom Hugh, 29 November 1924*). The Belgian Congregation
had been chosen because it was a modern organisation, dating from

1920. By 1927, it consisted of only three monasteries (Maredsous, Mont Cesar, and St. Andre) and was anxious to expand.

Early in 1925, Prior Hugh went to Rome and received every encouragement from the abbot primate to make an official application to the president of the Belgian Congregation on behalf of Mount St. Benedict. His application was accepted by Abbot de Kerchove, as well as the abbots of Maredsous and St. Andre on 23 May 1925 *(MSB, Abbot de Kerchove to Dom Hugh, 25 April and 4 August 1925).* This was the first step in the long process of affiliating the Mount to the Belgian Congregation. On his return to Trinidad from his European trip, Fr. Hugh convened the Chapter of the monastery, and on 25 June 1925, it unanimously agreed to seek affiliation with the Belgian Congregation. The document was signed by eighteen of the monks of the Mount. Two years later, on 16 December 1927, definitive affiliation of the Mount was granted by the General Chapter of that same Congregation. On 29 December 1928, the Sacred Congregation for Religious in Rome granted its decree sanctioning the above arrangement. Following on this, all the monks of the Mount changed their vows of stability to the Belgian Congregation.

Prior Hugh informed Dom Mayeul of all these negotiations, forcing the latter to examine the present situation regarding his vow of stability. In theory, the Benedictine vow of stability implied that a monk sink his roots in one place (monastery), and live there for the rest of his life. It has already been pointed out that Dom Mayeul had a problem committing himself, by a vow of stability, to any one monastery, whether in Belgium, Brazil or Trinidad. As the title of this biography suggests, he longed to belong, but had failed to find any place to which he could permanently belong. He had one last chance to rectify all this, now that he had reached the final stage of his life. There is no doubt that he expected to end his life in Florida, and that St. Leo Abbey would provide him with a permanent home where he could, at last, sink his roots. But, even at this eleventh hour, he still hesitated to commit himself. On 4 January 1926, he told Prior Hugh that he did not wish to break the solemn vow of stability, which he had made for the Brazilian Congregation in 1897. This implied that he had no intention of joining either the Belgian Congregation to which the Mount was affiliated, or the American-Cassinese Congregation, to which St. Leo Abbey was attached. He thus found himself, in a kind of 'no-man's land', during his first ten years in Florida (1924-34).

At irregular intervals, the Benedictine Order produces a catalogue of all the monks of the Order. Dom Mayeul was surprised to find himself listed in the *"Catalogus of 1926"* as a monk of Mount St. Benedict. Immediately, he wrote a rather unfriendly letter to Prior Hugh, asking the latter how his name had come to be included in the list of monks at the Mount. He requested that a thorough search be made in the archives of the Mount, to see if there was any document, showing he had taken a vow of stability for that monastery. When a reply was not immediately forthcoming, he wrote a second time, to Fr. Hugh, suggesting that his previous letter must have "made a detour via Japan!" *(MSB, Dom Mayeul to Dom Hugh, 11 April 1926)*. Prior Hugh chose to ignore this last remark, and eventually wrote to tell Dom Mayeul that no document had been found in the archives of the Mount, relating to a vow of stability taken by Dom Mayeul for Trinidad. The years went by, with further correspondence on this matter, mostly between Dom Mayeul and the abbot primate. The question of Dom Mayeul's monastic status was finally settled in 1935, when he was accepted into the American-Cassinese Congregation, taking a vow of stability for St. Leo Abbey.

Throughout his life, Dom Mayeul suffered from various health problems. When growing up in Cachtem, in the house of his uncle and aunt, he was considered a delicate child, and during his years at school he had been allowed exceptions in his diet. Later on, in Brazil, he survived two serious bouts of yellow fever. But it seems that his most serious health problem was chronic rheumatism, which he said had been his constant companion since the age of 7 years. He also had a weak heart, and had tried all kinds of cures over the years, with little or no effect. Now, in Florida, he found that most of his health problems disappeared, thanks to the climate, and the healthy diet of fresh fruit (oranges and grapefruit), vegetables, milk and eggs. The St. Leo Farm was out in the country, allowing him to take regular walks, and enjoy the beauties of nature. In his correspondence, he refers to the place as a Garden of Paradise. On 10 Aug 1924 he wrote about this to his nephew Gerard Decaigny:

> *I live here in the best place to write; I live in the villa of the abbey, about 7 kilometres away from the abbey, beautiful location,*

DOM MAYEUL IN FRONT OF THE FARMHOUSE

DOM MAYEUL AT THE LAKE, WITH THE FARMHOUSE IN THE BACKGROUND

in the midst of forests, orange orchards, adjacent to a lake full of fish. A promenade on the lake in the moonlight, in a small boat, is wonderful. It is very healthy here; we have excellent drinking water. It is semi-tropical and the climate is excellent against rheumatism. I share the villa with 2 brothers; one who is the cook, housekeeper and the other is the farmer, taking care of the orange orchard and the vegetable garden. It is much better here than at the abbey; it is much quieter and I have more time to write. I've been welcomed very well; it couldn't be better on this world! (F.A., F. De Caigny, Belgium)

He had, indeed, much to be grateful for. His life was idyllic, free from care, and suited to his new style of living, centred on prayer, reading and writing. He wrote about this on 21 May 1925 to his nephew Gerard De Caigny, the son of his elder brother Francois who had recently passed away:

Dear Gerard, thanks a lot for sending me the obituary. I was already informed of the death of your father by my sister Julie. I immediately offered Mass and I prayed a lot for him. I am grateful for the details I received on his illness and death, as well as on the funeral. Thanks for the beautiful obituary which is very well composed. Just follow now in the footsteps of your father. ... Thank God, everything goes well with me. Florida is for me the best area I ever stayed in; healthy climate and very quiet since I just wish to pray, study and write. I am including some pictures to give you an idea on the area (F.A., F. De Caigny, Belgium).

Although his day-to-day material needs were provided by the abbot and community of St. Leo, Dom Mayeul had two recurring financial worries during these early years in Florida. The first centred on his pension, which should have been paid in two instalments each year by the bursar of Mount St. Benedict, at the rate of one US Dollar a day. For the most part, this was paid regularly and on time. However, the financial situation in Trinidad deteriorated considerably, following on the Wall Street Crash (1929). During these post-1929 years, the monks of Mount St. Benedict, while honouring in principle their commitment to pay Dom Mayeul, sometimes found it difficult to come up with the money on time.

The second financial matter which interested Dom Mayeul was the non-payment by the abbey of Bahia of the annual allowance

Uw christene naastenliefde gedenke
de Ziel van Heer

FRANÇOIS DE CAIGNY

Weduwaar van Vrouw
SILVIE SCHELDEMAN,

Vereerd met het Burgerskruis van 2ᵉ klas. Voorzitter van
St Vincentius Genootschap
en van de Koorzangmaatschappij " DE KERELS ,,.
Lid van al de godvruchtige genootschappen.

geboren te ISEGHEM, den 4 October 1856,
en godvruchtig in den Heer
ontslapen te EMELGHEM, den 8 April 1925,
gesterkt door de laatste H. Sacramenten.

OBITUARY CARD OF DOM MAYEUL'S BROTHER,
FRANCOIS (1856-1925)

to Trinidad, as arranged by Abbot Visitator Zeller, at the General Chapter of the Brazilian Congregation in 1915. The total sum came to 50 Brazilian Contos, to be paid to the Mount over ten years. The money was paid for the first few years, but in 1924 the abbot of Bahia refused to pay any further instalments. He believed that the Trinidadian foundation had already received more than its rightful share of money from the mother house of Bahia considering that Dom Mayeul had brought with him from Bahia to Trinidad in 1912, the capital sum of about US$90,000. Relations between Trinidad and Bahia became very strained as a result of this question of financial endowment. Dom Mayeul regretted that the original arrangement had not provided for the total sum of 50 Contos to be made to Trinidad in one payment, thus avoiding the annual headaches, and the breakdown of relations between the two monasteries *(MSB, Dom Mayeul to Dom Hugh, 1 Dec. 1926)*. This financial problem was an ongoing subject for comment between Prior Hugh and Dom Mayeul in their correspondence. They eventually brought the matter to the attention of the abbot primate, who threw his weight behind Mount St. Benedict. Under threat of being reported to the Roman authorities, the abbot of Bahia changed his mind and decided to pay the money. The last payment was made in November 1929, by the newly elected Abbot Rupert, who sent five million Brazilian Reales (5 Contos), or 128 pounds sterling, to Dom Odo van der Heydt. In acknowledging this money, Dom Odo wrote a very friendly letter to Abbot Rupert on 18 February 1930:

> As this is the final instalment of the money for Trinidad from the monastery of Bahia, I want to take this opportunity to extend to you our sincere and humble thanks. God will bless your brotherly charity towards our new undertaking *(MSB, Dom Odo van der Heydt Papers)*.

Normal relationships were thus restored between the two monasteries, a situation which was a relief to all concerned.

To anyone who knew Dom Mayeul, it came as no surprise to learn that he found it impossible to remain locked up in his hermitage for very long, without making some kind of sortie from time to time. In fact, during his stay in Florida (1924-39), he made no less than three lengthy trips to Europe, in 1928, 1932 and 1935. He justified these journeys to Europe on the grounds that he needed to keep in touch with his family and friends, as well as with the abbot primate in Rome, and his former superior, Mgr. Gerard van Caloen, then living in retirement in the South of France. There were other reasons that drew him to Europe. In 1932, he brought with him the draft of his book, *"The Ascetical Commentary on the Magnificat"*, to be censured, and prepared for publication, by the abbot of Clairvaux in Luxembourg. He had also consulted Dom Olphe Galliard, the abbot of the Benedictine monastery in the Rue de la Source, Paris. He made some tentative promises to give a share of the royalties on this book to the Benedictines of both Luxembourg and Paris. This became a matter of legal dispute after his death. Also, during his 1932 trip, he had to prepare the publication of his *"Trilogy on Thérèse of Lisieux"*. He hoped it would be his most important work, as he had done thorough research into her life and spirituality.

How he succeeded in finding the money for the three trips he made across the Atlantic (1928, 1932, 1935) is another matter, especially as travelling, even second-class, was quite expensive. Yet, he never seemed to lack money to pay for these journeys. His pension from Mount St. Benedict would hardly have covered all his travel expenses. He appears to have supplemented his pension by receiving money from his family, and also payment for lectures and conferences, which he gave to various religious communities and parishes throughout Europe. He was also fortunate during his first trip in 1928 to get a very favourable rate of exchange for the US dollar, against the main European currencies.

On arrival in France in 1928, his first call was to Lisieux, to put his European trip under the protection of St. Thérèse. She had been beatified in 1923, at a ceremony in Rome attended by Dom Mayeul, but he had missed out on the canonisation ceremony in 1925, when she was declared a saint. His main ambition in 1928 was to seek interviews with St. Thérèse's four blood sisters, in the hope of getting first-hand knowledge of the Saint. Three of these sisters were Carmelites in Lisieux: Marie (Sr. Marie du Sacre-Coeur), Pauline (Sr. Agnes de Jesus), Celine (Sr. Genevieve de la Ste. Face), and Leonie (Sr. Francoise-Thérèse), who belonged to the religious Order of the Visitation of Holy Mary in Caen. According to Dom Mayeul, the idea of the book came from Sr. Emmanuel, a Carmelite of Lisieux and secretary of Sr. Agnes. Dom Mayeul's book was to be as a kind of *"discussion within the family on the meaning of St. Thérèse's life" (St. Leo, 'An Apology for the Trilogy' by Dom Mayeul – A Ten-page article in Dom Mayeul's handwriting, dated 4 Jan 1935)*.

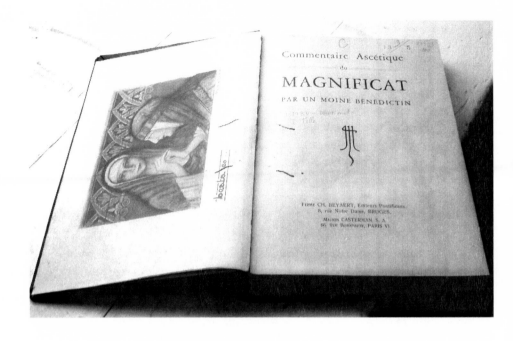

THE ASCETICAL COMMENTARY ON THE MAGNIFICAT

The tomb of St. Thérèse de Lisieux at the Carmelite convent

The basilica de Lisieux, a most beautiful basilica visited each year by the hundreds of thousands.

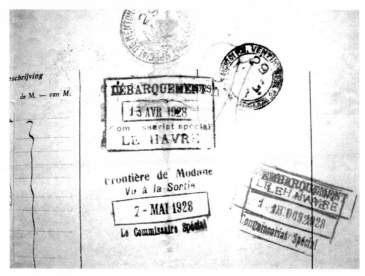

1928 PASSPORT OF DOM MAYEUL ISSUED IN WASHINGTON
BY THE BELGIAN EMBASSY
(ON TOP: ENTRY-STAMP OF LE HAVRE, FRANCE.)

THE MARTIN FAMILY, THE PARENTS AND SISTERS OF ST. THÉRÈSE

Considering the number of people, mostly reputable authors from all over the world, who were interested in writing about the life of St. Thérèse at this time, it is quite amazing how Dom Mayeul succeeded in getting access to the sisters of St. Thérèse. During the decade 1925-35, the worldwide interest in St. Thérèse was at its highest point. The Carmelite convent in Lisieux was a hive of activity. In one of the letters from Lisieux, written in 1927, there is reference to the great number of letters received, as many as 700-800 letters any day, asking for favours, relics or leaflets. The sisters in the Carmelite convent of Lisieux were certainly overtaxed dealing with this correspondence, and had little or no time for anything else. So how did Dom Mayeul ingratiate himself into the good books of the sisters, and thereby receive special treatment?

One suspects that he used his charm, more than anything else, to win their attention and favour. In such a situation, Dom Mayeul was in his element. He presented an imposing figure – the ideal prelate – tall, dignified and good-looking, dressed impeccably, in full abbatial regalia, with pectoral cross and ring. It would have been hard to resist him. But more important, he had, of course, prepared everything beforehand. Ever since his first visit to Lisieux in 1923, he had written regularly, especially at Christmas, to Sister Marie du Sacre Coeur, and again on the anniversary of her religious profession. He also sent monetary contributions to the Carmelites of Lisieux, first for the chapel to be built in Alencon, the birthplace of St. Thérèse. And later towards the basilica, in honour of St. Thérèse of Lisieux, on which construction was begun in 1929, though it was not completed until 1954. We have no way of knowing how much money he gave, but in her letter of 6 June 1927, Sr. Marie du Sacre Coeur wrote to thank him for his gift for the basilica: *"I am asking our little Saint to show her appreciation, by granting you all the graces you desire both for yourself and your family"* (St. Leo, Sr. Marie du Sacre Coeur to Dom Mayeul, 6 June 1927). It is interesting to note that Sr. Marie du Sacre Coeur always addresses Dom Mayeul as her "brother". At some early date, Dom Mayeul had asked the Martin sisters if they would accept him as their 'adopted brother'. The Martin family consisted of five girls, but no boys. They seemed very happy to welcome Dom Mayeul into the family circle as a surrogate 'brother'.

According to his memoirs, in 1928 he had long interviews with all the sisters of St. Thérèse *(Vol. II, 239)*. Normally the Carmelites kept a very strict enclosure, and when speaking with outsiders, kept the curtain drawn in the parlour, so that there was no eye contact. However, in the case of Dom Mayeul they made an exception. On another occasion, he was given special permission to enter the convent and view all the souvenirs of the life of St. Thérèse *(Vol. II, 248)*. When visiting the fourth sister, Leonie, in the convent in Caen, he was allowed to hold the crucifix which St. Thérèse had in her hands when she was dying. Leonie (Sr. Francoise-Thérèse) seems to have forged the special brother-sister relationship with Dom Mayeul, and addressed him by a pet-name: *"Frère Gateau"* *(Brother Cake) (Vol. II, 239)*.

All in all, some 80 handwritten letters, addressed to Dom Mayeul from the four blood-sisters of St. Thérèse, have survived, dating from 27 December 1924 to 3 February 1939. For the most part, they consist of acknowledgements of Christmas or feast day greetings, as well as thanks for financial help. They also offer spiritual reflections or advice to Dom Mayeul on some aspect of his proposed book, as well as information on the extraordinary worldwide devotion to the Saint of Lisieux, in the 1920s and '30s. They are warm and affectionate in tone, though embroidered with the usual religious 'cliches' of the time. Following on these many letters, as well as his three visits to Lisieux, in 1923, 1928, and 1932, Dom Mayeul felt he knew enough about St. Thérèse to produce his promised Trilogy on the Saint. The book, entitled *"Trilogie S. Thérèse de l'Enfant Jesus"*, was published in Belgium in 1934. Although called a trilogy, it consisted of one volume, being a study of St. Thérèse under three headings: (i) Lover of the Bible (ii) Doctor of the Way of Spiritual Childhood, and (iii) The Angelic Seraphim of Love. The name of the author was given simply as "A Benedictine Monk". The reason for this anonymity is difficult to explain. Perhaps he just wanted to play the Benedictine card, believing it would sell more books than his own name. The book is a solid piece of writing, though perhaps over-analytical, scientific and academic in style. We have no idea how many copies were sold in this first and only French edition. Dom Mayeul tried several times to have it translated into English, but failed to find anyone prepared to undertake this enormous task.

Dom Mayeul sent one of the first copies to the Carmelites in Lisieux, who received it with considerable enthusiasm and interest.

TRILOGIE

S. THÉRÈSE
DE L'ENFANT-JÉSUS

CONSIDÉRÉE COMME

I. Amante de la Bible
II. Docteur de la voie d'enfance spirituelle
III. et Séraphin d'amour

PAR UN MOINE BÉNÉDICTIN

FIRME CHARLES BEYAERT
EDITEURS PONTIFICAUX

DOM MAYEUL'S BOOK, TRILOGY ON ST. THÉRÈSE DE LISIEUX

Sister Agnes de Jesus (Pauline), who at this time was prioress and busy dealing with the growing correspondence arriving daily at the convent in Lisieux, asked her secretary, Sr. Marie Emmanuel, to read *"without delay"* Dom Mayeul's book *"in order that we might give you our appreciation" (St. Leo, Sr. Emmanuel to Dom Mayeul, 30 November 1934)*. However she was not pleased with everything she read in Dom Mayeul's book, and especially deplored the many misprints. While admitting that in general the book enhanced the honour and glory of St. Thérèse, she regretted that Dom Mayeul had adopted such a rigorist critical attitude towards some established authors, who had already written on the life of St. Thérèse. Sr. Emmanuel pulled no punches and was quite frank, if not blunt, in her letter to Dom Mayeul:

> *You have entered into the 'blame-game' by contesting, without any clear necessity, the opinions of certain authors, whose works we have already given our full approval: P. Martin and P. Petitot. It would be very difficult for us to recommend your Trilogy with these blemishes, especially as your thesis would not suffer if they were omitted. By writing this, you add a note of dissension, which may well lead to some displeasure among your readers, when they see the divergent viewpoints proposed by various authors. In other places you falsify entirely, without meaning to do so, the real character of St. Thérèse, i.e. her moral portrait. While these views may not diminish your own personal devotion to our Saint, your readers will not necessarily agree with you. We have had occasion before this of pointing out the danger of distorting, even with the best intentions, the true image (physiognomy) of our little Saint Thérèse. It is very painful for us to make these reservations on your interesting Trilogy, as it obliges us to await a second corrected edition, before we could recommend it to our friends (Ibid. Sr. Emmanuel to Dom Mayeul 30 Nov. 1934).*

This sharp critique of his book came as a great surprise to Dom Mayeul, as is evident from his lengthy reply to the letter of Sr. Emmanuel, a summary of which he wrote between the lines of Sr. Emmanuel's original letter. First of all, he explained the problem of the misprints. He was not in Europe when the book was going through the press, but had given the task of making corrections to a member of the Benedictine abbey of Jouarre, Paris. This particular sister had apparently slipped up more often than she should. He admits that he made a great mistake in not showing the book in manuscript, before publication, to the community in Lisieux, when they would have been able to give their opinion and suggestions. Again, the fact that he was in Florida and not in France, made it difficult for him to consult the Lisieux community during the final phases of publishing his Trilogy. He insists that he has done his best to honour St. Thérèse, and has never doubted her sanctity and power to help people. He would continue to call on her help in all his needs.

Strangely enough, he makes no allusion in his memoirs to this exchange of letters between himself and the sisters of Lisieux, in the aftermath of the publication of the Trilogy. It is possible that he was too embarrassed, or disappointed, to make any further reflections on the matter. However, in 1935, during his last trip to Europe, he visited for the last time, the blood-sisters of St. Thérèse, with whom he corresponded extensively until his death. Dom Mayeul gradually drifted away from the written word in book form, to a more direct approach of communication. During the last years of his life, apart from his private correspondence, he concentrated on the spoken word as a means of communication, mainly by preaching retreats to communities of religious men and women in the United States, Canada, and as far as the Caribbean.

More importantly, one is led to ask why Dom Mayeul continued to write his books in French. He had learned sufficient English while in Trinidad. We also know from the study of his vast correspondence while in Florida, almost entirely written in English, that he was fluent in that language. Living on his own in the outlying college farm, with only two non-American lay brothers as his companions, may have prevented him becoming a fully integrated English-speaking person. He may even have resisted any effort to become americanised. We know from his letters that he often received the Belgian newspaper "De Standaard". All the evidence suggests that he continued to live very much in the past, becoming a prisoner of his age and his spiritual and cultural upbringing. Though living in the New World, he remained very much a European, holding on to his Old World values and mentality. This is obvious from the fact that he wrote his memoirs, as well as his last three books, in French. He never threw himself into 'the melting pot', which America became for millions of other Europeans. However, it is difficult to say if his books would have done well, had they been written in English. And also, had they been written in English, a French version for Europe still had to be made, considering that the sales potential of his books in Europe was for sure much higher than in the USA. He certainly took the wrong road towards achieving literary success in America by writing only in French. But from a sales point of view he made the right decision. And perhaps, he had also realized that he had not mastered the English language, sufficiently well enough, to write a highly complex and analytical spiritual or religious work.

CHAPTER XX

The Hermit in St. Leo Abbey, Part II

APART FROM his literary interests and endeavours, and the problems relating to the payment, or non-payment, of his pension, and the canonical status of his vow of stability, Dom Mayeul had a number of other matters to occupy his mind and attention during the fifteen years he spent in St. Leo Abbey. The key to all this lies in his vast correspondence, which he carried on right up to the time of his death in 1939, as well as in a careful reading between the lines of his memoirs. There is a certain ambivalence in all that Dom Mayeul writes and does. He fluctuates between playing the role of the perfect 'hermit", while at the same time yearning for news of the outside world, anxious to be loved and respected by his many friends and acquaintances. Thus, at one moment he is quoting from the autobiography of St. Thérèse of Lisieux: *"What happiness to be completely hidden away, so that no one thinks of you, to be unknown, even to those among whom you live. I just want to be forgotten"* (Vol. II, 189). And again: *"My principal function is to live all by myself (Solus Soli), and to act as becomes a priest of Nature"* (Vol. II, 212). Yet, he admitted that his life as a hermit was not without a certain monotony, if not loneliness. All his life he had been surrounded by people, every moment filled with activity: preaching, teaching, administration, hearing confessions, counselling etc. Now, in Florida, no one came near him, and he found himself feeling somewhat uneasy, if not frustrated. While his literary work was progressing favourably, and proving very satisfying, he still yearned for human companionship. He was a born communicator, and he also had a deep social side to him. These needs had to be satisfied, sooner rather than later.

In October 1927, Abbot Charles asked Dom Mayeul, as a personal favour, to accept the appointment, for a term of three years, as ordinary confessor for the Benedictine sisters. He felt he couldn't refuse and that same evening the abbot presented him to the prioress. At first, this involved nothing more than hearing the confessions of the local Benedictine nuns and their students, and giving some spiritual conferences to the novices and younger sisters. However, as the convent was quite near to his hermitage, and Dom Mayeul found the work congenial, he began to visit the place almost daily. He soon discovered that the community had some serious problems regarding religious practice and fervour. Apparently, it had virtually been abandoned and left to go its own way over a number of years. Dom Mayeul, with his vast experience of governing religious men and women, took up the challenge and introduced reforms and changes which were initially not always fully understood.

One of the areas he took a particular interest in was the convent and school library. The library contained over 3000 books, but there was no catalogue and most of the books were in a sad state of disorder. Dom Mayeul spent long hours classifying the books. He was especially appalled to see that a great number of them were novels. This led him to do something to improve the kind of reading available to the nuns and their students. After consulting with the prioress, those novels which he thought unsuitable were replaced by what he called 'good books' *(Vol. II, 243)*. The community had the good fortune to experience the influx of new recruits during his time there, which pleased Dom Mayeul, though it meant added work for him. He soon found himself giving conferences and lectures to these young sisters. In 1930, at the end of his three-year term, he severed all connection with the local Benedictine convent and school. Reading the annotations on this topic, on the side of the page in his memoirs, it seemed that he had become frustrated by the little progress made in their spiritual life. Apparently, the high level of his teaching on how to raise their spiritual life to a higher standard was not adapted and proved a notch too high for them.

On 29 March 1931 Dom Mayeul entered into his 70th year. The fact of reaching this age surprised him, as he apparently had not expected to live that long. Such musings led him to think of his family in Belgium, and he resolved there and then that he should visit them the following year, 1932. In the meantime he was greatly saddened at the death of Abbot Charles Mohr of St. Leo Abbey, on Good Friday, 3 April 1931. He never forgot the debt he owed

DOM MAYEUL IN 1928 DURING A VISIT WITH THE VAN COLEN FAMILY,
LIVING IN TOLEDO, USA.
THE VAN COLEN FAMILY WAS RELATED TO DOM MAYEUL.
HIS FATHER'S SISTER WAS MARRIED TO A VAN COLEN.

to Abbot Charles, for offering him the hospitality of St. Leo Abbey in 1924, and thus opening up a new life for him. He was greatly relieved when the new abbot, Dom Francis Sadlier, let him know that he could remain on at the college farm. In fact, Abbot Francis held Dom Mayeul in such high regard that he immediately asked him to preach the pre-ordination retreat to four of the monks of St. Leo, three of whom where soon to be raised to the diaconate, and the other to the priesthood. The retreat was a six-day affair, lasting from 23 to 28 May 1931. This was only one of many such retreats he gave to the community of St. Leo during the remaining years of his time there. Throughout the 1930s, he was invited to give retreats to several communities of men and women up and down the United States. This kind of work appealed to him for many reasons, not least because it helped to boost his financial situation.

In late March 1932, Dom Mayeul sailed from New York to Europe, where he spent the next six months, visiting his family and friends in different parts of the continent. Thanks to the very favourable exchange which he got for the US dollar, he was able to undertake several extensive trips and pilgrimages. On 12 April, he presided at the silver jubilee of profession of his sister Marie in the Convent of our Lady of Refuge in St. Andre, Bruges, and on 12 September, he was present at the silver jubilee of his sister, Helene, at the convent of Iseghem, in Flanders. In each case, he preached the homily in honour of the jubilarian. He also took the opportunity of visiting his parents' grave.

During the summer months, he made a number of pilgrimages. The first was to Lourdes, which he had visited at least twice before. After that he went to Fatima in Portugal, and then to Our Lady of Czestochowa, "The Black Madonna", in Poland, both for the first time. He was very impressed by the devotion to Mary shown in these two latter places. In Fatima, he met the mother of the three children who had witnessed the apparition, and was allowed to sleep in the little house of one of the sisters. In Czestochowa, he was given the privilege of presiding at the ceremonies which accompany the daily raising and lowering of the curtain, which covers the miraculous statue of Our Lady (*Vol. II, 248*). While in the city of Warsaw, he was introduced to a Polish lady, Madame Helene de Bisping. They became friends, and corresponded with each other in French over the following years. She was the patron of a Catholic girls' boarding school, called in French "Fondation de la Providence", and hoped that Dom Mayeul would help them financially, by providing a scholarship for one of the poorer pupils. Helene had apparently been to the USA several times, and claimed to have met three presidents: Coolidge, Hoover and Roosevelt *(St. Leo, H. de Bisping to Dom Mayeul, 9 Nov. 1932)*.

Finally, while in Europe, Dom Mayeul made two final pilgrimages: one to Avila, the beautifully preserved city of the great St. Teresa of Avila, and the other to Lisieux, where he again had the pleasure of seeing and speaking with the sisters of St. Thérèse de Lisieux. Back in Belgium, on 15 August, he celebrated Pontifical Mass in the church of Emelghem, his first communion parish, surrounded by his family and friends. The occasion was the silver jubilee of his abbatial blessing in Bahia in 1907. Afterwards, there was a banquet given by his nephew, Gerard, in his honour. As he rose to thank his nephew and friends for their kind reception, he expressed his gratitude to God, for showering so many blessings on his family. If he belonged anywhere on this earth, it was surely this area to which he could make claim. Sadly, his memories of the few years he lived there were vague and blurred, and, sadder still, now, in the evening of his life, he had to admit that he was a stranger to most of its inhabitants.

As a Benedictine monk, Dom Mayeul had a problem attaching himself by a vow of stability to any one monastery. It was an unusual situation, and considered an anomaly by Benedictine standards, where a monk is attached for life to a particular monastery, normally that of his final profession. Dom Mayeul had made his first monastic profession in Olinda, Brazil, in 1898, and his final profession in St. Andre, Belgium, in 1901. But he never became a fully-fledged member of either of these monasteries. At some stage or other, he had lived in no less than nine monasteries (St. Trond, Beauplateau, Maredsous, Olinda, Santa Cruz, Rio de Janeiro, Bahia, Trinidad and Florida). Because of his continual moving from one monastery to another while in Brazil, he had opted, as far back as 1898, to pronounce a vow which covered the Brazilian Congregation, rather than any one specific monastery. Even when he moved to Trinidad, and later to Florida, he continued to keep his Brazilian connection. The reason for this lay in his having been abbot of Bahia from 1908 to 1915, and his reluctance to break off all

IN CAP D'ANTIBES (SOUTH OF FRANCE) WITH THE FAMILY BOUDET, ON HIS WAY TO THE ABBOT PRIMATE IN ROME TO DISCUSS AND RESOLVE THE PROBLEM ON HIS VOW OF STABILITY.

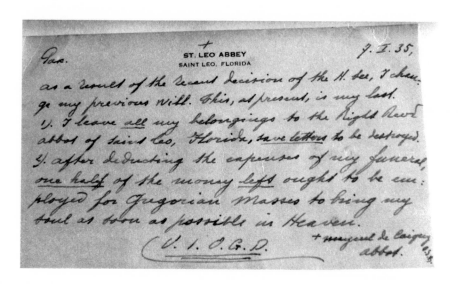

A LITTLE CARD, WITH THE CORRECTION OF A PARAGRAPH IN HIS LAST WILL, AFTER HE CHANGED HIS VOW OF STABILITY TO ST. LEO ABBEY.

connections with his former abbey. Added to which was his deep love and appreciation of the Brazilian language and way of life. Circumstances, which have already been described, forced him to leave Bahia and Brazil in 1912, though his heart continued to remain there even after he moved to Trinidad and Florida. He always considered himself, in his heart of hearts, "a monk of Bahia" *(APR, 613, # 4, Dom Mayeul to APR, 20 Jan. 1936)*. However, Abbot Primate von Stotzingen was not happy with this arrangement. It took twelve years (1924-1936), a trip to Europe and a drawn-out correspondence, for the abbot primate to convince Dom Mayeul that he should renounce his allegiance to the Brazilian Congregation. The final solution, which was reached on 8 December 1935, satisfied all parties. By this arrangement, Dom Mayeul opted to take a vow of stability for St. Leo Abbey, which was affiliated to the American-Cassinese Congregation. At long last, he gave his allegiance to a particular monastery, which he could call his 'home'.

During his time in Florida, Dom Mayeul carried on a correspondence with a great number of people. It is impossible to do justice to this side of Dom Mayeul's life, mainly because he had so many correspondents. The majority were women friends, some new, some going back to his years in Brazil and the Mount. He had an extraordinary knack of keeping friends. He could not be accused of 'using' his friends, but he certainly needed them. Some could be classified as his spiritual daughters, to whom he became a kind of "agony uncle', and who poured out their hearts and problems to him. Others were people he had met along the way, with whom he struck up an acquaintance. For the most part, the incoming letters are preserved in the archives of St. Leo Abbey, Florida. His correspondents wrote from many countries: USA, Canada, Trinidad, Brazil, Belgium, France, Italy, England, Luxembourg, etc. Unfortunately, we have very few of the dove-tailing letters, i.e. his letters in reply to theirs. He seems to have been quite happy dealing with this everincreasing workload of correspondence, considering it just another side to his 'apostolate of the pen'.

Undoubtedly, one of Dom Mayeul's most interesting and fascinating correspondents is a lady called Rowena Lamy (she sometimes signs herself "Carina"). She wrote some 126 letters to Dom Mayeul between 18 August 1924 and 28 January 1935. Dom Mayeul had known her in the Mount, where she was one of the oblates.

She travelled a great deal, as is evident from the ever changing addresses: 18 Albion St., Port of Spain, Trinidad; Reading, England; Edinburgh, Scotland; and Tihany, Hungary. Some of her language is very poetic and exaggerated, though it probably reflects the religious climate of the day. Carina is in and out of the Catholic faith, and at one time calls herself "an agnostic". He never loses interest in her, and despite her moods and personal difficulties, shows great patience with her. They seem to have remained friends right up to the end. There is a high quality of literary excellence in her letters, many of which run to ten pages or more.

Another woman who wrote frequently to Dom Mayeul during his time in Florida was a Russian-born lady called Ms. Elizabeth Nekludov (Neckludoff). She signed herself "Lizok", probably a pet-name given her by her family. Eighty-nine letters of hers have survived in the archives of St. Leo Abbey. Her father had been Russian ambassador to the US under Czar Nicholas II. After the revolution of 1917, the family remained in the USA and never returned to Russia. She wrote from two different addresses: 36 East 72nd St., New York, and the Villa Maganosc, Nice, France, always beginning her letters with "Mon cher Mayeul". She adopted a very affectionate and personal tone, though her letters read more like a sister writing to a brother. It is difficult to know what holds their friendship together, except loyalty and the religious dimension. They also had some common interests, such as music and religion. Lizok was a very spiritual person, and had several Russian saints among her ancestors (*St. Leo, File H, "Lizok" to Dom Mayeul 10 Dec. 1928*).

Many of the letters which have survived are from different convents of religious women in USA. Of special importance is a series of letters, written during the years 1934-39, from the superiors of the Little Sisters of the Poor, in Savannah, Georgia, Germantown, Pennsylvania, Richmond, Virginia and Baltimore. During this time, Dom Mayeul was in constant demand by the Little Sisters of the Poor to preach retreats, and also to preside at ceremonies of profession and clothing. The Little Sisters of the Poor had been founded in France at the end of the 19th century, and many of the Sisters who came to US were French-speaking. Dom Mayeul preached most of these retreats in French, and became close friends with members of several communities of the Little Sisters of the

Poor. One of them, who signed herself either "Abi" or 'Soeurette", wrote frequently to him. Among other things, she sent Dom Mayeul her spiritual diary "The History of a Soul" (in French) *(St. Leo, File C. no. 9)*. The Little Sisters of the Poor had a number of nursing homes catering for elderly men and women. Dom Mayeul spent his final days, in 1939, in their care in the hospital of Savannah, Georgia.

One final correspondent worth mentioning is Magdelena, the young woman Dom Mayeul had brought from Brazil to the Mount, and claimed to have saved from a life of prostitution. After Dom Mayeul had left Trinidad in 1923, Prior Hugh sent Magdelena back to Brazil, on the grounds that he could not control her. From her letters to Dom Mayeul, one gets the impression that, by the 1930s, she had become a reformed person, if that is the correct word. In any case she continued to rely on Dom Mayeul, as she says in one of her letters, written in Brazilian-Portuguese from Rio de Janeiro:

> *I don't know how I continue to live like this. Without God's grace and your holy guidance to sustain me, life would have been even more difficult and empty. I long to hear from you. How is your health? Are you eating well? Are you happy? I love you very much, and I think that you are suffering on my account. While I am very grateful to you for your kindness, I have the impression that I stood in the way of your holiness. I want to be sure of your salvation and this causes me to be worried. When I attend Holy Mass, I pray that you will persevere in your sacred vocation and maintain your sanctity. I pray that God in His mercy will forgive all my sins and grant me the grace of everlasting salvation. We shall surely meet in Heaven, where love is pure and holy (St. Leo, Magdelena Gomes Saavedra to Dom Mayeul, 3 Oct. 1935).*

Some of Magdelena's letters are truly inspiring. She was no fool or simple soul, but possessed deep feelings of humility and gratitude. By the mid-1930s, she was a very spiritual person, and had come to realize how much Dom Mayeul had suffered on her account. One last quotation is worth giving, as it is an acknowledgement of Dom Mayeul's genuine pastoral concern, and the influence for good that he had on people. He had a special attentiveness for the poor and those excluded from society:

My dear Father, I realize how much you endured on my behalf, and I appreciate your persistent efforts to save me. It was not easy to guide this poor lost sheep to her place in God's flock. God alone can reward your kindness. Priests like yourself are hard to find, and it is your dedication that led me from iniquity to virtue (Ibid. 24 Dec. 1935).

Another example of his genuine kindness is shown in a letter (6 Feb. 1927) to his nephew Gerard De Caigny. In this letter Dom Mayeul shows his emotional side when he writes about the moral status of his youngest brother, and godchild, Alois. After Alois had lost his wife Silvie Callewaert, (she had died from cancer at the age of 49), Dom Mayeul understood very well Alois's grief and state of mind:

What makes me very sad is the moral state in which Alois currently is. His excessive sadness, his desperate mindset does him no good and is a burden for others. If he loves God with all his heart he will not give up fighting at this point. You need to support and help him in a soft way and treat him as a sick man by <u>showing affection</u> without talking about the cause of his sadness (F.A., F. De Caigny, Belgium).

Up to the end of 1934, Dom Mayeul seems to have been faced with financial problems. In almost every letter he wrote to Prior Hugh of the Mount, he added a reminder that his pension had not yet been paid. He failed to appreciate the serious financial situation at the Mount, and how difficult, if not impossible, it was for them in the aftermath of the Wall Street crash in 1929. Early 1934, Dom Hugh, the prior, informed Dom Mayeul that it was impossible for them to make any future pension payments:

Dear Lord Abbot, I regret very much that I am quite unable to send your allowance. Our financial position is becoming more difficult. And I don't think this is difficult for you to imagine considering the severe losses we have sustained as explained in my last letter. If times are not soon becoming better we shall get into severe difficulties. At present we are sinking and if there comes no change for the better we shall have to give up. I am always mindful for all you have done for this monastery and your great kindness to me personally. On account of all these sentiments I feel very much grieved.

THE YOUNGEST BROTHER, AND GODCHILD, OF DOM MAYEUL, ALOIS DE CAIGNY
(1875-1946) AND HIS WIFE SILVIE (1875-1925).
(PICTURE TO THE BOTTOM TAKEN FROM HIS MEMOIRS VOLUME III)

Now I have to give up because there is no money. Still I trust
that God will come to our rescue (Dom Hugh to Dom Mayeul
9 Feb 34).

Then, by the summer of 1936, a great change came over Dom
Mayeul, when he realized that he had more money than he needed
for his everyday expenses. Three things seem to have brought about
this change in his situation. First of all, in December 1935 he had
settled the question of his vow of stability, and became a full-mem-
ber of the St. Leo community. As such, he was no longer treated
like a guest, but had all the same rights and privileges, including
financial security, as the other monks of that monastery. Secondly,
his books, the Trilogy and the Magnificat, in spite of the initial
hiccups at the time of their publication, had begun to sell very well
in Belgium and France. Devotion to St. Thérèse and to the Blessed
Virgin Mary, were still major factors in Catholic circles in Europe
throughout the 1930s. The result was a substantial royalty cheque
in 1936 from his publisher, with a promise of more cheques in the
years to follow. It was the first time, since leaving Trinidad, that he
felt financially independent. This gave his self-confidence a great
boost, as he came to realize that his books were appreciated by so
many people. In spite of him needing the money, Dom Mayeul left
the royalties from the Brazilian version of *"The Ascetical Commentary*
on the Magnificat" for the abbey of Bahia:

> *The abbot of Bahia wrote to me on 23 March 1934, congratulat-*
> *ing me on the work, and expressing his wish to have it translated*
> *into Portuguese. As regards the royalties accruing from the sale*
> *of this translation, I gave all the profits to the Abbey of Bahia*
> *(Vol. II).*

In 1938 he published, also in French, his third and last book
"The Ascetical Method of St. Benedict", which was also well received by
readers in Europe. It was based on his many talks to his communities in Bahia and Trinidad, on the Rule of St. Benedict.

The third factor was the success of the retreats he gave throughout the US, and beyond, from 1934 onwards. He wrote on 15th
July 1934, from the priory, Nassau, Bahamas, where he had been
preaching a retreat to the Jesuits on the island. His trip from the
USA to the Bahamas was his first time on an airplane. He was paid
at least a hundred US dollars for each retreat, and received other

emoluments for presiding at the religious professions in various convents throughout the USA. All in all, he was a very busy man, a much sought after preacher, constantly on the road, and hardly recognizable as the hermit of the college farm.

One immediate result of his improved financial situation was his change of attitude towards the payment of his pension by the monks of the Mount. There were no more letters asking for his pension payment. Instead, he now was prepared to come to the aid of his beloved Mount St. Benedict. In March 1937, he wrote as follows to Prior Hugh:

> *I have just returned from preaching a number of retreats in the North of USA, for which I received very generous payment. I notice that your situation at present is not brilliant, so I have taken the resolution to help you out financially (MSB, Dom Mayeul to Dom Hugh, 1 March 1937).*

Dom Hugh van der Sanden replied on March 25th :

> *Dear Lord Abbot, your kind letter and generous donation were received with sincere gratitude. I appreciate highly your charitable spirit and the love you continue to bear for the Foundation that has cost you so much labour and pain. Thank God, matters begin to look brighter in Trinidad.*

His first payment was US$100, and there was more to follow over the next three years. Undoubtedly, this helped to restore some normality in his relationship with Trinidad. For obvious reasons, during the previous decade (1924-34), there had been very little communication between Dom Mayeul and the members of the Mount, apart from Prior Hugh. Soon after Dom Mayeul's contributions began arriving, Dom Odo van der Heydt, who had started researching the history of the Mount, wrote to Dom Mayeul, asking for information regarding the early days of the monastery. He hoped that Dom Mayeul would send him a copy of his memoirs, or at least the pages which mentioned the Mount. Dom Odo also wanted to find out the name of the person who had donated the three big Bells to the monastery (*MSB, Dom Odo to Dom Mayeul, 2 Feb 1938*). Dom Mayeul replied telling him that the donor was a certain Viscountess de Coetlosquet, a Belgian lady. During his final years at the college farm of St. Leo Abbey, Dom Mayeul seems to have mellowed considerably, a fact which allowed him to take a new interest in the progress and welfare of the Trinidadian foundation.

In trying to understand Dom Mayeul's changed relationship with the Mount, there were two factors which may have influenced him. The first occurred on 12 August 1934, when Archbishop Dowling made a remarkable speech in the capital city of Trinidad, Port of Spain, praising the monks of the Mount. A few days later, the archbishop wrote a long article on the Benedictines, in the diocesan weekly newspaper *The Catholic News*. His opening words were as follows:

> *The greatest outstanding event in the Archdiocese these past twenty-five years has been the introduction of the Benedictine Monks into Trinidad, and it will be appropriate to publish details of it. Today I am going to devote several pages to them alone. They highly deserve this recognition of their services to the archdiocese, and I am sure that the Clergy and the Laity will be pleased at their receiving it, and receiving it in this official and lasting way. (The Catholic News, 14 August 1934)*

He then gave a detailed account of the founding of the monastery, and its subsequent history. When taken in the context of his treatment of the monks in earlier days, it sounds like a complete turn-about on the part of the archbishop. Obviously, he made no reference to the difficulties he had encountered, down the years, with Dom Mayeul and Prior Hugh, over the parishes.

The second factor was the occasion of the silver jubilee of the foundation of the Mount on 6 October 1937, when Archbishop Dowling celebrated High Mass at the Mount and preached a sermon, in which he referred to Dom Mayeul as a "remarkable man". Dom Mayeul inserted copies of the newspaper accounts of these two events in his memoirs. There is no evidence that these eulogies made Dom Mayeul change his mind about Archbishop Dowling. Yet, he was inwardly pleased for the monks of the Mount, in that the monastery was at last recognized as an integral part of the archdiocese of Port of Spain. Regarding the silver jubilee of the foundation of the Mount, on 6 October 1937, Dom Mayeul decided to stay away, but told Prior Hugh that he "would be with him in spirit". There was no way he could bring himself to come face to face with Archbishop Dowling, considering their former strained relationship.

By 1937, Dom Mayeul had become more friendly and relaxed in his relations with the Mount, the monks, in their turn, reciprocated these feelings. This was especially true of Prior Hugh, who wrote a particularly flattering letter to Dom Mayeul, on 23 September 1937, congratulating the latter on the golden jubilee of his priestly ordination, which occurred on 11 October 1887:

> On the occasion of the golden jubilee of Priesthood, I offer you my heartfelt congratulations. Many souls have profited during this half century by your sound teaching, wise counsels and great charity. Among this great number I have to count myself, and I shall always be grateful to God for having given me during the first years of my monastic and priestly career such an experienced guide.
>
> It is surely gratifying, when looking back, that God made use of you for so many important works for His glory and the welfare of souls. Mount St. Benedict is one of these great works which needed vivid faith and unrelenting strength. Although the foundation has not given you the material satisfaction as a consequence of the sacrifices and hard labour you generously bestowed upon it, God has a far more precious reward in store for you.
>
> The monastery will be celebrating its silver jubilee on 6th October. That its Founder will not be present is surely something which some of us will keenly feel. I know, however, that Your Lordship will be present in spirit (St.Leo, Dom Hugh to Dom Mayeul 23 Sept.1937).

Mount St. Benedict had made great progress on all fronts since 1923, mainly due to the enterprise and administrative ability of Prior Hugh van der Sanden. By 1937, there were 23 solemnly professed monks, 2 simple professed, 5 choir novices, and 6 lay brothers, making in all 36 monks. By right, the monastery should then have been raised to the status of an abbey. However, Archbishop Dowling had made it clear that he would never tolerate another prelate in his diocese. Thus the monastery had to wait until 1947, after the death of Archbishop Dowling and under his successor, Archbishop Finbar Ryan, before becoming an abbey.

Photographie de l'Eglise de l'abbaye de Bahia prise à l'occasion de la messe célébrée pour le Jubilé d'or de mon ordination sacerdotale

CHURCH OF BAHIA.
MASS CELEBRATED ON 11 OCTOBER 1937 AT THE OCCASION OF DOM MAYEUL'S
GOLDEN JUBILEE OF PRIESTHOOD. HE STILL HAD A LARGE FOLLOWING OF PERSONS
AT BAHIA WHO HELD HIM IN HIGH REGARD, SO MANY YEARS AFTER HIS DEPARTURE.

AERIAL VIEW OF EXPANSION OF THE ABBEY MOUNT ST. BENEDICT -
CONSTRUCTION OF THE NEW CHURCH

MOUNT ST. BENEDICT, THE CHURCH

THE PORT OF SPAIN GAZETTE: "HUGE CROWDS IN ATTENDANCE" AT THE
MOUNT IN 1931, SHOWING THE ONGOING SUCCESS OF THE FOUNDATION

CHAPTER XXI

The Finale
(1938 – 1939)

IN JANUARY 1939, Dom Mayeul replied to the New Year wishes he had received from his brother Alois De Caigny, wondering what the future had in store. He had already lost three of his sisters (Pharailde in 1901, Leonie in 1903 and Julie in 1929), and his elder brother François who had died in 1925 at the age of 68. His younger brother, Medard, a very talented man, had died in 1889 at the age of 25. His youngest brother and godchild, Alois, who had stayed on the farm, had lost his wife Silvie in 1925; she was only 49. He had six boys to take care of. One of them, Remi, was the father of Monique De Caigny, mentioned in the prologue. So only two sisters, Helena and Maria, and his brother Alois were still alive. Dom Mayeul never wrote much about the death of his siblings. And when he did, it was not in an emotional way; just a few facts. Once he had finished his novitiate at St. Trond as a Redemptorist, he never again mentioned in his memoirs, his aunt and uncle who had taken him in their house at the age of five. They had been very good to him and had cared for him for many years. Unfortunately there are no letters in the archives from them to Dom Mayeul. Perhaps there weren't any. There is no reference either in his memoirs about their death, in 1911 and 1916.

It is hard to really understand, but perhaps it is because he was raised outside his family that he coped differently with his emotions, especially when he lost a family member. Didn't he write in his memoirs that as a young boy he felt like a stranger in the presence of his family? Of course he had loved them all very much and he did care about them, but something had been missing. Perhaps in his old age, he may have now regretted, more than ever, not having known them to the fullest.

My dearly loved brother and godchild, I read your best wishes for 1939 with great joy. I hope 1939 will be a blessed year for you and the whole family. My dear school friend, Charles de Keyser, from the minor seminary died. We are only 3 left from my class. Thank God, all is well with me. I wonder though what this year will bestow on me? (F.A., F. De Caigny, Belgium)

At different moments during his final years in St. Leo Abbey, Dom Mayeul thought of his pending death. This led him to draw up a number of last wills and testaments, in which he bequeathed his personal belongings, such as his manuscripts, books etc. to different institutions and persons. The date of his first will is 26 May 1930, in which he appointed Abbot Charles Mohr, of St. Leo Abbey, as his sole executor. Money should be put at the disposal of the abbot of St. Maurice in Clervaux, Luxembourg, to publish his new manuscripts. The balance and the revenue of his published books were to be divided as follows: one third to the Order of St. Benedict of St. Leo, Florida, one third to Mount St. Benedict, Trinidad, and one third to the Benedictine monastery, Bahia, Brazil. Third, his pectoral cross, rings, mitres and other pontifical insignia should be left to St. Leo Abbey. Fourth, his old manuscripts were to be given to Dom Gualbert Van De Plas, Mount St. Benedict, Trinidad and all other papers and letters should be burned. That Bahia is mentioned in this will comes as no surprise since at that time (1930) Dom Mayeul still belonged to the Brazilian Congregation.

A second will was drawn up on 14 February 1932, and a third one on 27 May 1934. Both contained many of the provisions listed in the first will. However the will of 1934 is in his own handwriting and full of religious quotes, expressing his deep belief in the Blessed Trinity and in God's will. The will also refers to the fact that it is possible that he may need the money for doctors and hospital bills:

I know that our Lord may give me that Great Love in one moment (sudden death) if He likes to do it; but perhaps He will give it only after many years of trial and in that case I may be in need of money to pay doctors and hospital bills not wishing to put such burden on the Abbey. (St. Leo Last Will 27 V 34)

The will further states that after paying the expenses for his funeral, the balance was to be divided between the abbey of St.

Leo, the abbey of Bahia, Brazil, and the monastery of Mount St. Benedict, Trinidad. The abbot was free to decide where to bury his body. All manuscripts should be sent registered to the monastery of Bahia; smaller ones with all the letters ought to be immediately burned, especially the correspondence with the Carmel of Lisieux at its request. The notification of his death needs to be sent to his brother, Mr. Alois De Caigny; his niece, Miss Helene De Caigny; Abbot Placido, San Sebastian Abbey, Bahia; Prior Hugh van der Sanden, Mount St. Benedict; Abbaye des Dames Benedictines, Jouarre; Abbaye des Dames Benedictines, Lisieux; Monastere du Carmel, Lisieux.

However, there was a serious flaw in all these wills: they ran contrary to the Canon Law of the Catholic Church and contrary to Benedictine tradition. By his vow of poverty, a monk renounces the right to own private property. This means that anything a monk acquires belongs to the monastery of his profession, and he cannot dispose of it privately or personally. It is true that Dom Mayeul had for years been a kind of floating entity, unattached to any one monastery. However, when he took a vow of stability for St. Leo Abbey, confirmed by the Holy See in Dec 1935, he was bound by the laws of the Church, and could no longer claim the right to own anything. All his personal assets, his pension from the Mount, money from his retreats and royalties from his books, his manuscripts, etc., were automatically transferred into the assets of St. Leo.

He probably felt himself bound by the promises he had made to a number of people, granting them a share in the profits from his books. It seems that between 1932 and 1934, he had given the rights to some of the profits from his books to Abbot Galliard of the Rue de la Source, Paris, and a small percentage of the same to the monks of St. Maurice, Luxembourg (*St. Leo, Dom Mayeul to Abbot O. Galliard, 8 Nov. 1936, 5 April 1937, 23 Nov. 1938*). But of course, all these promises were invalid, and would never stand up in a Church court of law. At the end of the day, Abbot Galliard of the Rue de la Source, and the monks of St. Maurice, Luxembourg, lost whatever claims they had to a share in the inheritance of Dom Mayeul. The Canon Law of the Catholic Church dictated how his personal belongings should be disposed of, thus overriding Dom Mayeul's wishes in this matter.

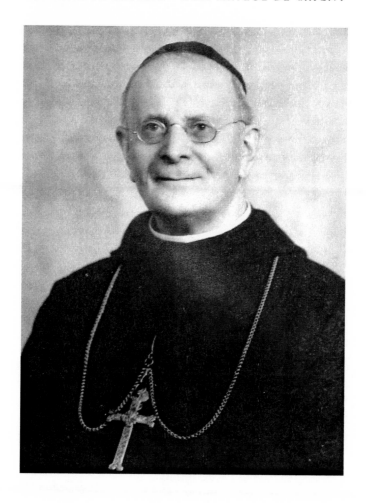

PUBLICATION OF DOM MAYEUL'S PHOTO IN ST. LEO COMMUNITY BOOK

The last seven years at St. Leo Abbey had been very rewarding and a blessing. He enjoyed the solitude of the abbey farm in combination with the hectic schedule of giving retreats and conferences, while still finding time for his spiritual publications and keeping up with his correspondence. In 1938 he published his last book, which got very good reviews by readers in Europe and he supervised the translation into English of the Trilogy of St. Therese de Lisieux, by the Benedictine Sisters of Pittsburgh. He confirmed his peace of mind in his memoirs:

> *How admirable are the ways of Divine Providence! Following of the persecutions in Bahia, I was led to Trinidad to make a new foundation there, which has become a much frequented place of pilgrimage, in honour of our Holy Father St. Benedict. This foundation being well established, God led me to Florida, where during 10 years I enjoyed complete solitude, during which time I was able to write a number of works of piety. Then, having completed these works, another field of activity providentially opened up for me, which I could never have found in Bahia, nor in Trinidad: that of preaching and conducting religious retreats, a work which pleases me greatly, and which has been blest by our heavenly Father. No doubt my life has been externally full of movements; but internally, I enjoyed a great tranquillity, in allowing myself to rest with confidence in the arms of God: "My destiny is in Your hands" (Ps. 30, 16) (Vol. II, 256).*

He was a happy and proud man. His publications were well accepted and he was in much demand for his spiritual conferences. After each of his retreats and conferences, a flow of correspondence followed, confirming the spiritual and other benefits the people had received. People loved him! At St. Leo Abbey he became more and more involved giving retreats and spiritual guidance and he received congratulations from the abbot of Bahia for his spiritual works. He was finally recognized. In 1938 he even entertained the idea of outsourcing the translation of his other books into English. He had met with an author who was willing to take on this difficult task of translation. He wrote to his sister Godelieve on 1 Dec 1938: *"I met with a very interesting person, an author, well educated, who wants to translate my books. I will see if it is serious"* (F.A., F. De Caigny, Belgium).

However Dom Mayeul had some serious health problems during his last years at St. Leo. Old age had caught up with him, especially during his last two years, 1937-39, when he had several spells of sickness. In September 1937 he was in hospital in Savannah, Georgia, and again before Easter 1938. However, he recovered sufficiently to continue with his work. Throughout 1938 he was occupied giving retreats and he speaks about his spells of sickness at various times in his memoirs:

I preached all these conferences, in spite of recurring and violent attacks of rheumatism. I was relieved to return to my dear solitude of St. Leo.

At the beginning of June 1938, I preached the Retreat to the community of St. Leo Abbey. This was the second time I had done so. The subject was my Commentary on the Magnificat, which apparently pleased the monks. Soon after this I had an attack of malaria, and was cared for in the infirmary of the Abbey (Vol. II, 257).

Over the last years, his handwriting in his memoirs had changed and the number of entries diminished although he found himself recovered and in excellent health. His last entry, dated January 1939, reads:

After these 9 retreats in 1938 I returned to St. Leo, in excellent health. My general condition seemed better than ever, thank God. These apostolic works were a great consolation to me. In the beginning of 1939, the Abbot of St. Leo indicated to me that he would like me to give a weekly conference to the novices. I accepted this task with pleasure (Vol. II, 259).

After this last entry on page 259, all pages remained untouched except from page 280 on, where in 1930 Dom Mayeul had included a full chapter on his genealogy. It looks like he left the few blank pages from 259 on for us to complete......

On 24 April 1939, a telegraph, of The West India and Panama Telegraph Company, arrived at Mount St. Benedict. Prior Dom Hugh van der Sanden read the message:

Benedictines Trinidad, Abbot Mayeul died today
Ex Abbatia S. Leonis
Saint Leo, Florida 24 April 1939.

† Franciscus Abbas.

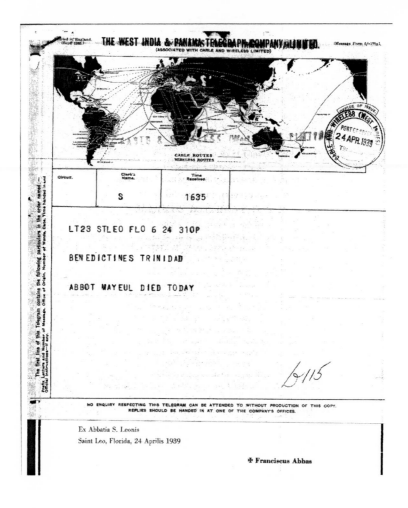

THE WEST INDIA AND PANAMA COMPANY, A TELEGRAPH FROM ST. LEO ABBEY,
ANNOUNCING THE DEATH OF DOM MAYEUL

A detailed record of Dom Mayeul's last weeks and days on earth is provided in several letters. Abbot Francis Sadlier of St. Leo Abbey gave a detailed account to the numerous people, asking for more information on Dom Mayeul's passing. Letters from the Little Sisters of the Poor, Savannah, and from the Sisters of Mercy at St. Joseph's hospital, give additional information. These letters, sent to Dom Mayeul's blood sister Godelieve and to Miss Nellie de Verteuil in Trinidad, are kept in the De Caigny family archives in Belgium. Fortunately, Miss Nellie had forwarded the letters she had received to Sister Godelieve, Prioress at Nieuwpoort, Belgium.

We all feel the loss of Abbot Mayeul very keenly. The thought that he has gone to his well deserved eternal reward must be a consolation to you as it is to us. For about two years he was showing that old age was creeping on him. One could see that he was gradually getting weaker and he had several times a serious spell of sickness. In September 1937 he was in the hospital of Savannah and before Easter in 1938 he took sick whilst giving a Retreat in New Orleans, and was taken to the hospital but he was able to come home on Holy Saturday, still a sick and feeble looking man.

After a few weeks he picked up and was able to resume his activity in the line of giving conferences and in June he gave our retreat. Two weeks later he had a serious attack and he was in the infirmary for ten days. One day he had a weak spell and it looked as if then the end was near. He got well and he was able to give a number of retreats and he was away nearly all fall till December.

Around New Year he was in good health and he himself expressed it that he was good for many years. But towards the end of March he had another spell of vomiting and whenever he ate something he felt nauseating.

On his birthday, March 29, he had made arrangements to go to some friends in Tampa but was not able to eat the birthday dinner, practically the whole time he was laying on a sofa. When he returned in the evening he called for me and I saw at once that he was a very sick man and we made at once arrangements to have him taken to Savannah. Next day he was in the hospital. He wanted to go to Savannah as he was with a certain physician and he liked the hospital.

The doctor had little hope for his recovery. For two weeks there was no improvement. Then he seemed to be a little better and the doctors advised an operation. On April 15th at 13.30 he was operated but the doctors could do nothing for him. He had liver sclerosis.

Then it went slowly towards the end. By Friday the following week he had a sinking spell and it was then only a question of a few days. Saturday night he was not expected to live through the night. Sunday, he was unconscious until the end on Monday April 24, at 10.05 in the morning. He had a beautiful death, plus we feel he was ready and well prepared after so many useful years in the service of God.

His body was brought here and the Solemn Funeral was on Thursday, April 27th. The Bishop of St. Augustine, Mgr. Patrick Barry, celebrated the pontifical requiem and I preached the sermon. After the Absolutions the body was carried to the cemetery were the burial took place. The abbot of St. Bernard Alabama was the only Abbot present besides myself.

His death was a shock to his many friends and we received numerous letters from different parts of the world. His influence was great, and the circle of his friends very large. He has left in his books a treasure of his teaching. Although he is dead, his work lives on and through the three books that he published his teaching and spiritual doctrines are still at the disposal of the people. Abbot Francis Sadlier May 18th 1939 (F.A., F. De Caigny, Belgium).

Sister Mary Theresia, at St. Joseph's Hospital, and Prioress Sister Patrick at the Little Sisters of the Poor, gave the following written account from Savannah:

Our dear father Abbot had the choice of hospital between Tampa, Florida, and St. Joseph's Savannah. He chose the latter so as to be nearer to the priests of his Order, as well as to the Little Sisters. Father Abbot looked an ill man, his colour was almost bronze. He could not eat and he was miserably thin. He had changed a lot since we last met him a year ago.

The doctors treated him for several weeks, X-rayed him and had several tests made. All seemed to point to a diagnosis of cancer of the liver. The doctors felt that if he could stand an operation they could at least give him temporary relief. So they operated but found that nothing could be done. Father was only given a local anesthetic, and after a small incision it was discovered that the gall bladder had completely dried up, after which the doctors decided that it was useless to proceed and they closed the wound.

We visited him daily, he was happy and our visits gave him pleasure. His only desire was to be able to get well so as to celebrate Holy Mass for our Centennial Celebration. Father Abbot was saying all the time that our Dear Lord wanted him to suffer so he would willingly bear all for Him. At the time of death, a priest, two nuns and several nurses were with him. Just following death our Bishop and a number of priests were with him. His remains were placed in the church of the Benedictine parish and was in state two nights and a day, before taken to St. Leo Abbey in Florida.

Father Abbot's resignation was most beautiful, we consider it a real privilege to have had such person in his last moments and we feel that he will intercede for us in heaven.

He was certainly a living saint – his kindness, patience and submission to God's will, were something that I will never forget. His death has been a great loss and we dreadfully miss him (May 14th 1939, F.A., F. De Caigny, Belgium).

Abbot Francis Sadlier, in his letter dated 2 June 1939 to Sister Godelieve, mentioned that the funeral was very impressive and that many people were not able to attend because of the large crowd. Bishop Patrick Barry, of St. Augustine, Florida, celebrated the pontifical requiem Mass, while Abbot Francis Sadlier preached the homily. Bishop Patrick Barry was very touched. He said that it was the most impressive funeral he attended. Dom Mayeul was buried immediately afterwards in the abbey cemetery. Following an old monastic custom, a crucifix and two candles were placed for thirty days at the place in the refectory occupied by Dom Mayeul when he happened to be at the abbey (*F.A., F. De Caigny, Belgium*).

The obituary, printed in the St. Leo Abbey Newsletter of June 1939, ended with:

St. Leo Abbey and community were blessed by the presence of a living saint during the time Abbot Mayeul was residing among them. His holiness and quiet demeanour marked him as an outstanding individual.

A Belgian lady, Genevieve Baroness Leon Gilles de Pelichy was on her way to visit Dom Mayeul and arrived in San Francisco a few days after his death. She wrote the following account to Dom Mayeul's sister, Prioress Godelieve at Nieuwpoort:

> When I called St. Leo I learned that Dom Mayeul had passed away a couple of days ago. I decided to travel from San Francisco to Saint Leo anyway. It was hard for me to accept his death. He was a unique friend. His death is touching me very hard. All his letters are in a safe, but I was allowed to look at some souvenirs. There is no tombstone as yet on his grave, but it is covered with flowers (F.A., F. De Caigny, Belgium).

Dom Mayeul's very last will is dated 14 April 1939, the day he underwent the operation at St. Joseph's Hospital, Savannah, and ten days before he died. The two page document, in pencil, is in his handwriting and shows clearly the pain and suffering he was in. His hand must have been shaking from pain, but he expressed his hope and confidence in what was to come after life. At this final moment of his life he realized he was getting closer to his final belonging. He accepted this in the name of God. His last will is written on hospital-headed notepaper and addressed to the abbot of St. Leo:

> St. Joseph's Hospital, Sisters of Mercy
> Savannah, Georgia
>
> Rev. and dear Father Abbot,
>
> Yesterday night I was anointed by one of our Fathers, as it is the custom here before operations. Today at 13.30 I will be operated. This is the advice of Dr. Egan and Dr. Broderick. There is hope of help in this operation although not certainly of complete recovery. Our Lords Will be done!
>
> In case of God willing me, you will find the money spared in the black handbag in the working room. Please burn all the letters and manuscripts which are not mine.
>
> You may keep the manuscripts of my Souvenirs of 25 years of missionary work in the tropics; also my manuscripts in French and Flemish, my Florilgium biblicum (Flowers from the Bible) and Meditations on the Sunday Masses.
>
> You will find a manuscript (i.e. memoirs Volume II) of my interior life as a child of Mary and a zouave of the Pope, but my

positive will is not to read it and not to give it to read during 10 years after my death.

If I am to die, I offer my life in union and for our Lord, in the faith and hope of Blessed Trinity. Amen.

Last will made in St. Joseph's Hospital 14 IV 39

That in all things God may be glorified" (Ut in Omnibus Glorificetur Deus).

(St. Leo archives)

On 27 April 27, the prior and subprior of Mount St. Benedict wrote a letter to Abbot Sadlier thanking him for informing them on the death of Dom Mayeul and to tender their condolences:

Abbot Mayeul was the Founder of the monastery and its first conventual prior. We remain grateful to him and to his memory for the great work he has done during the ten years he was with us. A new foundation, like ours, has of necessity to pass through many and great trials and tribulations and to overcome many difficulties before it reaches its full development. As a debt of gratitude and charity we are saying the Gregorian masses for the repose of the soul of the Abbot Mayeul and each priest will say three masses. A solemn Mass of Requiem has been announced in the local papers for Wednesday May 3rd to which also the clergy is invited. Our Community is also very grateful to you for the charitable hospitality accorded to the late Abbot in his sad hours of trial, and we pray that God may reward you for it in his own way superabundantly. Any particulars concerning the death of Dom Mayeul shall be the most welcome to us. Towards the end of July seven of our monks will be raised to the priesthood, the number of priests in our community shall then be 25. So under God's blessing the little seed thrown by the now defunct Abbot has born fruit and it is promising well for the future of Trinidad. May the prayers of the Founder obtain a long and fruitful existence for his Foundation for the greater glory of God and for the good of many souls (St. Leo, Dom Odo to Abbot Sadlier).

The foundation is flourishing, with seven new priests; Dom Mayeul would have been very proud. It is obvious from this letter that, at Mount St. Benedict, the community members who had known Dom Mayeul have been reminiscing and evoking the early days at the Mount and how Dom Mayeul had left his footprint on their future. They remember not only the early hardships, but also the beautiful moments, especially the thousands of pilgrims. What is most touching is that, as many as 16 years after Dom Mayeul had left Trinidad, their words indicate that they remember the sad hours of trial that Dom Mayeul went through, as something that he had been subjected to and not as something which was caused by himself. For them, he was innocent of any wrongdoing. Regardless of their relation with Dom Mayeul and regardless of how they felt about the circumstances in which they had left Bahia, they all agreed that without Dom Mayeul there would not have been a Mount St. Benedict. And without Mount St. Benedict, Trinidad would not have been the same. Their life in Bahia would probably have been more complacent, better housing, beautiful church, huge library and many more material advantages to be found in a big city, but for sure much less rewarding since at the Mount, so many Trinidadians were profoundly touched by the Benedictine presence. Dom Mayeul and his early companions started on the top of the hill, far away from the hustle and bustle of the big city, in the middle of nature; and in nature one finds God. Nowadays, that is still very much the case.

On 3 May 1939, Catholics from all parts of Trinidad and the members of the Benedictine community in Trinidad, paid tribute to their founder and first superior during a Solemn Requiem Mass. Besides the whole Benedictine community, no less than 10 members of the clergy representing other religious orders, and secular priests of neighbouring parishes and of Port of Spain were in attendance. This indicates that, after all these years, the local clergy had come to appreciate and understand Dom Mayeul. Absent was Archbishop John Pius Dowling, who had offered Mass at his private chapel for the repose of the soul of Dom Mayeul. One can only wonder what had gone through his mind while offering mass. Adding to the solemnity of the ceremony at the Mount and representing the pontifical dignity, a mitre and purple stole were put on a catafalque. Prior Dom Hugh van der Sanden was the celebrant of the mass, and Dom Fr. Sebastian Weber, who had been with Dom Mayeul from the very beginning in Bahia and Trinidad, gave a homily straight from his heart. Here are a few extracts from his long homily which are found, word for word, in the Port of Spain newspaper *(Thursday May 4th 1939 POS Gazette)*:

Requiem Mass For Abbot Mayeul De Caigny

Founder Of Mount St. Benedict

GIFTED PREACHER AND LEARNED THEOLOGIAN

Tribute By Dom Sebastian Webber

Catholics from all parts of the island joined with the members of the Benedictine Community in Trinidad in paying tribute to the memory of the late Rt. Reverend Dom Mayeul de Caigny, O.S.B., founder and first Superior of Mount St. Benedict, when they attended a Solemn Requiem Mass for the repose of his soul at the Priory Church, Mount St. Benedict, yesterday morning.

Dom Mayeul died on Monday, April 24 at St. Leo's Abbey, Florida, where he had been living in retirement for a number of years.

On Tuesday morning last His Grace the Most Reverend Dr. John Pius Dowling, O.P., D.D., Archbishop of Port of Spain, offered a Mass at his Chapel for the repose of the soul of the late Abbott.

Members of the Clergy representing other religious orders in the Colony and Secular Priests were in attendance at the Mass celebrated on the Mount yesterday.

In a panegyric of the life of the late Abbot the Reverend Father Sebastian Webber, O.S.B., Parish Priest of San Fernando, who had been in close association with him for over a period of years, paid fitting tribute to his services in the cause of salvation.

Dom Sebastian described him as a gifted preacher and a learned theologian. Further, he said that the late Abbot had raised his spiritual life to a standard of saintliness.

INTERESTING CAREER

Born in 1862 Dom Mayeul entered the Congregation of Redemptorists. He was ordained Priest in 1887.

THE NEWSPAPER, PORT OF SPAIN GAZETTE, A REPORT ON THE SOLEMN REQUIEM MASS. A MOST IMPRESSIVE, WORD FOR WORD, ACCOUNT OF THE HOMILY DELIVERED BY DOM SEBASTIAN WEBER WAS INCLUDED IN THIS ARTICLE.

By casting a retrospect upon his long life we can not help describing it as a very remarkable and eventful career, all devoted to the service and Glory of God, and to the salvation and sanctification of souls. Dom Mayeul, as its founder, shall be for ever gloriously associated and linked up with Mount St. Benedict. He selected this spot with his strong bent for solitude. It was a solitary, quiet, elevated spot, a sort of little Monte Cassino, away from the noise and din of the world, favourable for prayer and contemplation. A place that a priestly visitor called: where the advantages of grace and nature are blended.

Divine providence had endowed him with truly outstanding gifts and nature, which he made good use of. He was a gifted preacher, a learned theologian and a most winning personality, and his kindness, courtesy, attention and sympathy towards all, especially towards the poor will be held in lasting memory.

He used to repeat for us the sentence of the Holy Law "Honour all men".

He taught that every human being, being however lowly he may be, must be attended to with all respect.

Pilgrims from all over flocked here to pray in front of the statue of St. Benedict that Dom Mayeul had brought here. They sought advice and consolation from the Fathers but especially from the lips of Dom Mayeul whose exquisite kindness and charity won the hearts of all. The people were encouraged by his winning personality and his interest in their welfare.

The late Abbot had raised his spiritual life to a standard of saintliness. He was strongly convinced, and left behind in writing, that few souls reach to the height of pure love in this world. We can never thank God enough for the grace of religious vocation, as likewise, we can never enough ask pardon for the lack of faithful correspondence to such grace.

Let us address to him these beautiful words: Well done, thou good and faithful servant. Enter in the joy of thy Lord.

Dom Sebastian's homily included a full history on Dom Mayeul's life, with plenty of details on his early religious life as a Redemptorist and Benedictine and on the events that happened in Rio de Janeiro and Bahia. Reference was even made to the day that Dom Mayeul delivered the very famous sermon, *"Simon, art thou asleep? Town of Bahia, art thou asleep? People of Bahia, are you asleep?"*, trying to stop the persecution and preventing the destruction of the Bahia abbey church. What is interesting to note is that reference to Dom Mayeul's resignation was made in the homily: *"serious problems of administration put Dom Mayeul in difficulties. He consulted the Holy See about it and he decided to tender his resignation"*.

Several newspapers covered Dom Mayeul's death: the *Savannah Daily*, *St. Leo Chronicle*, *Tampa Daily*, the Belgian newspaper *De Standaard* and the *Savannah Evening Press*. The St. Leo Chronicle gave, besides the history of Dom Mayeul's life, more details on the funeral ceremonies at St. Leo Abbey. People from as far away as Alabama and Georgia, attended the funeral.

> *The funeral Pontifical High Mass was conducted in the new Abbey church crypt by the most Rev. Patrick Barry, Bishop. Attending the mass and participating in the absolutions ceremony conducted around the body were Rev. Boniface Seng, OSB abbot of St. Bernard Alabama, Rev Francis Sadlier, abbot of St. Leo, Rev. Boniface Bauer, OSB superior of the priory Savannah Georgia, Rev. John Schlicht, OSB prior St. Leo Abbey. Other visiting clergy attending were: Rev. Aloysius Menges, Director of the St. Bernard College Alabama, Rev Patrick Nolan of Lakeland, Rev. Cuthbert Bender of St. Bernard. After the funeral mass the body of the Abbot Mayeul was carried in procession to the Abbey cemetery and laid to rest.*

On 25 April 1939 Dom Placidus Staeb, abbot of Bahia, wrote to Abbot Francis Sadlier at St. Leo Abbey, thanking him for having informed the Bahia community of the death of Dom Mayeul:

> *We have ordered for the repose of his soul the usual suffrages and for the second of May we have announced a solemn Pontifical Requiem at which we look for a great attendance of the faithful. The Abbot has still a large circle of friends in Bahia.*

> *The news of his death came unexpectedly for he wrote me for the New Year that he was in good health and had all hope still for some years to come to give to God his life and service.*

Much has he worked and much has he suffered in the vineyard of the Lord. Now the Lord of the Vineyard has taken him to himself and given him the reward for his faithful service.

We thank you and your community for the charity with which you surrounded him. He will reward you by his intercession in heaven (St. Leo letter 25 April 1939).

Abbot Sadlier of St. Leo got numerous requests from all over the world, asking for more information about Dom Mayeul's death or asking for a picture of Dom Mayeul, and thanking him for the hospitality he had shown to Dom Mayeul. People were even asking for a personal souvenir of Dom Mayeul. Numerous letters from convents and monasteries explained how deeply Dom Mayeul had enhanced the spiritual life of the religious people that attended his retreats and conferences. For many he was a saint.

In 1940, the abbot of St. Leo asked the Court of Florida to decide on the various requests from France, asking for a share of the royalties generated by Dom Mayeul's publications. The Court granted all income to St. Leo Abbey. St. Leo made further attempts with a New York publisher to publish some of Dom Mayeul's books in English.

In 2007, Father James Hoge at St. Leo Florida, who was a novice in 1937, remembered Dom Mayeul as follows:

When I met Dom Mayeul for the first time, from the very beginning I felt like I was introduced into the presence of a true representative of Christ. He was truly an Alter Christus. He radiated a joy, warmth, peace, an aura of mystique that I never experienced since. It is difficult to express, but he was the kind of person that you could go up to and embrace. Even though one knew he was a stranger one felt he was outgoing, willing to communicate. He had that peace and contentment in his very being that attracted anyone to him. He conducted a monastic retreat at St. Leo with a daily high mass that he celebrated in the traditional Latin Gregorian chant. Despite his European accent the singing was angelic, clear and warm. During my retreat I never again heard a mass as he prayed it and sang it. It was an enchanting experience.

Dom Mayeul had expressed the hope, that the story of his life, answering many questions and explaining many controversial events that occurred during his life, would be made public and explained.

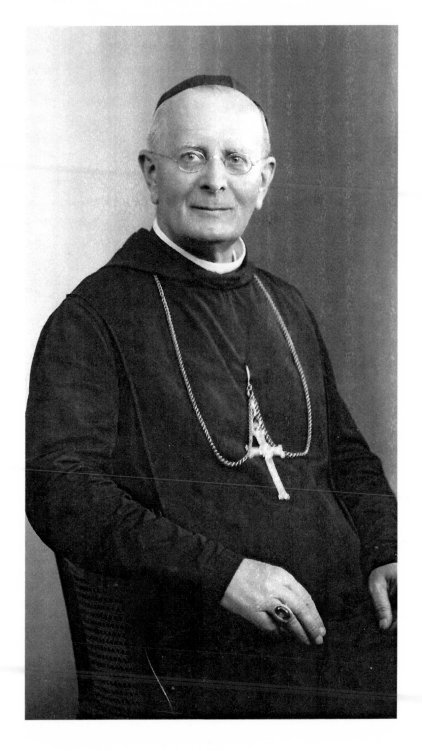

List of Archives

a. APR : Archives at Sant'Anselmo, Rome. Abbot Primate Fidelis von Stotzingen papers

b. ASAR de Hemptinne Papers : Archives at Sant'Anselmo, Rome. Abbot Primate de Hemptinne papers

c. Bahia, Chapter Bk. : Brazil, Abbey of Bahia archives, Chapter book

d. F.A., F. De Caigny, Belgium: family De Caigny archives held by F. De Caigny

e. MSB Dom Mayeul papers: Dom Mayeul papers at the Archives of Mount St. Benedict, Trinidad

f. MSB: Archives of Mount St. Benedict, Trinidad

g. POS, Benedictines or POS, Ben. : Port of Spain, Archives at the archdiocese, files on the Benedictines

h. POS, Dowling Papers: Archives Archbishop Dowling, Port of Spain Trinidad

i. SAZ, G.v.C. Papers: Archives of Saint Andre, Zevenkerken, Bruges. Dom Gerard van Caloen papers

j. St. Leo, Dom Mayeul papers: Archives at the Abbey of St. Leo Florida

k. Vol. I, II, III : Dom Mayeul memoirs Volume I, II or III at the archives of Mount St. Benedict, Trinidad

CPSIA information can be obtained at www.ICGtesting.com
Printed in the USA
LVOW060113180712

290406LV00005B/1/P